Chaoid Cinema

Chaoid Cinema

Deleuze and Guattari and the
Topological Vector of Silence

Colin Gardner

EDINBURGH
University Press

Edinburgh University Press is one of the leading university presses in the UK. We publish academic books and journals in our selected subject areas across the humanities and social sciences, combining cutting-edge scholarship with high editorial and production values to produce academic works of lasting importance. For more information visit our website: edinburghuniversitypress.com

© Colin Gardner, 2021, 2023

Edinburgh University Press Ltd
The Tun – Holyrood Road
12 (2f) Jackson's Entry
Edinburgh EH8 8PJ

First published in hardback by Edinburgh University Press 2021

Typeset in 11/13 Monotype Ehrhardt by
Manila Typesetting Company

A CIP record for this book is available from the British Library

ISBN 978 1 4744 9402 1 (hardback)
ISBN 978 1 4744 9403 8 (paperback)
ISBN 978 1 4744 9404 5 (webready PDF)
ISBN 978 1 4744 9405 2 (epub)

The right of Colin Gardner to be identified as author of this work has been asserted in accordance with the Copyright, Designs and Patents Act 1988 and the Copyright and Related Rights Regulations 2003 (SI No. 2498).

Every effort has been made to trace the copyright holders for the images; if any have been inadvertently overlooked, the publisher will be pleased to make the necessary arrangements at the first opportunity.

Contents

Acknowledgements vii

Introduction – 'Stratigraphic Silence': Chaoid Cinema and its Centripetal/Centrifugal Functions 1

1. 'The *Multiplicity* is Among Us': Silence and the *Machinic* Phylum in Fritz Lang's *M* (1931) 22

2. Ecosophical Chaoids: Towards an 'Infinite Cinema' with Hollis Frampton's *Zorns Lemma* (1970) and *Gloria!* (1979) 54

3. 'There is No Film. Let Us Proceed to the Debates!': Immanence as 'Syncinema' in Maurice Lemaître's *Le film est déjà commencé?* (1951) and Guy Debord's *Hurlements en faveur de Sade* (1952) 74

4. The Children of Barthes and *Paris Match*: Godard, Prostitution and the Rhetoric of the Image 102

5. 'Tricontinental Tropicalism': The Convulsive Carnival of a Syncretic Populism in Glauber Rocha's *Terra em Transe* (1967), *Der Leone Have Sept Cabeças* (1970) and *A Idada da Terra* (1980) 149

6. 'See You at Mao': the '60s Left Returns to Zero with the Dziga Vertov Group 188

7. Silencing Interpellation: Gorin, Althusser and the Ideological State Apparatus 227

8. 'We're Projectorists!': Concrete Duration and the Spectacle of Attractions in Malcolm Le Grice's *Little Dog for Roger* (1967), *Threshold* (1972) and *After Lumière – L'Arroseur Arrosé* (1974) 263

9. On Truth and Lie in an Extra-Formal Sense: Silence as Resistant *Punctum* in Abbas Kiarostami's *Chorus* (1982), *Homework* (1989) and *Close-Up* (1990) 283

Conclusion – 'The Abyss Also Looks Into You': From
Syncinema to 'Sin' Cinema in Mike Figgis's *Leaving Las Vegas*
(1995) and Harmony Korine's *Trash Humpers* (2009)   318

Bibliography   334

Index   352

Acknowledgements

I would like to give special thanks to Gillian Leslie at Edinburgh University Press for her ongoing support for this project as well as to Carol MacDonald for her encouragement during the last ten years for all of my Deleuze and Guattari-related research. I am also grateful to Helen Bleck for her brilliant copy editing, Eddie Clark, Richard Strachan and Caitlin Murphy for her wonderful work on the cover design.

Certain sections of this book started out as research papers delivered as keynote lectures or Deleuze and Guattari Conference papers at a number of international institutions in Lisbon, Stockholm and Royal Holloway College in Egham, England. I would like to thank in particular my hosts at Nanyang Technological University in Singapore – Vladimir and Tatjana Todorovic (currently faculty at the University of Western Australia) – who invited me to give a paper on Hollis Frampton's *Zorns Lemma* and Guy Debord's *Hurlements en faveur de Sade* as part of the university's Visiting Scholar Scheme and Lecture Series in the School of Arts, Design and Media. I'm particularly grateful for the generous input of Vibeke Sorensen, Ben Webster, Andrea Nanetti and Jeremy Fernando who helped to kickstart the project in its earliest stages.

Needless to say, my Deleuze and Guattari Conference cohort over the course of the last decade have been a major source of inspiration, in particular my writing partners Patricia MacCormack and Felicity Colman as well as my regular co-panellists Silke Panse, Dennis Rothermel, renee hoogland, Charles Stivale and Alina Cherry. In addition, I have shared a great deal of research with Tanya Shilina-Conte and Justin Remes, both of whom were instrumental in turning me on to the groundbreaking work of Abbas Kiarostami. Frida Beckman's work on 'control culture' has also been inspirational.

Any book grounded in specific case studies is heavily influenced by suggestions made by colleagues and acquaintances – mostly on the lines of 'You've got to check out such and such', or 'Surely you've seen (fill in the blank), it's full of sound drop-outs'. In this respect, I owe huge thanks to Darin and Toni Scott (*The Big Combo*), Michael Imperioli (*Rififi*), Clara Sherley-Appel and David Reed (*The Magicians*), Maiza Hixson

(*Trash Humpers*), Eric Prieto (*Borom Sarret*), Peter Bloom (the films of Béla Tarr) and Janet Walker (Fritz Lang's *M*). Special mention should also go to Daniel Martini Tybjerg for his insightful work on the Lettrists, Nikolaj Lübecker on Harmony Korine, James Nate Nichols for his research on the film theory of Raúl Ruiz and David Martin-Jones's insightful writings on Enrique Dussel and world systems theory. Many thanks also to Rosamund Felsen for her encyclopedic knowledge of the work of Paul McCarthy and Mike Kelley, to Troy Small for his invaluable tech support and last but not least to Dick Hebdige for his major support of my research over the past four years.

This book was largely written during a period of self-isolation due to the Covid-19 pandemic and wouldn't have been possible without the loving support of my wife Louise and the irresistible attention of our Golden Retriever, Spiffy. As ever, this work is dedicated to them.

INTRODUCTION

'Stratigraphic Silence': Chaoid Cinema and its Centripetal/Centrifugal Functions

1. The Sounds of Silence

One of the most memorable and visceral scenes in the entire history of *film noir* occurs approximately thirty minutes into Joseph H. Lewis's 1955 classic, *The Big Combo*. Police Lieutenant Leonard Diamond, played by Cornel Wilde, is on a personal crusade to bring down the crime syndicate run by the sadistic gangster, Mr Brown (Richard Conte). However, Diamond has been kidnapped by Brown's hired thugs, Fante and Mingo (Lee Van Cleef and Earl Holliman) and as he sits unconscious, tied to a chair, Brown's second-in-command, the hearing-impaired Joe McClure (Brian Donlevy) is itching to torture him for information. Despite Brown's insistence on a hands-off approach – for legal reasons he doesn't want to draw blood or show any marks – McClure defies orders and pays Fante and Mingo $100 each to turn a blind eye so that he can give Diamond the third degree. Enter Mr Brown: 'I told you not to touch him ... The trouble with you McClure is you never took time to learn *technique*.'[1]

Brown proceeds to demonstrate: he tells Fante to turn on the radio, then takes McClure's hearing aid – 'I only want to borrow it, Joe'. Brown inserts the device into Diamond's ear: 'We're going to give the lieutenant a little concert.' Mingo turns up the radio. 'How's that?' After an ineffectual grilling with no response they torture Diamond by screaming and blasting loud jazz, courtesy of Shorty Rogers and His Giants, into the hearing aid's amplifier. When Diamond still refuses to talk, Brown delivers the *pièce de résistance* – 'You like crazy drums, lieutenant? Have a good time.' Suddenly, an ear-splitting drum solo from Shelly Manne causes Diamond to pass out. Mr Brown pulls out the hearing aid: 'I think Mr Diamond needs a drink. Got any liquor?'

---

[1] Author's italics. All other italics throughout this text are in the original quote unless otherwise stated.

The scene is an exemplary example of Hollywood spectacle at its most primordial: an overdetermined synchronisation of sound and image for maximum affective return, whereby the cinema audience *feels* the diegetic character's agony as if we ourselves were helplessly sitting in the torture chair. Significantly, the tables are turned, both narratively and formally, towards the end of the movie. In the mistaken belief that he has bought the allegiance of Fante and Mingo, the resentful McClure attempts a coup against Mr Brown, luring his boss into a false rendezvous down a back alley where he will be unceremoniously gunned down by his two minions. Instead, the ever-loyal Fante and Mingo aim their machine guns at a shocked and horrified McClure. As he begs for his life Brown shows an uncharacteristic act of compassion: 'I feel sorry for you Joe. I'm going to do you a favour. You won't hear the bullets.' He removes McClure's hearing aid and the soundtrack drops out entirely as we cut to the blazing machine guns. The sound is then restored as we hear Mr Brown's footsteps, casually walking away.

In this case, the desynchronisation of sound and image not only deconstructs and counteracts the excessive spectacle of Diamond's torture scene earlier in the film, but it also marks a deliberate shift in audience response from affective identification to a more conceptual distanciation – a contracted form of sensation – as if we had switched philosophical planes. This doesn't necessarily make McClure's death any less violent: if anything, our ability to judge it without dramatic spectacle makes it all the more calculated and indelible. Indeed, as we shall see in our discussion of Guy Debord's first film, *Hurlements en faveur de Sade* (1952, *Howlings for Sade*) in Chapter 3, the two scenes seem to illustrate Jean Isidore Isou's objective in his seminal 1951 Lettrist film, *Traité de bave et d'éternité* (*On venom and eternity*) in which he averred, 'I want to separate the ear from its cinematographic master: the *eye*' (Isou 2019: unpaginated), thereby creating a 'discrepant montage' which subjugates the image to the visceral power of the soundtrack. 'I'd rather ruin your eyes than leave them indifferent! But in this visual disarray, the voice alone will be coherent and terrible' (Isou 2019: unpaginated).[2]

More importantly, *The Big Combo* taps into a key point made by Michel Chion in his influential book, *Audio-Vision: Sound on Screen*, where he notes that,

> the impression of silence in a film scene does not simply come from an absence of noise. It can only be produced as a result of context and preparation. The simplest

---

[2] 'Je voudrais séparer l'oreille de son maître cinématographique: *l'œil*'; 'je préfère vous abîmer les yeux que de les laisser indifférents! Mais dans cette pagaille de la vision, la voix seule sera cohérente et terrible' (Isou 1964: 16; 24).

of cases consists in preceding it with a noise-filled sequence. So silence is never a neutral emptiness. It is the negative of sound we've heard beforehand or imagined; it is the product of a contrast (1994: 57)

– in this case, a contrast between loud jazz as tortuous violence and the merciful absence of machine-gun bullets.

In effect, it is necessary to have sounds and conversation so that the formal and technical interruption of the soundtrack can accentuate (and consequently delve deeper into) the affective phenomenon of silence.

However, the radical elimination of the soundtrack is a rare technical device in sound film as the audience tends to assume that something has gone radically wrong with the projection (or, in the case of DVDs, the digital transfer). As Chion reminds us:

this zero-degree (or is it?) element of the soundtrack that is silence is certainly not so simple to achieve, even on the technical level. You can't just interrupt the auditory flow and stick in a few inches of blank leader. The spectator would have the impression of a technical break (which of course Godard used to full effect, notably in *Band of Outsiders*). Every place has its own unique silence, and it is for this reason that for sound recording on exterior locations, in a studio, or in an auditorium, care is taken to record several seconds of the 'silence' specific to that place. This ambient silence can be used later if needed behind dialogue, and will create the desired feeling that the space of the action is temporarily silent. (1994: 56–7)

This ambient 'silence' is often called 'room tone' and might include the barely audible ticking of clocks and subtler forms of reverberation (e.g. the rustling of clothes and curtains) which accentuate and foreground the removal of louder sounds such as traffic noise and aircraft flying overhead (or spoken dialogue) in order to give a great sense of silence without going to sonic extremes. This is played out to perfection in Jules Dassin's 1955 heist film, *Rififi*, where the thirty-two-minute bank robbery sequence, although not technically silent, is nonetheless devoid of all dialogue and musical score, all the better to highlight the subterfuge and meticulous planning of the operation by forcing the audience to pay attention to the unfolding tactics of the crime.

Although this book focuses exclusively on the Godardian type of silence as 'technical break' (indeed, we will discuss *Bande à part – Band of Outsiders* – in Chapter 4) we are also cognisant of John Cage's famous dictum in his 1961 collection of lectures and writings, ironically misnamed *Silence*, that 'There is always something to see, something to hear. In fact, try as we may to make a silence, we cannot' (1973: 8). This is of course exemplified by Cage's own composition, *4'33"* (1952), in which the ostensible pianist – originally David Tudor – sits at the piano and passes the time not by playing actual notes but by fiddling with the score and fidgeting on his stool while the audience coughs and murmers impatiently in the background. More recently, one of the best videos on YouTube shows the same piece 'performed' by the Austrian death metal band, Dead Territory as they stand silently facing the camera, nodding their heads to an unheard, interior rhythm, while Markus Itzenberger, the bass player, is unable to resist the urge to scrape his strings with his fingernail. As Cage argues, here,

> silence becomes something else – not silence at all, but sounds, the ambient sounds. The nature of these is unpredictable and changing. These sounds (which are called silence only because they do not form part of a musical intention) may be depended upon to exist. The world teems with them, and is, in fact, at no point free of them (1973: 22–3).[3]

Then, as if screaming in frustration, he declaims in strident capital letters: 'THERE IS NO SUCH THING AS SILENCE. GET THEE TO AN ANECHOIC CHAMBER AND HEAR THERE THY NERVOUS SYSTEM IN OPERATION AND HEAR THERE THY BLOOD IN CIRCULATION' (1973: 51).

This is perhaps a good moment to introduce Gilles Deleuze and Félix Guattari's insightful analysis of Cage as their work on chaoids forms the philosophical centre of this book. In Chapter 10 of *A Thousand Plateaus* – '1730: Becoming-Intense, Becoming-Animal, Becoming Imperceptible . . .' – they contextualise silence as a nonpulsed freeing of time as a precursor to what Deleuze will later call the time-image (or more specifically, the crystal image/hyalosign) in *Cinema 2: The Time-Image*:

> It is undoubtedly John Cage who first and most perfectly deployed this fixed sound plane, which affirms a process against all structure and genesis, a floating time against pulsed time or tempo, experimentation against any kind of interpretation, and in which silence as sonorous rest also marks the absolute state of movement. The same could be said of the fixed visual plane: Godard, for example, effectively carries the fixed plane of cinema to this state where forms dissolve, and all that subsists are tiny variations of speed between movements in composition. (Deleuze and Guattari 1987: 267)

Inspired by Nathalie Sarraute, Deleuze and Guattari then proceed to make a distinction between two planes of writing that are equally applicable to

---

[3] In the filmic context, we are always distracted in cinemas by the coughing, sneezing and murmuring of the audience, and even at home it's impossible to watch a DVD without the distraction of neighbours' power tools, gardeners' leaf blowers and the sound of police or ambulance sirens in the far distance.

sound and image. First, we have the transcendent plan(e) – the plan(e) that *organises* forms into specific genres (and their corresponding themes and motifs) and assigns them their corresponding subjects in the form of characters and personages. Second, we have a liberating plan(e) of consistency or composition that reduces forms to a shifting set of relations of movement and rest, speed and slowness, a plane that is inherently molecular and deterritorialising as opposed to molar and functional. Cage (and also Pierre Boulez), fall into the second category, for their music is composed of speeds and slownesses that challenge the integrity of the plan(e). 'As Cage says,' argue Deleuze and Guattari, 'it is of the nature of the plan(e) that it fail. Precisely because it is not a plan(e) of organization, development, or formation, but of nonvoluntary transmutation' (1987: 269). As we shall see, the planes are not mutually exclusive but in constant interaction as one passes over into the other.

2. Chaoids and the Body without Organs

Inspired by early Lettrist experiments (explored in detail in Chapter 3) 'discrepant' cinema (where sound and image 'drop-out' or cease to move at all) has recently become an extremely fruitful area of analysis in contemporary film theory. One thinks specifically of Justin Remes's *Motion(less) Pictures: The Cinema of Stasis* (2015), *Absence in Cinema: The Art of Showing Nothing* (2020) and his studies on Abbas Kiarostami where the director encourages the spectator to fall asleep during the screening of his *Five: Dedicated to Ozu* (2003):

> I do not believe in nailing the audience down at all. In certain films, you cannot miss a moment, but when the film is finished, you will have lost the whole film, your nerves, and your time. I declare that you can nap during this film. (Cited in Remes 2016: 235)

Similarly, Tanya Shilina-Conte's *Black Screens, White Frames: The Interstices of Cinema* (2021) and her two groundbreaking articles examine black space in both cinema and literature (Shilina-Conte 2015 and 2016). She has also made a video remix entitled *This Video Does Not Exist*, composed of announcements and signifiers that the image has been withdrawn or censored, so that we have an image that is present (as text) all the better to announce, aporetically, that it is absent.

Drawing specifically on a number of case studies – works by Fritz Lang, Hollis Frampton, the 'Syncinema' of Maurice Lemaître and Guy Debord (where silence is used as a deliberate spur to audience discontent and impromptu insurgency), Jean-Luc Godard and Jean-Pierre Gorin, Glauber Rocha, Malcolm Le Grice, Abbas Kiarostami, Mike Figgis and Harmony Korine – this book will extend the idea of 'Discrepant Cinema' by exploring the specific use of periods of silence – in this case a literal drop-out – in sound film as a means of accessing and connecting Deleuze and Guattari's three designated planes (outlined in *What is Philosophy?*) and their 'taming' of chaos through the creation of what they call 'chaoids', i.e. 'the realities produced on the planes that cut through the chaos in different ways' (1994: 208).

Chaos thus has three 'daughters' depending on the specific plane that cuts through it: the chaoids of art (composition), science (organisation/development) and philosophy (immanence/consistency) – each constituting different forms of thought and creation. As for the brain's role, '*The brain is the junction* – not the unity – *of the three planes*' (1994: 208). All three planes intersect and intertwine but never synthesise as a single totality. Thus, philosophy attempts to *save* the infinite by laying down a plane of consistency or immanence, utilising concepts to generate events; science *relinquishes* the infinite via a combination of reference and function, creating specific states of affairs; while, most importantly for our purposes, art *restores* the infinite through a finite composition of monuments and sensations. For Deleuze and Guattari, all art, including cinema, is both a simultaneous struggle against, and alliance with, chaos as a means of overcoming the deadening effects of *doxa* and opinion through a combination of affect, sensation and fabulation. As they put it,

> Art is not chaos but a composition of chaos that yields the vision or sensation, so that it constitutes, as Joyce says, a chaosmos, a composed chaos – neither foreseen nor preconceived. Art transforms chaotic variability into *chaoid* variety [...] Art struggles with chaos but it does so in order to render it sensory ... (1994: 204–5)

In cinema, this is accomplished by tearing hiatuses and holes (or, for our purposes, silences) in the surface of the sound and image track as a means of triggering the incommensurable event that is itself a form of unrepresentable time (Deleuze's Stoic-inspired immanent and cyclical time of Aion that connects past, present and future as pure crystalline becoming as opposed to the more dialectical or chronological time of Chronos). There are no longer any forms or developments of forms, no subjects or formations of subjects, no structure or genesis, 'There are only relations of movement and rest, speed and slowness between unformed elements, or at least between elements that are relatively unformed, molecules and particles of all kinds' (Deleuze and Guattari 1987: 266). This is what Deleuze and Guattari, following the terminology of the German biologist, Jakob von Uexküll, call ethology, a Spinozist *potentia* which defines a body not by its species or genus but by counting its affects and how they enter into a relationship of movement and rest with the molecules and particles of other bodies to create a still more powerful body, with an increased capacity to affect and be affected in turn (defined as a *haecceity*). As Deleuze describes the process in his essay, 'Ethology: Spinoza and Us':

> If we are Spinozists we will not define a thing by its form, nor by its organs and its functions, nor as a substance or a subject. Borrowing terms from the Middle Ages, or from geography, we will define it by *longitude* and *latitude* ... We call the longitude of a body the set of relations of speed and slowness, of motion and rest, between particles that compose it from this point of view, that is, between *unformed elements*. We call latitude the set of affects that occupy a body at each moment, that is, the intensive states of an anonymous force (force for existing, capacity for being affected). In this way we construct the map of a body. The longitudes and latitudes together constitute Nature, the plane of immanence or consistency, which is always variable and is constantly being altered, composed, and recomposed, by individuals and collectivities. (1992: 629)

The result is a dynamic vector of non-subjectified affects and collective assemblages; in short a war machine of displaced affects. Obviously, the Spinozist connection here reconfigures the ostensible subject-as-image as an intrinsic part of the object, as a manifestation of the finite woven into infinite. This necessarily entails a focus on 'subjectivity' – which is processual and fluid – rather than the 'subject-as-is' (as a homogenised entity). Subjectivity is by its very nature pragmatic and speculative: it must be carried out in the contemporary world (avoiding, as much as possible, received opinion) and is largely future-oriented. Subjectivity is thus the subject's very connection to an outside, the finite-infinite relationship in-itself. More importantly, this immanent ontology is predicated on the fact that the object always precedes the subject. This embedded quality of subjectivity as something always already lived on the plane of immanence allows it to escape the logic of doubt and negation and provides the springboard for Deleuze and Guattari's passive synthesis of life as joyful auto-affection.

This Spinozist, ethological connection to the plane of immanence/consistency has an added libidinal component insofar as Deleuze and Guattari also relate it to the Body without Organs (BwO) in Chapter 6 of *A Thousand Plateaus*, thereby tying the philosophical plane directly to bodily desire and the unconscious (which is, of course, a significant factor in how we read a film which has disturbingly jarring narrative breaks and fissures).[4] This is entirely consistent with Spinoza's *Ethics*, where thought, like bodily extension, is but an attribute of the substantive whole: 'Therefore, there is nothing outside the intellect through which a number of things can be distinguished from one another except substances, *or* what is the same, their attributes, and their affections' (Spinoza 1994: 87). By accepting the continuum of all substances in intensity and all intensities in substance, Deleuze and Guattari are able to define the BwO as immanence *and* an immanent limit, arguing that

> The BwO is the *field of immanence* of desire, the *plane of consistency* specific to desire (with desire defined as a process of production without reference to any exterior agency, whether it be a lack that hollows it out or a pleasure that fills it). (1987: 154)

Although the BwO is largely ignored in *What is Philosophy?*, in *Anti-Oedipus*, it has a specific negatory role in a larger schema of desiring-production where the subjective 'One' is depicted as a processual formation, and the BwO constitutes a 'disjunctive anti-production' in relation to the primary process of 'Connective' Desiring-Machines (a case of this *and* that or 'and *then* . . .') which mobilise the libido through a combination of actions and passions via forces of attraction. When the relationship with the BwO is inclusive it is called a 'Miraculating Machine' ('either/or . . . or . . . or'); when it is exclusive it is a Paranoiac Machine (pure Thanatos: everything stops dead). As Deleuze and Guattari argue:

> Machines attach themselves to the body without organs as so many points of disjunction, between which an entire network of new syntheses is now woven, marking the surface off into co-ordinates, like a grid. The 'either . . . or . . .' of the schizophrenic takes over from the 'and then': no matter what two organs are involved, the way in which they are attached to the body without organs must be such that all the disjunctive syntheses between the two amount to the same on the slippery surface. (1983: 12)

The 'Connective and Disjunctive machines' conjunctive synthesis is called the 'Celibate Machine', which consolidates intensive qualities into a surplus desiring subject which sees desire in the form of a revelatory

---

[4] This 'double duty' of terms – the plane of immanence is also the BwO – is not unusual in Deleuze and Guattari, for as Manuel DeLanda points out, 'Gilles Deleuze changes his terminology in every one of his books. Very few of his concepts retain their names or linguistic identity. The point of this terminological exuberance is not merely to give the impression of difference through the use of synonyms, but rather to develop a set of *different* theories on the same subject, theories which are slightly displaced relative to one another but retain enough overlaps that they can be meshed together as a heterogeneous assemblage.' (2002: 202).

retroactive discovery: 'So that's what it was', or 'So it's *me*!' Its intensive qualities constitute states of pure naked intensity, stripped of shape and form and are often manifested as hallucinations and delirium, projected and internalised (much like the *dementia praecox* symptoms of Freud's famous Daniel Paul Schreber case history). 'A genuine consummation is achieved by the new machine,' argue Deleuze and Guattari, 'a pleasure that can rightly be called autoerotic, or rather automatic: the nuptial celebration of a new alliance, a new birth, a radiant ecstasy, as though the eroticism of the machine liberated other unlimited forces' (1983: 18).

As a manifestation of desire as sensation and affect (and in extreme cases, delirium), art's role is to ally itself with chaos – to embrace it in part as a means of restoring the infinite – to rip holes in the umbrella of opinion, pre-existing *doxa* and cliché in order to create afresh through such new alliances. Here, as Deleuze and Guattari argue in *Anti-Oedipus*:

> the value of art is no longer measured except in terms of the decoded and deterritorialized flows that it causes to circulate beneath a signifier reduced to silence [. . .] It is here that art accedes to its authentic modernity, which simply consists in liberating what was present in art from its beginnings, but was hidden underneath aims and objects, even if aesthetic, and underneath recordings or axiomatics: the pure process that fulfills itself, and that never ceases to reach fulfillment as it proceeds – art as 'experimentation'. (1983: 370–1)

In this respect, silence has the potential of creating the ultimate philosophical 'effect' because it allows us to see through the surface of representation and figuration to perceive events, affects, passions and sensations that were never meant to be seen, such as the difference between the two acts of violence in *The Big Combo*, one purely affective (the plane of composition), the other more conceptual (the plane of immanence).

3. The Three Planes and Stratigraphic Time

In *What is Philosophy?* Deleuze and Guattari define philosophy in three interconnected parts as three *de jure* elements: 1. Concepts; 2. The plane of immanence; 3. Conceptual personae. Philosophers create and lay down their concepts on a specific plane and communicate them through conceptual persona. Thus, when Descartes engages with Plato to create a concept (such as the *cogito* – 'I think therefore I am') and lay out his own plane he doesn't converse with Plato as a historical person (via his writings) but through his conceptual persona (Socrates) via his own (the Idiot). Similarly Nietzsche engages with Socrates through Zarathustra. As Craig Lundy argues, 'Conceptual personae, put simply, personify concepts; they are the means by which philosophers converse with concepts, present or past' (Lundy 2012: 163). Similarly, when philosophers criticise each other (as friends in quest of the truth) it is always on a plane different from theirs: it never takes place on the same plane. When they criticise the concept, it vanishes when it is thrust into a new milieu so it must be recreated to give it the forces it needs to return to life. Everything else is just *ressentiment* (as Nietzsche might put it). For Deleuze and Guattari, Socrates is the worst culprit of the latter, making all free discussion impossible: 'He turned the friend into the friend of the single concept, and the concept into the pitiless monologue that eliminates the rivals one by one' (1994: 29).

Deleuze and Guattari also draw a key distinction between Conceptual Personae and Aesthetic Figures which will prove to be important in our analysis of the relationship between artistic affects and sensations and the thoughts/concepts that they trigger into existence. Thus,

> The difference between conceptual personae and aesthetic figures consists first of all in this: the former are the powers of concepts, and the latter are the powers of affects and percepts. The former take effect on a plane of immanence that is an image of Thought-Being (noumenon), and the latter take effect on a plane of composition as image of a Universe (phenomenon). (1994: 65)

Thus both art and philosophy cut across chaos and confront it but they use different planes, even though they may intersect and overlap: 'In the one there is the constellation of a universe or affects and percepts; and in the other, constitutions of immanence or concepts. Art thinks no less than philosophy, but it thinks through affects and percepts' (1994: 66).

In his groundbreaking book, *History and Becoming*, Lundy attempts to rescue history from Deleuze and Guattari's tendency to dismiss it as a suffocating historicism and instead sees it as a creative vector of becoming and transformation. He also gives us a key diagram of how this might work through the stratigraphic overlaying of the different planes akin to the different layers in Henri Bergson's famous cone of virtual memory, first published in *Matter and Memory* in 1896 (Figure I.1).

The ellipse AB at the base of the cone constitutes the totality of memory which potentially extends to infinity. Point S is the sensory-motor body or self in contact with the present (shown as the rectangle or the plane P). However, AB includes within itself all the intermediate layers or planes of memory – A′ B′, A′′ B′′, etc, that, for Deleuze,

> measure the degrees of a purely ideal proximity or distance in relation to S. Each of these sections is itself *virtual*, belong to the being in itself of the past. Each of these sections or each of these levels includes not particular elements of the past, but

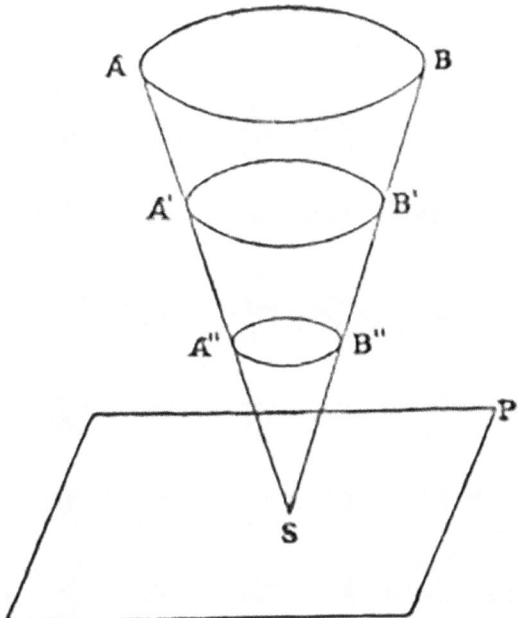

Figure I.1 Henri Bergson's Cone of Virtual Memory.

always the totality of the past. It includes this totality at a more or less expanded or contracted level. (Deleuze 1988a: 59–60)

Also, point S is not static but progresses inexorably towards an immediate future while simultaneously being linked to an immediate past. This is not the chronological time of Chronos but the non-linear time of Aion mentioned above: it is always amorphous and in constant flux. It exists concurrently with the present and each point in the future splits into a 'present that passes' and a 'past that is preserved'. Without this immanent bifurcation there could be no motion through time: time would not move if the present could not pass. In short, 'Bergsonian duration is, in the final analysis, defined less by succession than by coexistence' (1988a: 60).

Lundy builds on this planar flux, firstly pointing out that every order that arises from (and subsequently returns to) chaos is, as a result, a slice or plane of chaos. Deleuze and Guattari confirm this in *What is Philosophy?*, stating that, 'The plane of immanence is like a section of chaos and acts like a sieve' (1994: 42). The use of the word 'sieve' is significant, suggesting that there is an innate permeability between the planes that allows concepts, affects and functions to interpenetrate and transform each other while at the same time retaining their specific parameters as a plane of difference. As Lundy sums it up:

> if these slices of chaos that order difference differently were to be stacked on top of one another, they would form a diagram akin to Bergson's cone of virtual memory. Each slice of the cone is a plane of immanence that circumscribes chaos according to the singular curvature of its conic section. Although each conic section is itself infinitive and contains the whole of reality, since it does so in varying degrees of difference each plane is but one among a plurality: 'There are innumerable planes, each with a variable curve' [*What is Philosophy?* 1994: 76]. Each conic section can also be said to act like a sieve, sifting through difference according to particular level of contraction-détente. In this way, each plane regulates (resonates) difference respective to the level of specificity required. (2012: 154)

In this way our ability to extract different concepts, affects and functions depends upon the specific plane that lays it out and gives us access. In the case of philosophy, concepts may group together or separate themselves according to the points of view constituted by their different personae.

More importantly, following the architecture of Bergson's cone, this planar spatio-temporal structure is stratigraphic, as if we were mining the holes in the surface sieve to discover conceptual and affective riches beneath the surface as layered strata. As Deleuze and Guattari argue,

> We can only make headway with these questions if we give up the narrowly historical point of view of before and after in order to consider the time rather than the history of philosophy. This is a *stratigraphic* time where 'before' and 'after' indicate only an order of superimpositions. (1994: 58)

Thus the different strata of the plane of immanence lie above or below each other rather than linearly in chronological time, thereby causing shifts in orientation in the nature of concepts and images that defy easy resolution while at the same time guaranteeing creative transformation: 'It is true that very old strata can rise to the surface again, can cut a path through the formations that covered them and surface directly on the current stratum to which they impart a new curvature' (1994: 58–9). If we read the impact of this stratigraphic structure on the role of silences in film, the latter act as sonic ruptures in the surface plane of composition, encouraging us to mine the different strata that lie beneath and re-connect them in and through other concepts and silences.

However, this is not just a vertical downward thrust, akin to shaft mining or shaft sinking in civil engineering projects but rather a zig-zag, *transverse* trajectory, a series of bridges across and between planes that encourages us to flash back or flash forward to similar instances of silence within the same film (or groups of films by the same director) and thus discover new and ever-changing conceptual strata. For Deleuze and Guattari,

> Philosophical time is thus a grandiose time of coexistence that does not exclude the before and after but *superimposes* them in a stratigraphic order. It is an infinite becoming of philosophy that crosscuts its history without being confused with it. [. . .] Philosophy is becoming, not history; it is the coexistence of planes, not the succession of systems. (1994: 59)

The result is a contracted form of sensation that is ultimately unlocalisable, not unlike the excesses of exhaustion that Deleuze finds in the television work of Samuel Beckett (Deleuze 1997) and Virginia Woolf's cry to 'Saturate every atom' and 'keep only the saturation that gives us the percept' (Deleuze and Guattari 1994: 172). In this sense, a stratigraphic silence would also act as a form of affective saturation.

This transverse saturation works through the agency of a deterritorialising vector which ties the plane of consistency directly to a virtual continuum composed of multiplicities, thereby creating an extremely pliable and durational topological space. So what is a topology? According to Brian Massumi, it is a continuous and multiple space directly tied to the virtual, so that you might, for example . . .

> Take the images by the virtual centers. Superpose them. You get an overimage of images of self-varying deformation: a unity of continuous separation from self. It is there that the virtual most literally, parabolically appears. That is to say that the virtual is best approached *topologically*. Topology is the science of self-varying deformation. A topological figure is defined as the continuous transformation of one geometrical figure into another. (2002: 134)

Massumi then uses the example of a pliable coffee cup whereby you join the brim, enlarge the handle and stretch it into equally thick sides to form a doughnut, then twist the whole thing into complex knots. Although the new forms look like a complete desecration of the original (try drinking out of that!), all are versions of the same topological figure.

> The overall topological figure is continuous and multiple. As a transformation, it is defined by vectors rather than coordinate points. A vector is *transpositional*: a moving-through points as speed rather than movement. Because of its vectorial nature, the geometry of the topological superfigure cannot be separated from its duration. (2002: 184–5)

Thus a vector is always in the process of undoing coordinate points and treating them instead as way-stations and bifurcating linkages on a continuous journey of becoming. You pass through points so that you can remain on the line, NOT travel on the line in order to arrive at a point. It's a question of *speed* rather than *movement*, for as Deleuze and Guattari explain,

> Movement designates the relative character of a body considered as 'one', and which goes from point to point; *speed, on the contrary, constitutes the absolute character of a body whose irreducible parts (atoms) occupy or fill a smooth space in the manner of a vortex*, with the possibility of springing up at any point. (1987: 381)

This is not unlike an endless journey on the London Underground or Paris Métro with no termini like Cockfosters on the Piccadilly Line or Robinson on the RER to act as a network-imposed final destination, just endless transfers, interchanges and *correspondences* (like Châtelet-Les Halles in central Paris). One thinks of Jorge Luis Borges's brilliant 1941 short story, 'The Garden of Forking Paths' (*El jardin de senderos que se bifurcan*), which Deleuze, in *Cinema 2*, sees as 'Borges's reply to Leibniz: the straight line as force of time, as labyrinth of time, is also the line which forks and keeps on forking, passing through *incompossible presents*, returning to *not-necessarily true pasts*' (1989: 131).

This has obvious ramifications for the whole concept of chaoid cinema, for the viewer's experience of a deterritorialised and bifurcating narrative structure is always in a state of becoming. As Massumi summarises cinematic topology as a form of recycled synaesthesia (where sounds and colours are experienced as events), he notes that aesthetic experience . . .

> is not in any recognized thing or place. It is in them all, but in each under a different heading. Experience, as it happens, is in difference-of-heading before it goes in any determinate direction. The space of continuing experience is a pure or absolute space of differential heading: an indeterminate vector space infusing each step taken in Euclidean space with a potential for having been otherwise directed. The whole of vector space is compressed, in potential, in every step. (2002: 192)

Massumi then argues that this intensive vector space, which encompasses qualitatively different planes such as memory, proprioception, language and colour, is always a reaccessing of the already perceived but under new and different circumstances (thus no two or three silences are ever the same), like a perceptual Moebius strip, or what he calls a biogram: a previously experienced vector space. In effect, 'Biograms cannot be described without resorting to topology: centers folding into peripheries and out again, arcs, weaves, knots, and unthreadings' (2002: 188), not unlike the zig-zag effect of Bergsonian, stratigraphic time that we discussed earlier.

Significantly, Godard uses this Moebius strip analogy when describing the complex relationship between fiction and documentary which, like Kiarostami (especially in his 1990 film *Close-Up*), he sees as central to

> the problems of the cinema, where the real and the imaginary are clearly distinct and yet are one, like the Moebius curve which has at the same time one side and two, like the technique of *cinéma-vérité* which is also a technique of lying. It's pretty disconcerting to say the least. (Cited in Narboni and Milne 1972: 214–5)

André Malraux saw this as akin to hearing with one's ears the sound of one's own voice, which we are used to hearing with the throat. As Godard puts it:

> The voice issuing from the loudspeaker we eventually accept as our own, but even so in our ears it is something else, or to be very precise, it is other people, so one is faced with a very difficult thing which is to listen to other people with one's throat. This double movement, which projects us towards others while taking us inside ourselves, physically defines the cinema. (Cited in Narboni and Milne 1972: 215)

By this definition, *all* cinema can be seen and heard as a form of biogram.

4. Chaoids and Film Theory – Centripetal and Centrifugal Images as an Enfolding and Unfolding Aesthetic

Following this logic, biograms and their different vectorial comings and goings can be directly tied to classic and recent film theory through the concept of 'deframing' and its corrolaries, the centripetal and the centrifugal. Deleuze cites in particular Pascal Bonitzer's seminal essay, 'Deframings' (first published as 'Décadrages' in *Cahiers du Cinéma* 284, January 1978), which draws a clear distinction between cinema on the one hand, and painting and theatre on the other. Cinema tends to be centrifugal, i.e. dependent upon a continous and logical succession of shots and countershots to explain and normalise detail in an otherwise deterritorialised single shot via a more comprehensive set or something temporarily unrevealed: for example, the inverted point of view of a man hanging upside down who has yet to be shown in an explanatory subjective reaction shot. In contrast, painting and theatre are centripetal, self-contained and bound by the picture frame or proscenium. As Bonitzer explains,

> Any solution of continuity clearly calls for a repairing, a putting together again. At this point, it might be noted that this solution of continuity is twofold: narrative and scenographic. The two shots do not overlap one another. The second is produced by the first, in the sense that making of the frame [*cadre*] a masking [*cache*], thus the

setting up of an enigma, is necessarily to get the story rolling. It falls to the story to fill the hole, the terra incognita, the hidden part of the representation. ([1978] 2000: 199)

However, on occasion, these individual framed shots remain disconnected or unnormalised, as in the case of Robert Bresson, where they often remain unpragmatised, or in Yasujiro's Ozu's so-called 'pillow shots' (the term comes from Noël Burch), which act as independent interstices rather than establishing shots, a technique brilliantly lionised by Kiarostami in his aforementioned 2003 film, *Five Dedicated to Ozu*, which consists of five long takes shot by the Caspian Sea that re-contextualise Ozu's dead zones as an overdetermined documentary trope. As Deleuze explains, 'Bonitzer has constructed the interesting concept of "deframing" [*décadrage*] in order to designate these abnormal points of view which are not the same as an oblique perspective or a paradoxical angle, and refer to another dimension of the image' (1986: 15).

However, Bonitzer is quick to acknowledge that this is nothing new, for the distinction between frame (*cadre*) and masking (*cache*) is also central to André Bazin's realist film theory, outlined in two key essays, 'Painting and Cinema' and 'Theater and Cinema: Part Two'. In terms of film's relation to painting, for Bazin:

> The outer edges of the screen are not, as the technical jargon would seem to imply, the frame of the film image. They are the edges of a piece of masking that shows only a portion of reality. The picture frame polarizes space inwards. On the contrary, what the screen shows us seems to be part of something prolonged indefinitely into the universe. A frame is centripetal, the screen centrifugal. Whence it follows that if we reverse the pictorial process and place the screen within the picture frame, that is if we show a section of a painting on a screen, the space of the painting loses its orientation and its limits and is presented to the imagination as without any boundaries. Without losing its other characteristics the painting thus takes on the spatial properties of cinema and becomes part of that 'picturable' world that lies beyond it on all sides. (1967a: 166)

In other words, an object within the pictorial frame of a painting loses its relation to lived reality and is completely incorporated into the centripetal, artificial reality of the artwork. In contrast, cinema treats all boundary markers as a form of masking, indicating that it is just one of several ways to view the world represented. In this way we acknowledge the framing but remain completely involved in the vectorial, topological space of the real world, a space that the image is unable to completely absorb.

Bazin has a similar view of traditional theatre, which is itself an architecturally framed centripetal microcosm setting up its own self-contained world. He states,

> Everyone knows that when the actor 'retires to his apartment' from the yard or from the garden, he is actually going to his dressing room to take off his make-up. These few square feet of light and illusion are surrounded by machinery and flanked by wings, the hidden labyrinths of which do not interfere one bit with the pleasure of the spectator who is playing the game of theater. Because it is only part of the architecture of the stage, the decor of the theater is thus an area materially enclosed, limited, circumscribed, the only discoveries of which are those of our collusive imagination. (1967b: 104–5)

Bazin then continues:

> Its appearances are turned inward facing the public and the footlights. It exists by virtue of its reverse side and its absence from anything beyond, as the painting exists by virtue of its frame. Just as the picture is not to be confounded with the scene it represents and is not a window in a wall. The stage and the decor where the action unfolds constitute an aesthetic microcosm inserted perforce into the universe but essentially distinct from the Nature which surrounds it. It is not the same with cinema, the basic principle of which is a denial of any frontiers to action. (1967b: 104–5)

This is all well and good but of course it doesn't take into account a hybrid director like Sergei Eisenstein, who in many ways is over-concerned with the aesthetic world constructed within the (centripetal) frame through the sanctity of the single shot, all the better to set up a dialectical 'montage of attractions' *between* shots to create a centripetal 'shock effect' that would otherwise be diffused through a traditional aesthetic of masking (thus the dialectical 'collision' between the Tsarist troops and the spectators in *Potemkin*'s Odessa Steps sequence accentuated by jarring changes in camera angle). The latter works *because* of its innate theatricality, not despite it. We find a similar aesthetic in the films and theoretical writings of the Chilean film-maker, Raúl Ruiz (1941–2011), particularly his influential article, 'The Six Functions of the Shot', where film's centripetal and centrifugal functions once again play a key role. According to Ruiz:

> Every shot is independent of those that together with it make up the film. A film is a collection of independent shots. *When we see a film of four hundred shots, we do not see a film, we see four hundred films* [my italics]. Each shot is the figure of one or more events captured from a point of view. In each shot there are events and a point of view. When the point of view changes (when the camera moves), the event, in a certain sense, is settled by the change in the point of view. When a given set of objects that make up a given event are settled in the change of point of view, we shall

> say that the scene is closed. Yet a scene, a series of convergent and divergent actions, according to a more or less precise logic, will often open and close provisionally. The provisional closures form a weak film that follows the main film (the official story) as a shadow or a faithful dog. (Ruiz 2004: 57)

For Ruiz (unlike Eisenstein, who stresses a dialectical totality produced through montage itself), a film has neither a beginning nor an end simply because every shot is an individual world (in effect a staged *event*) innately separate from other shots. However, that doesn't mean that shots are not linked to other shots (the way points are linked to other points in a multiplicity). Ruiz calls these linkages the 'function' of the shot which ultimately form a provisional totality. In what sounds like a propitiously Deleuzian statement, Ruiz stresses the vectorial function of these relations in and between shots:

> We have to imagine a variety of overlapping shots that, according to the centrifugal function, search for each other and respond to each other. Though these are shots that should, once the centrifugal function has been activated, produce a double movement, so that on the one hand one can follow the sequence of shots from '1' to 'n', and on the other, due to the centripetal function, stimulate our immersion into each shot. (2004: 62)

If we extend these provocative centrifugal and centripetal models to our examination of silence in sound film, it seems obvious that 'drop-out' exploits both functions. It is centripetal insofar as it is overtly theatrical, in the Brechtian sense of drawing audience attention to the cinematic device and alienating us, through a form of *Verfremdungseffekt*, from a psychological absorption in the drama. As we noted earlier, our initial response is, 'What happened there?'; 'Where's the sound?'; 'Is the projector broken?' – not unlike Brecht's didactic strategies in the Epic Theatre and Godard and Gorin's disclosure of the latent Althusserian ideological state apparatus in the Dziga Vertov Group films. On the other hand it is also centrifugal, stratigraphically linking, through different vectorial topologies, different silences on different planes and strata, not unlike Ruiz's function of the shot. More importantly, these centrifugal linkages also metacommunicate the inevitable breaks and fissures between shots that are such a central element in Deleuze's time-image in *Cinema 2*, especially the chronosign ('an image where time itself ceases to be subordinate to movement and appears for itself' – 1989: 335) and its conceptual corollary, the noosign ('an image which goes beyond itself towards something which can only be thought' – 1989: 335).

As is well known, the chronosign disrupts and breaks conventional narrative edits that cover over the different strata of discrepant time through an action-oriented movement-image (thus, for example, the audience easily and efficiently fills in the gaps when a woman leaves her apartment, hails a taxi, and arrives at the station without having to see the entire duration of her journey, although a film-maker like Béla Tarr would probably devote a full fifteen minutes to showing every move in a single take). Instead, with the chronosign, we become aware of hidden time in all its chaoid fury, for in Deleuze's crystalline regime,

> the actual is cut off from its motor linkages, or the real from its legal connections, and the virtual, for its part, detaches itself from its actualizations, starts to be valid for itself. The two modes of existence are now combined in a circuit where the real and the imaginary, the actual and the virtual, chase after each other, exchange their roles and become indiscernible. (Deleuze 1989: 127)

Significantly, the Ruiz scholar Adrian Martin sees a direct relation to the Chilean film-maker's own form of 'Discrepant Cinema', noting that,

> there are visible shots in cinema but, equally, the less visible *intervals* between shots, or the fleeting *interstices* between them – not only, technically, the literal black spaces between film frames on celluloid (so much a part of cinema's peculiar metapsychological effect for the spectator), but also conceptually. This expandable interval between shots, both material and immaterial, is a crucial factor for Ruiz also. (2012: unpaginated)

With the interstice (as opposed to the edit), spaces-as-intervals are exhausted and superseded – they become, in effect, events or multiplicities.[5]

We might usefully conclude our introductory relation of silence as topological vector to contemporary Film-Philosophy via another durational paradigm, that of the baroque Leibnizian fold through what Laura U. Marks calls '*enfolding-unfolding aesthetics*' (Marks 2009: 87) whereby the past-as-virtual (Bergson's Cone of Memory) is not forgotten but rather enfolded as matter and simply waiting to be unfolded as information or image (which in turn mediates it before enfolding it back to its origins). As Marks explains it:

> The terms *enfolded* and *unfolded* (or their Latinate synonyms, *implicate* and *explicate*) echo Deleuze's explication of the baroque aesthetics of Leibniz. Leibniz's principle that the smallest element of matter is a fold makes it possible to conceive of what Deleuze and Guattari term the *plane of immanence* as composed of infinite folds. The actual is thus infinitely enfolded in the virtual. The past, then, reaches us or becomes actual to us through selective unfolding, in a relationship among Experience,

---

[5] For more on the interstice, see Tom Conley (2000), 'The Film Event: From Interval to Interstice'.

Information, and Image. I posit that each of these three levels is a plane of immanence: a membrane in which an infinity of stuff lies virtual, or enfolded. Now and then certain aspects of those virtual events are unfolded, pulled up into the next level. Images, perceptible representations of history, come into the world and retreat back into Experience in a ceaseless flow of unfolding and enfolding. (2010: 234–5)

Marks also points out how this model, like Deleuze's 'unfolding' of the movement-image in *Cinema 1*, relates directly to Charles Sanders Peirce's three semiological levels of Firstness (the infinite but latent history of all interrelational Experiences); Secondness (Information as a highly selective sifting of material and images from the totality of Experience: what we call 'the actual' – dominated by *doxa* and the cliché and epitomised in cinema by the action-image and the narrative cut/edit rather than the interstice); and Thirdness (the Image-based relation between Experience and Information). Thirdness can often reinforce *doxa* (this is the basis of Deleuze and Guattari's critique of history as historicism) but also – as in Brecht, Godard and Kiarostami – metacommunicate it through the defamilarising power of deterritorialisation and affect.

Thus, as Marks is quick to point out, Images are never direct reflections of Experience but represent selective unfoldings, so that . . .

> those Images that do arise from Experience are often selected, or unfolded, by political and economic interests that deem them to be useful as Information. Nevertheless, anyone can unfold any aspect of Experience to become a public Image, and artists (and others) do so in order to allow other aspects of Experience to circulate. We cannot perceive Experience as such, it has to be mediated through an Image; but films can emphasize the quality of Experience – its presence, detail, strangeness, noninstrumentality, infinity. (2010: 236)

The latter tactics are particularly important in non-western films, whether it be Arab cinema (Marks's own area of interest) but also the neo-colonial legacy of comprador culture in African cinema (Ousmane Sembene's *Xala* – 1975) or the hybrid anthropophagy of Brazilian films. Marks notes that in such cases, the Image can unfold from enfolded Experience and use a more critical form of Secondness/Information to reveal latent and buried native identity and difference that might then be activated in rebellion against organised *doxa*. She argues,

> This is especially relevant in viewing some remarkable works of Arab cinema, which, like other peripheral cinemas, represent history agonistically. Given the power struggles (neo)colonial and local, in the Arab world in the past century, the telling of history in the Arab world is absolutely fraught: the victors' dominant accounts are patently fraudulent, the accounts produced to please outsiders are simple pandering,

and the accounts that people most fervently wish to claim are fragile and difficult to sustain. (2010: 233)

Given this approach – which is of course not limited to the Arab world – Deleuze and Guattari's plane of immanence, now re-read as a Leibnizian fold, is absolutely immanent to/as an auto-affective 'Life itself'. In that sense, it cannot try to avoid or bypass capitalism's stranglehold on the information age but must actively engage with it. This is also, as Marks reminds us, a fundamentally Nietzschean strategy, for,

> Given that the fundamental nature of the unfolding and enfolding universe is constant flow, trying to stay enfolded or 'below the radar' of information is a form of suicide. Given the ubiquity of regimes of information, a better strategy is to cultivate enigmas. An enigma, we might say, retraces its historical path in the cycle from the universe of images, to information, to image, back to the Earth, to be unfolded in a new way, or to stay latent. This movement of enfolding is a way of understanding what Nietzsche calls the Eternal Return. (2009: 98)

It is also directly related to our previous discussion of the centripetal and centrifugal, for the former is clearly a form of enfolding (a return to the virtual world of Experience) while the latter is an unfolding (an outward vector to another form of Experience disclosed and transformed via Images and Information). That the two are inseparable and mutually enfolded is obvious – they work inextricably in tandem, with silence as film history's agent of becoming, in constant advance and retreat as it fulfils its genealogical function at disclosing the hitherto unknown and unrepresentable, for as Nietzsche argues,

> the genuine historian must possess the power to remint the universally known into something never heard of before, and to express the universal so simply and profoundly that the simplicity is lost in the profundity and the profundity in the simplicity. (1983: 94)

As we shall see in the case studies that follow, this fusion of profundity and simplicity can take on many guises, from cultural cannibalism to Maoism, from child killers to intimidating homework assignments, prostitutes to alcoholics, Lettrist poets to trash humpers. Clearly, as Foucault declared in a now famous statement, 'Genealogy is history in the form of a concerted carnival' (1984: 94). Glauber Rocha would have no argument with that!

CHAPTER 1

'The *M*ultiplicity is Among Us': Silence and the *M*achinic Phylum in Fritz Lang's *M* (1931)

It seems fitting to begin our series of case studies at the dawn of the sound era to see how the new medium influenced directors' audio-visual choices both in terms of narrative continuity/discontinuity and suggestions of off-screen space (whether centripetal or centrifugal). As is well known, *M* (1931) was Fritz Lang's first sound film and because of his sparing use of the new technology – there are at least sixteen sequences with no sound at all and many dialogue scenes have no ambient sound such as 'room tone' or street noises – there has been significant debate among film historians as to whether the film is still stubbornly stuck in the past or creatively integrating both sound and silence as an intrinsic part of both the diegesis and pro-filmic exegesis. Thus, as Noël Carroll argues on the more conservative side,

> *M* is what might be called a silent sound film. Other examples would include Dreyer's *Vampyr*, Lang's own *Testament of Dr. Mabuse*, Vertov's *Enthusiasm* as well as *Three Songs of Lenin*, parts of Pudovkin's *The Deserter*, Buñuel's *L'Âge d'Or*, and Clair's early sound films, especially *À Nous la Liberté*. Calling these silent sound films is not meant disparagingly. Each of these represents a major achievement. Yet that achievement in each case derives from a penchant for asynchronous sound based on a paradigm of montage juxtaposition as a means to manipulate, to interpret, and to reconstitute pro-filmic events. (1978: 16)

This position is endorsed by Sergei Eisenstein, Vsevolod Pudovkin and Grigori Alexandrov in their famous 1928 statement on sound where they argue against the realist illusionism of synchronous sound in favour of the dynamics of dialectical montage:

> ONLY A CONTRAPUNTAL USE of sound in relation to the visual montage piece will afford a new potentiality of montage development and perfection. THE FIRST EXPERIMENTAL WORK WITH SOUND MUST BE DIRECTED ALONG THE LINE OF ITS DISTINCT NON-SYNCHRONIZATION WITH THE VISUAL IMAGE. And only such an attack will give the necessary palpability which

will later lead to the creation of an ORCHESTRAL COUNTERPOINT of visual and aural images. (Eisenstein et al. 1957: 258 – caps in the original)

Much of this argument is reinforced by the technical nature of the sound editing process at that time, for as Anton Kaes points out,

> Early sound cinema employed special editors who recorded the sounds separately from the images in order to finesse and 'edit' the soundtrack, working with scissors to produce collage effects. Images and sound became joined on one strip only at the very end. (2001: 21–2)

As a result, synchronicity or disjuncture of image and sound could be delayed until the last moment so that silence was in many ways a latent 'ground zero' waiting to be filled in (or not, as the case may be). That doesn't mean that early sound film was structured like, say, Ousmane Sembene's first short, *Borom Sarrett* (1963), which was shot silent on the streets in Senegal with the entire soundtrack added post-synch in the studio. The one split-second sound drop-out is thus not an intentionally expressive sonic interstice but more of a technical glitch in the final editing process. In contrast, argues Kaes,

> For Lang, it was not a matter of adding a soundtrack to a silent film, but one of making the new technology a structural feature of the narrative itself. Sound became a signifying code that radically reconfigured the nature of the image, of vision, of film in general (2001: 18)[1]

Of course, it's also important to emphasise (as we shall reiterate in the next chapter when discussing Hollis Frampton's appropriation of silent

---

[1] One should note in particular the important influence of Walther Ruttmann's *Weekend* (1930), an eleven-minute short that features a black screen with a sound collage that throws together film, radio, disembodied voices and various noises to evoke weekend activities. According to Kaes, Paul Falkenberg, Lang's sound editor, drew direct inspiration from *Weekend* for his work on *M*, using the cross-fade to mix a smorgasbord of separate sounds but also disparate locations (a key technique in *M*'s ability to suggest the idea of fear and paranoia through the press and media's sonic 'contagion'). As Michael P. Ryan notes, '*Weekend*, for example, is divided into six parts: 1) "Jazz der Arbeit" ("Jazz of Work"); 2) "Feierabend" ("After work"); 3) "Fahrt ins Freie" ("Drive into the Country"); 4) "Pastorale" ("Pastoral"); 5) "Wiederbeginn der Arbeit" ("Return to Work"); and 6) "Jazz der Arbeit"' (2013: 269). A hodgepodge of sounds represents each milieu, as if we were caught in a hybrid format between a film and a radio play. Indeed, *Weekend* was not only broadcast over the radio but was also 'screened' in a Berlin cinema with the curtains closed in May 1930. It was later presented at the Belgian International Congress of Independent Film as an example of German avant-garde cinema, despite the lack of images.

film footage in *Gloria!*) that 'silent' films were never actually screened without some form of musical accompaniment, whether solo piano or full orchestra (especially at world premieres). In the case of Lang, one of his last pre-synchronous sound films, *Spione* (*Spies*, 1928) is always screened with a full score whose variations in rhythm and texture dictate audience response to the images by increasing or lowering tension, adding and subtracting humour and suspense. Thus Donald Sosin's hard-driving score for *Spione*'s 2004 Kino International release on DVD has no pauses or silences for quiet reflection or introspection whatsoever. Although the sheet music from Werner Richard Heymann's original orchestral score (written for *Spione*'s world premiere) is now missing, we know from the composer's 1931 article, 'Sound Film Music as a New Musical Form' (originally published in *Film und Ton*, a weekly insert in *Licht-Bildbuehne*), that Sosin's modern variation is very true to Heymann's original intentions. The latter had already written scores for F. W. Murnau's *Faust* (1926), Alexander Korda's *A Modern Du Barry* (1926), and Arthur Robison's *Der letzte Walzer* (*The Last Waltz*, 1927) and in his essay/manifesto he outlines a specific evolution in the sound-image relationship from incidental accompaniment to organic integration. Thus:

> To take a clear, objective position on this matter, one must first draw a clear line between those films with incidental songs and musical underpinning on the one hand, and on the other, those in which the filmic portrayal has a homogenous relationship to music and song. In the former category, which could actually be termed a 'surrogate sound film', the music and song play a passive role just like the musical illustration in earlier silent films, only with the distinction that the acoustic portion is simply mechanized. For this reason, this category can only be of limited interest to the film composer. Not to mention the downright incongruous attempt to violate musical stage works and transport them to the screen. (Heymann 1931: unpaginated)

Heymann then goes on to describe his second category, which is exemplified by his score for *Spione*,

> in which music as the primary element actively engages in the plot and is constantly inspirational and vitalizing, offers the imagination of the composer a wide range of possibilities for creative work, which, undertaken in close collaboration with the director, lead to the new musical form of the sound film. If the music and song contribute to – or better yet support – the organic construction of the plot, emphasizing the character of individual situations, this new form thus grows out of the unique laws of filmic portrayal itself. (1931: unpaginated)

It's some measure of Lang's commitment to the new sound medium that he eschews both of Heymann's categories, for *M* has no accompanying musical score whatsoever (thus allowing him to focus diegetically on the child murderer Hans Beckert's whistled refrain – 'In the Hall of the Mountain King' from Grieg's 1888 *Peer Gynt Suite No. 1*, Op. 46 – as the leitmotif of a murdering psychosis, instilling fear in mothers and their children throughout late Weimar Berlin). Instead, as we shall see, Lang creates three interconnected levels of communication throughout *M*, notably through sound, silence, and hapticity in order to draw political, economic and class correspondences and discrepancies as part of an overall series of machinic singularities and assemblages, what Deleuze and Guattari call the machinic phylum.

Made for Seymour Nebenzal's Nero Films, *M* was largely written by Thea von Harbou, Lang's wife at that time. The screenplay's earlier titles included *Mörder unter Uns* (*The Murderer is Among Us*),[2] *Eine Stadt sucht einen Mörder* (*A City Searches for a Murderer*) and *Dein Mörder sieht dich An* (*Your Killer Looks at You*), and it was loosely based on the activities of contemporary serial killers such as Fritz Haarmann (the Ogre of Hanover), Carl Grossmann, Karl Denke, and most notoriously, Peter Kürten (aka the 'The Vampire of Düsseldorf'), although Lang himself denies the import of the latter. In an interview with Gretchen Berg, published in *Cahiers du Cinéma* (1965–6), Lang states:

> Contrary to what many people think, *M* wasn't taken from the life of the infamous killer of Düsseldorf, Peter Kürten. It happened that he had just begun his series of murders at the time Thea von Harbou and I were writing the screenplay. The script was completed before he was caught. In fact, the first idea for the subject of *M* came to me when reading an article in the newspaper. I always read newspapers for a point of departure of a story. (Berg [1965] 2003: 72)

---

[2] In what may be an apocryphal story – Lang vacillated between endorsing and denying it in equal measure – Lang told Gretchen Berg that, 'When I tried to make *M* in 1931 (its original title was *The Murderer Among Us*), I received menacing anonymous letters, and I was then told that the main studio at Staaken was off limits. "But why such an incomprehensible conspiracy against a film about a child killer in Düsseldorf?," I asked the studio director. "Ah, I understand," he said, and with a big smile, he gave me the keys to the studio. But I had already seen the Party insignia on the back. I then understood that the Nazis thought the title applied to them. When they found that the film was based on Peter Kürten, the killer of Düsseldorf (whom I knew personally), they consented to let me make the film. The title had to be changed to *M*, for murderer' (Berg [1965] 2003: 55). Later, in the same interview, Lang denies the Kürten connection, suggesting that the explanation given to the studio director was a deliberate misdirection.

In addition – and this helps to explain the extraordinary detail of the procedural aspects of *M* – Lang states that,

> At that time, I was working with 'Scotland Yard' in Berlin (at Alexanderplatz), and I had access to certain confidential files. These were reports on certain unnamed killers like Grossman in Berlin, the terrible Ogre of Hanover [Fritz Haarmann] (who had killed so many young people) and other criminals of the same ilk. (Berg [1965] 2003: 72)

Clearly, Beckert is a composite figure, not a real-life case study.

The film opens with a black screen punctuated by a loud gong (a deliberate reference to the connection of sound and time using contemporary radio techniques, where the gong was often used to announce the start of a news broadcast, a new scene in a radio drama or simply mark the hour of the day) before giving way to the voice-over of a young Girl (Hanna Maron), who chants the opening lines of a children's 'elimination game': 'Just you wait, it won't be long . . .' We then fade up to a sharp angle down on the Girl, who stands in the middle of a circle of nine other children playing in the central courtyard of a Berlin Mietkaserne or tenement block as she continues her macabre tale, pointing her finger at all the children in turn on the sound of each word . . . 'The man in black will soon be here. With his cleaver's blade so true. He'll make mincemeat out of *you*!' She then points decisively to a girl at the bottom right of the screen: 'You're out!'

Lang then pans up to the balcony overlooking the courtyard where a pregnant housewife carries a laundry basket as she walks past a line of washing. She looks down in disgust: 'I told you to stop singing that awful song! Didn't you hear me? That same cursed song over and over!' Unconcerned, the Girl continues her rhyme off-screen as we hold on the now empty balcony. The result, as Thierry Kuntzel notes, is

> Radical alterity: the children do not respond. The woman goes off. The camera remains on the empty and silent balcony, a void and a silence which, far from a metaphysical heaviness à la Bergman, have the weight of a narrative *suspense*, waiting and absence are inscribed in the text and not in an interpretation of the world. (Kuntzel 1978: 46)

The housewife climbs the stairs to another level and delivers the laundry to Mrs Beckmann (Ellen Widmann), who is busy making lunch and laying the table for her daughter Elsie, who is late coming home from school. Over the next five minutes the tension builds as neither two of Elsie's school friends, nor the local newspaperman who comes to deliver the latest crime *feuilleton*, have seen Elsie and the kitchen cuckoo clock marks the inexorable march of time with its penetrating refrain.

Lang underscores a clear class divide as he cuts to the exterior of the school as the children stream out to meet their parents for lunch. The more middle-class parents clearly have enough free time to escort their children home at a time of city-wide fear of the child murderer's invisible 'presence', while the working class Mrs Beckmann (whose husband is never shown throughout the film, if he exists at all) is obliged to stay at home to prepare Elsie's lunch in her kitchen. Thus when we finally see young Elsie (Inge Landgut), she is immediately shown to be vulnerable: after saying goodbye to two school friends by a 'Schule' sign, she steps distractedly into the street and is almost knocked down by a passing car. She hurriedly retreats to the pavement just as a policeman enters from the left and dutifully stops the traffic in order to help her across the road.

As her mother continues to lay the table for her lunch, Elsie bounces a ball as she approaches a Morris column (*Litfaßsäule*) and for the first time we become aware of the full extent of the serial nature of the immanent child-murdering threat. As Elsie continues to bounce her ball against the column (again, like the children in the tenement courtyard, attempting to override death and murder with the innocent rhythm of childlike play), Lang pans up to a large poster in German Gothic print. It reads:

10,000 MARKS REWARD
WHO IS THE MURDERER?
Since Monday, 11th June this year, the following have disappeared: the schoolchildren Klaus Klawitzky and his sister Klara, who live at 470 Müller Street. Various evidence leads us to believe that the children were victims of a crime similar to that committed last autumn against the Doering sisters. (Von Harbou 1968: 17; 1973: 100–01)

Suddenly, the shadowy outline of a hat, facial profile and shoulders spreads across the poster from the right. It's Hans Beckert (Peter Lorre), who speaks acousmatically from off-screen: 'What a pretty ball you have there.' He leans in and down. 'What's your name?' The naïve and trusting Elsie replies: 'Elsie Beckmann.' We cut back to the kitchen as Elsie's mother continues to prepare lunch – peeling potatoes and putting them in a tureen – just as we cut once again to a close-up of the cuckoo clock: it's now 12:20 (in effect, twenty minutes of diegetic time has been reduced to 1′ 20″ of screen time, expressing the inexorability of *M*'s losing race against 'time-as-death').

This inevitability is quickly borne out as we cut to a high angle down on Elsie and Beckert as he pays a blind balloon seller (later revealed to be Heinrich, played by Georg John), while whistling his *Peer Gynt* leitmotif. Elsie takes a number of balloons fashioned in the shape of a large, bulbous doll, curtseys in grateful thanks to Beckert and the pair exit right, Beckert still whistling his refrain. Lang expresses her unseen death (and the outward signs of Beckert's psychosis) by cutting back to her empty table setting, then to her ball rolling across a patch of grass and finally to her balloon caught in the telephone lines overhead before being blown away by the wind.

Elsie's murder then gives Lang the opportunity to not only express the high degree of anxiety among the general public but also how it is fed by the sensationalist media, so that innocent bystanders are attacked and accused at the slightest provocation. In addition, even though these scenes were cut from the final edit (see Kaes 2001: 81–2 for the full transcript) a number of citizens are writing to the police and the press admitting to the crimes, either as a means of hogging the limelight or deliberately wasting police time. The latter self-aggrandisers include Beckert himself, whom we see from the rear sitting at his window ledge, writing a letter to the papers as he once again whistles his *Peer Gynt* refrain: 'Because the police did not publish my first letter, I am writing now directly to the press! Proceed with your investigations. All will soon be confirmed. But I'm not done yet!'

Beckert's letter – and the resulting pressure on the Chief of Police (Ernst Stahl-Nachbaur) from the City Minister (Franz Stein) – enables Lang and Von Harbou to set up two parallel investigations in order to showcase their differences and mutual alliances as part of a larger machinic assemblage. The first, led by homicide Inspector Karl Lohmann (based on the real-life Berlin police detective Ernst Gennat[3] and portrayed by Otto Wernicke) follows modern (albeit often inefficient) investigative techniques using field work such as collection of evidence – cigarette packets, candy wrappers, etc. – which are then traced on a city-wide map in ever-widening circles using a large compass (as if an investigation followed the rules of mathematical geometry); fingerprinting, handwriting analysis, and finally examination of the records of recently released psychiatric patients who might have a history of violence against children. This eventually extends to frequent raids on the haunts of known criminals such as the Crocodile Club, a seedy basement bar notorious for harbouring prostitutes, pickpockets and burglars.

---

[3] According to Kaes (2001: 32), Lang drew heavily on Ernst Gennat's articles published in the journal, *Kriminalistische Monatshefte*, from January to April 1930 during the widespread search for Peter Kürten. Two more articles on the trial were published later (May and June 1931) and included details that Lang used in *M*, such as the murderer's letter being written in pencil on a wooden surface.

Lohmann's tactics eventually lead to the discovery of Beckert's rented rooms, where he and his Assistant find evidence of the window ledge's rough wood grain that left an imprint on the murderer's confession letter to the press as well as shavings from the red pencil that he used to write it. However, the police are so lacking in initiative that their only subsequent tactic is to lie in wait for Beckert's eventual return so that they can arrest him. This, of course, could take days or even weeks and generate countless more deaths. Fortunately for public safety, the frequent police raids and intense questioning of known criminals has so disrupted the underworld's day-to-day business activities (and profits!) that Schränker, the crime boss (Gustaf Gründgens) calls a meeting of all his division leaders – the Pickpocket (Paul Kemp), the Bauernfänger/Con-man (Theo Lingen), Franz the Burglar (Friedrich Gnaß), and the Cheater/Hustler (Fritz Odemar) – to see how they might organise their own manhunt, for time is of the essence. This strategy was actually ripped from the headlines of the day, for as Lang described it in the German newspaper *Die Filmwoche*, No. 21, 20 May, 1931:

> There is one motif used in this case that seems to illustrate particularly well how fantastic real events have become: the idea that the criminal caste, Berlin's underworld, would take to the streets of its own initiative to seek out the unknown murderer so as to evade greater police activity is taken from a factual newspaper report and seemed to me such compelling cinematic material that I was constantly living in fear of someone else exploiting this idea before me. (Lang [1931] 2001: 139)

The underworld's solution is to use the street beggars' existing organisation to carefully allot them specific streets and tenements for surveillance and have them identify and tail the perpetrator with the eventual hope of trapping and abducting him. This is, of course, a far more efficient and effective plan than Lohmann's as it involves ground-level observation and meticulous organisation. As is well known, Beckert's *Peer Gynt* refrain proves to be his undoing as it is recognised by Heinrich, the blind balloon seller while on the street: he makes an immediate sonic connection to Beckert and Elsie during their first encounter. Heinrich promptly warns his young underworld cohort, Leeser (Carl Balhaus), who outlines the letter 'M' (for *Mörder*) in chalk over similar-shaped lines on his own palm and, pretending to trip over, slaps the letter on the back of Beckert's left shoulder as the killer attempts to seduce yet another victim. After Leeser hurries away, the young girl spots the mark and offers to clean it off, but a horrified Beckert now realises that he is being extensively surveilled and he flees the scene, abandoning the girl.

Trapped on a nighttime street with members of the underworld covering every exit, Beckert has no option but to hide inside a large office building just before the workers clock out for the evening at 6:00pm. The cordon of beggars contact Schränker, who arrives disguised as a police officer and dupes his way through the security gate with the help of the unsuspecting night watchman, Damowitz (Karl Platen). Schränker's minions join him, and the Con-man tortures Damowitz for information: it turns out that there are still two watchmen on the premises. The gang eventually catch Beckert as he hides quivering with fear in the attic but Damowitz gets a modicum of revenge against Schränker's gang by ringing an alarm that is connected to the local police station, triggering a ticker-tape machine that prints out the building's exact location (another case of a machinic connection between the authorities and local business).

Although the criminals manage to escape in the nick of time before the police arrive, Franz the burglar is not so lucky – waylaid by breaking through the ceiling into a neighbouring savings bank, he is apprehended as he attempts to climb a rope ladder back to the floor above. Lohmann then tricks him into giving evidence by falsely claiming that Damowitz died as a result of injuries sustained during the break-in and that Franz will be tried for murder if he doesn't admit the real reason for the crime – i.e. to find Beckert – and reveal where he has been taken. As Franz comes clean, the criminals drag a screaming Beckert to an abandoned distillery where he will be tried before a kangaroo court, i.e. a large silent crowd of thieves, prostitutes and con men led by Schränker and his crime lords. Although Beckert is granted a modicum of legal rights – he has a defence lawyer (Rudolf Blümner) who argues for a 'Paragraph fifty-one' plea of insanity clause – the underworld jury is ruled by blood lust and revenge, screaming for the death penalty. Beckert makes an impassioned defence of his actions, contrasting his own crimes to those of the underworld:

> What would you know? What are you talking about? Who are you anyway? Who are you? All of you. Criminals. Probably proud of it, too – proud you can crack a safe or sneak into houses or cheat at cards. All of which it seems to me you could just as easily give up if you had learned something useful, or if you had jobs or if you weren't such lazy pigs. But me? [His hands clutch at his chest. Desperately . . .] Can I do anything about it? Don't I have this cursed thing inside me? This fire, this voice, this agony?

Beckert then pleads to be handed over to the police. Similarly, his lawyer points out that the presiding 'judge' (i.e. Schränker) is wanted on three counts of manslaughter, and that it is unjust to execute an insane man.

Then, just as the enraged mob rushes forward to kill Beckert, the police arrive to arrest both him and the criminals.

The film ends as a panel of judges prepares to deliver their verdict at Beckert's 'official' (i.e. legal) trial. As we hear 'In the name of the people . . .' Lang immediately cuts to three of the victims' mothers, with Mrs Beckmann in the middle. She is pragmatic rather than vengeful, arguing that true justice must be a community enterprise: 'This will not bring our children back. One has to . . . keep closer watch . . . over the children!' We then fade to black but instead of the film's opening sound of the radio gong, we hear the mothers' crying and Mrs Beckmann's last line: 'All of you!'

'All of you' is a telling closing statement/plea because it suggests the pre-existence, but also the increasing need for the expansion, of a panoptic society in which modernity, technologies of perception and policing are brought together as a hybridisation of wartime and peacetime methods. In his seminal essay, 'The Cold Gaze: Notes on Mobilization and Modernity', Kaes notes that during a tracking shot where Lang's camera follows a father and daughter along the street after they have given a coin to a 'blind' beggar/informer, we catch a brief glimpse of a poster for G. W. Pabst's *Westfront 1918*, one of the most important war films of the era. Although this may have been a contemporary reference to a film released just prior to *M*, or an industry in-joke (*Westfront 1918* was also produced by Nero Films), Kaes sees,

> a link between the two films despite their seemingly quite different topographies. For is Berlin not shown in *M* as a battlefield, a west front 1931, a city in a state of total mobilization prepared to fight the enemy, who takes the form of an invisible serial murderer? (1993: 105)

Indeed, public fear of Peter Kürten was called 'War in Düsseldorf' by the press, which Kaes sees as marking 'The enemy as beast and phantom: this vocabulary also reached back to World War I. A flood of war novels, memoirs and picture books, from the far right to the far left, inundated the book market at the time' (2001: 42–3), the most popular being Erich Maria Remarque's 1929 *All Quiet on the Western Front*.

However, this association of late Weimar Germany with a wartime footing took on sociological and ideological ramifications through the common mechanism of the panopticon. Just as the police and underworld pull out all the stops to surveille Beckert's unseen presence in a city gripped by fear and paranoia, so the Great War was the first instance of using new technologies such as aircraft, Zeppelins and camera surveillance to keep a strategic eye on the enemy's movements. The key theorist in this regard was the war veteran and political advocate for a new form of nationalism, Ernst Jünger (1895–1998), whose 1930 essay 'War and Photography' ('Krieg und Lichtbild') anticipated Paul Virilio's *War and Cinema* (1989) by exploring the connections between the new technologies of warfare and their corresponding expansion of human perception during peacetime. As Kaes argues,

> In World War I reconnaissance planes photographed enemies' positions and weapons were equipped with optical devices for navigation. Perception itself became increasingly technological: the artificial eye of the camera could penetrate fog, haze, and darkness, extending into realms inaccessible to the human eye. (1993: 106)

Writing in the television and computer age, Virilio takes this a step further in 'The Overexposed City' by relating the resulting new urbanism to a proliferation of speed and instantaneity rather than concrete material space or place:

> This overexposure attracts our attention to the extent that it offers a world without antipodes and without hidden aspects, a world in which opacity is but a momentary interlude. Note how the illusion of proximity barely lasts. Where once the *polis* inaugurated a political theatre, with its *agora* and its *forum*, now there is only a cathode-ray screen, where the shadows and spectres of a community dance amid their processes of disappearance, where cinematism broadcasts the last appearance of urbanism, the last image of an urbanism without urbanity. This is where tact and contact give way to televisual impact. (2002: 444)

The key point here is that where Virilio, like Foucault, is critical of this 'overexposed' non-space, Jünger, as a war veteran, was a fervent advocate of the dematerialisation of both modern warfare and Modernist urban existence. Because both the military and civilian enemy is virtually undetectable and can strike, like Beckert, at any time, modern humanity needs to cultivate a heightened perception – the panopticon as a form of *aesthetic* experience that hybridises both the war and peacetime experience (after all, isn't the modern city full of dangerous, even deadly incursions such as speeding cars and motorcycles, not to mention dangerous criminals and psychopaths on a par with tank and trench warfare on the Western Front?). As Kaes argues, 'Jünger wanted to extend into civilian life the acute, often apocalyptic sense of peril he experienced on the war front' (1993: 107) as a means of creating the new Modernist metropolis. As Jünger himself put it in his 1926 essay, 'Big City and the Countryside' ('Grolkstadt und Land'):

> We must penetrate the forces of the metropolis, which are the real powers of our time: the machine, the masses, the worker. For here lies the potential energy from which will arise the new nation of tomorrow; and every European people is now at

work trying to harness this potential [. . .] The Great War itself is a good example of the way that the essence of the city has begun to take possession of the whole range of modern life. The generation of the trenches went forth expecting a joyous war in the old style, a field campaign. But just as the landscape of this battlefield proved to be no natural landscape but a technological landscape, so was the spirit that animated it an urban spirit. Urban, too, was the 'battle of materials' and still more the mechanized 'battle of movement' that developed from it. Today any kind of revolt that does not begin in the urban centers is doomed from the start to failure. (Jünger 1926, translated and cited in Werneburg 1992: 47)

It is through the camera and technologically recorded sound and radio broadcasts that urban dwellers can overcome the inherent fears of a wartime psychosis because they generate a more detached, 'second consciousness' which allows the subject to see themselves as an object that can stand outside the 'sphere of pain' and torment and connect up with fellow citizens through modern technology. In this sense, a film like *M* – although critical of the new detached urbanism – also reinforces it (albeit self-reflexively) by reducing human relations to this very same machinic 'second consciousness'. As we shall see, it's exactly this ambivalence that makes *M* such a brilliant case study of both a character type and a key moment in history (i.e. the Nazi rise to power).[4] As Kaes argues, 'Unlike Jünger, who embraces fascist discipline, Lang realizes that the camera in the service of surveillance and social order will produce a society ready at a moment's notice to be mobilized for war and collective violence' (1993: 117).

The transformation of the modern autonomous subject (and their accompanying liberal-humanist orthodoxies) into Jünger's utopian 'second consciousness' necessarily creates a new type of worker, one fully integrated into a machinic assemblage through a form of 'total mobilisation'. As Kaes points out,

> In his treatise of 1932, *Der Arbeiter* [*The Worker*], Jünger develops a right-wing utopian image of a radically technological civilization in which a new breed of men, the workers (as worker-soldiers), exist in a constant state of mobilization. Jünger sees modern industrial labor in military terms; Fordism for him is the militarization of the workplace, which he welcomes. The new type of man (*Typus*, as Jünger calls him) who supersedes the bourgeois individual of the 19th century could already be seen in the millions of World War I soldiers, all looking alike under their steel helmets. (1993: 111)

---

[4] Joseph Losey's 1951 remake of *M* transfers the Weimar context to Cold War era Los Angeles, whereby the relationship between the peace-ego and the war-ego (and their corresponding paranoia) are re-contextualised in terms of the McCarthy witch hunt and blacklist. For a comparison of the two films see Gardner (2017).

Lang himself had expressed this vision in *Metropolis* (1927), where we see hoards of workers, all dressed alike, shuffle in unison to start their day shift, then in a horrifying fantasy, to their death in the cauldron-like jaws of Moloch. 'The toll of World War I – 13 million dead, and many millions crippled – was not forgotten by the mid-1920s,' argues Kaes. 'To the individual, Ernst Jünger wrote in *Der Arbeiter*, the renunciation of individuality means an impoverishment; it signifies death. But to the *Typus* (which replaces the individual) it provides a key to another world' (cited in Kaes 1993: 111).

The obvious counter-argument to Jünger's *Typus* is Walter Benjamin's 'The Work of Art in the Age of Mechanical Reproduction', which argues that the aestheticisation of technical means leads to fascism, not to a radical change in property values. Thus he argues that,

> The logical result of Fascism is the introduction of aesthetics into political life. The violation of the masses, whom Fascism, with its *Führer* cult, forces to their knees, has its counterpoint in the violation of an apparatus which is pressed into the production of ritual values. All efforts to render politics aesthetic culminate in one thing: war. (Benjamin [1936] 1969: 241)

Then, as if in response to the objectification of mankind's 'second consciousness', he ends with his famous dictum that,

> Mankind, which in Homer's time was an object of contemplation for the Olympian gods, now is one for itself. Its self-alienation has reached such a degree that it can experience its own destruction as an aesthetic pleasure of the first order. This is the situation of politics which Fascism is rendering aesthetic. Communism responds by politicizing art. ([1936] 1969: 242)

Jünger's 'total mobilisation' immediately reminds us of Deleuze's oft-quoted statement on contemporary fascism in *Two Regimes of Madness*. There, he notes that old-style fascism looks positively quaint and folkloric in comparison to the current model:

> The new fascism is not the politics and the economy of war. It is global agreement on security, on the maintenance of a 'peace' just as terrifying as war. All our petty fears will be organized in concert, all our petty anxieties will be harnessed to make micro-fascists of us; we will be called upon to stifle every little thing, every suspicious face, every dissonant voice, in our streets, in our neighborhoods, in our local theaters. (Deleuze 2006a: 138)

It is also extremely reminiscent of Foucault's concept of the *dispositif*: 'a thoroughly heterogeneous ensemble consisting of discourses, institutions, architectural forms, regulatory decisions, laws, administrative measures, scientific statements, philosophical, moral and philanthropic propositions – in short, the said as much as the unsaid. Such are the elements of the apparatus' (1977: 194). A key aspect of this new apparatus that is relevant to *M*'s coordination of police and underworld investigations is that instead of the old binary opposition between the permitted and the prohibited, the lawful and unlawful, the *dispositif* constructs an optimal mean or average alongside 'a bandwidth of the acceptable that must not be exceeded. In this way a completely different distribution of things and mechanisms takes shape' (Foucault 2007: 6). Under this regime the new equation is surveillance + diagnosis + classification = discipline as security (which, in *M*, is only achieved through the *joint* efforts of the police and the underworld). Like Jünger (although critically rather than enthusiastically) Foucault sees the people not as a series of individuals or subjects but as a multiplicity, so that the specific space of security is largely concerned with setting up a milieu where a series of possible events might unfold and circulate within a given time and space, allowing for an open field of potential transgressions that can always be contained by the status quo. Thus for Foucault, 'it was a matter of organizing circulation, eliminating its dangerous elements, making a division between good and bad circulation, and maximizing the good circulation by diminishing the bad' (Foucault 2007: 18). In short, Foucault collapses the milieu into the *dispositif* to allow for maximum political contingency. The results, like Jünger's, are thus pragmatic, functional and multiplicitous.

Deleuze is extremely useful here in helping us to understand Foucault's *dispositif* not only as lines of organisation, connecting points like so many vectors, but also in terms of fissures, holes and fractures. In 'What is a Dispositif?' he describes his own idea of an apparatus, which, as we shall see, has many of the characteristics of a machinic phylum:

> First of all, it is a skein, a multilinear whole. It is composed on lines of different natures. The lines in the apparatus do not encircle or surround systems that are each homogenous in themselves, the object, the subject, language, etc., but follow directions, trace processes that are always out of balance, that sometimes move closer together and sometimes farther away. Each line is broken, subject to *changes in direction*, bifurcating and forked, and subjected to *derivations*. Visible objects, articulable utterances, forces in use, subjects in position are like vectors or tensors. (2006b: 338)

The apparatus, through the distribution of variables by different curves (and the regimes of utterances they engender), thus makes provision for lines of flight, for minoritarian deterritorialisations as part of its very nature. In this sense it is not unlike Henri Lefebvre's 'abstract space' with its dominance of exchange value over use value, as if the city were modelled on the rationality of the Taylorist/Fordist factory production line. Lefebvre notes,

> The space that homogenizes thus has nothing homogeneous about it. After its fashion, which is polyscopic and plural, it subsumes and unites scattered fragments or elements by force. Though it emerged historically as the plane on which a socio-political compromise was reached between the aristocracy and the bourgeoisie (i.e. between the ownership of land and the ownership of money), abstract space has maintained its dominance into the era of conflict between finance capital – that supreme abstraction – and action carried out in the name of the proletariat. (1991: 308)

However, as we can see in the case of Beckert, not all lines of flight are containable in such a space and this is largely due to a breakdown in the integration of the *Typus* into a war and peace economy. Beckert is so psychopathological that a single panoptic gaze isn't enough to comprehend or contain him, for as Kaes argues, 'While Lang examines the nexus between total mobilization, surveillance and social control, he also insists on an unknowable remainder, a scintilla of resistance which defies categorization' (2001: 49). As we shall see, this *aporia* is expressed through the film's silences, which in turn explore the machinic phylum as a series of incompatible singularities and aggregates.

Freud is extremely useful in helping us to understand Beckert's pathology in relation to peacetime war neuroses. In his short 'Introduction' to the 1921 collection *Psycho-Analysis and the War Neuroses*, Freud argues that many ex-soldiers had a difficult time in readjusting back to peacetime conditions because of the unresolved conflict between their peacetime ego – 'Thou shalt not kill!' – and their wartime ego – 'It's kill or be killed'. Beckert illustrates this ego-conflict dilemma perfectly in his impassioned plea to the kangaroo court:

> Who knows what it's like inside me? How it screams and cries out inside me when I have to do it! Don't want to! Must! [He screams in agony.] Don't want to! Must! And then a voice cries out, [he throws himself against the wooden barrier in a paroxysm, covering his ears with his hands] and I can't listen anymore! Help! I can't! I can't! I can't.

As Freud explains:

> The conflict takes place between the old ego of peace time and the new war-ego of the soldier, and it becomes acute as soon as the peace-ego is faced with the danger of being killed through the risky undertakings of his newly formed parasitical double. Or one might put it, the old ego protects itself from the danger to life by flight into the traumatic neurosis in defending itself against the new ego which it recognises as

threatening its life. The National Army was therefore the condition, and fruitful soil, for the appearance of war neuroses; they could not occur in professional soldiers, or mercenaries. (1921: 2–3)

War neurosis thus takes the form of what Gregory Bateson calls a 'double bind', whereby no matter what a person does they can't win: he or she lacks the ability to sublimate or to metacommunicate their dilemma through a form of linguistic distancing ('Oh, I'm still haunted by my wartime phobias: get over yourself!'). In addition, argues Bateson, 'It is hypothesized that a person caught in the double bind may develop schizophrenic symptoms' (Bateson 2000: 201), much like *M*'s *doppelgänger* effect.

More importantly, and this is highly relevant to Beckert's condition, this double bind between the war- and peace-egos is highly sexualised but lacks peacetime's positive ability to channel the libido through a healthy transference or cathexis. Instead, it treats sex as a threat, like a wartime enemy, and it too must be vanquished, albeit through repetition compulsion. Thus, argues Freud:

In the traumatic and war neuroses the ego of the individual protects itself from a danger that either threatens it from without, or is embodied in a form of the ego itself, in the transference neuroses of peace time the ego regards its own sexual hunger (libido) as a foe, the demands of which appear threatening to it. In both cases the ego fears an injury; in the one case through the sexual hunger (libido) and in the other from outside forces. (1921: 4)

Communicating this ego rupture in the context of the Weimar *dispositif* is Lang's chief aim in *M*, and he does it through the interaction of two main planes of composition: sound and hapticity (whose lines help to connect the points to help mobilise the *Typus* within the abstract space of Berlin), but also silence, which acts as a buried libidinal undercurrent, an unassimilable body without organs within the plane of immanence's machinic phylum that represents Freud's death drive and Deleuze and Guattari's disjunctive synthesis.

One of the most important uses of sound in *M* is to express the contagion of fear and panic spread by the media. Thus, shortly after Elsie's disappearance, a number of newspaper vendors hit the streets yelling 'Extra! Extra!' and as one cries out, 'Who is the murderer?' we cut to Beckert's back as he writes his confession letter to the papers, whistling the *Peer Gynt* refrain (thus further stoking the media fires). Just as Beckert concludes the last line of his letter, we hear a male news vendor's voice-over shout: '10,000 marks reward'. We then cut to a police poster announcing the same and 'Who is the murderer?' as we hear two disembodied voices: Woman: 'Christ, here we go again!' Man: 'This is horrible!' Rather than act as a redundancy however, these statements initiate a series of audio dissolves that link different sites in the city as if they were all part of the same listening audience. As Lang zooms out to reveal the backs of a small group of citizens standing in front of a wall of posters (including the police announcement) a series of voices call out from the gathering: 'The print's too small. We can't read it.' 'You in front, read it out loud!' The man closest to the poster obliges, reading: 'The terror in our town has found a new victim.' Lang zooms out further to reveal an even larger gathering. 'Louder!' 'We can't hear a word!' At this point, we have a distinct audio segue to another, slightly older male voice-over: 'Certain evidence leads us to believe that this is the same murderer who has already claimed eight victims from among our city's children. We must emphasise once again that . . .' We then cut to a claustrophobic angle down on five middle-class men seated at circular bar/restaurant table – known as a *Stammtisch* or informal gathering of friends – smoking and drinking while the eldest in the group continues the text, but this time reading it aloud from a newspaper:

> it is, now more than ever, every mother and father's sacred duty to alert their children to this ever-present danger and to the friendly guise it is likely to assume. A little candy, a toy, or an apple can suffice to lure a child to his or her doom.

While Tom Gunning agrees with the above description (that the second part of the voice-over is read exclusively from the newspaper) (Gunning 2000: 176), Noël Burch argues that the second off-screen voice was actually that of a radio announcer before segueing to the man in the café (1991: 23). Kaes takes a middle ground, noting that the voice, 'disembodied at first, could easily have been that of a radio, carrying the news everywhere, disregarding distinctions between outside and inside, public and private' (2001: 39). However, Michael P. Ryan gives a far more insightful reading, arguing that

> German radio announcers regularly based their news reports on the daily newspaper and they were even known to read the newspaper aloud over the airwaves. In fact, the connection between the two media was so strong that radio news was commonly referred to as 'die gesprochene Tageszeitung' ('the spoken newspaper') during the Weimar era. Nevertheless, at stake here is not whether or not we are listening to a newspaper being read aloud in a bar or in a broadcast studio; on the contrary, at stake here is what the disagreement about this sequence reveals. In my view, it reveals that *M* has provided us with a brilliant representation of the intermedial fog that had enveloped Weimar's modern media landscape. (2013: 271–2)

This transmission of rumour and innuendo through sound segues and cross-fading continues with the café scene that follows. As the older man reads from the newspaper, he repeats the news vendor's earlier shout from the street: 'Who is the murderer?' [As if in accusation, Lang cuts to a man holding a curved cigar-holder seated at the table to the right.] 'What does he look like? Where is he hiding? No one knows him, yet he is among us. Anybody sitting next to you could be the murderer.' This incites a Bald Man seated to the far left to accuse the cigar smoker of pederasty. The latter is outraged at such slander and lunges at the camera: 'You're crazy, you dirty swine!' The Bald Man stands up: 'Who's the swine? Me, or a man who chases little girls?' The Bald Man then accuses him of murder, leading the cigar smoker to run around the table to attack him. Meanwhile, the older man reading from the newspaper tries to calm them down: 'Gentlemen!' All to no avail:

> Cigar Smoker: 'I'll see you in court!'
> Bald Man: 'I'll have you locked up!'
> Cigar Smoker: 'Slanderer! Trying to ruin my reputation!'

On the word 'Slanderer!', Lang match cuts to the bedroom of a bourgeois apartment which has clearly been searched by the police as we hear the bitter, off-screen voice of its occupant, Mr Jäger: 'Damn slanderer! [His wife enters, crying . . .] Besmirching a man's good name! And the police fall for it! [A Policeman enters carrying his notebook as Jäger follows him in.] A search warrant!' Then, after his wife bemoans the disgrace that has fallen upon her family, her husband denounces the tide of rumour that is driving the police investigation: 'Searching a man's house based on an anonymous letter!' The Policeman predictably responds that the police are only doing their job and understands fully why the Jägers are in constant fear for their children: 'You see? That's why the police must follow up every lead. Any man on the street [Suddenly we cut to a little man on the street. He is about sixty, smartly dressed and wearing a bowler hat and spectacles with round metal rims as he stops under a street lamp to read his newspaper] could be the murderer.'

Again, Lang uses the smooth linkage of dialogue and voice-over to spread the rumour mill to different parts of the city, this time the brutal accusations against the little man after he is approached by a young girl who asks him for the time (unfortunately he also asked her where she lived so he must be the killer!). As Michel Chion argues,

> a word or phrase spoken by a character serves as a pivot between scenes. Thus the word of 'child murderer' – Kindermörder – pronounced by one character in one

scene leads to another scene that either shows the criminal or shows another social group repeating the word, suggesting the thaumaturgic power of a magic spell, where what is named appears. (2009: 48)

As one might expect, Lang continues this supernatural 'spell' of rumour by linking the public attack on the little man to the next victim in line. As the mob shouts: 'He's the murderer!' 'Call the police!' 'Never around when you need 'em!' 'Officer!' we cut to another policeman arresting a pickpocket on the top floor of a double-decker bus. When the thief complains, 'Sure, you can catch pickpockets! Why don't you catch the murderer instead!' we cut to the gathered throng at the bottom of the stairs. Brainwashed by the media, they just hear the word 'murderer' and assume the worst: the pickpocket is the culprit. 'The murderer . . . That's him . . . the murderer!' For Chion, 'textual speech eventually threatens to spread like a cancer with no master narrator to assume control over it and channel it' (2009: 48).

However, Lang does use montage as a form of master narrative to channel the contagion of sound through the contrasting and parallel investigations led by Lohmann and Schränker respectively. Together they help to consolidate and spread the mechanics that make up the *dispositif*. This is expressed through a long sequence of cross-cutting between police and underworld meetings as they attempt to come up with viable strategies to identify and locate Beckert. Lang stresses both their similarities and their differences. Thus, a police officer, adopting a military tone fully in line with Jünger's advocacy of 'total mobilisation' suggests that they 'Step up ID checks, comb the entire city, and raids – relentless, ever tougher raids!' We then cut to Schränker's Con-man: 'We need informers! We must know the police's plans almost before they do themselves!' Franz then chimes in: 'The girls gotta work the cops more! How often has one of us been nabbed 'cause his gal ratted on him to the cops? Now they can rat on the cops!' Lang's montage then gives the impression that police and criminals are all part of the same discussion, albeit in different spaces. A Plain-clothes detective suggests that, 'Every resident, every landlord, every property owner must be forced to consent to meticulous searches of his property for the slightest of clues.' The Pickpocket 'responds':

> We have our connections. What if we put an article in the papers that our syndicates – I mean, our organisation – doesn't wish to be lumped in together with this pig, and that the cops should look for this guy somewhere else. He's not even a real crook!

Lang suggests the difficulty of such a tactic by cutting back to the police:

> This man may well be – when not engaged in the actual act of killing – a harmless, upstanding citizen who wouldn't hurt a fly. In his right mind, perhaps he plays marbles with his landlady's kids or plays cards with friends. Without what I'll call the innocuousness of these murderers' private lives, it's inconceivable that someone like Grossmann or Haarmann could have lived right next door to their neighbours for years without arousing the faintest trace of suspicion!

In one case, Lang matches a line of dialogue from a police conversation with an underworld meeting to show how the two groups have made similar progress but at different levels of advancement. Just as Lohmann and his Assistant discover Beckert's heavily grained window sill and the red pencil shavings, Lohmann proclaims, 'My God, finally! We're finally on his trail.' We then cut to Schränker as he sits wearing his bowler hat, back to the camera. The Cheater is on the phone opposite him:

> Cheater: 'What? They're on his trail?'
> The Con-man bursts into shot from right: 'Did they find him?'
> Pickpocket: 'The beggars found him.'
> Burglar: 'His whistling gave him away.'
> Pickpocket: 'They put a mark on him.'

The phone conversation then allows us to cut diegetically to another space where we discover that the Cheater's caller is Leeser, sending in the latest news from the streets: 'They're following the mark. He isn't out of sight for a second. [Beckert walks down the street with another Little Girl]. His every move is being watched.'

In this case Lang uses sound matching (via the words 'We're finally on his trail') to link the two investigations but also to underline how the underworld tactics are far in advance of Lohmann's, thus creating a form of discrepant time-image, for although the two organisations mesh uncomfortably together, they are also independent in both their methods and objectives. As Deleuze argues in *Cinema 2: The Time-Image*,

> in *M* the collaboration passes through a speech-act which becomes independent of the two parties concerned, because a phrase begun by the commissioner will be continued, extended, or transformed by the leader of the gang, in two different places, and will make visible a problematic interaction of parties which are themselves independent, as a function of 'circumstances' (sociology of situations, of circumstances). (1989: 228–9)

Leeser's comment that 'They're following the mark. He isn't out of sight for a second' gives rise to the importance to a second plane of composition in *M*, that of hapticity and indexicality, which also serves to reinforce the integration of the *Typus* into the *dispositif*. In her groundbreaking 2015 article, 'Indexing Identity: Fritz Lang's *M*', Kata Gellen shows that

> *M* posits a view of individual identity that is determined not by personality or interiority but by the physical traces a person leaves behind and are left behind on him. Identity, thus, becomes a function of identification – something outward and external. In this way, Lang exposes and critiques how identity is conceived and established in modern society – as something cold, objective, and impersonal. (2015: 426)

'Cold and impersonal' echoes Jünger's ideal of a detached 'second consciousness', but it also underlines the new urbanism as a series of interlocking indexes of identity, epitomised by the letter 'M' that Leeser imprints on Beckert's shoulder, an accusing imprimatur that evokes, as Gellen points out, various associations: murderer (*Mörder*), grieving mothers (*Mütter*), urban crowds (*Massen*), power (*Macht*) and, most significantly for our purposes, mobilisation (*Mobilmachung*). More importantly, the haptic qualities of mark-making and the leaving of impressions focus the audience's attention on the human body (both as subject and object), its visibility and invisibility.

M is filled with indexical signification, using not only sound (as we saw earlier) but also touch and physical impression as a means of setting up contiguities and metonymic connections between different bodies and spaces. The most obvious is Leeser's 'branding' of Beckert's upper back, but this is repeated at the kangaroo court when Heinrich the balloon seller touches Beckert on the shoulder just prior to giving evidence against him, and at the very end when a policeman reaches in to arrest him. We have already seen that the latter is common police practice when making an arrest because the same happens to Franz after he is interrogated by Inspector Groeber (Theodor Loos) at the police station. As Groeber says, 'Take him away', a hand reaches in and taps Franz on the shoulder. He dutifully stands and exits left.

Similarly, Beckert is tracked down by the police not by his personal appearance or a mug shot (or even Francis Galton-type physiognomy studies), but by the indexical wood grain impression left on his letter to the press and the physical traces of his red pencil. Again, as Gellen rightly argues,

> Roughly, *M* suggests that identity is no longer determined or guaranteed by physical appearance or the personal name, much less by mental and emotional states. It consists instead of physical traces of bodily actions, marks that we make and marks we are forced to bear. Inscription, then, is not only a way to transmit language and images but an indexical marker of identity. Lang's film criticizes this modern view of identity, which is determined not by individuals but by impersonal organizations and institutions that enact dehumanizing processes of identification and classification. (2015: 428)

This is particularly true of the acoustic indexical trace that finally leads to Beckert's recognition and capture by the beggars – his *Peer Gynt* refrain. According to Gellen, this is a different type of index from that of haptic imprints. The latter capture the trace of the physical nature of something and always involve touch: it is the mark of something that happened in the past, that 'which has been', much like C. S. Peirce's footprint as indexical sign. In contrast, Beckert's refrain is divorced from the thing it represents and is placed firmly in the present (or even the future as a form of repeated leitmotif), not the past. It is a deictic index representing 'hereness' and 'nowness': the murderer is here now!! However, the deixis can be remembered or recorded (as in the case of Heinrich's recall) so that it can become an index of trace (and therefore usable as evidence at the trial). In other words, Beckert's refrain is an agency of deterritorialisation when it is actually whistled (unfolding), but of reterritorialisation when it is recalled and re-indexed as an inscription (enfolding). Gellen sums up Lang's cross-fertilisation of sound and indexicality/hapticity as the predominant plane of composition as follows:

> If *M* does not generate its narrative drive in the manner of a whodunit, what propels the story? The answer lies in the film's virtuosic parallel editing of the two investigations, one led by the police and one led by the mobsters. Though the mobsters do 'win' – they are able to identify and locate Beckert before the police do so – this fact is less important than a recognition that the race to identify and seize Beckert is a *contest of inscription*. (2015: 431)

So where does that leave silence as a vector for the exhumation of the plane of consistency? Firstly, we have a diegetic reference to the psychological importance of silence given during Beckert's defence plea at the kangaroo court. As he clutches his hands together in anguish, he states:

> I have to roam the streets endlessly, always sensing that someone's following me. It's me! I'm shadowing myself! Silently . . . but I still hear it! Yes, sometimes I feel like I'm tracking myself down. I want to run – run away from myself! But I can't! I can't escape from myself! I must take the path that it's driving me down and run and run down endless streets! I want off!

Here Beckert suggests that even his own silent self-surveillance – representing one half of the *doppelgänger* – is still audible to the other half: an obvious split personality. Then, he continues:

> And with me run the ghosts of the mothers and children. They never go away. They're always there! Always! Always! Except . . . when I'm doing it . . . when I . . . [He makes a strangling motion with his hands, then lets them fall limply at his sides.] Then I don't remember a thing. Then I'm standing before a poster, reading what

I've done. I read and read . . . I did *that*? I don't remember a thing! But who will believe me? Who knows what it's like inside me? How it screams and cries out inside me when I have to do it! Don't want to! Must! [He screams in agony.] Don't want to! Must!

Only when Beckert is in the act of committing the murders do the ghosts disappear and the tormenting screams stop: silence is his only sublimating solution to his innate double bind, caught as he is between wartime and peacetime egos.

Tom Gunning makes an excellent point when he argues that Beckert's psychosis takes the form of a film within a film, one with continual screenings which he cannot control or end – a Syncinema (where the audience is let in on the device of Beckert's self-punishing psychic theatre) that evolves into a form of 'sin cinema', a veritable snuff film.[5] As Gunning argues,

> The child always gives way to the bogeyman, the child-bride and her loving mother become vengeful ghosts. He can only live with this horror by becoming a horror himself and eradicating his child audiences. But now he has been recognized by others, who will end his private drama with a theatrical performance of their own. (2000: 191)

It's significant that many of those present at the trial nod in understanding and empathy – they've obviously been through this too – a criminal repetition compulsion. Thus Beckert's plea gives us a new motive for his actions:

> He commits them in order to stop the infernal repeating drama, the imaginary snuff film on an endless projection loop, to give himself relief, to make himself unconscious. [. . .] The murder is the blind spot of his torment, the release from the constant images and torture – oblivion. (Gunning 2000: 195)

Or, for our purposes, chaos as silence as chaos. It's an abyss of total unconsciousness achieved only when he kills a young child. His libidinal drives are killed off in the very act of killing others – but only in his fantasy world. In reality he always returns to consciousness and being tortured by his ever-present ghosts: 'One awakes from an imagined/attempted death/suicide only to find the private movie is still unreeling' (Gunning 2000: 195).

---

[5] We will discuss this evolution from Syncinema to 'sin cinema' in more detail in the Conclusion when we discuss Mike Figgis's *Leaving Las Vegas* and Harmony Korine's *Trash Humpers*.

Lang expands Beckert's self-willed silence into the main fabric of the film itself, not only to express the murderer's retreat into the act of killing, but also to show how this psychosis has spread throughout the entire fabric of the city and becomes an intrinsic (if virtual or latent) part of the machinic *dispositif* as a whole. Significantly, *M* opens with a framing silence, each side of the announcing gong and as a lead-in to the children's elimination game, as if to suggest an unseen and unheard 'presence' that will pervade everything that follows. This is fully borne out in the sequence with Elsie's mother cooking lunch, where Lang uses the shrill sound of her voice to mark her increasing panic. Thus she moves to the kitchen window, opens it and looks out with her back to the camera: 'Elsie! Elsie!!!' We then cut to the overhead, vortex-like shot of the tenement's inner staircase (which will become a Lang staple in many of his films to follow) as Mrs Lohmann cries out in desperation from off-screen: 'Elsie!!!' Cut to the attic: empty except for some clothes hanging out to dry. Again, 'Elsie!!! [Even more shrill] Elsie!!!!' We then get the first extensive use of silence as Lang cuts to an angle down on Elsie's empty lunch setting: 'her clean plate, her spoon, and her folded serviette' (von Harbou 1973: 102; 1968: 19). Cut to a

> Medium close-up of a patch of scrubby ground. Out of the undergrowth, rolls Elsie's ball. It stops in the middle of the frame. The big, doll-shaped balloon floats up and catches momentarily in some telegraph wires, until the wind shakes it free and carries it away. (von Harbou 1973: 102; 1968: 19)

While the sound of Mrs Lohmann's cry of 'Elsie!' links the first set of shots as a form of objective correlative of her own subjective fear and horror, the silences switch us to that of Beckert, whereby the immanence of death fuses with his own respite from his self torture: it's as if the rolling ball and the doll-shaped balloon represent the release of his demons and not just Elsie's death.

More importantly, Beckert's silences are an intrinsic part of the *dispositif* as a form of machinic drive that intersects with, but also differentiates itself from, other parts of the larger social machine: State, military, police, capitalism, the underworld. Guattari's ecosophical model is extremely useful here as it helps us to avoid a Freudian, Oedipal reductionism based on a simple 'double bind' or split subject. Thus Guattari writes that 'In order to counteract reductionist approaches to subjectivity, we have proposed an analytic of complexity starting with an ecosophic object with four dimensions' ([1992] 1995: 124). These four dimensions can be outlined as follows (with their corresponding Freudian terms in the right column):

GUATTARI	FREUD
1. Material, energetic and semiotic **Fluxes**	Unconscious (Libido)
2. Concrete and abstract machinic **Phylums**	Drives
3. Virtual/Potential/Incorporeal **Universes** of value Ecological Becomings of new Subjectivities Unrepresentable re-singularisations	Complexes/Sublimation (Value)
4. Finite existential **Territories** Transversality via New media	Transference (Self)

Guattari translates Freud's unconscious into a series of interconnecting fluxes, a cybernetic interaction and feedback of living organisms and social structures. Instead of the Oedipus Complex we have heterogenesis; the talking cure (speech) is replaced by assemblages of enunciation, while the unified subject becomes molecular points of singularity arranged into temporary, ever shifting aggregates. However, none of these elements are autonomous – all entail cybernetic interaction and feedback with larger social structures (like Beckert's pathology with the *dispositif*). As Guattari explains,

> it is as much a matter of establishing a transversalist bridge between the ensemble of ontological strata which, each in their own way, are characterised by specific figures of chaosmosis. Here one is thinking of the visibilised and actualized strata of material and energetic Fluxes, of the strata of organic life, of those of the Socius, of the mecanosphere, but also of the incorporeal Universes of music, of mathematical idealities, of Becomings of desire ... Transversality never given as 'already there', but always to be conquered through a pragmatics of existence. ([1992] 1995: 124–5)

In other words, Guattari's four figures of chaosmosis are strata, becomings and universes: putting into effect a metabolism of the infinite and a politics of immanence.

The machinic phylum, which supersedes Freud's notion of drives (and which is much closer to Deleuze and Guattari's 'Desiring-Machines') is based on the relationship between singularities and aggregates. For Deleuze, a singularity is a form of conceptual island, a given point that can be joined to another point by a vector, thereby producing series and correspondences where perception can be felt in movement (as speeds and slownesses) on both a micro and macro level, thereby joining the infinitesimal to the infinite. Singularities work through a combination of attraction and bifurcation which give rise to different 'traits of expression'. In *A Thousand Plateaus*, Deleuze and Guattari state that, 'We may speak of a *machinic phylum*, or technological lineage, wherever we find *a constellation of singularities, prolongable by certain operations, which converge, and make the operations converge, upon one or several assignable traits of expression*' (1987: 406). The machinic phylum is also self-organising, bringing order out of chaos (as a chaoid) in terms of both biological phenomena and inert matter. As Manuel DeLanda puts it, this self-organisation includes 'all processes in which a group of previously disconnected elements suddenly reaches a critical point at which they begin to "cooperate" to form a higher level entity' (1991: 6–7).

But what if the singularities diverge within a given material or context, perceptual or otherwise? In that case we have to recognise two different phyla. Deleuze and Guattari give the example of the iron sword – descended from the dagger – and the steel sabre – descended from the knife (1987: 406). One might also add Beckert's knife (as weapon) that he uses as a tool to crack the lock in the attic – two different phyla, reinforced ontologically by the sound drop-out that envelops the scene in silence. Thus, 'Each phylum has its own singularities and operations, its own qualities and traits, which determine the relation of desire to the technical element (the affects the saber "has" are not the same as those of the sword)' (Deleuze and Guattari 1987: 406). However, it's important to note that all phyla are tied together by

> a single phylogenetic lineage, a single machinic phylum, ideally continuous: the flow of matter-movement, the flow of matter in continuous variation, conveying singularities and traits of expression. This operative and expressive flow is as much artificial as natural: it is like the unity of human beings and Nature. But at the same time, it is not realized in the here and now without dividing, differentiating. (Deleuze and Guattari 1987: 406)

As DeLanda argues, 'It is as if the principles that guide the self-assembly of these "machines" (e.g., chemical clocks, multicellular organisms or nest-building insect colonies) are at some deep level essentially similar' (1991: 7). In ideological terms, the *dispositif* is thus a unified whole but composed in and through difference. The same machinic model could obviously be applied to *M*'s internal 'cooperation' between the criminal underworld, the police, the legislature and capitalism as a whole, with the *Typus* (what DeLanda calls 'robot consciousness') as the individual unit of such 'cooperation'.

So what is an assemblage and what role does it play? 'We will call an *assemblage* every constellation of singularities and traits deducted from the flow – selected, organized, stratified – in such a way as to converge (consistency) artificially and naturally; an assemblage, in this sense, is a veritable invention' (Deleuze and Guattari 1987: 406). Assemblages thus cut the phylum up into differentiated lineages but without negating its continuity of matter-as-movement: the machinic phylum always cuts across them all, deserting or excluding one all the better to resurface again in another, or acting as an 'included middle' between the two so that they may co-exist. Deleuze and Guattari explain:

> It is thus necessary to take into account the selective action of the assemblages upon the phylum, and the evolutionary reaction of the phylum as the subterranean thread that passes from one assemblage to another, or quits an assemblage, draws it forward and opens it up. *Vital impulse?* [. . .] There is indeed a machinic phylum in variation that creates the technical assemblages, whereas the assemblages invent the various phyla. A technological lineage changes significantly according to whether one draws it upon the phylum or inscribes it in the assemblages; but the two are inseparable. (1987: 407)

For our purposes, the machinic phylum, like Beckert's presence (and absence) in *M*, is always fleeting and in process, never reducible to a static aggregate or one singular point. Indeed,

> the *machinic phylum* is materiality, natural or artificial, and both simultaneously; it is matter in movement, in flux, in variation, matter as a conveyor of singularities and traits of expression. This has obvious consequences: namely, this matter-flow can only be *followed*. (1987: 409)

Thus the need for a street organisation of beggars that can track it, follow it, arrest it, and put it on trial.

Lang highlights the machinic qualities of Beckert's urges in three sequences where he is framed by a shop window, all linked by sound drop-outs. The first two are cross-cut with Lohmann's Assistant examining Beckert's room for clues prior to discovering the window sill and pencil shavings, as if to express a plane of immanence (in this case a botched body without organs) beneath the 'normal surface' of Beckert's domestic life as a nondescript, unassuming tenant of Elisabeth Winkler. As the Assistant rubs his hand over the smooth surface of a round dining table and sifts through the rubbish in his waste basket, Beckert stands by a fruit-seller's barrow, innocently eating an apple. What could be more commonplace? However, Lang breaks the silence with the sound of car horns and a street car as we see two men walk past the window of J. A. Henckels cutlery and silverware shop. Beckert emerges from the left, eating another apple. He stops in front of the shop and is joined by a taller man to the right, who glances at the window display and then moves on. Lang then drops out the sound as we reverse cut to a shot through glass from inside the window as Beckert looks in, 'his face framed in the reflection of a diamond-shaped display of knives. The reflections of other cutlery form geometric patterns around him' (von Harbou 1968: 58; 1973: 139). The silence continues as we cut to a point-of-view shot of the knives arranged in semi-circles in front of the diamond mirror display at the rear. Various knives and scissors are also laid out in a series of display cases on a table, an obvious objective correlative of Beckert's state of mind (the need for symmetry and objective order as a means of keeping his impulses in check).

However, there is more to it than that, because Deleuze and Guattari make a direct connection between the machinic phylum and the deterritorialising effects of metal and metallurgy. In Aristotle's hylomorphic model, for example, which sees Being as a compound of matter and form, the latter are always kept separate by an intermediary dimension so that clay, for example, can be seen specifically as matter, while a mould determines its form. 'In metallurgy, on the other hand,' argue Deleuze and Guattari, 'the operations are always astride the thresholds, so that an energetic materiality overspills the prepared matter, and a qualitative deformation or transformation overspills the form' (1987: 410). The result is a material vitalism that is usually kept hidden or made unrecognisable. 'Metallurgy is the consciousness or thought of the matter-flow, and metal the correlate of this consciousness' (1987: 411). In the case of this particular scene, the corresponding singularity of Beckert and the knives creates a form of 'pan-metallism', an aggregate pulled together by the machinic phylum that expresses the immanent power of corporeality in all matter (human and non-human). More importantly, Deleuze and Guattari also state that 'Metal is neither a thing nor an organism, but a *body* without organs' (1987: 411), suggesting that the entire *mise-en-scène* represents a disjunctive synthesis of a botched Desiring Machine.

The connection of this metallic phylum to immediate sexual desire is marked by an immediate change in Beckert's expression: still framed by the knives he suddenly stops eating and a strange look appears on his face. We cut to his point of view: 'Reflected in the mirror he can see a little girl leaning against the railings on the sidewalk, the image framed with knives' (von Harbou 1968: 58; 1973: 139). We reverse cut back to Beckert, who rubs his mouth and his eyes start to bulge. We cut back to the girl in the mirror, nonchalantly leaning on a railing, clearly waiting for someone. Beckert is taken aback, his arms fall limply to his sides. He sways, eyes closed, trying to catch his breath. He recovers, but only in time to see the girl exit to the left. Lang then fades up the street sounds of car horns as Beckert gathers himself and starts off in pursuit, once again whistling the *Peer Gynt* theme. The sequencing of this scene suggests that the Grieg refrain is the signifier of his acting out his pathology rather than internalising it as pure machinic desire (represented by silence).

After cutting back to the silent scene of the Assistant picking up an empty sweet carton from Beckert's bedside table and taking some notes, we return to the same street and the little girl. She has now moved on to another shop window, this time a bookshop, 'where a cardboard circle with a spiral design turns endlessly while a huge arrow shoots up and down. The little girl stares fascinated by the continual motion, until she turns away distracted by something else' (von Harbou 1968: 59; 1973: 139–40). That something else turns out to be Beckert's off-screen whistle, which trails her movements as the camera tracks to the right. Suddenly, at the sound of a car horn, she turns and delightedly runs into the arms of a smart young woman who has entered shot from the right. Beckert's whistling stops abruptly. Girl: 'Mummy! I wanted to meet you halfway!' Her mother hugs her as they move off left: 'Child, you mustn't do that. You know why.' Foiled again, Beckert is left with the kinetic consolation of the shop window display, whose machinic properties are both an expression *and* a suppression of his desire. As Kaes rightly argues,

> The same hypnotic spiral had appeared in Walter Ruttmann's 1927 documentary, *Berlin Die Sinfonie der Großstadts (Berlin, Symphony of a Big City)* where it connoted an urban vertigo effect. Inspired by Marcel Duchamp's experiments with rotary glass plates and optical machines, the spiral was used as an advertising gimmick in 1920s window displays. In *M*, the manically moving objects correspond to Beckert's agitated state. His feral desire and lust radiate outward, animating all objects around him. (2001: 59)

Beckert's inability to sublimate these drives is made clear in the next scene, where he retreats from the prying eye of Lang's camera (which is in itself an agency of surveillance) behind an outdoor café trellis. Several shots of cognac are unable to quench his insatiable thirst and he leaves quickly, once again whistling his refrain before we cut back to Lohmann's office.

The final machinic/sexual connection to Beckert occurs after Leeser has marked his back with the letter 'M' and, accompanied by silence, the underworld systematically tracks his movements on the street after he has been 'spotted' by Heinrich, the balloon seller escorting another little girl. Echoing the interior shot of J. A. Henckels cutlery and silverware shop, we now see Beckert and the girl stop in front of a toy store display. There are various dolls, teddy bears and toys, and the moving legs of a marionette/jumping jack dangling into top of frame. He talks to her enthusiastically and she points out a particular toy toward the left of the window (her right). After we cut to a street shot as they approach the store entrance, the silence is broken by the film's big reveal: she points out the chalked 'M' on his back. His silent reverie is shattered, literally and figuratively.

The marionette/jumping jack serves several conceptual and affective purposes in this shot. Firstly, it once again evokes the machinic phylum but also Heinrich von Kleist's essay, 'The Puppet Theatre', which stresses the importance of coordinating a puppet's limbs not by using separate strings for each section (which allows for independent expression) but to a common centre of gravity (or deterritorialised aggregate of consistency):

> it sufficed if this, inside the figure, were controlled; the limbs, which were nothing but pendula, followed without further interference, mechanically, of their own accord. He added that this movement was a very simple one; that whenever the centre of gravity was moved *in a straight line* the limbs described a *curve*; and that often, if shaken by accident, the whole thing was brought into a kind of rhythmical activity similar to dancing. (2004: 411–12)

Because of the single wire, all the other limbs (which would be the mark of affection or self-awareness), are dead. As a result, the discovery of the self and self-consciousness is seen by Kleist as an irretrievable fall from grace – it would therefore separate Beckert and those with similar pathologies from the real world and from his own Self because he is perpetually perceiving himself as Other. In addition, the marionette's legs, which open and close like spread legs, resemble the sexually aggressive letter 'M' in Peter Flötner's *Menschenalphabet* (1534), a mark therefore that is not only inscribed on Beckert's back but which also frames his face: a sexual profile that marks him as both the puppet *and* puppetmaster of his own marionette theatre.

Of course, Beckert is not the sole actor in this production: he is fully integrated into the *dispositif* as yet one more cog in the machine. Thus, when he first composes his letter to the press using the red pencil, Lang accompanies the scene with Beckert's whistled *Peer Gynt* refrain, but when it is actually published in the newspaper and read by the police, Lang cuts the soundtrack entirely, as if to suggest that Beckert's machinic pathology is deepening through his exploitation of media coverage and must now inevitably involve both the underworld and Lohmann's more 'legitimate' investigation. Thus it's no accident that Leeser's chalking of the letter 'M' on his palm, Lohmann and his Assistant's discovery of the red pencil, the street beggars' tracking of Beckert, and Damowitz the night watchman's contact with a passing policeman on his beat are all linked by silence as a unified politics/surveillance of immanence.

This plane of immanence also extends to a broader sexuality where the Desiring Machine, capitalism, the underworld and the policing machine unite through the common trope of prostitution. Inspired by the Minister's complaints about lack of progress in the investigation, the Chief of Police outlines their tactics on the phone (intercut with actual examples in the field) before admitting that 'the investigation has not yet yielded the slightest results, nor have nightly raids in the criminal districts'. This inaugurates ninety seconds of silence as we cut to prostitutes and their clients on the street in the red light district at night. A Prostitute playfully bumps into a potential client (a plain-clothes policeman, according to the script) who goes on his way. She moves on towards the camera. Further on, under a streetlamp, another girl talks with a client while an angle down on a wet side street sees a couple disappear into a seedy hotel, as a detective, standing under another street lamp, left, looks on. Eventually, the whole area is filled with detectives as they arrive in squad cars and the call girls are manhandled into the hotel for questioning. The whole enterprise is run with military precision and timing, ending with a Jünger-type fantasy of five plain-clothes detectives walking in line in front of seven uniformed cops as they approach the high-angled camera. Lang then cuts to a side view of the procession from a side alley before breaking the silence with a loud human whistle (a criminal?) followed by a police whistle (the force of law). The raid on the Crocodile Club follows. This is obviously a carefully choreographed example of 'total mobilisation', presented in contrast to Beckert's 'lone wolf', perverse sexuality that escapes the d*ispositif*'s sublimation of sexual desire into exchange value and Taylorist production.[6]

Finally, Lang uses silence to create a direct link between Beckert's psychosis and that of the underworld, suggesting that the eventual emergence of Nazi Germany has deeper roots in Schränker's pathology rather than the pseudo-militarisation of Lohmann's forces. Thus as the Crime Lord and his men leave the office building with a restrained Beckert before heading to the distillery, Lang cuts to a series of silent shots showing the results of their violent incursion: an angle down on Damowitz as he lies unconscious on the floor, wrists handcuffed together; two other Watchmen, slumped in a corner gagged and similarly handcuffed; a smashed door outside BALAJ & Co.; a view along the attic passageway, smashed compartment slats to the left, a brick wall to the right; and finally an angle down on Franz's hole in the floor as a torch beam sweeps across the floor of the room below and rises towards the opening. The latter is clearly used as a more benign

---

[6] In Chapter 4 we will explore Godard's expression of a similar *dispositif*, where he presents all capitalist exchange as a form of prostitution, only this time indexed by a cacophony of urban sound. It is the silences-as-interstices that suggest an alternative vector.

contrast to the former shots (a non-violent burglary rather than a premeditated felony).

This view is more than confirmed at the kangaroo court, which Lang opens with an extended thirty-second pan to the right across the vast crowd of underworld 'jurors'. The scene is shot in complete silence as we eventually rest on Schränker and his men, before the silence is broken by Beckert's frenzied calls for help. In the context of the whole film we can't help but connect Beckert's role as a botched body without organs to the larger machinic phylum of the underworld's perverted sense of justice. Thus when the soundtrack returns, we hear a series of cries from the mob: 'There's only one thing right for a man like you – death!'; 'Right! Kill him!'; 'Kill the rabid dog!'; 'Put the animal to death!' Then, when the defence attorney fights back and attempts to plead Beckert's case – 'I will not let you shout me down! I will not allow a murder to be committed in my presence. I demand that this human being . . .' – an off-screen voice protests: 'That's not a human being!'

Even though *M*'s last silence is framed by the off-screen voice of the police officer who has come to arrest Beckert – 'In the name of the law . . .' – and the legitimate Judge who proclaims 'In the name of the people . . .' at Beckert's legal trial, this sense of criminal law conquering all is not what we take away from the film, despite Mrs Beckmann's appeal to be vigilant and watchful. Instead we remember Schränker's leather jacket and cane – the outward 'uniform' of an SS officer – the extreme rhetoric of final solutions, the systematic elimination of outsiders, and the euthanasia of mental patients. More importantly, in just a few years, Beckert's 'M' will resurface as the Star of David and Pink Triangle as outward markers of anti-semitic and homophobic extremism, while in what amounts to the film's biggest irony, Beckert's impassioned courtroom speech (and his yearning for silence, just to make the screams stop!) will be appropriated as part of the 1940 racist documentary *The Eternal Jew* (*Der ewige Jude*, directed by Fritz Hippler) 'to show simultaneously the dominance of the Weimar cinema by Jews (such as "the Jew actor", Lorre) and as a portrayal of psychotic Jewish behaviour' (Gunning 2000: 198).

It also shows that the machinic phylum serves multiple duties, both metallic and sensate, as a generator of singularities *and* aggregates. Returning once again to Kleist, as Deleuze and Guattari, argue, 'He presents us with a becoming-weapon of the technical element simultaneous to a becoming-affect of the passional element (the Penthesilea equation)' (1987: 400). After all, 'Affects are projectiles just like weapons; feelings are introceptive like tools. [. . .] Weapons are affects and affects weapons' (1987: 400). That's why we have to be vigilant and watchful. All of us!

CHAPTER 2

Ecosophical Chaoids: Towards an 'Infinite Cinema' with Hollis Frampton's *Zorns Lemma* (1970) and *Gloria!* (1979)

In an oft-quoted 1937 letter to the German writer and translator Axel Kaun, Samuel Beckett advocated Modernist literature's role as a radical fracture of what he deemed to be the superficial continuity of language by tearing fissures or interstices into its artificial surface:

> It is to be hoped the time will come [...] when language is best used where it is most efficiently abused. Since we cannot dismiss it all at once, at least we do not want to leave anything undone that may contribute to its disrepute. To drill one hole after another into it until that which lurks behind, be it something or nothing, starts seeping through – I cannot imagine a higher goal for today's writer... (Fehsenfeld and Overbeck 2009: 518)

More importantly, Beckett extends his mission beyond literature to include music, and by extension, the visual image, arguing that the disruption of language's signifying function is akin to the way that intervals (and silences) carve up and interrupt the tonal progression of a piece of music:

> Is there any reason why that terrifyingly arbitrary materiality of the word surface should not be dissolved, as for example the sound surface of Beethoven's Seventh Symphony is devoured by huge black pauses, so that for pages on end we cannot perceive it as other than a dizzying path of sounds connecting unfathomable chasms of silence? (Fehsenfeld and Overbeck 2009: 518–19)

Hollis Frampton's *Zorns Lemma* (1970) and *Gloria!* (1979) are particularly apt cinematic examples of this process, for both dislocate the innate structures of language by using silence as semantic and sonic hiatuses, literally tearing holes in the material surface of sound and image to disclose a more 'chaotic', topographical structure beneath that folds together the finite and the infinite, life and death. In his essay, 'Impromptus on

Edward Weston: Everything in its Place', Frampton relates these hiatuses to the differentiating, infraliminary role of the interstice, noting that:

> Again and again, we find texts that amount to nothing other than minute descriptions, in flat, declarative sentences, of spaces, of objects disposed within those spaces, of the surface and volumetric attributes of those objects. In Beckett, in Robbe-Grillet, in Borges, we are accustomed to notice, at first, that nothing appears to be happening. Causality and temporality having been dispossessed from the text, we are left free to enjoy the gradual construction of the space within our consciousness that the text will occupy, as we experience the process of reading in a time – that of the spectator – which is explicitly and entirely disjunct from the atemporality of the text itself. (2009a: 72)

Thus it is the reader or spectator who actively 'constructs' the text, either from the inside (by subjectively tying together its structural logic – in Frampton's case, set theory), or from the outside by mentally unifying the artwork in the form of affective monuments (Deleuze and Guattari's plane of composition) that are often purely imaginary.

In order to highlight the 'exhaustion' of the central, silent section of the film (its main affective sequence, which demands audience participation), *Zorns Lemma* is framed by two overdetermined verbal 'bookends'. The first is a brief opening section featuring readings from the *Bay State Primer*, Euro-America's first grammar book, which was designed to teach late eighteenth- and early nineteenth-century children the alphabet. The epilogue features a couple and their dog walking away from the camera across a snow field as six female voices read selected passages in rondo, at one word each per second, from the 1225 treatise, *On Light, or the Ingression of Forms* by Robert Grosseteste, the Bishop of Lincoln (c. 1175–1253). In Frampton's hands, each text represents the systematicity of a different form of set theory. As Melissa Ragona explains, 'For Frampton, set theory permits the abstract representation of film's capacity to catalog intersecting planes of perception in infinite combinations, allowing him to perceive and articulate the expansive range of film in a way that semiotics could not' (2004: 99). She then argues that 'set theory offered a world free of intended speech, a world that could account for infinite sets of relations unhinged from a unidirectional matrix' (2004: 100). Thus it is in the silent middle section of *Zorns Lemma* that Frampton deterritorialises the narrative and semiotic structure of language by literally drilling into its surface fabric through a form of double replacement. First, cyclical fragments of New York City street signs (words taking the place of concepts) are arranged in alphabetical order, one image per second, but then slowly replaced at random by real-time images of everyday activities and phenomena (but without the text), until all letters have been re-represented by a newly formed contiguous logic of production, movement and sensation.

In this respect the film constructs a powerful ecosophical project, for as Guattari argues in *The Three Ecologies*,

> There is no overall hierarchy for locating and localizing the components of enunciation at a given level. They are composed of heterogeneous elements that take on a mutual consistency and persistence as they cross the thresholds that constitute one world at the expense of another. (2008: 36)

In this respect, Frampton's fragments form silent, asignifying chains much like Schlegel's 'work of art', which is simultaneously complete and self-contained but also a fragment of a larger whole, for 'A fragment, like a miniature work of art, must be totally detached from the surrounding world and closed on itself like a hedgehog' (*The Athenaeum*: fragment 206, Guattari 2008: 36). *Zorns Lemma* thus creates the possibility of creative proliferation at the very point that discursive chains (in this case the alphabet) break with meaning and form their own theoretical and practical auto-constructibility, for every image is potentially replaceable by another. For Guattari,

> These focal points of creative subjectification in their nascent state can only be accessed by the detour of a phantasmatic economy that is deployed in a random form. In short, no one is exempt from playing the game of the ecology of the imaginary! (2008: 38)

In short, that which forces us to think is the SIGN – specifically the contingency of its encounters. Deleuze expands this point in *Proust and Signs*, arguing that art is the ultimate world of signs, a dematerialised avenue to ideal essence. Art – and by extension, film – reacts on all the other signs, integrating sensual signs and colouring them with aesthetics, thereby teasing the essence out of them. 'This is why all the signs converge upon art; all apprenticeships, by the most diverse paths, are already unconscious apprenticeships to art itself. At the deepest level, the essential is in the signs of art' (Deleuze 2000: 14).

As in the case of most of Frampton's films, *Zorns Lemma*'s search for essences is constructed around a series of paradoxes. In his 1976 essay, 'Notes on Composing in Film', Frampton argued that 'a paramount signified of any work of art is that work's own ontogeny', and that 'the understanding of an art consists in the recovery of its axiomatic substructure' (1976: 104–5). Then, 'Once the set of axioms has been isolated and disintricated, the artist may proceed to modify it in any of four ways: by substitution, constriction, augmentation, or by displacement' (1976: 106). Film art thus consists of its own self-reflexive expression through a combination of reading and misreading its internal axiomatic structure: 'The incorrectly read or imperfectly disentangled compositional assumption invariably remains to haunt the intellectual space usurped by its successor. Thus new works building upon axioms derived by misreading from the structural assumptions of older works, must be forever contingent' (1976: 107). Against the established morphology that assumes that films are isolated objects and that understanding them involves little more than determining their precise location on a predetermined grid – e.g. through genre, auteur studies, national cinemas, types of montage, etc. – Frampton proposes another, radically different morphology, 'one that views film, not from the outside, as a product to be consumed, but from the inside, as a dynamically evolving organic code directly *responsive* and *responsible*, like every other code, to the supreme mediator: consciousness' (1976: 109). As we shall see in the next chapter, this places Frampton's oeuvre in direct alignment with Isidore Isou's *phase ciselante* or chiselling phase of cinema, which renounces all subject matter *external* to the medium and focuses instead on its internal form.

As the film's title suggests, in this case Frampton appropriates German mathematician Max Zorn's 'lemma' as his structuring principle. Here, the eleventh axiom of set theory proposes that, given a set of sets, there is a further set composed of a representative item from each set. Thus, according to Frampton,

> *Every partially ordered set contains a maximal fully ordered subset*. You may multiply instances at your leisure. For one or more things to be 'ordered', they must share a perceptual (provable) element. So there are many ordered *subsets* within the set of all elements that make up the film, e.g. all shots containing the color red. (2009c: 195)

Although Frampton's film doesn't exactly demonstrate Zorn's axiom, his use of a set of sets to structure the film suggests that he subscribes to an 'existential axiom' as the chief governing device of film narrative. In this sense Frampton is a structuralist film-maker *par excellence* because his set of sets is the lowest common denominator of the film shot, itself composed of twenty-four still frames per second. Thus on the micro level every shot is an ordering of the twenty-four frames which constitute it, while on the macro level, as we shall see, Frampton structures his film's narrative into further series of twenty-four (in terms of both sound and image). In this sense Frampton uses set theory centripetally and centrifugally. On the one hand, he isolates his schema into a totalising logic, withdrawn from the world like Schlegel's curled-up hedgehog, on the other he uses the fragment to expand and unfold his sets into an infinite connectivity with other sets, like Guattari's deterritorialising ecology of the imaginary. As Allen Weiss neatly puts it:

> This disposition by means of seriality, exemplification, listing, and cataloguing operates within the limits of two antithetical functions. Either such listing is a subversive activity, destroying all taxonomic schemes, or lists serve as formal imperatives, constituting structures and systems. In the former case, a hermeneutic schema entails a de-centering and de-totalizing logic of events, operating according to the aleatory conditions of existence. In the latter, a hermeneutics entails a centering and totalizing logic of structures and formal systems, constituting a determinate axiomatics. (1985: 119)

This two-way system of expansion and contraction, unfolding and enfolding, is remarkably close to Deleuze's description of the movement-image in *Cinema 1*, particularly his analysis of the frame, shot and the cut, which he sees as a closed system composed of parts that belong to various sets. These may subdivide into subsets, or they may themselves be part of a still larger set, and so on to infinity. For Deleuze, closed systems never actually reach completion – they always refer outside themselves to a larger set, a new out-of-field connecting to the whole universe:

> The whole is therefore like thread which traverses sets and gives each one the possibility, which is necessarily realized, of communicating with another, to infinity. Thus the whole is the Open, and relates back to time or even to spirit rather than to content and to space. (1986: 17)

More importantly, Deleuze shares Frampton's view of cinema as an extreme mediator of consciousness, akin to C. S. Peirce's notion of Thirdness or mental relations, for

> The shot is like the movement which continuously ensures conversion, circulation. It divides and subdivides duration according to the objects which make up the set; it reunites objects and sets into a single identical duration. It continuously divides duration into subdurations which are themselves heterogeneous, and reunites these into a duration which is immanent to the whole of the universe. Given that it is a consciousness which carries out these divisions and reunions, we can say of the shot that it acts like a consciousness. (1986: 20)

Zorns Lemma plays out Deleuze's schema through three axiomatic structures, each tied in their different ways to the three daughters of chaos, reaching an apotheosis of ecosophical creativity only in the middle, silent section. Let us examine the two sound 'bookends' first. The prologue is five minutes long, consisting of a soundtrack against a black screen. A woman recites in a school-marmish voice twenty-four rhymes from the *Bay State Primer*, which ties twenty-four letters of the Roman alphabet (I and J, U and V are counted as one, respectively) towards a biblical stricture of collective guilt, oriented, as Frampton himself notes, 'towards death, towards acceptance of authority, a kind of rote learning in the dark' (Gidal 1985: 94). Thus, 'In *Adam's* Fall, we sinned all'; 'Thy life to mend, God's *book* attend'; 'The *Cat* doth play, and after slay'; 'A *dog* will bite a thief at night', etc. For Weiss, 'The mathematical axiom is operative in the alphabetical order of the text; the theological axiom is operative in the biblical content of the text. Thus a twofold axiomatic system is articulated according to a double coding: structural and ontological' (Weiss 1985: 120). The sequence ends with a more abstract assertion of set theory where each letter is shown in isolation against a black background at one image per second, once again tying the filmic shot (twenty-four frames) to a larger narrative set of twenty-four (Roman alphabetical sequencing).

Significantly, the primer's representation of the letter 'Z' takes the form of '*Zaccheus*, he Did climb the tree, His Lord to see'. In this first section the infinity of chaos is relinquished by the function of linguistic reference while it is also saved by the consistency of theological piety. However, like Zaccheus, we are unable to *see* the infinite Creator or his creation. In this sense, Part III's lyric form, manifested through the recitation of Grosseteste's *On Light*, is a neo-Platonic and Aristotelian attempt to express a theology, ontology and cosmology based on the propagation of light. It is, in effect, Hylomorphic, for as Amelia Sparavigna argues, 'We find that the firmament, which is the outermost heavenly sphere, is the simplest body of the world, composed of first matter and first form. To Grosseteste, the first form was light (lux)' (2014: 54). This is fully expressed in *Zorns Lemma*'s voice-over as the couple walk across the snow field into the infinity of pure light:

> The first bodily form I judge to be Light. For Light, of itself, diffuses itself in every direction, so that a sphere of Light as great as you please is born instantly from a point of Light. But Form cannot abandon Matter because Form is not separable and Matter cannot be emptied of Form. Form is Light itself or the doer of its work and the bringer of dimensions into Matter. But Light is of a more noble and more excellent essence than all bodily things. (Frampton 2009c: 194)

That the sequence ends with a flare-out as the film canister runs out of stock, filling the screen with a pure white light, suggests that Frampton is equating Grosseteste's cosmology to that of cinema itself. In this case both reference death (or at least an infinitude of chaos), for as Scott MacDonald correctly observes,

> the flare-out to white not only signals the end of the roll and the film, it is suggestive of the widespread observation by those who have had near-death experiences that, at the moment of death, we see a powerful light. Finally, since Frampton may have assumed that the coming of the light at the end of *Zorns Lemma* would be followed by the lights coming on in the theater and the audience filing out, the exit of the man, woman, and dog from the field is not only echoed by the viewers' exit from the cinematic incarnation, but is prescient of our ultimate exits from life, and the concluding moment of our intellectual growth. (MacDonald n.d.: unpaginated)

As we shall see, Frampton will push this analogy still further in *Gloria!*, which is not only a film about death but the enfolding and unfolding vectors of life experience and cinema itself through a combination of family genealogy, personal memory and the cinematic archive.

Thus, pinpointing a key line from Grosseteste's text: 'In the beginning of time, light drew out matter along with itself into a mass as great as the fabric of the world' (Gidal 1985: 98), Frampton takes this to be

> a fairly apt description of film, the total historical function of film, not as an art medium, but as this great kind of time capsule. It was thinking about this, which led me later to posit the universe as a vast film archive (which contains nothing in itself) with – presumably somewhere in the middle, in the undiscoverable center of this whole matrix of film-thoughts – an unlocatable viewing room in which, throughout eternity, sits the Great Presence screening the infinite footage. (Gidal 1985: 98)

However, because Grosseteste's text is spoken by a chorus of female voices, 'including those of artist and filmmaker Joyce Wieland, choreographer Twyla Tharp, and painter Rosemarie Castoro' (Frampton 2009c: 202 n.3), one word at a time in synch with a metronome, the final section is actually as fragmented as the second, undermining the illusion of homogeneity (and authority) of the source of enunciation, so that once again we have a simultaneous expression of the (word) fragment alongside the (seemingly) infinite image (which is itself made up of five 100-foot rolls, themselves broken down into twenty-four frames per second), the linguistic/representational hedgehog at odds with the ecosophical imaginary.

It is only in the silent middle section that Frampton overcomes this *aporia*, paradoxically by pushing his axiomatic structure to its limits by bringing the serial and the aleatory, contraction and expansion together, thereby forcing his spectator to connect with an incommensurable outside. As Deleuze and Guattari argue,

> Contraction is not an action but a pure passion, a contemplation that preserves the before in the after. Sensation, then, is on a plane that is different from mechanisms, dynamisms, and finalities: it is on a plane of composition where sensation is formed by contracting that which composes it, and by composing itself with other sensations that contract it in turn. (1994: 212)

Silence then would be a contracted form of sensation on the plane of composition that links it both to other sensations/contractions and concepts on the plane of immanence, much like the silence that conceptualises McClure's execution in *The Big Combo*.

Zorns Lemma's central section is forty-five minutes long and consists of, to quote Frampton,

> 2,700 one-second cuts, one-second segments, twenty-four frame segments, of which about half are words: the words are alphabetized. The reason for alphabetizing them really was to make their order as random as possible, that is, to avoid imposing my own taste and making them into little puns or something like that . . . (Gidal 1985: 95)

Thus, the first cycle starts with a cut-out form of the letter 'A', and moves through the words 'Baby', 'Cabinet', 'Daily', 'Each', 'Fabric', 'Gain', 'Hack', etc., each derived from street and shop window signage and posters in Lower Manhattan (although Frampton has a propensity to 'cheat' by breaking his own pre-set rules – he takes Dante's Divine Comedy as his model – 'Fox' was shot in Brooklyn, 'Humble' in Summit & Medina Counties, Ohio – MacDonald 1995: 57). Occasionally a suggestive pairing such as 'Limp Member' pops up, but in general we are more aware of the hiatuses between signs than the narrative continuity of the signs as a syntagmatic chain. This was deliberate on Frampton's part, for he wanted to stress the cut between shots rather than the shots themselves:

> what you see (consciously) most of all is the one-second cut, or pulse. So that what I imply is that the maximal fully ordered subset of all film (which this film proposes to mime) is *not* the 'shot' but the *cut* – the deliberate act of articulation. (Frampton 2009c: 196)

Again, this is reinforced by Deleuze's analysis of the movement-image whereby '*Cutting is the determination of the shot, and the shot, the determination of the movement which is established in the closed system*, between elements or parts of the set' (1986: 18). In addition, it is the cut rather than the shot that determines variation within the system, for not every image is exactly twenty-four frames in length. As Frampton explains, there are metrical errors in twenty-four instances: twelve images are only twenty-three frames long while another twelve are twenty-five frames long. 'Their positions were determined by another party [...] by chance operations specified by me, and then he destroyed the record of their location (without informing me)' (Frampton 2009c: 198). The result is an often imperceptible upsetting of the film's internal rhythm, creating a logic of sensation – something *felt* – that overrides the strict logic of the film's internal axioms.

Over the course of 107 cycles, Frampton gradually replaces each letter-word with an unrelated image that lacks an alphabetic reference. This is not an 'either or' process or a situation where the alphabetical *sign* becomes a non-sign, but rather one of 'inclusive disjunction' where letters and their reciprocal non-alphabetical images generate, as Deleuze and Guattari, put it:

> an immanent use that would no longer be exclusive or restrictive, but fully affirmative, nonrestrictive, inclusive. A disjunction that remains disjunctive, and that still affirms the disjoined terms, that affirms them throughout their entire distance, *without restricting one by the other or excluding the other from the one*, is perhaps the greatest paradox. 'Either . . . or . . . or', instead of 'either/or'. [Emphasis in the original.] (Deleuze and Guattari 1983: 76).

Frampton's multiplicity would necessitate less a linguistics of relational signs (à la Saussure) than one of flows, for

> What defines it is the AND, as something which has its place between the elements or between the sets. AND, AND, AND – stammering. And even if there are only two terms, there is an AND between the two, which is neither the one nor the other, nor the one which becomes the other, but which constitutes the multiplicity. (Deleuze and Parnet 1987: 34–5).[1]

As if to signify the cosmic unity of this replacement ontology, in effect a shift from semiotic structure to infinitude, the first four substitutions reference the four elements – fire (X), water (Z), air (Q) and earth (Y). This initial sequencing is in many ways a set-up, for as we are locked into an axiomatic mode of spectatorship due to the overwhelming structuring hegemony of the alphabet and its corresponding one-second interval, we persist in looking for alphabetic (or at least structural) connections with all subsequent replacement images. For example, could there be a set pattern

---

[1] We will discuss the import of this stammering effect in relation to Godard's *British Sounds* in Chapter 6.

of replacements (say, one every four cycles)? Can the replacement images be categorised as, for example, banal actions – a man painting a green wall white (K); a woman cutting star-shaped cookies from a sheet of dough (D); three men digging a hole (M); Frampton himself assembling a Tinkertoy chain (R) or changing a tyre (T), or everyday phenomena: an egg frying in a pan (B); a stark, single tree in winter (F)? Not surprisingly, it turns out that the system is internally variable. Thus there are no new image substitutions between the fifteenth and the twenty-eighth cycles, but there are two in the short interval between the seventy-fifth and seventy-ninth. Also, certain key images have far more screen time than others. The first substitution – the raging bonfire for X – first appears in the fifth cycle and repeats 102 more times (for a total of 103 seconds of screen time), while the final replacement image for letter C (a red ibis flapping its wings in the Bronx Zoo, much like a phoenix rising from the ashes of the fried egg that precedes it) exists for only one second in the entire film, suggesting an arbitrary value of rarity and exoticism for the ibis imposed directly by Frampton's specific editorial choices.

However, there is also a *performative* and affective logic that runs through the film's internal matrix: every act is completed by the end of the film. Frampton finishes his Tinkertoy chain (although the sequence was actually shot in reverse, with the film-maker taking apart the chain, in order to give an impression of skill) and changes his tyre; a man walks an entire block before disappearing around a street corner; a tangerine is peeled and eaten; a boot lace is tied. Colour also creates links across the matrix, breaking the alphabetical sequence through affective resonance – the red ibis triggers associations with Frampton's red sports car, the yellow yolk of the egg with flashing street lights at night. Moreover, there are also two meta-cinematic durations that once again tie Frampton's use of sets to his structural view of an infinite cinema. Frampton explains the structural logic of the latter in his key essay, 'For a Metahistory of Film: Commonplace Notes and Hypotheses' as follows:

> Before the invention of still photography, the frames of the infinite cinema were blank, black leader; then a few images began to appear upon the endless ribbon of film. Since the birth of the photographic cinema, all the frames are filled with images. There is nothing in the structural logic of the cinema film strip that precludes sequestering any single image. A still photograph is simply an isolated frame taken out of the infinite cinema. (2009b: 134)

Frampton plays this out metaphorically and literally through N's replacement image, which had shown a transparent container gradually filling with beans, so that by the end of the film the cinema screen is also completely filled, as if the mimetic, sculptural reality of the shot in depth had ultimately coincided with the non-sculptural flatness of the cinema frame (in effect a return to a kind of blank screen).[2] Similarly, the man painting the wall eventually covers the screen with white paint, again creating a meta-cinematic image but also creating a proleptic jump to the flare-out at the end of the film and Grosseteste's ontological treatise on light. In other words, the image as recognisable object is transformed into immaterial energy. As Frampton explains the process:

> The act of making a film, of physically assembling the film strip, feels somewhat like making an object: that film artists have seized the materiality of film is of inestimable importance, and film certainly invites examination at this level. But at the instant the film is completed, the 'object' vanishes. The filmstrip is an elegant device for modulating standardized beams of energy. The phantom work itself transpires upon the screen as its notation is expended by a mechanical virtuoso performer, the projector. (2009b: 138)

Frampton's film ultimately raises a key question in relation to the intersection of the three daughters of chaos, specifically whether the matrix of the cycle and set theory is compatible with Frampton's ideal of an infinite cinema, in effect a problem of folding the macro into the micro, the smooth into the striated. Deleuze's analysis of Nietzsche's dice throw and the eternal return can help us here, particularly the observation that there are always two moments of the game: 1. The dice that is thrown (on the Earth); 2. The dice that falls back (in the sky). As Deleuze explains,

> The dice which are thrown once are the affirmation of chance, the combination which they form on falling is the affirmation of necessity. Necessity is affirmed of chance in exactly the sense that being is affirmed of becoming and unity is affirmed of multiplicity. (1983: 26)

In this way Nietzsche – and one might usefully add Frampton to this equation – identifies chance with multiplicity, fragments, parts, chaos: he turns chance into affirmation as *amor fati*. This has important repercussions for the eternal return itself, for the latter is the second moment when the dice fall back – the affirmation of necessity, the number which brings together all the parts of chance *plus* the return of the first moment, the repetition

---

[2] Thus we can see how the insertion of black leader in a Lettrist film – particularly Guy Debord's *Hurlements* – and Godard would then constitute a return to a primordial infinite cinema.

of the dice throw which is also the reaffirmation of chance itself. Thus as Deleuze puts it,

> Universal chaos which excluded all purposeful activity does not contradict the idea of the cycle; for this idea is only an irrational necessity [. . .] What this means is that chaos and cycle, becoming and eternal return have often been brought together, but as if they were opposites. (1983: 28)

For chaos to be made circular – as becoming – it needs an act of an artist-philosopher who can impose the model of an idea upon it. Frampton does this by freeing the circle from the mathematical axiom in favour of the theological – through both the *Bay State Primer* and Grosseteste's treatise – and, more importantly, harness film as an ecosophical catalyst of the artistic fragment. This would make Frampton closer to Heraclitus than to Grosseteste's neo-Platonism, for 'Only Heraclitus foresaw that there is no kind of opposition between chaos and cycle' (Deleuze 1983: 28–9). Both affirm chance and not causality to affirm the number and the necessity that brings it back: an irrational necessity instead of a finality. As Deleuze, citing Nietzsche from the 1935 Friedrich Würzbach (Gallimard) edition of *La Volonté de Puissance*, argues:

> There was not first of all chaos, then little by little a regular and circular movement of all the forms: on the contrary, all this is eternal, removed from becoming; if there ever was a chaos of forces the chaos was eternal and has reappeared in every cycle. *Circular movement* has not come into being, it is the original law, in the same way as the *mass of force* is the original law without exception or possible infraction. All becoming happens inside of the cycle and the mass of force. (*La Volonté de Puissance* II 325 – circular movement = cycle = mass of force = chaos.) (Deleuze 1983: 29)

For Frampton, this is as true of cinema as it is of life, with *Zorns Lemma* as its axiomatic model, its paradigmatic chaoid.

Frampton brings this eternal return to full realisation in *Gloria!*, a ten-minute short that was designed to culminate in his ambitious *Magellan* cycle, a thirty-six-hour film in celebration of Ferdinand Magellan (1480–1521), the Portuguese explorer who was the first to circumnavigate the Earth. Whereas *Zorns Lemma* focuses on set theory and the alphabet as its organisational matrix, *Magellan* (which was nearing completion when Frampton died in 1984) was intended to be shown in a calendrical cycle over a total of 371 days (one film per day) with extra showings on special days such as the solstices and equinoxes. Of course, in the current era of watching films digitally through Netflix or DVD on home TVs, computers and phones, Frampton's cinematic ideal of tapping into an infinite, universal 'film archive' now seems questionable, for as Scott MacDonald argues:

> In fact, current institutions for film exhibition and distribution are ill-equipped for showing the film as Frampton presumably meant it to be seen. In this sense, *Magellan* offers a challenge to the current state of film accessibility, a challenge based on Frampton's admiration of epic literature, and particularly for Joyce's *Ulysses* and *Finnegans Wake*: For Frampton the challenge was to extend cinematic horizons so that the pleasures and revelations of cinematic thought could be as flexible, in terms of accessibility, as the experience of reading serious literature. (MacDonald n.d.)

Nonetheless, taken in isolation, a film like *Gloria!* can give us crucial insight into Frampton's interest in collapsing the spatio-temporal framings of life experience and cinema through the durational possibilities of art as meta-history. If *Zorns Lemma* is more Beckett-ian in its desire to fissure the surface of language, *Gloria!*, with its narrative roots in *Finnegans Wake*, is assuredly more Joycean as a hybrid mash-up of seemingly unassimilable monuments.

Whereas *Zorns Lemma* follows a tripartite structure based on Sound–Silence–Sound that roughly corresponds with different set theories pertaining to rote language–image/text–language-as-light, *Gloria!* follows the same pattern, but flips the order, opening and closing with silence over an early film clip based on *Finnegan's Wake*, an Irish-American comic folk ballad first published in New York in 1864, followed by an animated computer-based flow of unfolding typed text. These frame a central three-and-a-half-minute section featuring a blank, Kelly-green screen accompanied by the film's only sound track, a performance of the Irish hornpipe, 'Madame Bonaparte' performed by Finbar Furey. Thus the film opens with a blue-toned nineteen-second clip from *A Wake in 'Hell's Kitchen'* (1900) shot by Arthur W. Martin on the roof of the Bronx Biograph studio for the American Mutoscope and Biograph Company. Clearly based on a slapstick version of Finnegan, the film is a typical ethnic vaudeville routine akin to *A Gesture Fight in Hester Street*, which dates from the same year, but instead of exploiting Jewish stereotypes this film is set in an Irish slum in Hell's Kitchen and exploits the immigrants' penchant for excessive drinking.

Filmed in the tenement's parlour with a single image of a Christian cross on the wall, an open coffin lies dead centre, with the corpse's feet facing the audience. To the left, the widow (played, in the true tradition of vaudeville, by a man) stands holding a bouquet of flowers as she weeps and wails, wiping away her tears with an apron. To the right, two men in smart suits sit drinking beer. The two men talk, light their pipes as the widow turns away to conceal her grief. Suddenly, the 'corpse' rises up from the coffin, looks around and spies a mug of beer. He picks it up, gulps it down and lies back down again. However, when the widow places the bouquet in the coffin she notices the empty mug of ale and accuses the two mourners of drinking it. A heated argument ensues during which the 'corpse' tosses the flowers from the coffin, causing the widow to faint. Completely freaked, the two men rush away, inadvertently knocking over the coffin and spilling the 'deceased' onto his wife.

The second archive excerpt is a blue-toned print of *Murphy's Wake* (1903), directed by Alf Collins from a play by Dion Boucicault, also for American Mutoscope. In this case the traditional scenario starts a little earlier, with Irish revellers dancing in a back garden. Things turn nasty when two of the men argue over a woman. They stand off and fight with shillelaghs. The bearded man with a black eye patch knocks his hated opponent (i.e. Murphy) to the ground and continues to beat his head while he lies prone on the grass, then runs off past the camera. A priest closes Murphy's eyes and raises his arm in the air, thus pronouncing him dead, whereupon the others carry the corpse in a sombre procession, stage right. We then cut to the interior of the house where Murphy's wake is underway. The priest blesses the victim, then exits right as the wailing mourners keen and lament. As if on cue, Murphy suddenly sits up, looks around, drinks from a jug as the others are oblivious of his return from the dead. He pats his stomach and lies back down again. As the laments continue, he rises yet again to grab the jug. Unfortunately it's empty, so he throws it at the mourners in frustration. It hits one man, who gets up and protests. Murphy falls out of bed, jumps up, hands in the air, dances a jig as the frightened mourners run off and exit through a back door stage right. The key to understanding both the song and its filmic interpretations is that whiskey is seen as both a giver of life and death in a form of eternal return. It is derived from the Irish phrase *uisce beatha* which means 'water of life'. Thus in the original ballad Tim Finnegan is a hod carrier with an insatiable love of booze:

> Tim had a sort of a tipplin' way
> With a love of the liquor now he was born
> To help him on with his work each day
> Had a 'drop of the craythur' every morn.

One day, overly drunk, he falls from a ladder, cracks his skull and is believed dead. At his wake, the mouners get rough and rowdy and spill whiskey on his corpse, causing his resurrection:

> Tim revives! See how he rises!
> Timothy risin' from the bed,

Sayin', 'Whirl your liquor around like blazes
Thunderin' Jaysus! Do you think I'm dead?'

When Joyce appropriated the story for his own *Finnegans Wake* (1939) he also envelops life, death and resurrection together as a form enfolding/unfolding of the universal life cycle. We not only see whiskey as the 'water of life' but 'wake' itself alludes to both a passing into death and oblivion and a re-awakening from sleep. The lifespan *in between* (and *after*) thus forms a biogram where the vectors of life and death harness each other's universal energy. Significantly, Joyce removed the apostrophe from the original song's title so that instead of a single Finnegan we have a name standing in for all the Finnegans in the world (representing, in turn, all of humanity). In short, we all rise, fall, awaken and rise back up throughout eternity: that's the stuff of endless creation.

It's significant that Frampton decided to express this sense of eternal return by dropping out the soundtrack for both film sequences. As we noted in Chapter 1 in relation to Fritz Lang's *M*, films were never screened without some sort of live accompaniment in the so-called 'silent' era (i.e. films with no synchronised recorded sound). Music was usually provided by a pianist or theatre organist playing from sheet music or live improvisation. In addition, Japanese films were accompanied by so-called *benshi*, performers who stood off to the side of the screen and gave live narration or spoke the characters' dialogue out loud. By removing all sound accompaniment Frampton not only creates a form of 'drop-out', setting up a vectorial relationship between the two Finnegan films and the computer text, but he also returns the films to their archival status, as if they were raw material for Frampton's own active reconstruction of their bit-part in his larger cosmic archive, his infinite cinema that will also include the computer-based sections of the film.

Frampton brilliantly applies this matrix not just to his love of literature and lyric poetry but to his own family background and how together they shape his active role as the builder of a meta-history of cinema. According to Frampton:

> Among other things, there's a lot of loose punning about Irishness in the whole thing, which means certain things to me personally, but also has a certain flavor within literary modernism. For me, the most important part of English-language literary modernism is Irish. I must say that I am also somewhat moved by the film; it's relatively recent. It's not easy for me to get through it with a completely dry eye, I suppose. (2009d): 232)

It's thus no accident that the film is dedicated to his maternal grandmother, Fanny Elizabeth Catlett Cross (1896–1973), whose lifespan covers the birth of cinema (the Lumière Brothers' first films) and Frampton's own digital experiments.

Indeed, the latter begin in *Gloria!* immediately after *A Wake in 'Hell's Kitchen'* at the nineteen-second mark as we cut abruptly to a Kelly-green cathode-ray computer screen where white characters appear one by one at the bottom of the frame (as if typed on a computer keyboard) and gradually shift upwards to make way for the next line as we progress. Eventually Frampton gives us sixteen different clauses narrating the importance of his grandmother on his life and artistic development:

> These propositions are offered numerically, in the order in which they presented themselves to me; and also alphabetically, according to the present state of my belief.
> 1. That we belonged to the same kinship group, sharing a tie of blood. [A]
> 2. That others belonged to the same kinship group, and partook of that tie. [Y]
> 3. That she kept pigs in the house, but never more than one at a time. Each such pig wore a green baize tinker's cap. [A]
> 4. That she convinced me, gradually, that the first person singular pronoun was, after all, grammatically feasible. [E]
> 5. That she was obese. [C]
> 6. That she taught me to read. [A]
> 7. That she read to me, when I was three years old, and for purposes of her own, William Shakespeare's 'The Tempest'. She admonished me for liking Caliban best. [B]
> 8. That she gave me her teeth, when she had them pulled, to play with. [A]
> 9. That she was nine times brought to bed with child, and for the last time in her fifty-fifth year, bearing on that occasion stillborn twin sons. No male child was born alive, but four daughters survive. [B]
> 10. That my mother, her eldest daughter, was born in her sixteenth year. [D]
> 11. That she was married on Christmas Day, 1909, a few weeks after her thirteenth birthday. [A]
> 12. That her connoisseurship of the erotic in the vegetable world was unerring. [A]
> 13. That she was a native of Tyler County, West Virginia, who never knew the exact year of her own birth till she was past sixty. [A]
> 14. That I deliberately perpetuate her speech, but have only fragmentary recollection of her pronunciation. [H]
> 15. That she remembered, to the last, a tune played at her wedding party by two young Irish coalminers who had brought guitar and pipes. She said it sounded like quacking ducks; she thought it was called 'Lady Bonaparte'. [A] [Written vector to sonic interlude that follows: silence/text to sound/non-text].
> 16. That her last request was for a bushel basket full of empty quart measures. [C]
> (Frampton 2009e: 253–4)

Obviously Proposition 15 is the written genealogical cue for the single sound segment that follows (i.e. Finbar Furey's rendering of 'Madame Bonaparte', also known as 'Bonaparte's Advance' and 'Not Tonight Josephine'), but the difference between the numbers (the original ordering of Frampton's memory of his grandmother) and the letters (the present state of his belief) indicate an evolutionary becoming whereby memory is always superseded by the creative vector of immediate utility. In this sense the list of propositions represents a textual time-image on a par with that of the cinematic archive as a whole while at the same time Frampton is careful to return to his dedication at film's end, as we witness another scrawling text in blue on black along the bottom of the screen: 'This work, in its entirety, is given in loving memory of Fanny Elizabeth Catlett Cross, my maternal grandmother, who was born on November 6, 1896, and who died on November 24, 1973.'

Frampton's decision to dedicate *Gloria!* to Cross seems to be based on both macro and micro literary levels. The former is grounded in his friendly rivalry with Dante, for

> As long as I've known anything about Dante Alighieri and *The Divine Comedy*, I have been at once touched and annoyed by the dedication of that huge work to Beatrice Portinari, who presumably was an extremely attractive person. But Dante only saw her once for sure, and she was nine years old, and it's all very discorporate. And so *Gloria!* is also a very alive and very cumbersome work that is dedicated to a woman, who is extremely important to me but was by no means a spiritual and discorporate creature. She was my Irish Grandma with the style of a drunken sailor, and I think my final decision to do the *Gloria!* at that place and in that way devolved more heavily than anything else upon a conflict that I had always felt about the dedication of *The Divine Comedy*. (Frampton 2009d: 233)

The latter, more micro insight into understanding the genealogical and archival significance of this paean to Frampton's grandmother is actually not included in the sixteen propositions but cited by Alice Lyons as an epigraph to her superbly insightful essay, 'A Keyboard Mind: Hollis Frampton's *Gloria!* as Lyric Poem' (2016). Here, Frampton reminisces that '*I was three when I started reading. My grandmother taught me to read with a typewriter. It was easy and quick. The first two words I learned to recognize and to type on the typewriter myself were Cheese Ritz.*' Lyons argues that Frampton's creative formalism is that of a keyboard mind where typing one letter after another is not that dissimilar to editing one shot of twenty-four frames per second after another. Rather than meaningful words we instead get a non-linear sense of QWERTY as a self-contained non-signifier in and for itself in much the same way that Frampton deconstructs the alphabet in the middle section of *Zorns Lemma*.

In addition, Lyons also highlights Frampton's roots in lyric poetry via his friendship and correspondence with Ezra Pound. In this sense, his fourteenth proposition: 'That I deliberately perpetuate her speech, but have only fragmentary recollection of her pronunciation. [H]' is a deliberate attempt to hybridise lyric poetry with the fractured shards of the typewriter keyboard (introduced to him by his grandmother) via the digital medium of the cathode-ray tube computer screen. As Lyons explains,

> Mutlu Konuk Blasing says that lyric poetry 'remembers the history of the process of its own coming into being' and this memory includes our experience of being outside language as aliens before we are initiated into it. Nestled within that kernel of a notion is yet another notion: that Frampton's *Gloria!*, in enacting in filmic language its own coming into being, is not a 'poetic film' or even a 'poetry film' or 'film poem'. It is a lyric poem. [...] In the process of devising the materialities necessary to communicate this verbal *milieu* – he writes a code in which to create a digital, onscreen typewriter, his mother tongue, so to speak – Frampton demonstrates how cinematic tools can be freighted with lyric purpose. (Lyons 2016: unpaginated)

This lyricism unfolds on-screen as we follow the letter-by-letter unfolding of each word as if animated by an invisible cursor. The latter – the animated/animating figure of textual inscription – acts temporally, defining the instant that a letter is disclosed but also suggesting a 'letter or number to come', which will in turn form a word that will replace the words already typed out. Lyons notes,

> As such, what Garrett Stewart calls the 'acoustics of textuality' are conjured; the propositions are burdened with the phonic. This draws into the frame the body of the film's reader/viewer/listener, 'the body as the receptive site of textual activation', a ground on which the textual and cinematic materialities of the film are inscribed. (2016: unpaginated)

English readers of a certain generation might remember the TV sports show, *Grandstand* (1958–2007), which was aired on Saturday afternoons. At 4:55pm, we saw a close-up of a teleprinter typing out the football scores as they came live into the newsroom. Unlike the late and legendary Tim Gudgin, who read the final scores out loud after all the games were over and used a rising (winners) and falling (losers) intonation in order to accentuate and indicate the result (he used a flat intonation for draws), the teleprinter was strictly neutral and gave nothing away until all the letters and numbers were visible. Thus, on a given Saturday, we would read Q-U-E-E-N'S P-A-R-K R-A-N-G-E-R-S [2] (insert cries of despair from the viewer – 'We've lost!') B-R-E-N-T-F-O-R-D [3] (Yes!!!! Finnegan-like dancing and singing follows). The key is that the results were always in a state of becoming until the final score was typed out due to the very nature of the typewriter matrix. Similarly, as Lyons points out,

> In its rapid unfolding, *Gloria!*'s digital text behaves in much the same way as a cursor. Its leading edge, quickly 'running' from left to right, becomes a messenger, a figure that mimics the near simultaneous coming-into-being and disappearance of spoken language production. In one instant, the cursor instantiates the action of language, the making of a mark or an utterance; in the next it represents the not-mark, the not-sound of language. (2016: unpaginated)

One outcome of Frampton's strategy is to disembody the component parts of his image/text matrix all the better to resurrect them in a newly formed spatio-temporal continuum – i.e. his own personalised archive curated as a metahistorian of cinema. This creates an inherent problem of selection, for as Frampton argues in 'For a Metahistory of Film',

> The historian of cinema faces an appalling problem. Seeking in his subject some principle of intelligibility, he is obliged to make himself responsible for every frame of film in existence. For the history of cinema consists precisely of every film that has ever been made, for any purpose whatever. [...] The historian dares neither select nor ignore, for if he does, the treasure will surely escape him. (2009b: 136)

On the other hand, through the recycling (and reinvigorating) of silent footage and his own family history in *Gloria!*, Frampton takes on the role of inventor, the creator of a plane of composition that merges with and hybridises itself with a conceptual plane of immanence. Thus, in contrast to the film historian:

> The metahistorian of cinema, on the other hand, is occupied with inventing a tradition, that is, a coherent, wieldy set of discrete monuments, meant to inseminate resonant consistency into the growing body of his art. Such works may not exist, and then it is his duty to make them. Or they may exist already, somewhere outside the intentional precincts of the art (for instance, in the prehistory of cinematic art, before 1943). And then he must remake them. (Frampton 2009b: 136)

In this context, everything is equivalent to archive footage that may be reconstructed or reused as 'new' work in a new tradition. 'Wherever this is impossible, through loss or damage, new footage must be made. The result will be perfectly similar to the earlier work, but "almost infinitely richer"' (2009b: 136).

Through this statement Frampton deliberately moves beyond a Joycean, Finnegan-like playfulness and wit to a more Borgesian paradigm, specifically the latter's 1939 short story, 'Pierre Menard, Author of the *Quixote*'. As Borges states, Menard

> did not want to compose another *Quixote* – which is easy – but *the Quixote itself*. Needless to say, he never contemplated a mechanical transcription of the original; he did not propose to copy it. His admirable intention was to produce a few pages which would coincide – word for word and line for line – with those of Miguel de Cervantes. (Borges 1970: 65–6)

Even though Cervantes's original text and Menard's 're-write' are verbally identical, 'the second is almost infinitely richer. (More ambiguous, his detractors will say, but ambiguity is richness)' (1970: 69). Just as Menard is a metahistorian of literature, Frampton styles himself as a metahistorian of cinema, creating a complete tradition from nothing more than the obvious limits of its intrinsic parts: camera, projector, filmstrips, film canisters, etc. But, and this is a key caveat that transforms Frampton's monuments into conceptual personae – his grandmother, himself, Joyce, Finnegan, Borges and Pound, to name but a few – film is less material than conceptual:

> Now I expound, and attempt to practice, an art that feeds upon illusions and references despised or rejected by other arts. But it occurs to me that film meets what may be, after all, the prime condition of music: it produces no object. (Frampton 2009b: 138)

In this way Frampton turns the plane of immanence into a 'total film machine': pure sensation.

CHAPTER 3

'There is No Film. Let Us Proceed to the Debates!': Immanence as 'Syncinema' in Maurice Lemaître's *Le film est déjà commencé?* (1951) and Guy Debord's *Hurlements en faveur de Sade* (1952)

If Hollis Frampton's *Zorns Lemma* and *Gloria!* use silence to privilege the image over sound and the signifying power of language – the chaoid linked to an eternal return of non-signifying sensation-as-becoming – Guy Debord's proto-Situationist *Hurlements en faveur de Sade* (1952) does the reverse: a combination of silence and a spoken soundtrack deliberately and wilfully replace the hegemony of the image all the better to destroy cinema as spectacle and return creative and interpretative power to the audience itself (the fundamental basis of what came to be known as Syncinema or '*séance de cinéma*'). In this chapter we will examine *Hurlements* in some detail while at the same time acknowledging its debt to its Lettrist forebears (a structural enfolding and unfolding in Laura Marks's parlance), specifically Isidore Isou's *Traité de bave et d'éternité* (1951), Gil J. Wolman's *L'Anticoncept* (1952) and most importantly, Maurice Lemaître's *Le film est déjà commencé?* (*Has the Film Started Yet?*, 1951), which uses sound dropouts as the formal prototype for Syncinema's often scandalous, interventionist 'happenings' on the Left Bank ciné-club circuit.

As Debord famously wrote in *Society of the Spectacle* in 1967, 'In societies where modern conditions of production prevail, all of life presents itself as an immense accumulation of spectacles. Everything that was directly lived has moved away into a representation' (Debord 1983: parag. 1). Accordingly, the feature-length *Hurlements*, completed in June 1952, contains no images whatsoever. The soundtrack, which features the voices of Lettrist founder Isou as well as his regular cohorts Barbara Rosenthal, Serge Berna, Wolman and Debord himself, is accompanied by a completely blank white screen filled with bright light as they effectively declare the death of traditional cinema. As Debord retrospectively described *Hurlements* in the 1964 book, *Contre le Cinéma*,[1]

---

[1] From Jorn (1964), a collection of the scripts of Debord's first three films.

> These dialogues, which altogether total no more than twenty minutes, are broken up into short fragments amid passages of total silence totaling one hour (the final portion of the film consisting of an uninterrupted 24-minute period of silence). During the silences the screen, and thus the theatre, remains totally dark. (Cited in Debord 2003: 210)

Despite the film's title, the Marquis de Sade is barely mentioned except when Rosenthal self-reflexively states that 'no one talks about Sade in this film' (Debord 2003: 5). Instead, the focus is on cinema's detrimental relationship to the spectacle, for as Wolman argues in the film, 'A science of situations needs to be created, which will incorporate elements from psychology, statistics, urbanism, and ethics. These elements must be focused on a totally new goal: the conscious creation of situations' (Debord 2003: 4). After Debord declares that, 'Like lost children we live our unfinished adventures', the dialogue ends and we are left in complete darkness, waiting for cinema to reactivate itself yet again.

This combination of silence and darkness – with its apparent expression of pure absence – was particularly palpable during the film's first screening on 30 June 1952, at the Ciné-Club d'Avant-Garde in Paris. In *Off-Screen Cinema*, Kaira M. Cabañas's seminal book on the Lettrist Avant-Garde, Debord deliberately used magnetic tape – more commonly used for sound editing – to construct the opaque leader. As Cabañas explains,

> When magnetic tape passes through the gate of a film projector, it is utterly opaque and erases the borders of the film frame, creating, according to Keith Sanborn, a 'palpable, eerie void'. Moreover, when passing through the optical sound head of a film projector, it is silent (in contrast to the optical sound track on the clear leader). (Cabañas 2014: 160 n. 13)[2]

However, despite Debord's best attempts to avoid light and sound 'leakage' from the theatre projection, we also know that there is no such thing as complete darkness, just as we also noted in the Introduction, following John Cage's dictum, that there is no such thing as complete silence, for as Des O'Rawe rightly points out,

> Silence is not simply the absence of sound any more than black is only the absence of colour. Silence traverses all manner of contexts: it is never absolute and achieves significance in relation to what it denies, displaces, or disavows. It is impossible to think, speak or write about silence without invoking sound. (O'Rawe 2006: 395)

---

[2] Keith Sanborn, 'Return of the Suppressed,' *Artforum* 44, no. 6, February 2006, pp. 188–9.

As we shall see, the resulting environmental switch in emphasis from passive spectatorship to active *sonic* performance on the part of the audience becomes a vital component of Debord's *détournement* of Lettrist cinema in the first screenings of *Hurlements*.

At first glance, the film's dialogue appears to be a bricolage of verbal non-sequiturs, randomly juxtaposing extracts from the dry legal language of the French Civil Code – 'Article 516. Property is either real or personal' (Debord 2003: 2) – literary references to James Joyce's *Ulysses*, Jean-Paul Sartre's *Roads to Freedom* trilogy, and André Breton's *Lost Steps*, as well as films such as *Gun Crazy* (Joseph H. Lewis's *film noir* precursor to *The Big Combo*), and John Ford's *Rio Grande* (both released in 1950). These are juxtaposed with the seeming banalities of idle banter, romantic gossip and aphorisms about love. Thus, Rosenthal asks: 'Tell me, did you sleep with Françoise?' (2003: 2); Wolman: 'You know, I like you a lot' (2003: 3); or this disjunctive exchange that seems to come from the awkward fusion of two separate screenplays:

> Wolman: 'I love you.'
> Rosenthal: 'It must be terrible to die.'
> Wolman: 'See you later.'
> Rosenthal: 'You drink far too much.' (2003: 10)

However, the texts are also self-consciously revolutionary, both in relation to French history – 'Happiness is a new idea in Europe' is a direct quote from Louis-Antoine de Saint-Just's 1794 'Laws of Ventôse' (Debord 2003: 225, n. 3) – but also the Lettrists' own self-glorification as artistic and literary radicals. As in most Lettrist films of the period, self-referentiality and self-quotation are rampant in *Hurlements*. Thus, following the first extract from the Civil Code, Wolman cites the first line from Debord's 'Prolégomènes a tout cinéma futur', published in the first and only issue of the Lettrist journal *Ion* in April 1952, proclaiming that 'Love is valid only in a prerevolutionary period' (Debord 2003: 1).[3] However, later in the film Debord himself quotes the last line of the same essay in order to position *Hurlements* as a supersession and *détournement* of Lettrism: 'The arts of the future can be nothing less than disruptions of situations' (2003: 2).[4]

Détournement seems to be a particularly apt reading when one considers the Situationists' subsequent definition of the term in the inaugural issue

---

[3] 'L'amour n'est valuable que dans une période pré-révolutionnaire' (Berréby 1985: 109).
[4] 'Les arts futures seront des bouleversements de situations, ou rien' (Berréby 1985: 109).

of the Situationist International journal (*Internationale Situationniste*) in 1958. According to the editors, it is short for the

> détournement of pre-existing aesthetic elements. The integration of present or past artistic production into a superior construction of a milieu. In this sense there can be no situationist painting or music, but only a situationist use of these means. In a more primitive sense, détournement within the old cultural spheres is a method of propaganda, a method which testifies to the wearing out and loss of importance of those spheres. (Knabb 1989: 45–6, referring to the Situationist International journal, June 1958: 13[5])

Which isn't to say that Lettrism is completely superseded, for in the film Isou himself quotes from a letter that he had written to Debord: 'I know people only by their actions. In other respects they are indistinguishable from each other. In the final analysis, we are differentiated only by our works' (Debord 2003: 3; 225 n.3). Nonetheless, Wolman responds with a major caveat: 'And their revolts became conformisms' (Debord 2003: 3). In general, as Allison Field argues, 'with a wry and ironic tone, the film's quotations isolate parts of larger dialogues, texts, and fictional works which, through their isolation, are made ridiculous' (Field 1999: 64). This is particularly true of the extracts from the Civil Code, for, she notes,

> While these selections seem arbitrary, they all address issues of the rights of people in a society based on a fixed idea of normalcy of citizenship and legal participation. Outside the legal context, the passages seem ridiculous; given his criticisms of all organized social structures, Debord's citation of these passages seems to aim at undermining their authority and relevance. (Field 1999: 64)

How, then, are we to interpret the use of the black leader and silent passages? Are they also irrelevant absences and arbitrary voids? Or do they actually open up an interstice in the diegetic and narrational surface of the film in order to access one or more chaoid planes below, constructing, in effect, a non-dialectical, stratigraphic temporal structure where, as Deleuze and Guattari put it in *What is Philosophy?*, '"before" and "after" indicate only an order of superimpositions' (1994: 58)? Let's begin with a basic, albeit superficial reading. There are fourteen black-screen, non-sound sections in total, varying in length from thirty seconds to the final twenty-four-minute black-out. As one might expect, five allude specifically to scenarios of death. Two in particular frame references to the mysterious 1950 suicide of twelve-and-a-half-year-old Madeleine Reineri, a popular

---

[5] The SI journal archive is online, and this edition can be viewed at <https://www.cddc.vt.edu/sionline///si/is1.html> (last accessed 24 March 2021).

young radio actress who threw herself into the Isère River, 'after having placed her schoolbag on the bank' (Debord 2003: 4). Before the black-out, Debord himself laments, 'Little sister, we're not a pretty sight. The river and the misery continue. We are powerless' (2003: 4). It is after this black-out that Rosenthal says, 'But no one talks about Sade in this film', as if Madeleine's suicide were a masochistic supersession of Sade's apparent irrelevance. She is mentioned again later in the film, only this time *following* the black-out instead of before. Interestingly, Debord's response is far less fatalistic: 'Mademoiselle Reineri of the Europe Quarter, you still have your wonderstruck face and that body, the best of promised lands' (2003: 10). Debord mentions suicide again just prior to the fifth black-out, stating that 'The perfection of suicide lies in its ambiguity' (2003: 6) and this seems to be further expanded following Debord's reference to *Gun Crazy* and its violent depiction of the John Dall/Peggy Cummins murder spree, where the fusion of Eros and Thanatos take on almost existential proportions. 'You remember,' intones Debord. 'That's how it was. No one was good enough for us. Nevertheless [. . .] The hailstones on the banners of glass.' Then, just before the black-out, he insists, 'We won't forget this cursed planet', the supposed last words of the decadent nineteenth-century writer, Auguste Villiers de l'Isle-Adam (1838–89) (2003: 7; 226 n. 7).

Most of the other black-outs seem to signify the unrepresentable or incommensurable, such as the almost unfathomable extent of police power when Berna intones, 'The Paris police are equipped with 30,000 billy clubs' (2003: 9), or of the impasse between untrammelled, true romance and the necessary restrictions of the law. 'What is a one and only love?' asks Debord, to which Berna 'responds', 'I will answer only in the presence of my attorney' (2003: 6). Similarly, Berna earlier cites Civil Code Article 488: 'The age of adulthood is 21 years; a person of that age is capable of all acts of civil life' (2003: 3). In this case the subsequent darkness of the theatre could be suggestive of all the unviewable acts of adult civil life, including sex, perversion and ultimately a revolution 'yet to come'. That the latter is necessarily unknowable and unrepresentable is further expressed by black-out #12, prior to which Debord laments that 'We were ready to blow up all the bridges, but the bridges let us down.' Without the right tactics in place, Wolman's call for 'the conscious creation of situations' (2003: 4) will always be a work in progress, perhaps necessitating the thirty-second pause for thought expressed by black-out #3. In light of this reading, it's significant that the film's closing line, 'Like lost children we live our unfinished adventures', is sandwiched between two black-outs, (#11 and #12): as if to say that the true revolution is one long *dérive* or drift, irreducible to either conventional ideology (Marxist or otherwise), or to the traditional audio-visual forms of cinema.

A major clue to a more complex reading of the planar interstices of *Hurlements* is provided early on by Wolman's recitation of key moments in the history of cinema, which are clearly presented as precursors to Debord's own revolutionary contribution (ever the self-promoter, Debord's *Hurlements* concludes the list as an obvious apotheosis of formal innovation). In his essay, 'Dismantling the Spectacle: The Cinema of Guy Debord', Thomas Y. Levin makes a key point that,

> This whirlwind tour of landmarks in film history – genre classics of the early cinema (Georges Méliès), expressionist cinema (Robert Wiene), dada cinema (René Clair), Russian revolutionary cinema (Sergei Eisenstein), surrealist cinema (Luis Buñuel and Salvador Dalí), and socially engaged comedy (Charlie Chaplin) – also sketches the contours of a film aesthetic if one considers each entry as short-hand for a catalogue of formal devices and concerns. This is particularly true of the last two works listed prior to Debord's *Hurlements*, the extraordinary and largely unfamiliar films of Isidore Isou [i.e. *Traité de bave et d'éternité*] and Gil J. Wolman [*L'Anticoncept*] who, along with Maurice Lemaître, are the principal figures of what is known as Lettrist cinema, the cinematic avant-garde that was probably the single greatest influence on Debord's cinematic practice. (Levin 2002: 335–7)

This influence is irrefutable based on the textual evidence of the aforementioned Lettrist journal *Ion*, whose only issue was devoted specifically to expounding the tenets of Lettrist cinema. Debord's *Prolégomènes* is followed by a first, unrealised draft of *Hurlements* which, unlike the realised version that premiered two months later, has both an image track *and* a different accompanying soundtrack. At first glance, Debord takes great pains in his *Prolégomènes* to distance himself from Isou's advocacy of 'Discrepant Cinema' in *Traité*, gleefully announcing its demise:

> Finally, I come to the death of discrepant cinema by the *relation of two non-senses* (images and words perfectly insignificant), a relation that will be overtaken by a scream. But all of this belongs to an epoch that is finishing, and that no longer interests me. The values of creation are shifting toward the conditioning of the spectator, with what I have called *three-dimensional psychology*, and the *nuclear cinema* of Marc'O that begins another amplic stage. The arts of the future can be nothing less than disruptions of situations. (MacKenzie 2014: 50)[6]

[6] 'Enfin, je parviens á la mort du cinéma discrépant par le rapport de deux non-sens (images et paroles parfaitement insignifiantes) rapport qui est un dépassement du cri. Mais tout ceci appartient à une époque qui finit, et qui ne m'intéresse plus. Les valeurs de la création se déplacent la psychologie tridimensionnelle, et le cinéma nucléaire de Marc'O, qui commence un autre amplique. Les arts futures seront des bouleversements de situations, ou rien' (Berréby 1985: 109).

This may be true of the final version of *Hurlements* but the unrealised screenplay that immediately follows in *Ion* is, as Levin points out, 'a veritable catalogue of Lettrist cinematic strategies and citations' (2002: 341). In this respect, the superseded formal devices of 'Discrepant Cinema' form one of the key latent strata disclosed by the realised *Hurlements*' apparent absences, a plane of composition (Isou and Lemaître's) lying hidden beneath a more active plane of composition and immanence (Debord's).

So what are the characteristics of 'Discrepant Cinema' and how are they manifested in the unrealised version of *Hurlements*? In *Traité*, Isou's diegetic alter ego, Daniel, states that 'Film interests me because it contains potential for discovery, for ongoing progress. I like cinema when it is insolent and does what it shouldn't do' (Isou 2019: unpaginated).[7] This 'insolence' is theoretically outlined in Isou's own contribution to *Ion*, his 148-page *Esthétique du Cinéma* (1952), in which he outlines two successive tendencies in the development of all artistic media, including cinema. First we have the *phase amplique* or amplic phase, which is the period where an art medium perfects its stylistic vocabularies in order to explore and give expression to subject matter outside itself, such as the mimetic representation of a fictional diegesis or documentary subject. This would be represented by the classical phase of narrative cinema, marked by rigorous synchronisation of sound and image and the development of narrative techniques such as continuity editing, point-of-view shots, flashbacks and shot-reverse-shot montage. It would also encompass the development of specific genres such as westerns, musicals and horror films, as well as auteur studies, a significant interest of French cinéastes, especially those centred on *Cahiers du Cinéma*.

This is followed by the *phase ciselante* or chiselling phase, which usually occurs when the first phase has run out of ideas and entered a period of excessive decadence. As Daniel says in *Traité*,

> First and foremost, I believe that cinema is too rich. It's obese. It has reached its boundaries, its maximum. At the first attempt to expand itself the cinema will explode! This congested *over-fattened pig* will burst into a thousand pieces. I declare the *destruction of cinema*, the first apocalyptic sign of the disjunction and rupture of this *bloated and bulging* organism called film. (Isou 2019: unpaginated)[8]

---

[7] 'J'aime le cinéma lorsqu'il est insolent et fait ce qu'il ne doit pas faire' (Isou 1964: 13).

[8] '*Je crois premièrement que le cinéma est trop riche. Il est obese. Il a attaint ses limites, son maximum. Au premier movement d'élargissement qu'il esquissera, le cinéma éclatera! Sous le coup d'une congestion, ce* porc rempli de graisse se déchirera en mille morceaux. J'annonce la destruction du cinema, *le premier signe apocalyptique de disjunction, de rupture, de cet organisme* ballonné et ventru *qui s'appelle film*' (Isou 1964: 15).

For Isou, the first move is to destroy the autonomy and sanctity of the object (as in, say, Picasso's switch from representational painting to non-representation and collage), followed by renunciation of all subject matter external to the medium itself, thereby producing a radical deconstruction of cinema and its various devices. In short, don't make new masterpieces but, following the dictates of Oswald de Andrade's 'Cannibalist Manifesto', chew up and regurgitate those of the past, a clear precursor of Debord's Situationist *détournement* to come, for as he puts it in *Society of the Spectacle*, 'The spectacle is not a collection of images, but a social relation among people, mediated by images' (Debord 1983: parag. 4).

The two main formal strategies of 'Discrepant Cinema', which are prevalent in both Isou's *Traité* and the unrealised script of Debord's *Hurlements*, are: 1) *Montage discrépant* or discrepant editing, i.e. the purposeful non-synchronisation of sound and image; and 2) The *image ciselante* or chiselled image. As Cabañas neatly describes the process, in addition to printing images upside down and backwards,

> chiseling meant subjecting the filmstrip to a series of interventions, including scraping it with needles or painting on it with a brush to produce a chiseled image. The chiseled image track was to signify as both referential and abstract, iconic and indexical. (Cabañas 2014: 10)

Isou seemed to have a clear premonition of the final released version of *Hurlements* when he predicted that 'upcoming films will eliminate the *photo* from cinema' (*Esthétique du cinéma*, *Ion* 1952: 46, cited in Cabañas 2014: 14), which suggests that Debord perhaps had fewer strategic issues with Isou than we previously thought.

Isou's *Traité* is a model combination of discrepant montage and chiselled images or painted filmstrip (*pellicules brossées*). Firstly, all the characters in the film are represented by diegetic voice-overs in addition to the omniscient voice of the film's narrator (Bernard Blin), none of which are directly synched with the film's visuals. Thus the character of Daniel is portrayed by Isou himself on the image track, but his voice-over is post-synched by Albert J. LeGros, thereby introducing a performative bifurcation between image and voice, much like the dialogue of a foreign language film dubbed into English by another actor. At times, Isou also seems to be playing himself, especially when he interacts with the film's guest stars, Jean Cocteau, Jean-Louis Barrault, Blanchette Brunoy, André Maurois and Blaise Cendrars, as if to prove to the audience that the latter were actually recruited to be part of the diegesis, not edited scraps of found footage.

The film is divided into three chapters. 'Le principe' consists of shots of Isou and various Lettrists walking the streets and squares of Saint-Germain-des-Prés with a contentious ciné-club debate on the soundtrack, whereby Daniel is vainly trying to placate a hostile audience as he expounds the fundamentals of 'Discrepant Cinema'. 'Yes!' he cries. 'we must tear apart the two wings of cinema, the sound and the image' (Isou 2019: unpaginated).[9] Then over a random shot of his legs, walking, 'If until now, the word has only been commentary on the *pellicule*, from here on, whether it's necessary or not the *pellicule* will be the simple complement of the scream!' (Isou 2019: unpaginated).[10] A sound so emphatic and independent of the image that it will drive the audience mad: 'We should leave the cinema with a migraine! Every week there are so many films that people exit just *as stupid as when they entered*. I'd rather give you neuralgia than nothing at all' (Isou 2019: unpaginated).[11]

Chapter 2, 'Le développement', presents an intimate account of Daniel's cruel and caddish love life, where his various rendezvous with abortive loves such as Eve, Denise and Mimi are presented exclusively on the voice track against found footage appropriated from the trash bins of specialised film labs such as the Services Cinématographiques du Ministère des Armées. The latter is a significant choice as many of the (often inverted) images – fishing boats, military parades and manoeuvres, a metal machine shop) – reference France's so-called 'Dirty War' in Indochina (indeed, the disastrous battle of Diên Biên Phu was but a mere two years off). Maurice Lemaître was responsible for most of the chiselling and it's significant that only the faces of the military officers and colonial dignitaries are obliterated, leaving the foot soldiers and Vietnamese villagers unmarked, an obvious disclosure of his anti-imperialist political sympathies and a clear indication that Isou still had a modicum of interest in the ideological power of the image. Nonetheless, because we are forced to imagine the love affairs in our mind's eye, we are reminded of one of the ciné-club members' earlier complaints that, 'if photography doesn't count anymore, then it's no longer cinema, it's *radio*, it's *reading in an armchair*' (Isou 2019: unpaginated)'.[12] But Daniel (who has clearly seen Fritz Lang's *M*) fails

---

[9] '*Oui, il faut déchirer les deux ailes du cinéma, le son et l'image*' (Isou 1964: 15).

[10] '*Si jusqu'à présent la parole n'était que le commentaire de la pellicule, dorénavant la pellicule sera le simple complémentaire, nécessaire ou inutile, du* cri!' (Isou 1964: 16).

[11] '*Qu'on sorte du cinéma avec un mal de tête! Il y a tant de films, chaque semaine, d'où l'on sort aussi crétin que l'on y est entré. Je préfère vous donner des névralgies que rien du tout!*' (Isou 1964: 24).

[12] '*Mais si la photo ne comte plus, ce n'est plus du cinéma, c'est de la* radio, *c'est de la* lecture dans un fauteuil' (Isou 1964: 25).

to see a problem: 'Why not? Because of television, radio has become a type of cinema. Why shouldn't cinema, in return, become some sort of *radio?*' (Isou 2019: unpaginated).[13] The Narrator adds the icing to the cake: 'Daniel was thinking that he always liked to do something different: music in poetry, painting in the novel, and now the *novel* in the *cinema*' (Isou 2019: unpaginated).[14]

Finally, in Chapter 3, 'La preuve', Daniel and Eve attend a Lettrist recital and we are treated to cameos by Lemaître, François Dufrêne and Marc'O as all the elements of 'Discrepant Cinema' finally come together: more of the ciné-club debate intercut with the gutteral intonations of Lettrist poems, whereby language is reduced to the sound of a single letter, each paired with black and white abstract sequences as well as clear and countdown leader, thereby reinforcing the parallel between the whittling of semantics in speech and the abstract chiselled image on-screen. As Daniel's friend Pierre neatly sums it up,

> It's odd, you highlight the words as the element to overturn the picture [The p*ellicule brossée* or painted filmstrip shows a chiselled white squiggle over a ship's cable] but you like Letterism [*sic*], which is the destruction of words. Basically what you are interested in is creation, invention, and discovery. [The *pellicule brossée* switches to white squiggles over a colonial troop carrier.] Fundamentally it is creation. [Cut to black cross-hatching over a city street.] An incessant destruction of layers in order to reach the flow further underground. (Isou 2019: unpaginated)[15]

– or, as we have been arguing, a different, buried plane of composition. Indeed, Isou's alter ego, Daniel, directly relates this 'creation' to an embracing of chaos in-itself as he muses on the revolutionary nature of his next film, 'a preface of films to come':

> Daniel: 'I'll call my film "Drool and Eternity", or "Drool and Marble" or "Drool and Steel" to emphasize the distance between the speck of dust that is our speech and the stature of its power. I will highlight Nietzsche's phrase: "one must still have chaos in

---

[13] '*Pourquoi pas? La radio, par la television, est devenue une espèce de cinéma. Pourquoi le cinéma, en retour, ne devien-drait-il pas une espèce de* radio?' (Isou 1964: 25).

[14] '. . . *de la musique dans la poésie, de la peinture dans le roman et maintenant du roman dans le cinéma*' (Isou 1964: 25).

[15] '*Il y aura, sans cesse, un déplacement des valeurs dans ce film! Il y aura des photos pour dire qu'il faut être attentive aux paroles. Tu vanteras les paroles et tu créeras le lettrism qui est la destruction de ces paroles. To pourras raconteur l'histoire d'un amour pour te rappeler, à l'abri de cette histoire, un autre amour, plus précieux. Mais c'est ça, la création. Une incessante destruction des surfaces, pour l'atteinte d'un écoulement plus souterrain*' (Isou 1964: 77).

oneself to be able to give birth to a dancing star".' (Isou 2019: unpaginated; 'Il faut beaucoup de chaos en soi pour accoucher d'une étoile qui danse' Isou 1964: 85)[16]

This Nietzschean 'creative chaos' is at the very heart of Maurice Lemaître's Syncinema, which was in turn grounded in the specific context of the Parisian ciné-clubs and their well-established presentational protocols. Thus they usually followed a tripartite format that included: 1) A short introductory lecture; 2) The screening of the film itself; and 3) A post-screening debate (which, as we saw in Isou's *Traité*, could often be cantankerous and venomous). As Cabañas points out, 'For the Lettrists the ciné-clubs did more than provide an actual venue. The social form of verbal communication they engendered came to define both the content and the structure of Isou's and Lemaître's first films' (2014: 59). Like Debord with *Hurlements*, Lemaître preferred to stress the role of film not as a self-contained diegetic whole, but as just one part of a larger Deleuzian *event*, which, as we noted in the Introduction, doesn't exist in strictly physical form – i.e. it is not representable – but is attributed to bodies as happenings or becomings which exist in the time of Aion (rather than Chronos) – the 'split' moment that always evades the fixed present. Andrew V. Uroskie neatly summarises the link between Syncinema and the event as follows:

> Lemaître was adamant that his work not be described as a 'film', but rather as a '*séance du* [sic] *cinéma*'—roughly, a 'film *screening*'. Rather than stress the complementarity and interdependence of *séance* and *cinéma*, however, Lemaître insisted on stressing their difference. In so doing, he highlighted some of the subterranean linguistic properties concealed within the term *séance*. For if the English terms for the presentation of a film tend to suggest spectacles that are produced *for*, and directed *toward*, an observing audience, the relevant term in French, *séance*, is generally used to denote assemblies or meetings—activities in which a public is constituted and a variety of interactions take place. (2011: 37)

Séance thus takes on major political connotations (dating back to the French Revolution), for it suggests a *right* of assembly, where rules and rights are dictated by the act of assembly itself. Uroskie argues that,

> For Lemaître, thinking of his production in terms of a *séance du* [sic] *cinéma* is meant to underline a radically new emphasis on the idea of *film as event*. Rather than a material object, each film is a performance that occupies a particular place over a particular period of time. Lemaître wants to focus our attention upon this expanded cinematic situation, this performative, exhibitionary frame. (2011: 37)

---

[16] Nietzsche's original text states: 'I say unto you: one must still have chaos in oneself to be able to give birth to a dancing star. I say unto you: you still have chaos in yourselves' (Nietzsche [1883] 1976: 129).

Thus his *Le film est déjà commencé?* is riddled with references to Hollywood film studios like 20th Century Fox and RKO Radio Films, film processes like Technicolor, as well as advertisements for coming attractions ('PROCHAINEMENT SUR CET ECRAN' 'Coming Soon on this Screen') and advance warnings of possible plot ploys ('VOUS DECOUVRIREZ LE COUPABLE!' 'You'll find out who did it!') in order to break down its own diegetic frame and create vectors pointing to other films, other events and modes of production beyond its own limited world as a ciné-club attraction. In this way, Lemaître's film is but one small part of a much larger performance as public event. It's thus no accident that Lemaître deliberately incorporated his own local ciné-club phenomenon into his *séance de cinéma*, whereby *Le film est déjà commencé?* was first presented (at least in part) on 12 November 1951 at the Ciné-Club Avant-Garde 52 at the Musée de l'Homme, followed by its so-called world premiere on 7 December at the Ciné-Club du Quartier Latin at Cluny Palace on the Blvd St Germain. On both occasions, the regular ciné-club audience would already be well primed for any theatrical stimulus and manipulation that Lemaître's undercover professional minions might want to induce by deliberate acts of provocation.

Needless to say, it's impossible to recreate the complete spectacle of a séance when viewing *Le film est déjà commencé?* at home on a computer via UbuWeb Film[17] or through a DVD transfer, nor is it currently screened in cinemas for larger public consumption and intervention. Basically, all we can see and hear is the image and soundtrack. Indeed, all the profilmic elements can only be accessed (and mentally recreated) through reading the published screenplay (Lemaître [1952] 1999: 95–183) which is divided into three separate columns: SON – IMAGE – SALLE in order to indicate the synchronous activity on all three planes. As Cabañas reminds us, 'Here *salle* refers not only to the space of the theater but also to the audience, drawing attention to the environmental and, more specifically, spectatorial situation that occurs exterior to film's technological support' (2014: 59–60). As we shall see, one of the film's great innovations is to fold the 'son' (sound) and 'salle' (room) planes together to form a biogram or repetitive Moebius strip where the two endlessly interweave.

Let's start with the image track, which effectively carries on where Isou's *Traité* left off, creating a more extreme version of chiselling through a combination of discrepant montage and *pellicule brossés*. For the raw material of his imagery, Lemaître seems to draw upon much of the same

[17] The film is viewable at <http://www.ubu.com/film/lemaitre_film.html>.

military archive material that Isou used in *Traité*, only in this case much of the footage is colour-tinted and many of the shots are shown in negative and/or upside down, under- or over-exposed. Thus we see very brief glimpses of a tractor in a field, a child's doll, people disembarking from a ship, classical statues in a park, Isou walking in the street and other still portraits of Lettrists, a burning house, an angle down on men working on a boat, a man playing an accordion, a wedding procession, an orange-tinted shot of a Paris café interior with bucket seats, and a luxurious country chateau in a beautiful landscape. Continuing his chiselling work on *Traité*, Lemaître paints, scratches and draws over the film's surface emulsion, sometimes complementing the architectural lines of the shot and its frame [*cadre*], sometimes obliterating it entirely so that we are more aware of the shot as a masking [*cache*]. As Uroskie also points out, many of the images are 'deliberately scarred by light leaks, dust, debris, and holes punched through the surface of the celluloid. The film has been soaked in soapy water so that the gelatin structure of its base runs and reticulates, disintegrating before our eyes' (2011: 36). In addition,

> Old scraps of film taken from a processing laboratory have been intercut into the work, as well as pieces of film leader, and negative film in its unprocessed state. There are sections that produce a stroboscopic or 'flicker' effect through the alternation of pure black and white, with the occasional pure color frame thrown in. Words, numbers, and other kinds of symbols are presented in such short durations as to strain the viewer's cognitive abilities. (2011: 36)

It would be tempting to dismiss these exercises in chiselling as just another formalist experiment typical of post-war materialist film practice but Lemaître is careful to direct audience response (and its inevitable discomfort) towards an understanding of the film event as a spectatorial intervention. Thus on one level we strain to find a narrative coherence in the sound and image tracks and, for a more structural analysis, a detailed understanding of specific shots. Although on a computer we might have the added advantage of pausing the film to explore a shot or series of shots in greater detail – 'Is that an upside-down portrait of Marc'O in negative?' 'Is that the same wedding reception we saw earlier?' 'Didn't we see that boat in Isou's *Traité*? It's from a Vietnam film archive isn't it?' – the actual 'séance' audience wouldn't have enough time to 'read' the shot before it's immediately replaced by the next one (an example of Rául Ruiz's 'function' of the shot, which forms a provisional totality). Thus the filmic shot is no longer defined as either a frame or a transparent window on reality but rather as a vector to an outside that expresses a different compositional and psychological plane.

It is the latter function that the 'Salle' column in the screenplay enables as an active component of the work's disjunctive orchestration. Before the film actually starts, Lemaître describes the pro-filmic set-up, starting off in the street outside the ciné-club or cinema:

> As soon as night closes in and shadows stretch along the boulevard a pink portable screen will be set up at the entrance to the cinema whose neon signs will be off. Until the show begins and one hour beforehand an impassive projectionist will screen cinema classics such as *Intolerance* by Griffith, for example. 'Film on at 8:30 pm' will be written in huge yoghurt-white letters on the pavement right in front of the cinema, and an arrow will point to the pay-desk. A giant plain poster hung above the desk on the pediment will show the title of the film: 'The film has already started' (Lemaître [1952] 1999: 99)[18]

After describing a group of film-oriented photographs mounted under glass by the entrance (as if creating an outdoor cinema lobby), the script then outlines the first of a series of pre-orchestrated disruptions:

> Although the show has been advertised for 8.30 P.M. people will be left queuing till 9.30 P.M. Dusty carpets will be shaken, and buckets of water will be poured from the first floor of the building down on to the people who have been queuing for sixty minutes. Those who carry out this loathsome business will exchange insults with the particularly loud-voiced extras, paid by the cinema for stealing into the crowd. (Lemaître [1952] 1999: 101)[19]

Unbeknownst to those in the water-soaked queue outside, Lemaître has planted another group of hired extras inside the ciné-club who now come rushing out, stand by the pay desk and exclaim how awful the film is that they have just seen. As if to compensate, they proceed to content

---

[18] 'Un écran portative de couleur rose sera installé devant l'entrée du cinéma aux néons tous éteints, dès que la nuit se sera allongée sur le boulevard. Une heure avant la séance et jusqu'à celle-ci, un opérateur impassible y projettera des classique du film: "Intolérance de Griffith," par exemple. Sur le trottoir, devant la salle seront écrits en letters énormes, d'un blanc yaourt, les mots: "Ici, à 20 h 30, séance de cinéma" avec une flèche dont la pointe sera dirigée vers la caisse. Au dessus de cette caisse, sur le fronton, une gigantesque affiche, sans aucune illustration, indiquera le titre du film: "Le film est déjà commencé"' (Lemaître [1952] 1999: 99). Translation courtesy of the Getty Research Institute, Los Angeles, California.

[19] 'Bien que la séance ait été annoncée pour 20 h 30, on laissera la queue se former jusqu'à 21 h 30. Pendant ces 60 minutes d'attente, du premier étage de l'immeuble, on secouera des tapis poussiéreux et on jettera des seaux d'eau glacée sur la tête des personnes qui feront la queue. Des insultes seront échangées entre ceux qui accompliront cette répugnante besogne et les figurants, de voix particulièrement forte, payés par l'établissement qui se seront préalablement glissés dans la foule.' (Lemaître [1952] 1999: 101).

themselves by watching Griffith's *Intolerance* on the outside screen, shouting noisy approval. Given the disquiet, the Manager now addresses the waiting crowd from the pay desk and tries to dissuade them from wasting their money, even going so far as to offer to pay for certain couples to take a hotel room instead. Eventually, other extras persuade the Manager to let them in and they rush cheerfully into the dark amid shouts and exhortations.

However, Lemaître has made sure that there are no usherettes to show them to their seats and confusion reigns as a western (and not the advertised film) is shown on the screen. Fights break out, the screen is ripped with a knife and shot at, objects are dangled in front of it and as the western ends the projectionist begs the audience to evacuate the room. Then, a couple of cleaners enter, complaining about their job and how audiences make it impossible to clean the place properly and never leave tips. They air their grievances to the Manager and then exit, just as Lemaître himself heads for the stage:

> Maurice Lemaître will start reading a lengthy defense of his film and the extras will interrupt him with jeers. Holding the film loose in his hands, the cameraman will erupt onto the stage and standing next to the author, he will accuse him of making a film in contradiction with his own ideas and will start tearing it to pieces. Another character introducing himself as the producer will rush at him, trying to save as much of the film as possible. They will all go out, shouting. (Lemaître [1952] 1999: 107–9)[20]

And all this before the film has even started! As we shall see when we explore the interweaving of the 'salle' and 'sound' tracks, more is yet to come.

Interestingly, for all of its pro-filmic innovation, Lamaître's Syncinema or séance is actually a centripetal throwback to theatre (albeit in a radical guise) in the form of Filippo Tommaso Marinetti's advocacy of 'Variety Theatre', outlined in his 1914 tract, 'Futurism and the Theatre: A Futurist Manifesto'. As Marinetti avers (uncannily pre-empting Isou's Daniel in *Traité*):

> We have a profound disgust for the contemporary theatre, (verse, prose and music) because it wavers stupidly between historic reconstruction (a pastiche or a

---

[20] 'Ils sortiront en discutant tandis que viendra sur la scène l'auteur du film. Maurice LEMAÎTRE commencera à lire une longue défénse de son film, entrecoupé par les huées des figurants. L'opérateur de la sale, tenant dans ses mains de la pellicule en vrac, fera irruption à côté de l'auteur et, l'accusant d'avoir fait un film en contradiction avec ses propres idées, se mettra à déchirer cette pellicule. Un autre personage, se présentant comme le producteur du film se précipitera sur lui, essayant de sauver le maximum de pellicule. Ils sortiront tous en criant.' (Lemaître [1952] 1999: 107–9).

plagiarism) and the photographic reproduction of our daily life. On the other hand we assiduously frequent the Theatre of Varieties, (Music Halls, Café-chantants or equestrian circuses) which today offers the only theatrical spectacle worthy of a truly futurist spirit. (Marinetti 1914: 188)

Marinetti, suddenly sounding more like Lemaître's concept of a séance, then proclaims that 'It is necessary absolutely to destroy all logic in the spectacles in the Theatre of Variety, to exaggerate noticeably its extravagance, to multiply contrasts and to make the improbable and the absurd reign as sovereigns on the stage' (1914: 192). How is this to be done?

> To make the spectators of the pit, the boxes and the gallery take part in the action. Here are a few suggestions: put strong glue on some of the stalls, so that the spectator, man or woman, who remains glued down, may arouse a general hilarity, (the damaged dress-coat or costume will naturally be paid for on going out). (1. Yet somehow I hardly see this being done twice to the same public.). Sell the same place to ten different people; hence obstructions, arguments and altercations. (2. Haven't we already once too often pulled grandma's chair away from her just as she was sitting down?) Offer free seats to ladies and gentlemen notoriously whimsical, irritable or eccentric, calculated to provoke disturbances by obscene gestures, nudges to the women, and other eccentricities. Sprinkle the walls with powders which produce itching, sneezing, etc. (1914: 192–3)

Obviously, this may be seen as a centripetal return to theatre but it is also a centrifugal expansion from the confining architecture of the proscenium to a potentially limitless frame that is Life.

However, on another level, Lemaître is not as radical as he may seem (as Debord will reveal with *Hurlements*) for he enfolds this expansive unfolding vector back within the diegetic frame by having the film soundtrack duplicate and comment on the theatrical *salle* antics as a repetitive biogram: an eternal return of difference. Thus in a number of scenes, what is described by voice-overs on-screen are actually duplicated at the exact same time in the auditorium by extras acting out Lemaître's instructions. Thus at the 47' 30" mark, Voice 6 remarks that 'One of the extras will stand up and shoot at the screen. Another one will jab it with a knife and walking through it, will reach the backstage or launch an attack on the wall'[21] just as on the opposite page of the script the text describes the exact same action under 'salle', as if paying literal reference to René Claire's simulation of breaking the screen at the end of *Entr'Acte* (Godard pays a similar homage

---

[21] '*Un des figurants se lèvera dans la salle et tirera des coups de revolver sur l'écran. Un autre le déchirera à coups de couteau et passera de l'autre côté de celui-ci, dans les coulisses, ou s'attaquera au mur*' (Lemaître [1952] 1999: 168).

in *Les Carabiniers* as a cinematically naïve Michelangelo rips through the screen in literal pursuit of a projected image of a woman in a bathtub).

Similar events follow: the description and simultaneous acting out of stink bomb attacks, couples embracing, verbal and visual prohibitions against smoking in the theatre followed by immediate protests from extras in the audience. The film even stages its own enforced ending as the Manager diegetically addresses the audience from within the film over a fuzzy image of the film's title in reverse before cutting to FIN (also backwards) and PROCHAINEMENT SUR CET ECRAN:

> Ladies and gentlemen. This is the manager speaking. The projectionist has just told me he has not found the last reel of M. Lemaître's film. We do not know whether it has been lost or simply undelivered. We are sorry for having to put an end to the show.[22]

Suddenly, the room is filled with extras dressed as police who blow their whistles and clear the auditorium as a female usherette shouts 'Sweets, mints, choc-ice!' over the final title card: FIN.

Lemaître also turns the seemingly synchronous relationship between sound and 'salle' into a disjunctive time-image where virtual and actual are hybridised into a recollection or mnemosign, 'a virtual image which enters into a relationship with the actual image and extends it' (Deleuze 1989: 335). After a voice-over enumerates the film's various avant-garde attributes – ending pre-existing cinema and promoting a new medium; the first use of a Joycean sentence in a film, producing inarticulate sounds; the end of conventional screenplays; the absorption of the filmic séance into a cinematic self-destruction; the acceleration of discrepant editing and chiselling – a female voice announces: 'Dear listeners, Here is the film review. The evening news will follow. You can get it on 52 and 63.20 metres or 64 kilocycles. At 8:30 P.M., the rest of the news.'[23] Then over heavily damaged and chiselled stock with vibrating black dots, we hear Jean-Jacques Laurence's rapidly spoken general survey of the shows in Paris:

> Last night was screened in a Left Bank cinema the world Premiere of Maurice Lemaître's film. Its strange but nonetheless promising title was: 'The film has

---

[22] 'C'est le directeur de la salle qui vous parle. L'opérateur vient de me prévenir qu'il ne trouve pas la dernière bobine du film de M. Lemaître. Nous ne savons pas si celle-ci a été égarée ou si elle ne nous a pas été livrée. Dans ces conditions, nous regrettons, et nous nous en excusons auprès de notre aimable clientèle, de ne pouvoir assurer la suite de la projection' (Lemaître [1952] 1999: 182).

[23] 'Chers auditeurs, Voici maintenant le courier des spectacles. Ensuite, vous pourrez entendre sur 52 mètres et 63 mètres 20 ou 64 kilocycles le journal parlé de la soirée et, à 20 hours 30, la suite de nos informations' (Lemaître [1952] 1999: 172).

already begun?' The audience welcomed this unusual work with mixed feelings. So did the critics. Before commenting on the film itself, we shall give you a few examples of the criticisms that are to be found in today's Parisian press.[24]

If the film's actual audience is present at the premiere, Laurence's temporal reference of 'last night' creates a time discrepancy – according to the voice-over we're watching a film whose premiere has already taken place; or we're at the actual premiere whereby the soundtrack anticipates and reproduces a press reception to come.

As Cabañas rightly points out, 'Given the impossibility of premieres both yesterday and today, the fictive nature of the press reports reproduced on the film's sound track become increasingly aporetic' (2014: 52). On one level the film is 'ahead' of its immediate audience and published press reports because it has included the date of its premiere and reception within its diegesis, while on another level it is 'behind' them both because it cannot know the real circumstances of either (especially given the active role of the spectator in the séance context). Like any cinematic rebel trying the stave off the amplic appropriation of his film as either politically correct or reactionary, he makes all the reviews ideologically negative or trivial. To give but a couple of examples, writing in *Echo des travailleurs de la pellicule*, Roger Diamil saw the film as an outrage to leftist radicals:

> Whereas our exhausted workers are refused any salary increases when working long hours in capitalist factories, whereas they are denied the legitimate right to the holiday bonus they have been claiming for so long, so that they could send to the countryside their children weak from lack of sun and fresh air, a daddy's boy like Maurice Lemaître manages to chuck away money he has not earned by the sweat of his brow, money it is easy to guess where it comes from, to make a film with neither ideological nor artistic value which must have scorched the hands of our underpaid comrade technicians. Let's stick together facing this impending threat.[25]

---

[24] 'Hier soir, dans un cinéma de la rive gauche, a eu lieu la première mondiale du film de Maurice Lemaître au titre étrange et prometteur: "Le film est déja commencé."' (Lemaître [1952] 1999: 172).

[25] '*Pendant que l'on refuse des augmentations à nos travailleurs épuisés par un dur labeur journalier dans les usines des capitalistes, pendant qu'on leur nie le droit sacré à cette prime de vacances qu'ils réclament depuis si longtemps et qui leur permettra d'envoyer à la campagne leurs petits, étiolés par le manqué de soleil et d'air pur, des fils à papa comme Maurice Lemaître trouvent le moyen de jeter par les fenêtres un argent qu'il n'a pas gagné à la suere de son front, un argent don't on se doute un peu d'où il provient, pour faire un film sans aucun valeur, ni idéologique, ni même artistique, qui a dû brûler les main de nos camarades technicians aux salaires de famine. Tous unis devant la menace*' (Lemaître [1952] 1999: 174).

In contrast, writing from the perspective of the Christian right, Maurice de La Ruchardière laments in 'The Liberated Roman Catholic':

> One cannot help shuddering when one comes to think that some of our children may have been as unfortunate as to see Maurice Lemaître's film. One yearns to defend them against those hellish undertakings, obviously inspired by the devil to divert from God's way, suffering and seeking souls. Confronted with those films that intelligent censors willing to protect our children should have banned, a Christian does feel he must act as Christ's soldier, sustained in his effort by the mystery of Incarnation.[26]

By deliberately constructing his film's press reception *avant la lettre* Lemaître both constructs and *détournes* critical *doxa*, theatricalising its ingrained prejudices, all the better to champion his own film as a defamiliarising antidote. Uroskie has also noted this Brechian strategy, noting that,

> Lemaître returns to this framing of the cinematic event again and again on every level, traversing the 'inner' and 'outer' space of the spectacle, constantly plying the boundaries of the aesthetic experience itself. This is not a simple dissolution of 'art' into 'life' but a highly organized and scripted series of experiential encounters wherein the boundary or barrier between the aesthetic and the everyday can be seen to have been situated. Seeing these boundaries, the audience begins to experience them as such. (2011: 42)

This is a very different strategy to *Hurlements*, where Debord's lack of scripting reduces the amount of foregrounding of boundaries: the audience is encouraged to ignore the boundaries altogether rather than experience them critically.

So, what is the role of silence and sound drop-outs in this overall schema? On a single viewing, it's extremely difficult to make any formal sense of the film's sonic interstices because they are easily lost in the overdetermined sensory onslaught of the film's discrepant montage and chiselled imagery. However, on careful viewing, we can find five distinct instances that ultimately construct a relatively coherent conceptual vector and topology. The first occurs at the thirty-three-minute mark and is actually scripted

---

[26] '*Quand on pense que certains de nos fils et de nos filles auront pu, par malheur, assister à la présentation du film de Maurice Lemaître, on se sent frémir. Et on aspire ardemment à les défendre contre ces entreprises diaboliques, manifestement inspirées par le malin pour détourner du chemin de Dieu les âmes qui souffrent et qui cherchent. Le Chrétien, devant ces films, qu'une censure intelligente, et soucieuse de préserver nos enfants de ces mauvais exemples, devrait interdire, se sent vraiment un soldat du Christ, soutenu dans son effort par le mystère de l'Incarnation*' (Lemaître [1952] 1999: 176–8).

to be twenty seconds long (although it is actually cut to twelve seconds). It occurs when members of the audience complain about the lack of a credits sequence in Lemaître's film which leads to boos and whistles and the start of a repetitive football chant: 'The credits! The credits!' Meanwhile, the 'salle' instructions state that someone gets up from their seat and angrily approaches the screen.[27] Suddenly, a piercing voice yells out 'Silence', and the whole soundtrack drops out as we see heavily chiselled imagery on the screen. The silence is eventually broken when a planted member of the audience complains that there are also no stars in the film.[28] This is simultaneously echoed by a similar complaint on the soundtrack, forcing the Manager (as Voice 6) to explain: 'Ladies and gentlemen, on account of the present problems the French cinema has to face, and given the stars' unreasonable demands, we inform our patrons that there will be no stars in . . .'[29] Before he can finish, a couple on-screen say they're leaving while an actual couple leave from the theatre itself.

If the first sound drop-out shakes the audience into understanding the commercial limitations of avant-garde film-making as a viable concern, the second underlines its benefits as an innovative art form. It is here, at the fifty-minute mark, just as Lemaître states on the soundtrack how sorry he is for being unable to go on with the show, that the film runs its soundtrack backwards for thirty seconds so that all the voices are incomprehensible. However, this is far from being an innovative move (many Dada and Surrealist films had already run this tactic into the ground almost thirty years earlier). So Lemaître follows the reverse sound with ten seconds of silence as if to clear the slate for something far more innovative. As a voice-over proclaims: 'Ten seconds' silence will follow this piece of incoherent sound and then, to show how a Lettrist poem is *composed*, a Lettric symphony for a three-part chorus and two soloists will be played.'[30] As the Lettrist chorus chants in the background, a voice fades up to then outline all the innovations that the film has introduced into

---

[27] 'Quelqu'un se lève dans la sale et dans une rage folle se précipité vers le fond de la sale.' (Lemaître [1952] 1999: 145).

[28] 'Quelqu'un s'écrie: "Mais où sont les vedettes dans ce film?"' (Lemaître [1952] 1999: 145).

[29] 'Mesdames et Messieurs, par suite des difficultés financiers actuelles du cinéma français et étant donné les énormes exigencies des vedettes, nous informons notre aimable clientele qu'il n'y aura pas les vedettes dans . . .' (Lemaître [1952] 1999: 146).

[30] 'Immédiatement après ce morceau de son incohérent, on placera un silence de 10 secondes puis, pour montrer l'organisation d'un poème lettrists, on passera une "symphonique lettrique" pour trois chœurs et deux soloists' (Lemaître [1952] 1999: 170).

cultural history, focusing specifically on the transformation of the cinema performance into a theatrical event or happening.

Obviously, such artistic innovation has its ramifications, and the next two sound drop-outs frame the negative press response that we discussed earlier, and also Lemaître's possible self-doubts. Thus eight seconds of silence over the chiselled image of men gathered outside a government building leads into the next voice-over: 'Maurice Lemaître is wondering why he made such a film. Is it not a totally absurd venture?'[31] If we follow the internal vectoral logic of the silences, the answer to this question is clear: no it's not an absurd venture because Lemaître, like Hollis Frampton's homage to *Finnegans Wake* in *Gloria!*, is simply following in the footsteps of a great literary master, James Joyce. At the one-hour mark, just before the Manager closes down the screening because the final reel has been misplaced, the script calls for a complete break in both the sound and image tracks: 'At that moment, a long piece of transparent film (one minute long) will be integrated into the sound track. (This results in very deep silence making the noise of the camera audible).'[32] Although the silence is actually only fifteen seconds long, it does serve to underline the importance of what has gone before, most notably the biogrammatic repetition of a voice-over line stated earlier at the fourteen-minute mark: 'Nobody ever lived but Socrates, Dante, Joyce. He knows our passions die away, but the world is subject to one implacable law, one absolute determination: the law of creation.'[33] It is this 'law of creation' that ensures an artist's immortality, or as a concluding voice-over (presumably standing in for Lemaître himself) puts it, 'Immortality through their own works – and if I live long enough – the concrete immortality of their being.'[34]

Joyce is important to Lemaître because he equates his own Lettrist experiments in sound and séance with the writer's syntactical disjunctures and disassociative shifts in semantics as opposed to Isou's more subjective Proustian experiments through Daniel's interior monologues in *Traité*. Indeed, as we noted earlier, Lemaître's second example of his own film's

---

[31] '*Maurice Lemaître se demande pouquoi il a fait ce film? N'est-ce pas là une enterprise totalement absurde?*' (Lemaître [1952] 1999: 180).

[32] '[Ici on mettra dans la bande son un long morceau (1 minute) de pellicule transparante (ce qui donne un silence très profond et permet d'entendre le bruit de l'appareil de projection)] (Lemaître [1952] 1999: 182).

[33] '*Que personne n'a jamais vécu que Socrate, que Dante, que Joyce! Il sait que nos passions meurent. Mais que le monde est soumis à une seule loi implacable, une seule détermination absolue: celle de la création*' (Lemaître [1952] 1999: 114).

[34] 'L'immortalité par leurs propres œuvres et – si je vis suffisament – l'immortalité concrete de leur être' (Lemaître [1952] 1999: 182).

innovative contributions to film history is its 'First use of a Joycean sentence in a film finally bursting into a series of inarticulate sounds'. Thus, the sonic centrepiece of the whole film occurs around the forty-four-minute mark when a voice-over proclaims the following stream-of-consciousness mash-up of languages-as-sounds. Here's an excerpt:

> tiponimaiesche po ruski ia, nié *znaoui* dosvidanié tavaritchbrokchnovieff qu'est-ce qu'on joue sur les boulevards tu manes maintenant où tu t'en vas? I had a gal once at the end of town it was like l'Angleterrde 1697 24 april pleure le plus grand ses musicians: Henry Purcell mort à like dipping in a barrel of honé donnez-moi un paquet de gauloises si tu crois petite je ne sais pas ce qui lui a pris tu n'est pas ca-pa-ble-de il ne sait rien faire de ses six doigts heureusement qu'il a ses parent qui lui donnent à manger sans cela qu'est-ce-que tu ferias on vous appelle au téléphone duex tickets jusqu'au Trocadéro [. . .] il est mort en Espagne où quelque part en voulant rejoinder les forces françaises libres, I am terribly sorry gonna fuck you balls votre père est un sous-Apollinaire . . . (Lemaître [1952] 1999: 164–6)

This is immediately followed by the backward sound passages as if to illustrate that nothing that extreme can even begin to compete with Lemaître's Joycean alliance, a point that even Debord might concede, for in *Hurlements*, following Rosenthal's line that no one talks about Sade in the film, Wolman quotes directly from Joyce's *Ulysses*, Chapter 17: 'The cold of interstellar space, thousands of degrees below freezing or the absolute zero of Fahrenheit, Centigrade or Réaumur: the incipient intimations of proximate dawn' (Debord 2003: 5).[35]

Clearly, the first (unfilmed) draft of Debord's *Hurlements* owes a direct debt to Isou and Lemaître's discrepant techniques while at the same time instigating a *détournement* of their potential for amplic appropriation as yet one more example of the avant-garde as an easily dismissable cultural inoculation (thus one could criticise Lemaître's cinematic recycling of Joyce as a filmic equivalent of literary stream-of-consciousness that fails to critique disjunctive Modernist formalism *per se*). Nonetheless, Debord's initial debts to his Lettrist colleagues are palpably clear and unapologetic, for as Levin argues, they

> include acoustic material by (and/or references to) Dufrêne, Marc'O, and Isou, as well as improvisations of Lettrist poetry [François Dufrêne's poems, 'Marche' (*March*) and 'J'interroge et j'invective' (*I Question and I Accuse*) are also featured in Isou's *Traité*], citations of Apollinaire, shouts, noises, and music by Vivaldi.

---

[35] The full quote from Joyce reads: 'Alone, what did Bloom feel? The cold of interstellar space, thousands of degrees below freezing point or the absolute zero of Fahrenheit, Centigrade or Reaumur: the incipient intimations of proximate dawn.' (Joyce 1961): 704).

The image track, which includes newsreel footage (a boxing match, young people killed in the streets of Athens, the Indian army), images of Paris, of Debord, and of Marc'O, also contains much graphical work on language, black frames, and film scratched to the point of total destruction. At times, however, it is, as is spelled out on the screen, "T,e,l,l,e,m,e,n,t, v,i,d,e, à, h,u,r,l,e,r, à, h,u,r,l,e,r" (So empty one could scream, one could scream)' (Levin 2002: 341; Berréby 1985: p. 114).

A particularly interesting addition to the image track of this original version is Debord's use of 'rencontres', which are defined in the script as, 'all of the images whose eroticism will only be restrained by the existence, scandalous and scarcely believable, of a police'.[36] For example, Debord uses these sexually explicit images to accompany the accounts of Madeleine Reineri's suicide (which in the realised version of the film were framed by black-outs), as if to reference – and also reinforce – the popular media's exploitation of a tragic death for public titillation (Berréby 1985: 118). Debord also injects considerable sexual innuendo into otherwise innocent images and statements. Thus a series of *rencontres* are framed by images of parachutists jumping from a plane, as if to associate the act with sexual ejaculation. This is then followed by the line, 'He is lying down by swimming in a very hot river, a sea of oil',[37] an inescapably eroticised image given the sexual antics on-screen. Finally, as we noted earlier, in the realised version of *Hurlements*, the last line – 'Like lost children we live our unfinished adventures' – was framed by two black-outs, as if to underline the incommensurability of the task. As Field rightly points out,

> This expresses the Situationists' image of themselves as transitory wanderers through life, as exemplified in the film title (and the title of the 1989 ICA exhibition on the S.I.), *On the passage of a few people through a rather brief moment in time*. (Field 1999: 65)

However, the non-realised original script inserts an image of a deserted Saint-Germain-des-Prés before adding an additional clause: 'our adventures inordinately small'.[38] These lines are now juxtaposed with more scenes of *rencontres*, as if to create a frisson between the seriousness of Debord's ideological endeavour and the latter's frivolity. This discrepancy, reinforced by the audio-visual montage, is further exacerbated by

---

[36] 'Le terme *rencontres* désigne uniformément toute les image dont l'érotisme ne sera tempéré que par l'existence, scandaleuse et à peine croyable d'une police' (Berréby 1985: 113; cited in Field 1999: 61).

[37] 'Il est couché à la nage dans un fleuve très chaud, une mer d'huile' (Berréby 1985: 120).

[38] 'Nous vivons en enfants perdus, nos aventures incomplètes, nos aventures démesurément petites' (Berréby 1985: 122; cited in Field 1999: 66).

another added line, spoken over an image of Debord himself leaving the Escupade and strolling along the rue Dauphine, which runs between Saint-Germain-des-Prés and the Place Saint-Michel in the Latin Quarter: 'You know, none of this is of importance.'[39] We cut to a final black screen followed by 'very violent cries in the darkness'.[40]

Debord's presence at the conclusion of the unrealised version is the last of six appearances, each framed by a black screen or *écran noir*, situating the final version's use of silence and darkness as a self-inflating cinematic personality cult. The main recurring image, first published in *Ion*, is a black and white photograph of Debord shot at Cannes in 1951 on deliberately damaged stock, staring casually at the camera. It first appears following a colonial-era parade of Indian army troops and is followed by an image of a girl sucking on an ice lolly. Then, following views of Notre-Dame, it cuts to a girl seated with her face on a table, her hair splayed before her. Subsequent appearances are followed by a boxing match and a riot scene, while another shot shows him drinking in a bar, followed by verbal fragments from Dufrêne's '*J'interroge et j'invective*', howled aggressively and loudly. Allison Field makes an excellent point when she notes that,

> The association of Debord's persona with sex, puissance, macho drinking, and violent power is so prevalent in the film it suggests a self-conscious absurdity. Debord, the solitary artist, shown walking away alone at the end of the film, creates a romanticized autoportrait with this film. This self-portrait formulates the mythic persona of Debord with obsessive repetition of hyperbolic associations. (Field 1999: 62)

One might also add that far from being a successful Brechtian attempt at an estrangement from the spectacular, such hyperbole instead places the unrealised *Hurlements* firmly within it, as yet another amplic nod to auteurist cinema conventions, akin to the personal appearances of experimental film-makers such as Kenneth Anger and, of course, Isou himself.

As Debord wrote five years later in the Lettrist journal, *Potlatch*,

> Anyone who cannot conceive a radical transformation is propping up the *arrangements* of the status quo – practiced with elegance – and is separated only by a few *chronological preferences* from those consistent reactionaries who (whether politically of the right or the left) would like to see a return to earlier (*more solid*) stages of the culture that is breaking down. (Debord 2002: 53; in Berréby 1985: 250)

It is perhaps for this reason that a radical change occurred between the release of *Ion* in April and June 1952, when *Hurlements* finally reached

---

[39] 'Vous savez, tout cela n'a pas d'importance' (Berréby 1985: 123).
[40] 'Un cour silence, puis des cris très violents dans le noir' (Berréby 1985: 123).

the ciné-club screen. During this period Debord had clearly come under the influence of the second of the two Lettrist films cited in his cinematic roll of honour: Wolman's *L'Anticoncept*, and it is perhaps no accident that *Hurlements* is, in fact, dedicated to him. In contrast to Isou's use of discrepant editing, chiselled image and conventional use of theatrical projection in *Traité*, and Lemaître's 'séance de cinema', which privileges the extra-filmic space of the auditorium and street in *Le film est déjà commencé?*, Wolman's film, which was completed in September 1951 and first shown on 11 February 1952 at the Ciné-Club Avant-Garde 52 at the Musée de l'Homme, Paris, abandons the indexical image track altogether, reducing it to a pure white, circular light, interspersed with flickering black-outs, projected onto a spherical, helium-filled weather balloon, two metres in diameter. The actual filmstrip consisted of 35mm footage featuring a transparent disc framed in black (much like voyeuristic peephole shots) with Wolman covering the remaining images with opaque black paint. The film was then printed from this material (Cabañas 2014: 154, n. 2).

Wolman saw his film as a breakthrough into a new 'Phase Physique' or 'Physical Phase' of Cinema and as we shall see, this has important ramifications for the final cinematic form of *Hurlements*. Like Isou, Wolman stresses the soundtrack over the image track, and the film exacerbates a strong sensate response from the audience by stressing an extreme facet of Lettrist recitation called *mégapneumie*, a physical poetry based on breath rather than letters that evokes animal cries as opposed to human speech-acts. Unlike the film's opening poem, *TRITS*, which was actually scripted and takes the form of a series of consonant-dominated repetitions:

TRITS OB TRITS OB TRITS OB
OVIL GTON OVIL GTON OVIL GTON
TRITS OB TRITS OB TRITS OB
Voice 2
GAGNDOCBLEKIS – VRILEJA
GAGNDOCBLEKIS – VRILEJA
GAGNDOCBLEKIS – VRILEJA (Berréby 1985: 91)

. . . the closing three and a half minutes of superimposed *mégapneumie* were recorded and improvised directly, thereby denying the audience or reader a conceptual or linguistic grounding usually associated with the translation of speech into a meaningful utterance. Indeed, given the lack of diegetic engagement on the image track due to the removal of all iconic and indexical references, the naked audio was so disturbing that the audience left in droves during the first screening. As the film journal, *Cinéma* described the experience:

> A nonnarrative sound track, a kind of 'interior monologue', including physiological noise and as if 'musicalized'; an image track formed by the irregular alternation of black and white circles projected on a spherical screen. This 'light music' bathes the theater and creates in the viewer a 'physical movement' . . . To the objective and fixed concept [Wolman] opposes the anticoncept 'subjective and variable through the spectators' reactions'. (Cited in Cabañas 2014: 80)

In short, Wolman's film created a pure situation because, as Cabañas rightly states, '*L'Anticoncept* provided no alternatives to the space and time in which it unfolded' (Cabañas 2014: 81), leaving the audience with an unmediated irruption of the howling body into the otherwise passive space of cinematic spectacle. Wolman's emphasis on the primal embodiment of speech clearly evokes Deleuze and Guattari's definition of the body without organs (BwO) in *Anti-Oedipus*, where,

> In order to resist linked, connected, and interrupted flows, it sets up a counterflow of amorphous, undifferentiated fluid. In order to resist using words composed of articulated phonetic units, it utters only gasps and cries that are sheer unarticulated blocks of sound. (1983: 9)

We are also reminded of the BwO's theatrical source, Antonin Artaud's mélange of words, screams and effusions in *Pour en finir avec le jugement de Dieu* (*To have done with the judgment of God*) from 1947. In a particularly visceral passage, Artaud declaims:

> And truly must it be reduced to this stinking gas, my body? To say that I have a body because I have a stinking gas that forms inside me? I do not know but I do know that space, time, dimension, becoming, future, destiny, being, non-being, self, non-self, are nothing to me; but there is a thing which is something, only one thing which is something, and which I feel because it wants TO GET OUT: the presence of my bodily suffering, the menacing, never tiring presence of my body . . . (Artaud 1976: 566)

However, Wolman's use of the cinematic *apparatus* rather than live performance produces a separation of voice and body as opposed to Artaud's desire for a fusion of the two through a form of gestic utterance. 'The illusion of spatial distance between the listener and the recorded speech event is effectively breached,' notes Cabañas. 'Wolman vomits into our ear as he vomits into the microphone' (Cabañas 2014: 92). Not surprisingly, the film was banned by the French censors on 2 April 1952.

The impact on the realised version of *Hurlements* now seems obvious. The latent plane of composition expressed by Isou's 'Discrepant Cinema' that so dominated the initial script has been *détourned* and superseded in favour of the howling soundtrack minus the images. However, we also noted earlier that there are actually no howlings for Sade in the film itself. Indeed, apart from a very brief *mégapneumie* from Wolman that opens the film prior to the spoken credits and dedication, there are no Lettrist contributions in *Hurlements*. However, far from marking an overt absence or ellipsis in regards to the 'poetry of vomit or spittle', *Hurlements* simply redirects it onto another plane. What was originally diegetic in *L'Anticoncept* (howlings on-screen) is now strictly performative (howlings in the ciné-club or movie theatre), a shift from the plane of composition, with its emphasis on sensation and physicality, to the plane of immanence as philosophical interjection, not unlike the cantankerous ciné-club debates in Isou's *Traité*, except they now take place in real time during the screening of *Hurlements*, not on-screen. In this sense, *Hurlements* continues the precedent of the original script of Lemaître's *Le film est déjà commencé?* with its deliberately provocative delay of the actual screening of the film and anarchic disruptions inside the theatre. As a result, Debord's singular authorial voice, so overdetermined in the unrealised script, is deterritorialised onto the audience as a creative line of flight and it is the film's combination of silences and black screen that make this new topological space possible.

This shift was hinted at by Isou in his essay, *Esthéthique du cinema*, when he states that:

> At the point when the projection was to have begun, Debord would have gotten up on stage in order to say a few words of introduction. He would have simply said: 'There is no film.' I thought I would get involved and link up their destructive scandal with the theory of the constructive pure debate. Debord should have said: 'The cinema is dead. There can be no more film. Let us proceed, if you like, to the debates.' (Isou 1952: 147–8)

Isou himself appropriates Debord's role by speaking these words in the finished film, and it is clear that Debord relished the scandal invoked by the film's screenings when audience protests forced the management to shut it down. Indeed, at the film's second screening on 13 October at the Ciné-Club du Quartier Latin, following a fake opening lecture by a professor from the Cinémathèque of Lausanne, the Lettrists, now split into two rival camps, staged their own disturbances. The original group, led by Isou, erupted in howls and whistles, crying 'scandal', while Debord's breakaway Lettrist International responded from the balcony. Indeed, Michèle Bernstein 'remembers a series of "Hurlements en faveur de vous", whereby Debord would make a sign to prompt someone to scream. Bernstein responded to the prompt with her own "Hurlements en faveur de Guy'" (Cabañas 2014: 108).

As in the case of Hollis Frampton's *Zorns Lemma*, this is where *Hurlements* becomes a potential ecosophical project, connecting the materiality of film (ecology, the biophysical), the social (the cultural context of Lettrism and the Situationist avant-garde), and the perceptual, which treats the mind as an interactive system characterised by an exchange of information – images, sounds, looks and audibilities. Indeed, for Deleuze, as we noted in the Introduction, this is close to one of the chief characteristics of ethology, as defined by von Uexküll, which is concerned with the composition of relations or capacities between different things:

> a question of knowing whether relations (and which ones?) can compound directly to form a new, more 'extensive' relation, or whether capacities can compound directly to constitute a more 'intense' capacity or power. It is no longer a matter of utilizations or captures, but of sociabilities and communities. How do individuals enter into composition with one another in order to form a higher individual, ad infinitum? (Deleuze 1988b: 126)

One might argue that this process is completed but also extended when *Hurlements* is reduced to a discussion in a book chapter or public lecture. If we take Isou's directive literally – 'There is no film. Let us proceed to the debates' – by refusing to show the film or even selected extracts (or in the case of a book chapter, citations from the script), a speaker or writer allows the listening and reading audience to take over. Regardless of whether they stay in their seats or walk out, the plane of composition represented by the cinematic arts has been effectively *détourned* in favour of a plane of immanence or consistency more attuned to philosophical debate. This allows the discussion to pass on to another speaker, another topic. End of cinema, end of lecture/chapter: cue howls and whistles. Who needs de Sade anyway?!

CHAPTER 4

The Children of Barthes and *Paris Match*: Godard, Prostitution and the Rhetoric of the Image

We ended the last chapter with a casual dismissive shrug – 'Who needs de Sade anyway?!' It would perhaps be more appropriate, given Guy Debord and Maurice Lemaître's well-documented contempt for the French New Wave, to rephrase it as 'Who needs Godard anyway?!' Kaira Cabañas has acknowledged that Alain Resnais, Chris Marker and Godard were almost certainly present at Lettrist film screenings, and 'While largely unacknowledged, I wager that these filmmakers owe, at least in part, their development of certain aesthetic devices – from the use of imageless sequences with voice-over to heterogeneous montage aesthetics – to their early exposure to Lettrist film' (Cabañas 2014: 17). Indeed, despite the Lettrists' and Situationists' own propensity for shameless appropriation, Lemaître went so far as to accuse their New Wave successors of blatant plagiarism, as seen from his essay titles: 'Marguerite Duras: Pour en finir avec cet escroc et plagiaire généralisée' ('Marguerite Duras: To Have Done with This Crook and Generalized Plagiarist', 1970); 'Les Nouvelles escroqueries de Jean-Luc Godard' ('The New Scams of Jean-Luc Godard', 1989) (cited in Cabañas 2014: 17–18).

Part of the Situationists' complaint was that while Syncinema created a dialectical space between the screen and the audience – activating the latter as a political engagement that took the film out of the theatre and into the streets – the New Wave directors worked within the formal parameters of the history of film, falling back on Isou's discrepancy between sound and image in *Traité*, in effect returning the chiselling phase back into the amplic. To give one example of Situationist critique of Godard's retrograde tendencies, S. Chatel (the pseudonym of Sébastien de Diesbach) wrote an article on Godard's *Breathless* in *Socialisme ou Barbarie* #31 that proclaimed,

> Even if Godard presents people with an image of themselves in which they can undeniably recognize themselves more than in the films of Fernandel, he

nevertheless presents them with a false image in which they recognize themselves falsely. Revolution is not 'showing' life to people, but making them live. (Cited in Knabb 1981: 312)

They were even critical of Godard's Maoist period. In the Situationist International (SI) journal, No. 11 (1967), René Viénet wrote in an article entitled 'The Situationists and the New Forms of Action Against Politics and Art', that

> [Godard] will never be capable of anything but brandishing little novelties picked up elsewhere: images or star words of the era, which definitely have a resonance, but one he can't grasp (Bonnot, worker, Marx, made in USA, Pierrot le Fou, Debord, poetry, etc.). He really is a child of Mao and Coca Cola. (Viénet 1967, cited in Knabb 1981: 215)

Then as if to bang the last nail into Godard's political coffin, an anonymous 1969 review of *Le Gai Savoir* in the following issue, entitled 'Cinema and Revolution', argued that:

> This Maoist liar is in this way winding up his bluff by trying to arouse admiration for his brilliant discovery of a noncinema cinema, while denouncing a sort of ontological lie in which he has participated, but no more so than have many others. In fact, Godard was immediately *outmoded* by the May 1968 movement, recognized as a spectacular manufacturer of a superficial pseudocritical art rummaged out of the trashcans of the past. At that point Godard's career as a filmmaker was essentially over, and he was personally insulted and ridiculed on several occasions by revolutionaries who happened to cross his path. (Cited in Knabb 1981: 297)

Although these arguments might seem valid on the level of formal innovation – destroying established cinematic conventions from the outside in order to transform spectacle into situations through a form of *détournement* – they don't take into account Godard's more Brechtian (and equally legitimate) strategy of dislocating the sound and image combination *from the inside* in order to generate a *Verfremdungseffekt*, where the audience is both seduced and alienated by images at the same time. Godard's strategy will always be seen as 'untimely' (in Nietzsche's sense) because it is a form of *critical* amplic history aimed at transforming both film and its relation to Life. As Deleuze and Guattari state in *What is Philosophy?*, 'Communication always comes too early or too late, and when it comes to creating, conversation is always superfluous' (1994: 28). Thus Debord and Godard will always be on separate wavelengths because they are out of time with each other's plane of consistency.

Perhaps more relevant is Antonin Artaud's aesthetic approach, whereby he advocates the creation of

> a really significant work, the originality of which does not reside in numerous technical devices or external and superficial sequences of shape, but in a profound renewal of the plastic matter of images, a veritable liberation, by no means hazardous, but intricate and precise, of all the dark forces of the mind. (Artaud 1972: 68)

Which isn't to say that Godard's early 1960s work isn't concerned with deconstructing the society of the spectacle. He simply chooses to use a more Barthesian approach, taken from the latter's early works – specifically *Mythologies* ([1957] 1972) – and the later *Image, Music, Text* (1977), which explore the 'rhetoric of the image' through different semiological approaches. Godard's films use silence and disjuncture to create a proliferation of alternative readings within each individual sound-image relation. According to Barthes:

> The variation in readings is not, however anarchic; it depends on the different kinds of knowledge – practical, national, cultural, aesthetic – invested in the image and these can be classified, brought into a typology. It is as though the image presented itself to the reading of several different people who can perfectly well co-exist in a single individual: *the one lexia mobilizes different lexicons* . . . This is the case for the different readings of the image: each sign corresponds to a body of 'attitudes' – tourism, housekeeping, knowledge of art – certain of which may obviously be lacking in this or that individual. There is a plurality and a co-existence of lexicons in one and the same person, the number and identity of these lexicons forming in some sort a person's *idiolect*. (1977: 46–7)

Godard's films that predate his Dziga Vertov Group period (c. 1968–72), focus in particular on the power of connotation over denotation in order to illustrate the seductive power of the image to draw the audience into a spiralling vector of ideological and capitalist exchange value. This is best illustrated by Figure 4.1, which Barthes discusses in *Mythologies*:

> I am at the barber's, and a copy of *Paris-Match* is offered to me. On the cover, a young Negro in a French uniform is saluting, with his eyes uplifted, probably fixed on a fold of the tricolour. All this is the *meaning* of the picture. But, whether naively or not, I see very well what it signifies to me: that France is a great Empire, that all her sons, without any colour discrimination, faithfully serve under her flag, and that there is no better answer to the detractors of an alleged colonialism than the zeal shown by this Negro in serving his so-called oppressors. I am therefore again faced with a greater semiological system: there is a signifier, itself already formed with a previous system (*a black soldier is giving the French salute*); there is a signified (it is here a purposeful mixture of Frenchness and militariness); finally, there is a presence of the signified through the signifier. (1972: 116)

THE CHILDREN OF BARTHES AND *PARIS MATCH*   105

Figure 4.1 *Paris Match* cover, 1955

Godard explores this 'rhetoric of the image' or larger 'Empire of Signs' on two intersecting fronts: the enfolding and unfolding relations of Paris as the site of both literal and a more generalised ideological prostitution, and the complicity of text (particularly literary and cinematic references), image and sound, in furthering this endless exchange of commodities. As Colin MacCabe points out, 'Jean-Pierre Gorin summarizes Godard's entire career as "an assault on the notion of intellectual property". That assault includes both music and painting as well as literature and cinema' (2004: 122–3). In other words, for Godard, there is no such thing as an original text or image (or even character in a film): everything has always already been read, seen or heard (even silence). As Derrida would put it, all we have are traces – knowledge is a tracking down of an endless line of tracks, like Marx's general formula for capital: C-M-C or M-C-M where C = Commodity and M = Money, which Deleuze, following Noël Burch's idea of the 'Large Form', appropriates for his own formula for the movement-image: S-A-S' (Situation-Action-Situation') which accentuates the gap between the situation and a future action which transforms it, ad nauseam.

It's thus completely appropriate that in a 1979 interview, Godard once declared that,

> If you want to write a book about me then there is one thing you must put in: money. The cinema is all money but money figures twice: first you spend all your time running to get the money to make the film but then in the film the money comes back again, in the image. (MacCabe et al. 1980: 27)

In other words, the film-maker and his product are at the mercy of a capitalist system that turns everything into profit and exchange value. Colin MacCabe and his co-writers use the example of Godard's *Une femme mariée* (*A Married Woman*, 1964) to show how the construction of images of women is the main focus of attention but in this case the spectator's look is divorced from that of a diegetic male character, allowing the camera to escape a single given point of view or focalisation. Thus the main character, Charlotte Giraud (Macha Méril) escapes both the trap of looking and being seen as a unifying vision of herself.

> Charlotte's look, which is the only security that the narrative offers us, is radically insufficient for the task of harmonizing the sequence of looks in the cinema; spectators find themselves engaged in an active process of seeing as Charlotte's look refuses to work for them. (MacCabe et al. 1980: 37–8)

Thus her image is mixed up and confused with advertising images that both co-opt and redirect her look, so that 'where there is a look to be stimulated and satisfied then there is money to be made' (1980: 38). However, it is through montage that Godard disrupts this exploitative association, generating a discrepant visual field that is not reducible to the order of money (or, in Debord's terms, spectacle).

This association of female sexuality and monetary gain is one part of a general ideological critique in Godard's films, for as Richard Roud argues:

> a very important theme, and one that comes up over and over again, is that of prostitution – a subject which is both personal and social at the same time. The treatment

of prostitution begins on the personal level and slowly spreads, or rather enlarges itself, to take in social considerations as well. Or perhaps Godard simply discovered that the two are inseparable, as in fact they are. The tightest bond which links any of us to the social structure is what the Marxists call the cash nexus. We all have to eat, and to earn money in order to do so. And one of Godard's main contentions is that many of us earn that money by doing things we don't want to. (1967: 28)

Godard himself confirms this thesis, for when discussing *Deux ou trois choses que je sais d'elle*'s subject of prostitution, which was triggered by an anecdote in *Le Nouvel Observateur*, he states:

The thing that most excited me was that the anecdote it tells coincides basically with one of my most deep-rooted theories. The idea that, in order to live in Parisian society today, at whatever level or on whatever plane, one is forced to prostitute oneself in one way or another, or else to live according to conditions resembling those of prostitution. (Godard 1971: 17)

Apart from *Deux ou trois choses* (*Two or Three Things I Know About Her*, 1967), Godard deals with the subject in its literal form in *Vivre sa vie* (*My Life to Live*, 1962) and the sketch, *Anticipation, ou l'Amour en l'an 2,000* (1967) in the episode film, *L'Amour à travers les âges*. However, he also covers it in a more general sense, as we saw with *Une femme mariée* (where marriage was framed as a form of prostitution), in *Une femme est une femme* (*A Woman is a Woman*, 1961), where Anna Karina's Angéla 'sells' her body as a striptease artist in order to help cover the rent; *Le Mépris* (*Contempt*, 1964), where a playwright sells out to Hollywood in order to pay off his expensive flat and secure his wife's affections; *Bande à part* (1964), where a triangle of friends – Franz, Arthur and Odile – pull off a heist but rather than defy the system are easily co-opted by it; and *Alphaville* (1965), where prostitution is regimented by the state. Thus in *Le Mépris*, when Brigitte Bardot's Camille sleeps with the producer, Prokosch (Jack Palance),

her never-formulated excuse might be that if her husband can sell his brain to this man, she might as well – or even, is morally bound to – hand over the use of her body. Which can be taken as a growing realization on Godard's part that the personal and the social are inextricably intertwined. (Roud 1967: 31)

In this sense, Godard's overriding dictum with these films is stated by Fritz Lang, playing himself in the film, as he quotes from Brecht's 1942 poem, 'Hollywood': 'Every day, to earn my daily bread / I go to the market where lies are bought / Hopefully / I take up my place among the sellers' (Brecht 1987: 382). In this sense cinema could be seen as a great intellectual whorehouse ('sin' cinema) but also as a space for intellectual and affective redemption against an all-encompassing *dispositif* of desire-as-profit.

It is in the latter role that silence plays a key intervention in four of the films: *Une femme est une femme*, *Bande à part*, *Vivre sa vie*, and *Deux ou trois choses que je sais d'elle*, which we will analyse in turn.

Discussing the components of the filmic image in *Cinema 2: The Time-Image*, Deleuze notes that one of the key components of the French New Wave – and Godard's films in particular – was a predilection for irrational cuts over classical cinema's reliance on 'invisible' continuity editing between two series. Under the new regime,

> images and sequences are no longer linked by rational cuts; which end the first or begin the second, but are relinked on top of irrational cuts, which no longer belong to either of the two and are valid for themselves (interstices). Irrational cuts thus have a disjunctive, and no longer a conjunctive value. (1989: 248)

In this sense we can discern a more pedagogical, didactic basis for cinema, where conceptual lessons on the nature of things, images, texts (diegetic, such as books and magazines or extra-diegetic such as appropriated intertitles), colours, words, sounds and silences are generated in and for themselves as philosophical propositions, each moving towards a limit divorced from the continuous series of images which surrounds and defines it.

'Now', as Deleuze notes,

> this limit, this irrational cut, may present itself in quite diverse visual forms: whether in the steady form of a sequence of unusual, 'anomalous' images, which come and interrupt the normal linkage of two sequences [for example, the over-theatricalized musical dance numbers in *Une femme est une femme*, or the machine-gun fire in the street in *Vivre sa vie*, which interrupts the café scene between Nana and her pimp, Raoul]; or in the enlarged form of the black screen, or the white screen, and their derivatives. *But on each occasion, the irrational cut implies the new stage of the talkie, the new figure of sound.* This may be an act of silence, in the sense that it is the talkie and the musical which invent silence. It may be a speech-act, but in the story-telling or founding aspect which it takes on here, in contrast to its 'classical' aspects. (1989: 248–9)

This intercession of silence as interstice reaches its apotheosis in the films under discussion in this chapter, for here Godard reinvests the visual with sound (or conversely, with silence) in order to restore both to the body from which they have been extracted. In short, notes Deleuze, it 'produces a system of disengagements or micro-cuts in all directions: cuts spread and no longer pass between the sound and the visual, but in the visual, in the sound, and in their multiplied connections' (1989: 249).

Unlike Fritz Lang in *M*, where a long passage of silence was used to bind together the *dispositif* of prostitution, police surveillance and underworld profits, Godard does the opposite, harnessing multiple layers of sound – exterior street noises such as car horns, the cries of market-stall vendors and newspaper sellers as well as the interior cacophony of cafés and bars: cash registers, juke boxes and pinball machines – to express the unity of Paris as an urban site of unrelenting exchange value. Godard uses brief periods of silence to break through this surface plane of composition in an attempt to free up an alternative topological vector, a machinic phylum that might connect the viewer to a more constructive and affective plane of immanence. Thus, in the case of *Une femme est une femme*, although the plot is simple and absurdist enough – 'A woman wants to have a baby, just like that, all at once, the way you feel like having a piece of candy' (Godard in Manceaux 1972: 29) – the fact that it is filmed as a musical in Techniscope and Eastmancolor with multiple uses of book titles, magazine covers, neon signs and posters creates a complexity of image-sound rhetoric that exemplifies Deleuze's notion of irrational cuts.

Angéla (Anna Karina) is a young striptease artist who works at the Zodiac Club in the Strasbourg-St Denis district on the Right bank of Paris. She is not only desperate to get pregnant but it must be today – 10 November 1961 – because her Fertility Cycle Indicator tells her that it is the optimum time for conception. Unfortunately, her live-in lover, Émile Récamier (Jean-Claude Brialy) refuses to oblige – he is more concerned with his upcoming cycling meet at the Parc des Princes stadium that weekend and is scared that the sex will drain his energy. As a result, Angéla agrees to recruit his overly willing best friend Alfred Lubitsch (Jean-Paul Belmondo) to do the job for him. Alfred, of course, is named after the film's dedicatee, the famed German-born Hollywood director, Ernst Lubitsch, the master of elegance, sophistication and light-hearted wit in classic films such as *Ninotchka* (1939), *To Be or Not To Be* (1942), and *Heaven Can Wait* (1943), which earned him the stylistic soubriquet of 'The Lubitsch Touch'. The film, punctuated by countless song and dance interludes, then proceeds to unfold Angéla's dilemma whimsically (she eventually gets her way – with Émile) but not at the expense of scoring important points about the mechanics of prostitution as well as the economic, social and sexual ramifications of its integration into society. As Godard himself explained in a 1962 interview in *Cahiers du Cinéma*, he saw his films during this period as appropriations of spectacle (as opposed to Debord's Situationist *détournement*) to create a dialectical play between documentary and fiction, as if an Alfred Hitchcock screenplay had been filmed by the anthropological auteur, Jean Rouch. Godard stated that,

> If I analyse myself today, I see that I have always wanted, basically, to do research in the form of a spectacle. The documentary side is: a man in a particular situation.

> The spectacle comes when one makes this man a gangster or a secret agent. In *Une femme est une femme* the spectacle comes from the fact that the woman is an actress; in *Vivre sa vie*, a prostitute. (Cited in Narboni and Milne 1972: 181)

To expand the contradictions further, Godard saw the film as a 'neo-realist musical':

> It's a complete contradiction, but this is precisely what interested me in the film. It may be an error, but it's an attractive one. And it matches the theme, which deals with a woman who wants a baby in an absurd manner whereas it is the most natural thing in the world. But the film is not a musical. It's the idea of a musical. (Cited in Narboni and Milne 1972: 182)

In effect, it's nostalgia for the musical genre, which is ostensibly moribund, still awaiting the major revitalisation that it will receive in the form of Jacques Demy's *The Umbrellas of Cherbourg* (1964). Godard helps to resurrect it here by infusing it with large doses of the *cinema dell-arte* tradition, with its propensity for irrational cuts, discontinuity, changes in rhythm and radical breaks in mood. Thus, argues Godard,

> The characters perform and take their bow at the same time: they know and we know that they are acting, laughing and crying at the same time. It is an exhibition, in other words, but that is what I wanted. The characters act for the camera the whole time: it's a show. [. . .] In *Vivre sa vie*, on the other hand, one should feel that the characters are constantly avoiding the camera. (Cited in Narboni and Milne 1972: 182)

The film opens by showcasing its Brechtian credentials, with Karina's voice-over, imitating the commands of a film director, shouting 'Lights!' (BRIALY's name comes up on the credits); 'Camera!' (KARINA); 'Action!' (BELMONDO). During a brief sound drop-out, the film's title fills the screen in red letters over an interior shot of a café window looking out onto Blvd. de Strasbourg. We then hear the non-diegetic sound of Michel Legrand's soundtrack with Charles Aznavour singing *Tu t'laisses aller*, as Angela walks by, from right to left holding up a red umbrella. We pan left as she enters the café. She orders a white coffee and stares at the jukebox. Then, in reverse angle, a man approaches the bar and orders green coffee (thereby comically breaking Barthes' dictatorial 'regime of signs' in the very opening scene). She looks at him, moves to the jukebox and selects a record. She moves back to the bar, the non-diegetic music stops, and she watches the man drink his coffee. The same Aznavour song then blasts back in, suggesting that this is diegetic music from the jukebox (although they are both clearly post-synched). Angéla asks the barmaid for the time: it's 5:30 – she's late. Her coffee is too hot to drink so she heads for the door, breaking the fourth wall by winking at the camera as she exits. We then see her walking right to left on the busy street, her footsteps, barely audible as the ambient sound of the boulevard is faded down to a bare whisper. Suddenly we cut to another angle and the street sounds burst in loudly as Angéla approaches the camera, past a van to the right. We pan right to follow her, then left to take in two older men. She smiles at them as if flirting unashamedly. Suddenly Godard cuts to a high angle down on the same street, showing vendors carts, a VINI PRIX sign, and a 'France-soir' advertisement over a newsagents. This is accompanied by a brief three-second sound drop-out before the music bursts in again.

In an interview around the time of the film's release, François Truffaut was hyper-critical of this resort to non-ambient silence, most specifically because of its Syncinema switch from passive absorption in the diegesis to active, extra-diegetic audience involvement (which caused actual riots in Nice) even though Maurice Lemaître and Guy Debord would probably have (grudgingly) approved:

> It remains to be seen why it was that certain films, such as *Une femme est une femme*, didn't get across to the public. As far as this film is concerned, I would say that one can reach one's audience in almost any conceivable way, but not by assaulting their basic peace of mind. If one plays around with the sound-track and the images in too unusual a way, people start objecting – it is a normal reaction. They ripped up the seats at Nice because they thought the projection booth was not properly equipped. Of course one could explain things to people through articles, but in those cinemas where the film was put on the audiences were taken by surprise. Godard went too far for them in the sound mixing. When the girl comes out of the café, there's suddenly no sound, just complete silence. Straight away people think the projector has broken down. Although, of course, those spectators in Nice were not civilized – one simply does not knife cinema seats. (Truffaut, cited in Graham 1968: 100)

However, Truffaut's argument doesn't take into account any of the fundamentals of Reception Theory's empowerment of the audience to fill in the gaps, either through expanding their 'horizon of expectations' (in Hans Robert Jauss's term), or through Wolfgang Iser's 'concretisation of the text'.

Thus at this point we have no idea what the silence indicates, but all is made clear when Angéla enters the newsagents and runs into Émile, one of the employees, who is surrounded by magazines as he thumbs through a picture book while standing next to a young boy and girl. He puts the book back on the rack and makes eye contact with Angéla. To give him time to talk to the kids, she browses through the display, briefly touching *Le Cinéma* magazine, which features a close-up of Catherine Demongeot, the young star of Louis Malle's *Zazie dans le Métro* (1960), adapted from

Raymond Queneau's novel. Then we have the big reveal: she opens a copy of *J'Attends un Enfant*, Laurence Pernoud's popular self-help book of obstetrics. As Kevin J. Hayes points out in his excellent analysis of the use of book references in the film, 'Since its appearance five years before, Pernoud's work had gone through multiple printings and had become the authority on pregnancy and childbirth among French women. Glancing at the book, Angela demonstrates her newfound interest in having a child' (2000: 66–7). Significantly, after she puts the book back on the rack and makes brief eye contact with Émile, she picks up a copy of *Santé* magazine, which features a naked woman on the cover. As she lowers it and peeps over the magazine at him we get two conflicting (but also complementary) images of a woman's body. One is framed as pure sexual desire for the delectation of a male gaze (a scene repeated much later when Émile watches a striptease at the Zodiac Club and with each cross-cut between his face and the performer, the latter loses another piece of clothing until she stands topless), the other as a symbol of reproduction and motherhood.

As if to reinforce the latter as Angéla's ideal fantasy (as opposed to the former as her wage-slave day job), the sound drops out for a couple of seconds before returning to Émile as he tries to interest the two children in a copy of *La Belle au Bois Dormant* (*Sleeping Beauty*) (sorry, not sexy enough!). Hayes makes an excellent point when he argues that

> The image of the independent, smart-aleck Zazie, juxtaposed with that of a young woman reading a popular obstetric manual, combines the thrill of having a child with the fear of watching her grow up much too quickly. The juxtaposition captures the cycle of life from birth to childhood to motherhood. (2000: 67)

This is reinforced when, after cutting back to Émile, we realise that the little girl talking to Émile is actually Catherine Demongeot herself, an obvious in-joke but also a reminder that all fantasies have a reality check when you least expect it. While Émile is fully aware of this reality – indeed it's clear that he isn't ready to start a family because he has little idea of what is suitable reading material: the children are far too sexually mature for his limited understanding – Angéla has a different attitude. As Hayes rightly argues, unlike the Sleeping Beauty,

> Angela, being a modern woman, does not wait impassively for her prince to take action. She wants to get married and to have a child, though not necessarily in that order, and she will do what she must to accomplish her goals. (2000: 67–8)

It now seems clear that this first sound drop-out represents a subjective, immediate desire for motherhood on Angéla's part in a larger urban context of family planning, birth control and sexual diversion (i.e. paid-for sex). From a Brechtian perspective this seems to be an extremely conservative and traditionalist stance, particularly given the critical, class-conscious approach that we have come to expect from both Godard and his theatrical mentor. This is reinforced by another narrative vector: namely making Émile's surname be Récamier. As Godard explained in an interview with *L'Express* in 1961, 'I did that just for fun, so that Anna could want to become Mme Récamier. [...] I don't know whether it's a comedy or a tragedy. At any rate, it's a masterpiece' (Manceaux 1972: 29). Mme Juliette Récamier is, of course, the subject of Jacques-Louis David's celebrated (albeit unfinished) portrait from 1800 which features the French socialite and 'salonnière' reclining on a *Directoire*-style *chaise longue* sofa. Juliette's salon was a famous gathering place for leading literary, artistic and political aficionados of neo-classicism, so that projecting Angéla's future into such an elevated status (with a prospective heir to boot) would make her dreams the apotheosis of *embourgeoisement*. It seems clear that Godard is eschewing the more Marxist Brecht of the Epic Theatre's *Lehrstücke* or 'teaching plays' from the early 1930s, with their focus on *gestus* over mimesis, and instead embracing the Brecht of *Mother Courage and Her Children* (1939), which forces the spectator to identify with a character whose actions and ideals they cannot condone (in this case profiting from war), generating a response on the lines of, 'You've got to be kidding! Are you nuts? That's just what they want you to think. Talk about idiot factor!' As Walter Benjamin describes the character of Galy Gay in Brecht's *A Man's a Man* (1926), such characters are like 'an empty stage on which the contradictions of our society are acted out' (Benjamin 1998: 8).

Much the same can be said about Émile and Alfred, for both are blind to more revolutionary, anti-capitalist ideologies that might make them see the truth of their double bind. Émile has one brief moment of sound dropout (shared with Angéla), late in the film when they argue at the top of the stairs in their apartment building. She's adamant about having a baby, but he refuses to budge:

> Émile: 'Don't be indecent, Angéla!'
> Angéla: 'Don't be cruel, Émile!'
> Émile: 'That plaid skirt really doesn't suit you at all.'
> Angéla: 'That's all right. I don't want people to fancy me.'
> She gets up and pauses. (Godard 1984a: 50)

At this point we have complete silence as they stare at each other, then embrace in a passionate kiss. The soundtrack wells up and they start their argument over as he threatens to leave for Mexico. This constant to-ing and fro-ing between attraction and alienation has much to do with Émile's own lack of interest in traditional parenthood. Instead, judging from the proliferation of sports magazine covers on their apartment walls – featuring cycling and athletics – and his own tendency to cycle around the room instead of engaging in constructive conversation with Angéla, he is much more interested in stereotypical male activities, epitomised when he yells at Angela for not tuning in the radio so that he can listen to the Real Madrid vs Barcelona football commentary. Admittedly, this was the heyday of football brilliance, featuring international stars such as Alfredo di Stéfano, Ferenc Puskás and Luis del Sol, but it also underlines how football acts as the opiate of the masses, as one more spectacle designed to take the public's eye off real issues such as class iniquity (an issue taken up by Glauber Rocha in the Brazilian context in *Age of the Earth* – as we shall see in the next chapter).

Alfred's 'subtext' turns out to be far more sinister, harking back to Lang's examination of the criminal class and its relationship to the capitalist system in *M*. For his legitimate job, Alfred works for the city, putting traffic tickets on car windshields. Early on, just after Alfred and Angéla meet briefly in the street, Belmondo is approached by a man wearing a cap and raincoat who says that Alfred owes 52,000 francs to the Hotel Bikini. On 9 July he left there without paying his bill. Because Alfred keeps a daily record of all his activities he thumbs through his pocketbook, convinced the man is wrong. Only it's true. The man asks if he's going to pay him, Alfred walks away: 'No, never'. A slanging match follows, disclosing a darker side to Alfred that is probably unknown to Angéla (at least at this stage):

> Alfred: 'Cretin!'
> Man: 'Dirty bastard!'
> Alfred: 'Stinking queer!'
> Man: 'Dirty bugger!'
> Alfred: 'Bloody Jew!'
> Man: 'Fascist!'
> Alfred: 'Sodomite!' (Godard 1984a: 25)

Their earlier discussion was constantly interrupted by very brief sound drop-outs, suggesting that Alfred has disturbing tendencies buried deep below the surface of his cordial good-naturedness.

This suspicion is borne out later, when Angéla and Alfred sit together in a café and two blind beggars enter and ask Alfred for money. Of course they're scam artists and fail to recognise Alfred because it's hard to see while wearing such dark sunglasses. After they leave he tells Angéla that they're fellow informers, suggesting that he makes his real money working for the underworld. The casting of Belmondo is important here because it connects Alfred directly to his *doppelgänger* role as Michel Poiccard/Laszlo Kovacs in Godard's *Breathless* (1960). Indeed, Alfred makes an in-joke at one point, encouraging Émile and Angéla to hurry up and stop arguing as *Breathless* is playing on television that night. However, this darker vector becomes highly personal in the scene that follows because as they listen to Charles Aznavour's *Tu t'laisses aller* on the jukebox, Alfred shows Angéla an old black and white photograph of Émile with an ex-lover, only Alfred claims that it's current. Thus all the venom that Aznavour's lyrics aim at his lover in the song – 'Why should I even try and hide / Whatever I may feel inside / You lie, you curse and you provoke / And then you treat it as a joke [. . .] At times you're cruel beyond control' – could just as easily be aimed at Alfred.

Also, like Émile, Alfred is a master of creating a double bind whereby every unfolding is enfolded back into a seemingly never changing whole. Thus Émile will only have a child with Angéla if they get married, but he sets it up as a catch-22:

> Émile: 'We'll have a child as soon as we're married.'
> Angéla jumping up excitedly: 'Then let's get married . . . but I haven't got my birth certificate . . . I'll write to Copenhagen straight away.'
> [. . .]
> Émile: 'Oh, there's no hurry!'
> Angéla: 'But I don't understand . . .'
> She moves towards him, hands in pockets of her apron.
> Émile examining a bicycle part: 'Yes, Angéla . . . if we had a child, we'd get married right away . . . But that's not the case.'
> Angéla pauses, then turns away dejectedly. (Godard 1984a: 30)

Alfred pulls a similar number after the Aznavour café sequence above, when it turns out that neither he nor Angéla have enough money to pay the bill. He approaches the unsuspecting bar tender:

> Alfred to Barman: '*I'll ask you a question and you answer either* "yes" *or* "no", okay?'
> Barman: 'Okay. [. . .]'
> Alfred to Barman: 'If you answer "yes", I owe you ten thousand francs, and if you answer "no" you owe me the money. Okay?'
> Barman: Okay.
> Alfred: 'Here's the question, "Can you lend me ten thousand francs?"'
> Barman wiping his hands on a towel: 'No.'
> Alfred: 'Then that's how much you owe me! . . . I'll pay you back next week.'
> (Godard 1984a: 49)

Another key reinforcement of this criminal sub-current running throughout the film is the countless references to *Série Noire* novels or other heist stories. Thus Jeanne Moreau makes a short cameo appearance in a bar as Alfred asks her how Truffaut's *Jules et Jim* is coming along, while Angéla's friend Suzanne (Marie Dubois), who is also considering a move into prostitution having lost her job and Communist Party membership, is reading David Goodis's *Shoot the Piano Player* while standing on the pavement (the in-joke here is that she co-starred with Charles Aznavour in Truffaut's 1960 film adaptation of the same book). Similarly, in the famous scene where Angéla and Émile, their relationship reduced to non-stop name calling as they lie in bed, communicate exclusively by showing each other paperback titles taken from their two bookshelves, *Série Noire* thrillers play a prominent role. As Hayes points out,

> Taken together, these books provide an indication of Emile's and Angela's literary tastes and supply a sample of French book culture circa 1961. The books suggest that Emile and Angela take an interest in archeology and ethnology; that they enjoy popular fiction including American crime novels and French science fiction; and that they enjoy some serious novels from American authors and avant-garde French writers. (2000: 78)

This literary contagion will of course be extended even further in *Alphaville*, where the FBI agent Lemmy Caution, created by British writer Peter Cheyney (1896–1951), hits the screen yet again in the form of Eddie Constantine, a role that he had played seven times in earlier films dating back to *Poison Ivy* (directed by Bernard Borderie) in 1953.

Perhaps the ultimate irony of *Une femme est une femme*, given our Barthesian subtext of the 'rhetoric of the image' is that, according to Jay Hoberman, Anna Karina herself became pregnant during the course of the movie's production and she and Godard were married in March 1961, 'an event that made the cover of *Paris Match*' (Hoberman [1998] 2004: 7). Thus Godard himself becomes enfolded in the endless circulation of signs, which allows him to include himself in the Brechtian, *Mother Courage*, form of self-critique. As he put it earlier in this chapter, everything in film is about money, for the money always comes back again, in the image, and in this case, the personality cult of the film business as a whole.

The same is true, as we shall see, of the ending for *Bande à part* (*Band of Outsiders*, 1964) although the rest of the film expresses a far more ambivalent attitude towards ideology. Here, the characters eschew systematisation in favour of a more *instinctual* resolution of contradictions that they know will never last or permanently transform the status quo. Based on

Dolores Hitchens's novel, *Fools' Gold* (1958), which had been republished in France as part of the *Série Noire*, the film, as Julia Lesage describes it, 'is loosely structured like a "heist" story, but its protagonists' adolescent concerns and its pace – a rambling tour of grey, wintery, suburban Paris – give the film a nonchalant, even melancholy tone, rather than one of adventure or tension' (1979: 59). Set in Joinville in the eastern suburbs, the film focuses on Odile Monod (Anna Karina), who lives with her Aunt Victoria (Louisa Colpeyn) and her guardian Mr Stolz in a house by the canal. Her guardian (whom we never see until the very end) has a stash of money hidden away in a cupboard in his room, which Odile discovers. Meanwhile, she has become friendly with a fellow student in her Berlitz-style English class in Paris – Franz, played by Sami Frey – and she naïvely tells him of her discovery. In no time flat Franz – who is clearly a con artist – tells his friend and cohort Arthur Rimbaud (Claude Brasseur – obviously, a poet!) and the pair plan to use Odile as an accomplice (willing or unwilling) to obtain Stolz's room key so that they can steal the money. Unfortunately Arthur isn't the sharpest knife in the drawer, for as Godard described his character in the original 1964 press book, printed by Unifrance/Gaumont for the film's theatrical release:

> Arthur is one of those people for whom metaphors need never to be explained. He believes in outward appearances, in Billy the Kid in the same way as he believes in Cyd Charisse. Put another way, he is a boy for whom life is totally denuded of mystery, but with all the poetry that the word 'total' implies. [. . .] To play this role, Claude Brasseur was ideal, because he has the innocence and the madness of children when they play at marbles or at war, I mean both the necessary brutality and the sufficient frankness, or vice versa. (Godard 1964: 4).

This combination of naïveté and impulsiveness is borne out by his clumsy seduction of Odile – he is tender and violent by turns – and also his inability to keep a secret: he foolishly tells his aunt (Chantal Darget) and uncle (Ernest Menzer) and the latter immediately want in on the heist, using Arthur's ex-legionnaire cousin Roger (Georges Staquet) as their enforcer. Arthur pretends to go along with the family's plan but quickly tells Franz and Odile that they have to commit the robbery the following day to get a twenty-four-hour jump on their rivals. Fearing that Stolz already suspects that something is brewing, Odile confides in Franz, urging him to call the whole thing off. Clearly they are romantically attracted to each other because they also discuss escaping to the Far North or South America. Then, after conducting the fastest tour of the Louvre on record, they carry out the robbery. Unfortunately, the door to Stolz's room is locked (as is the outside window) and they are forced to use an extension ladder to enter from the outside. The window is also locked and Arthur punches Odile in frustration. They return the next day disguised as TV reporters (as Arthur puts it, 'TV is the open sesame') only to discover that they left traces on the ladder the previous day so all the locks have been changed. Odile urges Franz and Arthur to leave but they barge their way in, tie and gag Aunt Victoria, and stuff her into a downstairs closet. Unfortunately, there's no money – just a few francs in a couple of rooms (including Odile's) and a sizeable wad in the fridge. Before leaving, they check on Aunt Victoria: she seems to be dead.

The trio start to drive away but Arthur insists on going back to check on Victoria and look for the money. Franz and Odile continue on but U-turn when they spot the uncle's car heading to the house. It's cousin Roger, clearly on his way to steal the cash. Meanwhile, Arthur has found the money in an outdoor doghouse. As he readies to leave Roger sneaks up on him and shoots him five times as Arthur approaches him, gun drawn. He staggers each time he is hit but doesn't fall, then shoots and kills Roger as Franz and Odile look on from the far background. As Arthur dies, Godard's voice-over fades up:

> Arthur's dying thought was of Odile's face. As a dark fog descended on him, he saw that fabled bird of Indian legend which is born without feet and thus can never alight. It sleeps in the high winds and is only visible when it dies. When its transparent wings, longer than an eagle's, fold in, it fits in the palm of your hand.

Suddenly, Stolz returns home and picks up the spilled money by the doghouse, then heads for the front door. Aunt Victoria (yes, still alive), emerges from the house to greet him, as if to say, 'Let the working-class criminals shoot it out among themselves so the really crooked bourgeoisie can keep their own stolen spoils.' Indeed, it turns out that Stolz stole his money from the government: he obviously won't be informing the police. As Odile and Franz make their way back to Paris – they have enough money from the stash in the fridge to make a future for themselves – they discuss their feelings and he lets her decide on their ultimate destination: north or south. She chooses the latter. The film ends with them on a boat, headed for Latin America, declaring their mutual love.

Bande à part is famous for three specific scenes including all three characters – the complete sound drop-out in the café sequence that Michel Chion called 'the zero-degree . . . element of the soundtrack that is silence' (1994: 56–7) that we discussed in the Introduction; the Madison dance number in the same café a few minutes later; and the sprint through the Louvre just before attempting the robbery. Obviously, the silent sequence is of key importance for our purposes but it is directly related to its seeming antithesis in the other two. At the forty-six-minute mark, as they sit in the café, obviously tired from the overbearing nature of the English class and its pedantic teacher (Danièle Girard), Franz makes an odd suggestion:

> Franz: 'If there's nothing to say, let's have a minute of silence.'
> Odile: 'You can really be dumb sometimes.'
> Franz: 'A minute of silence can be a long time. A real minute of silence takes forever.'
> Odile: 'OK. One, two, three . . .'

Suddenly the ambient noise of the café cuts out and the silence begins. The three sit idly, staring into space for what seems like an eternity. At first glance Godard appears to be following his earlier tactic in *Une femme est une femme*, introducing a radical irrational cut in the soundtrack to enable the spectator to follow an alternative vector to that of the surface plane of capitalist consumption (and its corollary, prostitution). This is reinforced by Godard's statement that as a band of outsiders, his characters form a unity whereby they are more honest with themselves than with other people, purposefully leading their own lives through their natural reactions:

> It's not really they who live outside of society. It's society that is far from them. They go everywhere – you see them in the Louvre, in the bistros; they're no more withdrawn from society than the characters of *Rebel Without a Cause*. [. . .] These are characters right out of Jean-Jacques Rousseau. They're just the opposite of the hero of *Le Mépris*, Paul Javal, who is a bad offspring of civilization. (Godard, cited in Collet 1972: 44)

However, Godard cheats: after a mere thirty-six seconds, Franz breaks the silence: 'That's enough. I'll put a record on.' He gets up and exits right. On one level, Godard has done us a major disservice: we have been denied the full extent of the minute's silence (that can seemingly take forever) so that we can never feel either its somatic affect or its intellectual stimulation. One obvious vector that the sequence could have pursued is a plane of immanence represented by Henri Bergson's differentiation between the quantitative multiplicity of time (which can be measured, as if marked by a stopwatch) and the qualitative multiplicity of duration (which cannot be segmented). We also miss out on a potential example of Syncinema (bearing the silence in a cinema surrounded by other people – exchanging glances or deliberately coughing to set up a sense of community) or the alternative medium of watching the film on a computer at home, by ourselves and timing the exact length of the silence.

On another level it may be read as a Brechtian distanciation device, where Godard once again brings in the issue of money and commerciality. It's possible that he heeded Truffaut's critique of the sound drop-out in

Une femme est une femme (and the resulting riots in Nice) and attempted to show that he is willing to appease his audience's state of mind by eschewing technical excess, but it's more likely that he was using the sequence sarcastically and self-critically. However, the famous 'Madison' dance sequence that follows (it's actually different from the real Madison which originated in Columbus, Ohio in 1957), where the trio 'improvise' a carefully choreographed dance in the café, suggests that Godard is far more interested in spectacle than *détournement*, for the routine serves to tie together music, dance, sexual desire and café society as a self-conscious form of cinematic entertainment. It's no accident that the band, Nouvelle Vague, led by musicians Olivier Libaux and Marc Collin, appropriate this sequence for the music video of their cover of Lords of the New Church's song *Dance with Me*, sung by Mélanie Pain, thereby recycling the original New Wave spectacle for the YouTube audience.

Similarly, the sprint through the Louvre, which they complete in less than nine minutes, forty-three seconds, thereby breaking the record set by Jimmy Johnson of San Francisco, is another transformation of serious aesthetic contemplation into mindless competition (not unlike Monty Python's brilliant 'Summarise Proust in 15 Seconds' sketch).[1] However, as in the case of the sound drop-out, Godard is self-reflexively aware of such co-option. It's no accident that the trio run past Jacques-Louis David's *Oath of the Horatii* (1784) in the process, a reminder of the true nature of family sacrifice and loyalty to a larger cause whereby the three Horatii brothers agree to end Rome's war with Alba Longa by fighting the Curiatii brothers as singular representatives of their cities. This is, of course, in stark contrast to the characters in the film, where Odile 'betrays' her aunt and guardian and Arthur's uncle and cousin subvert their relative Arthur's heist.

It's also important to point out that the three scenes – the silence, the Madison, the Louvre – are ultimately subverted by the characters themselves, not Godard – i.e. it's a diegetic issue, not an extra-diegetic intervention. It's Franz who calls an early end to the silence, spurred perhaps by his *horror à vacui* (he can't even be silent for the full minute), which is tied to his need for superficial noise, money, consumption of any kind, stirring adventure and friendly company. Similarly, both Franz and Arthur cut out of the Madison dance before the music is over, leaving Odile dancing alone until the number ends. All three agree to the Louvre sprint, as

---

[1] One recalls Peter Cook's inspired version: 'Marcel Proust dipped his biscuit in his tea and remembered everything.'

if to pump up their adrenalin for the robbery that night. Godard has an interesting explanation for this impatience:

> The characters in *Bande à part* don't know how to discuss. They're little animals. Instead of being the wild animals of *Les Carabiniers*, they're domesticated animals, you might say. They're also the little suburban cousins of the Belmondo of *À bout de souffle* and of *Une femme est une femme*. Furthermore, *Une femme est une femme* almost had a title *On est comme on est* (You Are What You Are). (Godard in Collet 1972: 44)

In other words, Odile, Franz and Arthur are not dominated by any ideological technique or preconceived ideas – which leads to a strange equalisation of affect and politics:

> They know it's wrong to steal money. They have neither the mentality of thieves or of capitalists. They're like animals. They get up in the morning. They have to find a bird to kill so they can eat at noon, and another for the evening. Between that, they go to the river to drink. And that's it. They live by their instincts, for the instant. The danger would be to make a system of it. Whereas these characters correct themselves. For the moment, they're happy because they're not asking themselves any questions. (Godard in Collet 1972: 45)

Thus the silence, Madison and Louvre sequences don't cancel each other out or work dialectically but are equal outcomes (resolutions) of the characters' eschewal of systematisation. All are part of the same instinctual vector. The danger is that they may end up co-opted (by crime, wage slavery, the system of rote learning of Shakespeare – as in the English class – or the spectacular).

The latter is a particular danger, for as Keith Reader rightly points out, serious ideological issues such as colonialism are mentioned only in passing or as scattered readings from newspapers with little or no contextualisation. Thus Roger, Arthur's cousin, fought at Diên Biên Phu, the 1954 battle which ended the French colonial presence in South-East Asia, but we learn nothing more. Within just one year, in *Pierrot le fou*, Godard would make Vietnam a central theme. China, which Franz argues is rapidly replacing Britain as a major colonial power, will get a far more extensive reading in *La Chinoise* (1967), as will the division between the 'here' of Europe and the Global North and the 'elsewhere' of the Global South (which Godard, Gorin and Anne-Marie Miéville will make a central issue in *Ici et Ailleurs*, 1976). More important to contemporary audiences, argues Reader,

> is the reference to the former Belgian colony of Rwanda. This occurs when Arthur and Franz are waiting idly outside Odile/Anna Karina's house, reading passages from the newspaper to each other to pass the time. A couple of banal *faits divers* are

followed by a story about ethnic conflict between Hutus and Tutsis in Rwanda, which had obtained its independence only the previous year [. . .] What is perhaps most powerful about this reference is the banality of the context in which it is embedded. Ethnic cleansing – to use a term not then invented – is placed on an everyday, uneventful footing, as though in support of Debord's theses on the leveling, banalising effects of the spectacle. (Reader 2007: 83)

Much the same could be said of the film's ending, where, accompanied by a terrier dog on their transatlantic voyage, Franz and Odile speculate about their romantic future in Latin America:

Odile: 'Are there lions in Brazil?'
Franz: 'As well as croc . . . Odiles. Thinking of me?'
Odile: 'Obviously.'
Franz: 'In what way?'
Odile: 'The way you think about me. When guys think of girls they think about their eyes, legs and breasts. Girls think of guys in exactly the same way.'
Franz: 'So we're in love?'
Odile: 'Oh, we'll see soon enough . . .'

Well indeed, there are predator 'lions' in Brazil – one has just seized power against the civilian government of João Goulart in a coup d'état that culminated years of political unrest. This will be a central catalyst of Glauber Rocha's films, which we will discuss in the next chapter, and which Godard will recycle into his own *Le vent d'est* (1970), which features a personal appearance by the Brazilian director. But for now, as Godard's voice-over tells us,

My story ends here, like in a pulp novel, at that superb moment when nothing weakens, nothing wears away, nothing wanes. An upcoming film will reveal [On the Earth, rotating in the cosmos] in CinemaScope and Technicolor the tropical adventures of Odile and Franz.

In other words, money returns one more time as we evolve from a B picture Serie Noire to a big studio production. This raises an interesting, if speculative question: does this sequel end up being *Pierrot le fou*? (even though it's Eastmancolor?), with Franz/Ferdinand and Odile/Marianne ending up on the French Riviera and discovering their own ultimate chaoid – death!?

Death is also the chief 'subterranean' vector in *Vivre sa vie*, which continues Godard's use of Brechtian *V-Effekt* before reaching its apotheosis in *Deux ou trois choses*. Broken up into twelve tableaux, each introduced by an intertitle, the film stars Anna Karina as Nana (the Zola reference immediately sets up an obvious literary intertext) as a beautiful would-be actress who reluctantly leaves her husband Paul (André S. Labarthe) and young son in order to pursue her dreams. However, unable to pay her way via her job as a record shop assistant, she is evicted from her apartment and gradually slips into prostitution under the expert mentorship of her pimp, Raoul (Saddy Rebbot). However, just as she seems to have found true love in the form of a handsome young man and decides to ditch Raoul, the latter makes arrangements to sell her to another pimp. While making the exchange, the two men argue over money and Nana is killed during the ensuing gun battle (Godard parodies this scene in *Bande à part* as a mimed western shoot-out between Franz and Arthur, showing how diegetic death and tragedy in one film is immediately spoofable as quotable commodity in another).

Godard structures the film as a series of dialectics, contrasting specific speech-acts with a more generalised philosophical discourse, pitting diegetic and extra-diegetic sound against silence. Firstly, the film's diegetic dialogue is interspersed with metacommunicative interludes, so that almost all of the sequences take on the form of a language game describing different facets of love and affect: divine/spiritual; philosophical; theatrical (Paul accuses Nana of speaking in stage lines, 'parrot talk'); artistic; romantic; mechanistic, as commodity value; as free will; as affect; as betrayal; as failure of communication. The philosophical discussion culminates in Nana's chance meeting with the language philosopher Brice Parain in tableau eleven. Discussing her ongoing struggle to find the right word in everyday conversation, Nana poses a more provocative question: 'Why must one always talk? Often one shouldn't talk, but live in silence. The more one talks, the less the words mean.' The loquacious Parain is understandably sceptical: 'Perhaps, but can one? I've found that we can't live without talking.' Nana insists: 'I'd like to live without talking.' 'Yes, it would be nice, wouldn't it?' replies Parain, 'Like loving one another more. But it isn't possible.'

Although this sequence is both touching and entertaining, the most important dialectic in the film is that between sound and silence. This is established during the opening title sequence which is superimposed over three tight close-ups of Nana's face – left profile; full face; right profile – each lasting approximately fifty seconds and shot in deep shadow. The opening half of each set-up is overlaid by Michel Legrand's extra-diegetic score (itself divided into three variations on a simple theme) with the second half reduced to dead studio silence. The sequence ends with an epigraph attributed to Montaigne: 'Lend yourself to others and give yourself to yourself.' Superficially at least, the contrast between sound and silence seems to establish two sides to Nana's personality – the material world of the finite (with its association with the hard realities of survival and, by extension, prostitution), and the infinite possibilities of dream and fantasy (her creative ideal of being an actress, of giving herself to herself as a personal ethics). In this sense, music restores bodily affect to material exchange value, silence to its infinite incommensurability. However, we know in our discussion of Godard's other 'prostitution' films that commodification permeates all levels of intercourse under capitalism (whether sexual or textual), where reification and exchange value are the dominant modes of production, particularly in the world of commercial film. Thus although we might mistake the close-ups of Nana as the equivalent of screen tests or actress publicity stills, they could also be seen as police criminal mug shots, a reading further reinforced when Godard repeats the images during Nana's interrogation by the police for shoplifting during tableau 4. Given that Godard is also directing his real-life wife in the film, he may also be collapsing his own role as cinematic auteur into that of controlling pimp, as a directorial version of Raoul.

So if the Montaigne quotation, with its clear-cut divide between pragmatics and idealism, turns out to be a misleading key to understanding the sound–silence dialectic, then where is it actually grounded? The answer lies in a key scene in tableau 3, where Nana and her date attend the cinema to see Carl Theodor Dreyer's 1928 silent film masterpiece, *The Passion of Joan of Arc*. Godard introduces the scene with an establishing shot of the theatre with JEANNE-D'ARC emblazoned in neon (it's actually the name of the theatre itself, not simply a publicity title for the film) against a soundtrack of dead silence. He then cuts to a side view of Nana in the audience, facing the screen to the right. We hear the ambient sound of the theatre and the heavy footsteps of a patron as he leaves for the exit, frame left. We then cut to a huge close-up of Maria Falconetti as Joan (a clear manifestation of Deleuze's affection-image), also in complete silence. This is an obvious deceit on Godard's part for as Tony Pipolo has pointed out, the print – with its odd combination of intertitles and subtitles and narrow aspect ratio compared to recently restored archive prints (indicating an added soundtrack) – is clearly the 1951 negative of Dreyer's second version of *The Passion of Joan of Arc* found in the Gaumont Studios vaults by Joseph-Marie Lo Duca. Apart from illustrating the intertitles and adding subtitles, Lo Duca also included a baroque score. As Pipolo argues:

> It is highly unlikely he [Dreyer] would have approved the music of Bach or Vivaldi appended as mere accompaniment, and equally improbable that he would have been moved by attempts to make his silent film 'easier' to watch and hence more

commercially viable. He made his feelings about this sonorized version quite clear more than once. (1988: 309)

Indeed, Dreyer hated it:

> It is simply horrible: wrong music, wrong sound [. . .] gothic windows and other things of the same sort totally deceiving; there are no words which can express the way Lo Duca has made my film on Joan of Arc banal. (Cited in Pipolo 1988: 309)

Godard thus uses a bastardised print with an unsuitable soundtrack but cuts the sound completely – including the ambient sound of the projector. Instead, Godard uses artificial silence (and the history of silent cinema as a whole) as a form of hiatus within the sound-image surface of his own film as a means of naturalising the silent film image as a kind of latent or spectral plane of consistency as it intersects with the plane of composition of *Vivre sa vie* itself, creating in effect the conjunction of two chaoids.

It's significant that Godard selects the scene of Joan's encounter with Maître Jean Massieu (played by Antonin Artaud) at the very moment that he announces her death at the stake. Joan closes her eyes, opens them, barely able to control a facial spasm of horror. Godard then cuts to a full face close-up of an enraptured Anna in the audience, creating a direct match cut with Joan, as if to unite two affection-images through a common bodily passion. Significantly, we suddenly hear the ambient sound of the theatre, including a man's voice, as if to underline that at this point Nana's identification with Joan is still a material, affective one as Falconetti faces up to the reality of her *bodily* death. Godard then reasserts the silence of Dreyer's film as Artaud leans towards the camera with an ironical smile:

> 'How can you still believe you were sent by God?'
> Joan responds: 'God knows where he leads us, but we know the path of our journey.'
> Massieu is shaken by her self-possession as Joan continues: 'Yes, I'm his child.'
> Artaud is now seething with anger at such blasphemy: 'And the great victory?'
> Joan: 'It will be my martyrdom.'
> 'And the deliverance?'
> Falconetti, looks down, saddened: 'Death.'

Godard now cuts back to Nana who is silently weeping. More importantly, there is no longer any ambient sound: Nana is fully integrated into Joan's spiritual, affective space, the monument that is pure sensation, conjoined by their shared silence. The following intertitle – the repeat of the word 'Death' – directly links Falconetti and Nana in the infinite afterlife, transcending language and image through a common resort to the interstice.

It's tempting to see this conjoining of Joan and Nana's faces through intercutting as a transcendental moment but in fact it's more accurate to see them as a form of durational immanence, for as Godard explains:

> Cutting on a look is almost the definition of montage, its supreme ambition as well as its submission to *mise en scène*. It is, in effect, to bring out the soul under the spirit, the passion behind the intrigue, to make the heart prevail over the intelligence by destroying the notion of space in favour of that of time. (Godard [1956] (1972c): 39)

Again, there is a Spinozist moment here, for both Nana and Joan are able to access a larger reality beyond their immediate state of material existence through a form of intuitive speculation – Deleuze's 'transcendental empiricism' – for as he points out in *Bergsonism*, 'To open us up to the inhuman and the superhuman (*durations* which are inferior or superior to our own), to go beyond the human condition: This is the meaning of philosophy' (1991b: 28). The result is an actualisation of the virtual via an empirical ethics; a discovery of what our bodies – actualising machines – are capable. Godard retroactively marks the bounded limit of the scene by cutting to Nana and her date approaching a café as the ambient noises of the street fade up on the soundtrack.

It's important to stress, however, that Godard doesn't just use silence as a connecting portal to the infinite – in this case Joan's transcendental passion as an immanent, undifferentiated time-image – on an individual basis but expands this deterritorialised subjectivity to the surface fabric of imperial Paris as a whole. As Mark Betz points out in his analysis of Nana as a modern *flâneuse*, Paris isn't just an objective correlative of Nana's subjective state of mind, or even a contextual backdrop for her attempts to 'live her life', but is rather an integrated, immanent expression of her shifting subjectivity as a decentred being. Godard's views of Paris are directly linked to the body of his female protagonist, who traverses the city and is traversed in turn by its commodified surface. Thus *Vivre sa vie* is not a subjectivity tracing Nana's self-discovery via her contact with various 'others' (including herself as other), but is instead captured through the lens of an ethnographer who objectifies Nana as yet another subject of colonisation and violence. Thus, as Betz notes,

> although one might first consider the gun battle in the street as simply a generic nod to the American gangster films so coveted by the *Cahiers du Cinéma* group of critics and filmmakers, Raoul informs us in the next episode that the violence in the street 'had something to do with politics' – and the politics in Paris in 1961–62 means OAS terrorism, the Algerian war brought home. The fate of Nana,

the modern woman, is bound up in flânerie, prostitution, violence, death – and politics. (2009: 149)

In this sense, Godard's fracturing of the movement-image with the immanent world of affect has important philosophical ramifications, which is evident in the transition from tableaux nine to ten. At the end of the former, Nana does a seductive pole dance in a café in order to attract the attention of the young man she will fall in love with. The accompanying music is a loud, diegetic jazz piece playing on the jukebox, which continues over the beginning of the next intertitle, but cuts out into twenty-five seconds of silence for the start of the next scene. The latter features Nana smoking a cigarette backed by a mass of advertising posters, as if she were yet one more commodity on display in a city completely defined by exchange value. This is confirmed when she seductively purses her lips and we cut to Nana's point of view for six more seconds of silence as a young man passes from left to right before glancing directly at the camera. Godard then cuts to another seven seconds of a silent Nana before fading up the street sounds as Nana is joined by another prostitute and is eventually picked up by another client as we return to business as usual. However, the silence serves as an important hiatus in the sequence because it allows Godard to construct a gap or hesitancy between stimulus and response which allows access to the infinite as a realm of pure potentiality. In this sense the street scenes have much in common with those in André Breton's novel *Nadja* (a key literary inspiration for *Bande à part*, eventually replaced by Queneau's *Odile*) another Paris-based text riddled with silences and lacunae (not least the absence of Nadja herself). However, whereas Godard mines the interstice for the pure logic of sensation, as Raymond Spiteri argues, Breton grounds his novel in the surface appearance of another kind of politics –

> the politics of the marvellous – that operates in the interval between event, image and text. This strategy goes to the heart of the constitutive role of silence, interval and failure in the construction of *Nadja*, in which silence acts as an unsurpassable limit around which the narrative unfolds. (Spiteri 2003: 70)

Significantly, *Vivre sa vie*'s narrative exists in the gap between two deaths – that of Joan and Nana, one spiritual, the other seemingly banal and material. In this sense, Deleuze's description of temporality in Resnais seems very appropriate: 'Between one death and the other, the absolute inside and the absolute outside enter into contact, an inside deeper than all the sheets of past, an outside more distant than all the layers of external reality' (1989: 208). While Resnais' characters return from Auschwitz, Hiroshima or Algiers, either literally or spiritually, they also become philosophers, creatures of thought. For Deleuze,

> the philosopher is someone who believes he has returned from the dead, rightly or wrongly, and who returns to the dead in full consciousness. The philosopher has returned from the dead and goes back there. This has been the living formulation of philosophy since Plato. (1989: 209)

Is this not also an accurate description of Nana's path, revisiting the cinematic death of Joan in order to return to another, present-day death that is her own, a mental and affective journey – a passion – that can only be created on the plane of immanence through the intercession of the chaoid of sensation, itself wrought in the interstices of silence? As Deleuze sums up,

> From one pole to the other a creation will be constructed, which is true creation only because it will be carried out between the two deaths, the apparent and the real, all the more intense because it illuminates this interstice. (1989: 209)

– and, one might add, its accomplice: silence.

One might have thought that Godard would continue this trajectory in *Deux ou trois choses* – indeed the film includes publicity posters for both *Muriel* and *Vivre sa vie* as part of its *mise-en-scène* – but instead of unfolding this line of flight to infinity the film enfolds it back (like Schlegel's hedgehog) to an unresolveable impasse, requiring a new start from scratch or what Godard calls a 'return to zero'. Focusing on a day in the life of a prostitute, Juliette Janson (Marina Vlady), her radio ham husband Robert (Roger Montsoret), who passively listens to American forces broadcasts spouting Lyndon Johnson's war threats against Vietnam and China, and their two children, Christophe and Solange (Christophe and Marie Bourseiller), the film's context derives from two related sources. First, we have the re-planning of Paris under Paul Delouvrier, appointed by de Gaulle in 1961 as head of the Délégation Générale au District de la Région de Paris. In 1964 Delouvrier began a four year programme to develop eight new towns on the perimeter of the region, each containing its own distinct social, commercial and cultural centres. Godard specifically attacks the so-called grands ensembles', also known as HLMs or 'Habitation à Loyer Modéré' (Housing at Moderate Rent). It was here, in locations such as Sarcelles in the northern department of Val-d'Oise,[2] that

---

[2] Although, according to Jacqueline Levitin, Godard actually shot the film in La Courneuve, 'whose 4000 lodgings were completed in 1963' (2014: 259, n. 6)

pieds-noirs – French settlers and Jewish refugees from Algeria and Egypt – were transferred into high-rise apartment blocks. Godard makes his own views known throughout the film in a whispered voice-over commentary, divided into twenty-eight sections (in this respect, Godard himself is the 'I' of the film's title). In Commentary Number 3, over the image of twin AZUR petrol pumps with a high-rise apartment and a large crane in the background, he states that, 'I've already worked out that Paul Delouvrier, in spite of his fine-sounding name [it means 'of the worker'], began his career in the Lazard and Rothschild banking trusts' (Godard 1984b: 124). It's not surprising that this provocative line was cut by the censor but the following accusations – voiced-over shots of an apartment forecourt and a radio equipment shop – actually made it into the final film:

> Which presumably means that that the Gaullist regime, while claiming to modernize and to reform the system, in fact only wishes to record and to regulate the natural course of major capitalism. I also deduce that stratifying the directive and centralizing processes, the same authority accentuates the distortion of the national economy, and still more that of the underlying day by day morality. (1984b: 124)

It is the latter 'day by day morality' that is the focus of Godard's second source, three articles by Catherine Vimenet (two of them shared the same title) – 'Les Étoiles filantes' ('Shooting Stars') and 'Prostitution dans les grands ensembles?' (Prostitution in the 'Grands Ensembles?'), published in *Le Nouvel Observateur* on 23 March, 29 March and 10 May 1966 – which recount the phenomenon of daytime, clandestine prostitution by newly located housewives in the suburban HLMs. Unable to pay the rent or to keep their families in a comfortable lifestyle (given their husbands' equally low wages), they were forced to take on what they called 'overtime' activities. The articles spawned an anonymous letter to the editors by a woman named 'Stella', published on 4 May 1966, which authenticated the first two articles as Stella outlined her own initial fears and reluctance but also the eventual rewards from her new lifestyle:

> I've practiced this activity outside of office hours for seven years now. I always used to be short of money. Now I go to the hairdresser twice a week, and without being extravagant I buy myself whatever I like to wear. I was also able to buy my apartment, which to my tremendous concern was for sale. ('Stella' [1966] 2009: 13)

Stella's letter thus shows us how 'ensemble' can also be associated with another possible definition that plays an equally important part in the new economy – a combination of clothes (shades of Barthes and 'The Fashion System' as a combination of denotative and connotative axes), make-up and hairstyle that might make a housewife more attractive to potential clients. However, it was perhaps the following class-conscious comment that spurred Godard to make the film:

> Now you can tell the pack of the self-righteous who condemn prostitution officially, the better to enjoy it incognito, that the hundred francs they won't grant a female colleague for a monthly raise – thereby denying her professional experience, her work skills, her ability to back someone up, her efficiency (believe me, it's happened to me) – will be spent by them a few hours later for a brief moment with a woman, temporarily buying what she has in common with all her sisters: her sex. ('Stella' 2009: 12–13)

Significantly, Godard not only takes the concept of the *grands ensembles* as they appertain to Paris's redevelopment under Delouvrier and their economic relation to the family as 'ensemble' or 'complex' (not uncoincidentally, *grue*, the French word for crane, is also slang for 'prostitute', thus explaining Godard's tendency to follow Juliette's shifting gaze with moving cranes in the next shot), but he extends this loose 'totality' to include the complicity of American imperialism in Vietnam and also the degradation of language and texts in popular culture (Barthes's 'rhetoric of the image' as an endless syntagmatic connotation circumscribed by the prevailing ideology of capitalism). Thus in his original synopsis of the film, Godard describes its socio-economic context as follows:

> While the Americans continue to wage an immoral and unjust war in Vietnam, the French government, whose links with international capital are well known, builds round Paris enormous blocks of flats whose inhabitants, whether through boredom or because of the anxiety which this kind of architecture produces, or because of economic needs, are led to practice prostitution, for Americans returning from Vietnam among others. At the same time, this Society, which is building these blocks of flats, distributes, in the form of paperbacks, a cheap culture which is assimilated by the population in a fragmentary and lamentable way. All this goes on among a very loud noise of piledrivers, motors, cement mixers, and compressed materials which, to a certain extent, prevents communication. (Cited in Kustow 1968: 289)

This synopsis suggest that there are far more than 'two or three things' that Godard knows about 'her' (which many critics limit to: 1) his leading actress, Marina Vlady; 2) the fictional character she plays, Juliette Janson; and 3) Paris as a whole). Indeed, in the film's soundless trailer, intercut with selected scenes from the film, we have twelve texts that suggest additional meanings of the word 'elle':

> Learn in silence 2 or 3 things I know about
> HER

HER, the cruelty of neo-capitalism
HER, prostitution
HER, the Paris region
HER, the bathroom which 70% of the French do not have
HER, the dreadful law of the housing high-rises
HER, the physique of love
HER, life today
HER, the Vietnam war
HER, the modern call-girl
HER, the death of humane beauty
HER, the circulation of ideas
HER, the Gestapo of structures (Atack 1999: 53 and n. 25)

As Margaret Atack argues, contextualising Godard's advance role leading up to the events of May '68, 'The political themes of anti-capitalism, anti-colonialism, and anti-imperialism, together with the challenge to conventional sexuality and to conventional aesthetics as bourgeois, make Godard one of the prime articulators of *gauchisme* in the cultural sphere' (1999: 53).

Godard's tactic in expressing this larger 'ensemble' is, as usual, Brechtian, on one level using the latter's usual array of distancing devices – silences and loud sounds are used to both link and defamiliarise images that would otherwise be naturally and unobtrusively complicit – but also to present the whole film as an elaborate form of comic strip where his characters play out seemingly contrived and preconceived roles. However, far from being a simplistic reduction of ideology to stereotypes, Godard uses his own voice-over commentary to question the very status of his own film and his own relation to the subject. Thus on one level the whispered tones suggest conspiracy and subterfuge, as if Godard were a political ethnologist examining his subject all the better to destroy its comparative human structures, while on the other a form of confession or self-doubt as he poses narrative and compositional dilemmas. In this sense his words act as prompts to inaugurate a topological vector and then steer it in different directions to connect with deterritorialised (seemingly unrelated) points. Thus, as Michael Kustow argues, he is

> questioning why he should be filming these girls rather than those trees, asking himself where he stands in relation to his camera, the person he is filming, the society, the time of day, the universe. The tone of this commentary continues as it begins, in a whisper, urgent, tentative, trying to find a purchase in a world governed by the grind of bulldozers and the roar of trucks. (1968: 289–90)

In the end Godard moves from analytic distanciation to accepting (but also questioning) his own inescapable role in the maintenance of the 'grand ensemble'.

Godard's Brechtian approach begins with his deliberate reversal of fictional and documentary devices (a tactic which he and Gorin will pursue to its ultimate extreme in the Dziga Vertov Group films that follow – see Chapters 6 and 7). Thus, in relating his own practice to that of Jean Rouch and Robert Flaherty, he argues that,

> They take characters from reality and make a fictional story with them. It is somewhat like what I do, but just in the opposite way: I took fictional characters, and I made a story with them that in a way looked like a documentary. (Cited in Kovács 2007: 170)

This reversal takes place from the start as Godard, foregrounding the framing role he plays as the director, introduces in voice-over his main character, firstly as the actress, Marina Vlady (wearing a blue-grey sweater with two yellow stripes, of Russian descent with light or dark brown hair), then as the character she plays, Juliette Janson (with the exact same description). Then, as if Marina can hear Godard's every word and is in on the theatrical distancing device, she responds: 'Yes, to speak as though one were quoting the truth. Old Brecht said so. That actors must quote' (Godard 1984b: 124).[3] 'But who is it that the actor quotes?' asks Alfred Guzzetti in his landmark shot-by-shot analysis of the film. 'In one sense it is the character; in another, it is the author whose text the actor has memorized.' In the present case, as Marina Vlady reports, the process is short-circuited:

> I have, in effect, no text to learn, since Jean-Luc speaks the text to me at the moment the scene is shot . . . Jean-Luc gives me banal sentences to say, like 'pass me the salt', and then, at the same time, during the scene, he asks me questions, to which I must reply point blank, by means of a microphone which he speaks into and an earphone behind my ear. (Guzzetti 1981: 29, cited from Godard 1971: 120)

The film persists with this internal (albeit unseen) prompting, not only with Marina/Juliette but also with a number of other characters, including Juliette's husband Robert and a number of women whom Godard uses as case studies for the class-based issue of 'ensemble'. In this particular example, the scene also suggests that Godard knows more about

---

[3] In Brecht's own words, 'Once the idea of total transformation is abandoned the actor speaks his part not as if he were improvising it himself but like a quotation. At the same time he obviously has to render all the quotation's overtones, the remark's full human and concrete shape; similarly the gesture he makes must have the full substance of a human gesture even though it now represents a copy' (1978: 138).

Juliette than the actress who plays her, for at one point she says to the camera:

> Two years ago in Martinique. Exactly like in a Simenon novel. No, I don't know which one . . . yes, *Banana Tourists*, that's the one. I have to manage somehow. Robert earns one hundred and ten thousand francs a month, I think. (Godard 1984b: 124)

Clearly, Godard has whispered the Simenon title in her ear so that Juliette suddenly becomes Marina and the actress becomes a diegetic projection of Godard.

This combined cutting and re-suturing of the linguistic ensemble is another central theme of the narrative and enfolds the film's silences into its overall self-critique. In the other films discussed in this chapter, sound drop-outs are generally used to set up a vector to move the audience away from the surface plane of composition (ruled by desire as exchange value) to a more topological plane of consistency which allows for a more conceptual and affective critique (death as immanence). Although, as we shall see, this is used in a couple of instances here, Godard mostly uses silence to appropriate language and textuality (and by extension philosophical discourse) into the overall framework of the 'grand ensemble'. Thus, after Christophe has related a dream about the symbolic reuniting of North and South Vietnam through the merger of two twins on a cliff top, he asks his mother: 'Mummy, what does language mean?' She replies, paraphrasing Heidegger, 'Language is the house in which man dwells' (Godard 1984b: 129). Heidegger's original quote from 'The Letter on Humanism' (1947) reads as follows:

> Thinking accomplishes the relation of Being to the essence of man. It does not make or cause the relation. Thinking brings this relation to Being solely as something handed over to it from Being. Such offering consists in the fact that in thinking Being comes to language. Language is the house of Being. In its home man dwells. Those who think and those who create with words are the guardians of this home. Their guardianship accomplishes the manifestation of Being insofar as they bring the manifestation to language and maintain it in language through their speech. (1977: 193)

In many ways, Heidegger's binding of thought to the birth of Being, and Being – through language – as a form of birth, connects to Juliette's monologue in her kitchen as she talks to the camera while washing the dishes. She speaks of Being as if it were 'A kind of "message from beyond". [. . .] I was washing the dishes and I started to cry. I heard a voice saying to me [via Godard's concealed microphone?] [. . .] "You are indestructible." I, me myself, everyone' (Godard 1984b: 128). A brief fragment from Beethoven's String Quartet Number 16, Opus 135 links this scene to Juliette's response to Christophe's question, 'What is language?' As Guzzetti argues,

> It functions in the fashion of a leitmotif, connecting Juliette's answer to her phrase in the preceding scene: 'je, me, moi, tout le monde'. What was puzzling about that phrase (that it offers a linguistic paradigm where the context makes us expect a logical movement from part to whole) is explicated here: it is not logic that can secure the Cartesian path from the *je* to the world, but language, the manifestation of the ensemble, and, moreover, specifically by means of structuredness ('je, me, moi'). (1981: 67)

However, as Fredric Jameson would argue, this house of language is also a prison house, ruled by Ferdinand de Saussure's structuralist emphasis on static, synchronic axes at the expense of the becomings of history and time. In this case, Juliette's kitchen monologue is surrounded visually by advertising logos for cleansers such as PAX, over which Godard's commentary cynically whispers: 'Pax Americana [. . .] Super bargain-size brain-washing' (Godard 1984b: 127). Such brain-washing also extends to the textual references that interject throughout the film. Unlike the scene in *Une femme est une femme* where Angéla and Émile 'speak' to each other diegetically through hand-held book titles, in this case the book titles are extra-diegetically inserted by Godard as part of his overall commentary on the narrative. His choice of ten titles from the inexpensive Gallimard series called 'Idées' (*Ideas*) suggests that he is critiquing the appropriation of legitimate academic texts as part of a commercialised 'myth of culture'. Four of the inserts just use the series title – 'idées' – all shown with accompanying sound, while the remaining six display either the full title or an incomplete edit (four with no sound). The latter include 'dix-huit leçons sur la société industrielle' – the cover of Raymond Aron's *On Classes: Further Lessons on Industrial Societies* (1964); '(la lutte) de classes: nouvelles leçons sur les sociétés industrielles' – from Raymond Aron's *New Lessons on Industrial Society* (1964); Wolfgang Köhler's *Psychologie de la forme* (1964); and Lucien Goldmann's 'sociologie du roman' (*Sociology of the novel*) (1964).

A passage from the latter expresses Godard's position perfectly:

> The novel form seems to me, in effect, to be the transposition on the literary plane of everyday life in the individualistic society created by market production. There is a rigorous homology between the literary form of the novel [. . .] and the everyday relation between man and commodities in general, and by extension between men and other men, in a market society. (Goldmann [1964] 1975: 7)

Given the importance of Goldmann's thesis that monopolies are not only busy shaping the economy but also ideas, one might expect Godard to follow this insert, and its accompanying silence, with a serious ethnological scene to illustrate the point. However, he immediately cuts to a sequence featuring a black couple entering the poorly lit basement of a *grand ensemble*. We assume that she is a prostitute with her client but instead of pursuing a political argument concerning displaced *pieds-noirs* and the new economy, Godard forestalls the exchange because they can't find a suitable room for their liaison. We then immediately cut (with an accompanying sound drop-out) to the shot of an Azur petrol station as a red car pulls up to a pump for a refill, as if to crack a retrospective joke that the black client has 'failed to get serviced'. Godard reinforces this connection between textuality and the *grands ensembles* throughout the film by using silence (as well as music – specifically Beethoven string quartets – and construction noises) to link them together, as if writing, music, commerce and construction were all part of the same discourse.

It's also no accident that the Goldmann scene immediately follows a long café sequence at the Elysées-Marbeuf, where Godard intercuts between three completely fruitless conversations, where texts seem to exist purely for their own sake rather than for a greater critical end. They are linked by the fact that each scene is shot from a single, static angle in long takes, as if to homogenise both form and content. As Suzanne Schiffman, Godard's continuity supervisor on *Alphaville* states:

> Godard is the only director who never shoots a sequence from more than one angle. He takes the shot, and that's it – he goes on to the next one. He edits in the same manner, almost end to end; he doesn't make twenty different shots in order to have twenty different solutions. He has only one solution. During the editing, he reinvents certain solutions. (Cited in Cournot 1972: 48)

Although Guzzetti finds the sequence lazy (or even deliberately hostile to the audience), with its pointless talk and pretentious intellectualising, Godard's use of an alienating soundtrack is a clear attempt to present language itself as a *grand ensemble* that invites audience critique. Thus the continuous sound of a pinball machine that mechanically connects the various literary singularities (and their potential creativity as a vector) into a larger all-encompassing aggregate, much like a constraining, re-enveloping machinic phylum, serves to transform all language into yet another cog in the *dispositif*'s utopian 'second consciousness'.

The most famous scene is that featuring Bouvard and Pécuchet (named after Flaubert's two 'loser' copy clerks who attempt to create a comprehensive encyclopedia of all knowledge and instead become the paradigm of failure) who work their way through several stacks of books in much the same mechanical way that they eat their lunch. As Bouvard (Claude Miller) reads a number of unrelated extracts from a wide range of texts – a telephone directory, Henri Alleg's *La Question* (1958), Pierre Louys's *Aphrodite* (1896), and an attack on the Chinese by Nikita Khrushchev: 'I don't know which means will be employed to prevent the rash acts of madmen' – Pécuchet (Jean-Patrick Lebel), ever the dutiful copy-clerk, writes it all down. The conversations are no more fruitful. Robert, who is waiting for Juliette to join him, strikes up a conversation with a young woman, played by Juliet Berto (who will go on to play key roles in *La Chinoise* (1967), *Le Gai Savoir* (1969) and *Vladimir and Rosa* (1971)). Their discussion covers the issue of language, prompted by Robert's question: 'How could we talk together? I mean . . . really talk with total commitment on both sides?' As the camera holds exclusively on Berto, she replies:

> Berto: 'Well, we choose an interesting subject and talk it over, discuss it.'
> Robert: 'All right. We'll talk about sex then.'
> Berto: 'Sex, always sex.'
> Robert: 'Are you scared?'
> Berto: 'Of course not.'
> Robert: 'Well, I think you are scared.'
> Berto: 'If that's what you want, I'll say I'm scared. Why should I be scared?'
> Robert: 'Why on Earth are people always scared of sex?'
> Berto: 'But I'm not scared of it.' (Godard 1984b: 165–6)

As a test, Robert asks her to repeat a single line: 'My sex organs are between my legs.' She refuses, not because she's afraid but because it's stupid and obvious, not unlike Bouvard and Pécuchet's mindless repeating of extracts from texts simply for the sake of quoting and copying. Instead, when Robert later tells her that he works in a garage, Berto has a more interesting question:

> Berto: 'How do you know it's a garage? Are you sure you didn't get the name wrong and that it's not a swimming pool or a hotel?'
> Robert: 'Oh! Well, maybe . . . yes. Yes, it could also have a different name.'
> Berto: 'Right, exactly. What accounts for the fact that things have a specific name?'
> Robert: 'Because we give it to them.'
> Berto: 'And who gives it to them? You think you know everything, but do you even know yourself?'
> Robert: 'No, not very well?' (Godard 1984b: 169)

As Heidegger argues, naming allows Being to enter into the house of language, which guarantees our being-in-the-world, but unfortunately (unlike Juliette, in her earlier response to Christophe's question on language) neither Robert nor Berto are able to articulate the question in these terms.

Similarly, the third conversation, between Blandine Jeanson (who played 'Blandine' in *La Chinoise* and 'Emily Bronte' in *Weekend*) and the fictitious Russian Nobel Prize winner Ivanoff (Jean-Pierre Laverne) develops as a serious of platitudes until Blandine asks to confide something very personal to him. He's reluctant because he hardly knows her and she hasn't read any of his books.

> Blandine: 'I thought you would have more courage.'
> Ivanoff: 'It's probably not a matter of courage so much as one of . . . [he drinks] competence.'
> Blandine: 'Well then, it would be better if I wrote it down. I should be going now.'

All three scenes involve an impasse of language in which communication is constrained by writing's transformation into speech, which as Barthes puts it 'is nothing but a flow of empty signs, the movement of which alone is significant' ([1953] 1984: 18). Guzzetti correctly argues that:

> Even on first viewing, it is obvious that the theme of this sequence is writing. What may not be so obvious is that all three parts of it end in failures: the young woman will not speak Robert's line; Ivanoff will not hear the girl's question; and the two men are revealed to be Bouvard and Pécuchet, archetypes of incompetence. Insofar as the sequence constitutes a reflection by the film on its own methods – the method of direction, the process of asking questions, the reliance on quotation – the burden of this reflection is critical. This, I take it, is the beginning of the process which at the end of the film Godard describes as going back to zero. (1981: 297)

This impasse of 'writing' as a flow of empty signifiers extends to the film's political content, whereby the brut reality of Vietnam ('elsewhere') is contrasted to the mediated (through image and text) 'here' of suburban Paris. Thus in an early scene, introduced by a brief sound drop-out and the insertion of the cover of Raymond Aron's *On Classes: Further Lessons on Industrial Societies*, we are introduced to Robert and his friend Roger (played by Jean Narboni, *Cahiers du Cinéma* critic and author of the 1968 collection, *Godard on Godard*) as they listen in to American propaganda broadcasts from 'Saigon-Washington' on their short-wave radio. The scene is an almost direct verbal transposition of a Jules Feiffer political cartoon (Figure 4.2) featuring Lyndon Johnson as he makes increasingly escalated threats to bomb North Vietnam, Haiphong, Hanoi and then Peking.

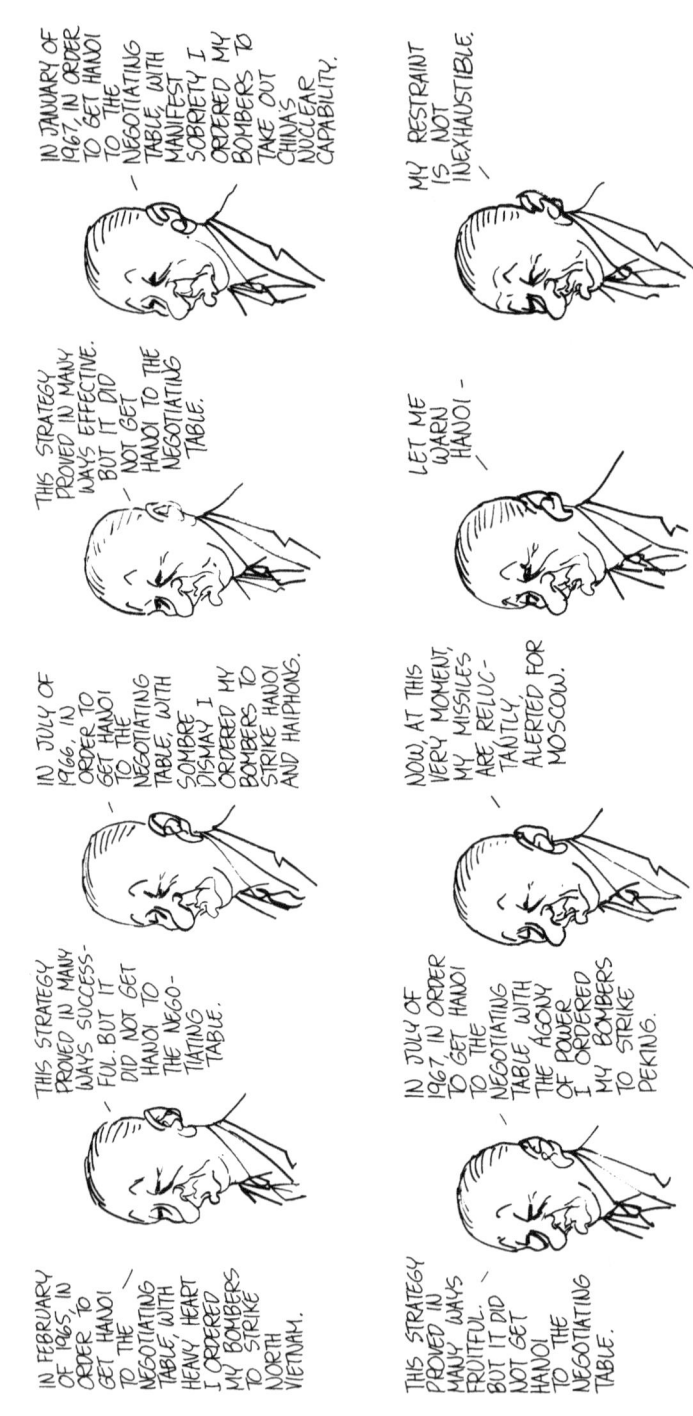

Figure 4.2 Jules Feiffer cartoon – a bellicose Lyndon B. Johnson

Not only is there no political analysis from either Robert or Roger – they simply parrot the broadcast's lines like the speech bubbles in the original cartoon – the scene proves Raymond Aron's main point that the labouring classes are simply puppets within the larger military industrial complex. The fact that the latter includes the trivialities of fashion as well as prostitution is underlined by Juliette's contribution to the scene, for after the radio suddenly cuts out she asks Robert:

> wouldn't you like it if I 'slipped into a pair of fake anklets or knee socks printed on tights designed by Louis Ferraud. They make an indecent dress look modest and are amusing as well as charming as long as your legs are perfectly slim and youthful-looking'. (Godard 1984b: 126)

After Robert tells her to stop talking nonsense, she says it's in *Madame Express* (so it must be true). When Robert says he's never heard of it she tells him: 'You're illiterate.'

This kind of 'fashion magazine literacy' mixed with the economy of prostitution spills over into the most overtly political scene in the film, when Juliette and her friend Marianne (Anny Duperey) 'entertain' John Faubus (played by the Belgian actor, Raoul Lévy, who would sadly commit suicide before the film's release), an American war correspondent and photographer for the *Arkansas Daily* who is taking a break from his posting in Saigon. As he puts it: 'I got fed up with the atrocities, with all the bloodshed. So I came here to get some fresh air!' (Godard 1984b: 160). The sequence is reduced to a series of clichéd signs of American imperialism, which, as we noted earlier, Godard links directly to the new economy of the HLMs. Thus Faubus wears a T-shirt bearing the stars and stripes, leading Marianne to proclaim, 'America Über Alles', as she reads a French translation of Ray Bradbury's 1959 collection of short stories, *A Medicine for Melancholy* (*Un remède á la mélancolie*). Faubus replies, proudly: 'Yes, but it's they who invented the Jeep and napalm.' Then, Faubus choreographs one of his favourite sex games, asking the women to walk naked around the hotel room wearing TWA and Pan Am flight bags on their heads, as if to proclaim the invincibility of American capitalism (little did anyone know that Pan Am would be bankrupt by 1991, TWA in 2001).

When Faubus asks Juliette to join Marianne in a more erotic sex act (which we never see), Marianne refuses and takes the opportunity to meditate on the difference between 'here' (the Paris hotel) and 'elsewhere' (Vietnam) and how her knowledge of the latter (as well as Godard's, as he candidly pointed out in his 'Camera Eye' segment in *Loin du Vietnam*, 1967) can only be mediated by commercialised images. In voice-over, she says: 'It's strange how a person living in Europe, on August 17, 1966, can be thinking about another person out in Asia. To think, to mean to say, that's not the same as writing, running or eating. No.' Godard then cuts to a close-up of the cover of *Life* magazine featuring a black and white photo of a wounded American soldier with bandaged eyes and an accompanying caption: WAR GOES ON. We cut back to Juliette as she continues:

> No, it's an internal process. [She hums a tune, looks over at Faubus and Marianne, then away to the left.] If someone asks me to go on singing this song. Well, I could, I could go on. What goes into that process? That knowledge that I can go on doing something? I don't know. [We now see a close-up of a colour still of a young Vietcong's frightened bloodstained face, an image that Godard will recycle, in black and white, in *Le Gai Savoir*.] For example, I can think of someone who isn't here. I can imagine him, or else I can bring up the subject all of a sudden. [On Juliette.] Even if he's dead. [She looks over to Faubus and Marianne.] For example, I declare . . . I'm hot . . . no, it's just that I'm impatient. (Godard 1984b: 162)

As if to reinforce the idea that Juliette's imagination is governed by commercial images and reportage, as Marianne once again cries 'America Über Alles', Godard cuts to a *Paris Match*-style series of photographs of war atrocities accompanied by the sound of machine-gun fire (which may be real or Christophe's toy machine gun) as the magazine text gives us the context: 'Van Tuong [. . .] These are the survivors. Four hundred tons of bombs have wiped out their villages' (Godard 1984b: 163). Juliette concludes the sequence with a revelation of her own:

> Now I understand how thought works. It's a matter of replacing the personal observation of reality with an effort of imagination. To say something . . . To want to say something. Yes, it may well be a muscular or a nervous reflex.

Adding emphasis to this discovery, the loud ambient sound – mingled with that of a construction site – which has dominated the scene throughout now gives way to Beethoven's String Quartet Number 16, suggesting that a new affective tonality is needed for this more somatic source of thought, a direction that Godard pursues through an extensive foray into phenomenology through the works of Maurice Merleau-Ponty (1908–61) and Francis Ponge (1899–1988).

We know of Godard's interest in Merleau-Ponty from an entry in his journal which was originally published in *Cahiers du Cinéma* in November 1966. Here he recalls (somewhat cryptically) that,

> Kissing Gilberte quickly on the corner of the mouth in a neon light at the Porte d'Auteuil, I had the feeling of passing through a slight and lukewarm event. She spoke to me about that invention – terrific, in her opinion – of Sartre's and Merleau-Ponty's, that of marrying the philosophic verb and the romantic adjective. In my opinion as

well. We spoke with emotion and tenderness, she of Ivitch, I of the confined one of Venice, she of *La Phénomènologie de la perception*, I of the study on Cézanne and cinema in *Sens et nonsense*. Michel Foucault, Lacan and the Marxist Alsatian would not do well to come to sit at our table. (1968: 298)

Derived originally from the writings of Edmund Husserl (1859–1938), phenomenology is less a philosophy than a *practice*: you don't think it, you *do* it. Unlike the work of Plato and Descartes, which begins with the thinking rational subject ('*I* think, therefore *I* am'), Husserl focuses initially on the object (the so-called *noema* or the *what* of experience), which undergoes a phenomenological reduction or bracketing off from the real world (known as *epoché*) so that it can be freed from the constraints of everyday *doxa* and utility – i.e. its role in the natural attitude or scheme of things. Thus, as Heidegger argues, we only know the true essence of a hammer 'in-itself' when it is broken and ceases to be a 'ready-to-hand' extension of ourselves. The second move is the *noesis* or *how* of experience, which is only linked to the subject or 'I' through intentionality. Thus there is no subject without an object, no object without a subject, ensuring that we must go back to the things themselves before we can understand our own being-in-the-world (*Dasein*). Merleau-Ponty summarises this interconnection perfectly in *Sense and Non-Sense* when he states:

> We must reject that prejudice which makes 'inner realities' out of love, hate, or anger, leaving them accessible to one single witness: the person who feels them. Anger, shame, hate, and love are not psychic facts hidden at the bottom of another's consciousness: they are types of behavior or styles of conduct which are visible from the outside. They exist on this face or in those gestures, not hidden behind them. (1964: 52–3)

Francis Ponge applies these principles to poetry. Indeed, he has been regularly called 'the poet of things' because simple objects like a plant, a pebble, a shell, a cigarette, or a bar of soap are the main subjects of his prose poems which were published in 1942 under the title of *Le Parti Pris des Choses* (roughly translated as 'The Things' View of It'). Language of course plays a major role in this process, because Ponge's objective was to get back to the basic naming of things (much like Juliet Berto's quizzing of Robert about the possibly mistaken use of the word 'garage' in the Elysées-Marbeuf café scene); in other words to treat objects as subjects. As Richard Stamelman explains it:

> Ponge's poems dramatize the radical transformation of the object of the poet's desire and his contemplation, the *objet-chose*, I will call it, into a different and original form, namely a text, an *objet-description*. This conversion is initiated, mediated

and accomplished through the operation of language, and, in particular, the language of description. All things, Ponge believes, yearn to express themselves, and they mutely await the coming of the word so that they may reveal the hidden depths of their being. The word penetrates through the tough skins and the closed surfaces of things, opening up a vast space and animating a dormant, microscopic world of unrevealed qualities which define the essential individuality of the object and its fundamental difference from all other things that exist or will ever exist. The word gives breath to the object, causing it to vibrate and its sounds to reverberate within the newly discovered interior landscape . . .' (1974: 689)

Although it's clear that Godard sees obvious limitations in the power of the spoken and written word to do the object justice, he nonetheless exploits the power of cinema – particularly the sound–image dialectic and radical use of silence – to develop another level of subject–object relationships through the freeing of new singularities. Indeed, Godard had shown an interest in Ponge as early as 1950 in a review of two films entitled '*Works of Calder* and *L'Histoire d'Agnès*', published in the *Gazette du Cinéma* on 4 October 1950. The former is a twenty-minute short on the work of the sculptor Alexander Calder (famous for his mobiles), produced by Burgess Meredith and directed by Herbert Matter. In his review, Godard waxes lyrical yet is clearly bound by a phenomenological approach to both object and image:

A young boy gazes at the sea, flowers and sand. Then he enters Calder's studio like Ali Baba discovering the thieves' treasure trove. Childhood is the open sesame to the bouquet of mobiles. Burgess Meredith's film not only bears the prestige of the most beautiful of beauties, but in passing defines the cinema, which consists simply of putting things in front of the camera. At the cinema we do not think, we are thought. A poet [i.e. Ponge] calls this the things' view of it. Not man's view of things, but the view of things themselves. *Works of Calder* is a propaganda film on behalf of objects. (Godard 1972a: 19)

Seventeen years later, Godard expanded this analysis in an insightful article he wrote for *L'Avant-Scène du Cinéma* (May 1967) entitled 'Ma demarche en quatre mouvements' [My Approach in Four Movements] which applied Ponge directly to *Deux ou trois choses*. After stating that the film describes 'a complex', he argues that

This 'complex' and its parts (Juliette being the one I have chosen to examine in greater detail, in order to suggest that the other parts also exist in depth) must be described and talked about as both objects and subjects. What I mean is that I cannot avoid the fact that all things exist both from the inside and the outside. This can be demonstrated by filming a house from the outside, then from the inside, as though we were entering inside a cube, an object. The same goes for a human being, whose face is generally seen from the outside. (Godard 1972b: 239)

He then proceeds to show how this unfolds strategically in four principal movements. He begins with an objective description, 'or at least attempt at description, Ponge would say' (1972b: 241) by showing objects such as houses, cars, cigarettes, apartments, shops, TV sets, etc., in addition to subjects like Juliette, Robert, Faubus, Marianne and beauticians. He will then attempt a subjective description of subjects, 'particularly by way of feelings, that is through scenes more or less written and acted', and of objects: 'settings seen from the inside, where the world is outside, behind the windows, or on the other side of the walls' (1972b: 241). Part 3 entails a search for structures (Part 1 + Part 2 = Part 3).

> In other words, the sum of the objective description and the subjective description should lead to the discovery of certain more general forms; should enable one to pick out, not a generalized overall truth, but a certain 'complex feeling', something which corresponds emotionally to the laws one must discover and apply in order to live in society. (1972b: 242)

As we have seen, this society is not a harmonious 'ensemble' but one ruled by exchange value and consumerism. The key here is that Godard makes no distinction between people and things (i.e. the complex is treated as a whole) so that the film's ethical 'conscience' lies in its cinematic process: film as thought.

Finally, Part 4 adds the previous three parts together as a form of Spinozan ethics or 'Life'. 'Maybe,' argues Godard, 'if the film comes off (I hope it will; if not all the time, at least in certain images and certain sounds), maybe then will be revealed what Merleau-Ponty calls the "singular existence" of a person – Juliette's in particular' (1972b: 242). Ultimately, all the movements are mixed together like a musical score.

So how do these movements work in practice? In a key scene, Juliette is seen at the beautician's getting her hair washed and a manicure. Godard makes a point of bifurcating Juliette's audible dialogue between what she is actually saying and what she is thinking so that it is difficult to tell inside and outside apart, creating an enfolding relationship between sense and non-sense (which, in French, is also a pun on the double meaning of *sens* – sense and direction). While this scene is a logical part of Juliette's daily self-grooming (it's all part of her job as a prostitute), it also has an objective parallel in the sequence that follows, where she takes her red Austin Mini to the car wash (as if objects too have to be groomed to look nice). While it's tempting to see the almost Taylorist mechanism of the car wash as a precursor to the long production line tracking shot at the Cowley factory that opens *British Sounds* (1969), Godard actually breaks up the sequence by presenting it non-chronologically and repeating certain shots (for example, Juliette is seen getting the car refuelled at the petrol pump twice, interrupting the car wash rather than preceding it). Moreover, he also uses it to explore how one can describe an event by paying equal attention to subjects and objects, to sense and non-sense. Thus, we see a tight angle down on feet walking left to right (*non-sens*) on a yellow arrow pointing in the opposite direction, right to left (*sens*) as Godard's voice-over states the obvious: 'Sense and non-sense'. Then, as Robert chats with Juliette at the petrol pump, Godard continues:

> Yes, how do you describe exactly what happened? Of course, there's Juliette, there's her husband, there's the garage. But do you really have to use those very words and those images? Are they the only possible ones? Are there no others? Am I talking too loud? Am I looking too close or from too far away? (Godard 1984b: 154)

Filled with self-doubt, Godard obviously realises that conventional language isn't working: 'Why are there so many signs everywhere so that I end up wondering what language is about, signs with so many different meanings, that reality becomes obscure when it should stand out clearly from what is imaginary?' (Godard 1984b: 155). Thus, while the Mini is being washed and polished by the attendants, he instead turns to Ponge:

> Images can get away with everything, for better or worse. Ordinary common sense reasserts itself before my very eyes and comes to the rescue of my shattered sense of logic. Objects are there, and if I study them more carefully than people it's because they are more real than people. Dead objects are always alive. Live people often already dead. (Godard 1984b: 155)

Finally, we hear the loud noise of the shiny and clean Mini emerging from car wash before the sound drops out completely and sparkling light reflects off the windscreen, as if to announce this 'dead' object's magical rebirth as a subject. Also, the silence connects the phenomenological subject to its previous association with 'Idées' book titles and construction cranes, suggesting that although it may be a vector of deterritorialisation onto another plane of consistency, it is also subject to potential co-option.

We see this play out in the scene's culmination where Godard's voice is heard over the gleaming Mini:

> My aim, for the simplest things to come into being in the world of humans, for man's spirit to possess them, a new world where men and things would interrelate harmoniously. It's really more of a political issue than a poetic one. (Godard 1984b: 156)

He then cuts to a tight angle down on the Mini's red roof reflecting the leaves from a nearby tree, thus fusing the object with nature, the abstract painterly surface (one thinks of Barnett Newman) with the political iconography of a red flag. Godard then concludes: 'In any case, it accounts for this passion for self-expression. Whose? Mine. Writer and painter' (1984b: 156). However, the red also recalls the PAX box from earlier in the film, which inspired Godard to comment, 'Pax Americana [. . .] Super bargain-size brain-washing', as well as Faubus's Stars and Stripes T-shirt in the hotel scene that follows: 'America Über Alles'.

Godard's Ponge discourse plays out far more successfully in a café scene where Juliette gives the brush-off to a potential pimp and subsequently sits at a table next to a couple who are busy reading. The woman leafs through the August 1966 issue of *Lui* magazine which shows suggestive pictures of women depicted as comic strip characters but also evoking fashion icons like Mary Quant and Twiggy. Godard's commentary lays out the dilemma of how to represent the scene and the problem of naming:

> That was how Juliette, at 3:37 p.m. came to be looking at the turning pages of an object which, in journalistic jargon, is known as 'magazine'. And that was how, about one hundred and fifty pages further on, another young woman, like her in every way, a kindred spirit, a sister, was also getting at the same object. Where then does truth reside? In full face or in profile. And anyway, what is an object? (Godard 1984b: 138)

Godard is in effect turning Juliette and the young woman into objects like the magazine, reinforced by a sound drop-out that links them both with the cartoon-like images. While capitalism links objects in terms of exchange value, the silence helps to dislodge objects from such connections and create new ones, based on a social collectivity or affective 'ensemble'.

However, sound returns with a vengeance as we once again hear the loud pinging of a pinball machine and a brief refrain from the Beethoven String Quartet as Godard outlines the potential drawbacks of this 'complex'. Over a close shot of a cup of coffee, he states that,

> Perhaps an object can provide a link, can enable one to go from one subject to another and so to live within society, to be together. But then, given the fact that social relationships are always ambiguous, given the fact that my thoughts create rifts as much as they unite, given the fact that my words establish contacts by being spoken and create isolation by remaining unspoken . . . (1984b: 139)

. . . what are we then to do? Godard's answer is to cut to an extreme close-up of the surface of the coffee and cut the ambient sound of the café completely for one whole minute. Removed from its original context as a customer's beverage, the coffee now takes on an ontological life as its own subjective essence as we zero in on the rotating bubbles as if they were a spiral nebula in the night sky, reaching out to the uncharted chaos of the universe. The microcosm and macrocosm thus fold into each other as overlapping and interpenetrating worlds, as if, read through Ponge's 'Things' View of It', the coffee was saying, 'my dark roast is as black as the unfathomable depths of the infinite cosmos'. Suddenly, we return to the ambient sound of the café as Juliette and the man exchange glances and Godard makes an existential comment about the need to go on listening and looking about him in order to embrace the world as a kindred spirit. The sound drops out one more time but the Ponge-like spell is broken when a sugar lump is dropped into the cup and we are returned to the banal reality of personal taste ('Wait, I don't take sugar!').

Guzzetti sees the juxtaposition of the silence of the coffee with the ambient sound of Juliette and the man as being informed

> by the prescription 'I must listen, I must look around me more than ever', that is, hear the sounds of the room, of the world, and look at *it*, not (to put it crudely) just at one's coffee. The shots of the coffee are not only self-absorbed and meditative; they *represent* self-absorption and meditation, especially the moral deficiency of those things. (1981: 145)

Obviously we disagree on this point because it's clear that the silence and coffee-as-vector are not deficient but act as both singularities and assemblages, escaping from the material world to chaos only to return to it as a new plane of immanence. In other words, this is the most affirmative use of the machinic phylum in the whole film because it incorporates both the topological and the biogrammatic. Thus, if we take Brian Massumi's example of a pliable coffee cup and replace it with the coffee itself, it is similarly transformable – from beverage to nebula to galaxy to the far reaches of outer space – but also continuous as well as multiple, always returning, like a Moebius strip, to a previously experienced vector space.

It's significant that Godard doesn't build on this singularity to suggest a possible way out of the *grands ensembles*. Instead he joins Juliette and Robert in acknowledging the impasse of their lives and the need to keep going until death intervenes. Thus, at film's end, they enter the kitchen and chat resignedly:

> Robert: 'Ouf. Here we are!'
> Juliette: 'Where?'
> Robert: (moving out of frame) 'Home.'
> Juliette: 'And what'll we do after that?'
> Robert off: 'We'll sleep . . . What's the matter with you?'
> Juliette: 'And after that?'
> Robert off: 'We'll wake up.'

Juliette taking out the groceries: 'And after that?'
Robert off: 'The same. All over again. [Juliette opens a cupboard and puts a package of Lustucru noodles on the shelf.] We'll work. We'll eat.'
Juliette: 'And after that?'
Robert comes back into shot and stands facing Juliette. He takes off his glasses.
Robert: 'I don't know. [Pause. He looks at his wife and puts on his glasses.] We'll die.'
Juliette: 'And after that?' (Godard 1984b: 174–5)

Godard then cuts to a petrol pump counter moving slowly, then accelerating from 00:00 to 01:15, as if to indicate that that clock's ticking and the price of petrol is rising.

Godard himself is resigned to a similar future (or at least 'Godard' as his own conceptual persona as opposed to that of a prostitute), for over another Ponge-like close-up (this time a glowing cigarette) he finally enfolds his own experience into that of the diegesis:

> I listen to commercials on my transistor radio. Thanks to Esso, I drive safely to the land of my dreams and I forget the rest. I forget Hiroshima, I forget Auschwitz, I forget Budapest. [Insert title card: *idées*] I forget Vietnam, I forget the SMIG [minimum wages], I forget the housing shortage, I forget the famine in India. (1984b: 177)

Then after cutting to a young couple in an advertisement for Hollywood chewing-gum, he concludes: 'I've forgotten everything except that, as I'm going back to zero, I'll have to use that as my point of departure' (1984b: 178). We then have the final sound drop-out as we . . .

> Zoom back to reveal a variety of consumer goods set out in such a way as to remind one of great blocks of flats in a housing estate. The ecstatic-looking couple advertising the chewing-gum is surrounded by boxes of Lava, Omo, Dash, Ajax, Schick razor blades, Lustucru noodles and various brands of cigarettes. (Godard 1984b: 177–8)

During a semi-fade to black, we hear three chords from a different Beethoven String Quartet (No. 12, Opus 127) and a sense that we are viewing the grand ensemble at night. However, as Guzzetti argues, it is no longer a found reality but an arranged and constructed one, a subject/object that could just as easily be deconstructed (Guzzetti 1981: 351).

The idea of a return to zero as a means of clearing the ground in order to enable a radical reconstruction on progressive lines has two pertinent sources. The first is Roland Barthes's 1953 book, *Writing Degree Zero* which argues for an objectified, concretised literature, which is 'no longer felt as a socially privileged mode of transaction, but as a language having body and hidden depths, existing both as dream and menace' ([1953] 1984: 5). Like Ponge, Barthes was advocating treating literature as an object in-itself, not a transparent, mimetic window on reality. In this sense,

> Mallarmé's work, finally, was the crowning achievement of this creation of Literature as Object, and this by the ultimate of all objectifying acts: murder. For we know that the whole effort of Mallarmé was exerted towards the destruction of language, with Literature reduced, so to speak, to being its carcass. ([1953] 1984: 6)

The objective would be 'to create a colourless writing, freed from all bondage to a pre-ordained state of language' ([1953] 1984: 64). The second source is another book in the 'Idées' series, *Gauche: année zero* by Marc Paillet, published by Gallimard in 1964,[4] which Godard cites at the end of *Made in U.S.A.* (which was filmed in 1966 simultaneously with *Deux ou trois choses*) and is the inspiration for the deconstruction of language in *Le Gai Savoir* and *Weekend*'s famous dictum: 'end of story, end of cinema'. Gilles Jacob translates *Gauche: année zero* as *The Lowest Point of the Left* and argues that it

> becomes a repeated outcry, the most serious Godard has made to this point – an outcry of anger, but also of despair. It is the tireless and anguished appeal of an artist who is keenly aware of the endangered freedom of expression, of the increasing presence of violence in daily life and of the pressure of the fingers of censorship tightening around his neck. (Jacob 1972: 158)

On the one hand, a return to zero combines a sense of defeat – due to a lack of coherent analysis – but also a necessary reassessment of the structures and language of revolution, a subject that will be at the core of the Dziga Vertov Group's films that we shall discuss in Chapters 6 and 7. Before then, however, we must take a necessary diversion (or bifurcation) into non-western paradigms, because a real return to zero cannot be exclusively Eurocentric, it must meld together the 'here' and the 'elsewhere', the Global North and the Global South into a new syncretic form. What better place to start than the films of Glauber Rocha and his own unique use of silence?

---

[4] The title is also a reference to Rossellini's *Germania, anno zero* (*Germany, Year Zero*, 1948).

CHAPTER 5

'Tricontinental Tropicalism': The Convulsive Carnival of a Syncretic Populism in Glauber Rocha's *Terra em Transe* (1967), *Der Leone Have Sept Cabeças* (1970) and *A Idada da Terra* (1980)

The bifurcating vector linking Godard's 'return to zero' in the context of the post-New Wave's rejection of Hollywood narrative cinema – manifested most directly in Godard's *Made in U.S.A.* (1966) – to Cinema Nôvo's similar opposition to traditional Brazilian cinema (with its predilection for expensive epics and cheap musical comedies known as *chanchadas*), can be found in Glauber Rocha's like-minded essay, 'Beginning at Zero: Notes on Cinema and Society'. Here Rocha eschewed an academic, Eurocentric approach to film form and history in favour of a specifically Brazilian analysis of the aesthetics of hunger and underdevelopment through *auteur*-based films 'where the movie-maker becomes an artist capable of tackling the great problems of his time; we want to make fighting films for a fighting age, and films to build a cultural heritage in Brazil' (Rocha cited in Viany 1970: 142).

Rocha is far less interested in continuing the legacy of groundbreaking film-makers such as Eisenstein, Rossellini, Bergman, Fellini, Ford or even Godard, than exploring specifically Brazilian issues, most notably the ineffectual response of populism and Marxism to the national crisis induced by the US-supported 1964 military coup (instigated by the Brazilian politician Carlos Lacerda, 1914–77), which overthrew the populist government of President João Goulart. The coup inaugurated a junta-led autocracy that lasted until March 1985, when power was eventually transferred back to the civilian government, five years after Rocha's death. This crisis is even more relevant in light of the election of far-right President Jair Bolsonaro on 28 October 2018 and his irresponsible policies regarding the environment (particularly the destruction of the rainforest through deforestation) and his nonchalant lack of an organised response to the spread of the Covid-19 pandemic. In March 2019, for example, Bolsonaro actually denied that the 1964 military takeover was a bona-fide coup d'état, yet nonetheless argued that the day of Goulart's removal by the military junta (31 March) should be appropriately commemorated.

With this reactionary history in mind, Rocha's statements in 'Beginning at Zero' take on even greater immediacy and relevancy:

> Is it worth the effort to make films that contribute nothing more to our culture? A growing awareness of the need to answer 'no' and therefore of the need for original films led to the creation of the Cinema Nôvo movement and to a new question: once imitation of North American films has been rejected, with what original formula does Cinema Nôvo propose to replace it? An underdeveloped country isn't obliged to have underdeveloped art. Cinema Nôvo, participating in the general unrest of Brazilian culture, rejects populist attitudes and the tendency of populism to manipulate the public. (1970a: 146)

Again, like Godard in *Les Carabiniers*, where the naïve mercenary Michel-Ange, sitting in a cinema, responds to a sequence as if it were reality – like the early impact of the Lumière Brothers' train entering a station – Rocha makes a similar homage to the foundations of silent cinema, not as a universal 'film archive in the sky' (like Hollis Frampton) but as the beginning of a *materialist* reconstruction of film as a weapon of decolonisation. As he puts it,

> Every film of the Cinema Nôvo begins at zero, like Lumière. When filmmakers decide to begin at zero, to create a cinema with new kinds of plot, interpretation, rhythm, and poetry, they begin the dangerous and revolutionary adventure of *learning at work*, of uniting the parallel activities of theory and practice, of reformulating theory at the outset of each practical move, of behaving according to Nelson Pereira dos Santos' appropriate phrase, when he quotes a Portuguese poet: 'I don't know where I am going; but I know where I am *not* going.' (1970a: 146)

As we shall see in our analysis of *Terra em Transe* (*Earth Entranced*, 1967) and *A Idada da Terra* (*The Age of the Earth*, 1980), which 'bookend' this chapter, Rocha exploits Brazil's carnivalesque and syncretic cultural traditions to overdetermine the idea of populism (all the better to defamiliarise it through Brechtian distancing devices) as a kind of trance, which situates it both as an *ally* of colonialism *and* as a potentially viable vehicle of national resistance. As Rocha argues,

> We wish to present our public with a new kind of cinema: technically imperfect, dramatically dissonant, poetically rebellious, politically unsure, violent and sad – much sadder than violent, like our carnival which is much sadder than it is gay. In our terms, new does not mean perfect, because perfection is a notion inherited from colonizing cultures which have decided upon their own definition of perfection, in the interests of a political ideal. (1970a:146)

Thus, although Rocha's 'return to zero' has formal and strategic parallels to Godard's, its objectives and processes are radically different due to the legacy of colonialism. Robert Stam hits the nail on the head when he states that, 'One cannot expect a Brazilian political film to have the icy theoretical distance of Godard's *Le Gai Savoir*, for leftist politics in Brazil is literally a matter of life and death, as it rarely is for left bank intellectuals' (Stam 1976: 51).

This is borne out by Rocha's rooting of resistance in an 'aesthetics of hunger', specifically through the use of allegory – all of his characters are reduced to types rather than psychologically subjective individuals – as a means of foregrounding underdevelopment whereby scarcity, starvation and poverty become signifiers of working-class identity. In short, deprivation is worn like a badge of honour. As Rocha wrote in his 1965 essay, 'An Aesthetic of Hunger',

> The hunger of Latin America, for this reason, is not only an alarming symptom: it's the nerve of its very society. Therein lies the tragic originality of cinema in relation to world cinema: our originality is our hunger and our greatest misery is that this hunger, while it's felt, is not understood. (Rocha [1965] 2019a: 43)

Just as this 'miserabilism' was a central feature of 1930s literature in Brazil, it is now the major subject of Cinema Nôvo, except that it is no longer the subject of a detached social critique but a major (and immediate) political problem. According to Rocha:

> We comprehend this hunger that most Europeans and Brazilians fail to understand. For the European, it's a strange tropical surrealism. For the Brazilian, it's a source of national shame. The Brazilian doesn't eat, but he's ashamed to say so. More importantly, he doesn't know where his hunger comes from. We know – we who made these ugly, sad films, these screaming, desperate films, in which reason hasn't always taken centre stage – we know that hunger will not be cured by government plans and that the cloak of Technicolor will aggravate rather than hide the physical evidence of this disease. Thus, only a culture of hunger, weakening its very structures, can overcome it in qualitative terms: and the most noble cultural manifestation of hunger is violence. ([1965] 2019a: 44)

Rocha's last line in this statement evokes the political philosophy of Frantz Fanon, where colonial subjects can only rid themselves of the psychological and material yoke of colonisation through a cathartic act of violence, an existential act that will destroy the mythology of Eurocentrism (and concomitant 'primitivisation' of the oppressed) by reducing everything to an equalising trance, all the better to annihilate it on every level. As Fanon argues in *The Wretched of the Earth*,

> The native who decides to put the program into practice, and to become its moving force, is ready for violence at all times. From birth it is clear to him that this narrow

world, strewn with prohibitions, can only be called in question by absolute violence. (1966: 30–1)

The colonial 'native' not only appropriates reality and transforms it into the pattern of his/her own customs, but also absorbs it into a general practice of violence that creates the cathartic breakthrough to what Sartre would call the 'road to freedom'. However, like Rocha, Fanon is also aware how this revolutionary spirit of violence can be easily co-opted (and blunted) by myths, sinking it into an ineffectual abyss. Thus, he is quick to point out that:

> We have seen that this same violence, though kept very much on the surface all through the colonial period, yet turns in the void. We have also seen that it is canalized by the emotional outlets of dance and possession by spirits; we have seen how it is exhausted in fratricidal combats. Now the problem is to lay hold of this violence which is changing direction. When formerly it was appeased by myths and exercised its talents in finding fresh ways of committing mass suicide, now new conditions will make possible a completely new line of action. (Fanon 1966: 46)

Whether Fanon had a direct influence on Rocha and his fellow Cinema Nôvo directors is still open to debate. On one hand, Ismail Xavier sees a direct connection, citing the following passage from 'An Aesthetic of Hunger':

> For *cinema nôvo*, an aesthetic of violence, rather than primitive, is revolutionary. Herein lies the first step enabling the colonizer to comprehend the existence of the colonized; only by recognizing violence as the only option of the colonized does the colonizer comprehend, in horror, the force of the culture that he exploits. As long as he doesn't take up arms, the colonized will remain a slave: that first policeman had to die in order for the French to be made aware of the Algerians. (Rocha [1965] 2019a: 44–5; cited in Xavier 2004: 21)

On the other hand, António Sérgio Alfredo Guimarães argues that Rocha had no recall of reading Fanon during this period but, on the recommendation of the playwright Antônio Pedro may have discovered his ideas by reading Sartre's 'Preface' to the Brazilian edition of *The Wretched of the Earth*, which was published in 1968 (Guimarães 2009: 166). On the other hand, Rocha was extremely suspicious of all outside ideological influences – especially European Marxism – so it's possible that the Fanon influence is far more syncretic than direct. As Rocha stated in a *Cinéaste* interview in 1970:

> In Brazil we resist a systematization of political thinking because we are on one hand colonized by the culture of 'mass cultures' and on the other colonized by the

European Left. Therefore, if we think that Hollywood is dangerous for us, so is Sartre, and very much so. We try to have a more profound relation with our reality in order to arrive at a more authentic political thinking. (Rocha, Crowdus et al. 1970: 7)

For Deleuze, this cathartic violence is the necessary trigger point for the creation of a decolonised 'people to come', who break through trance-like myth to create a national identity out of the hunger of underdevelopment. The roots of Deleuze's analysis of Rocha's films lies in his key distinction, outlined in *Cinema 2: The Time-Image*, between classical cinema (i.e. Hollywood and its European acolytes) and modern political cinema, most specifically in the Third World context. In the case of the former, the people are clearly present (even if they are oppressed, deceived, myopic, unconscious subjects). 'Hence,' as Deleuze argues, 'the idea that the cinema, as art of the masses, could be the supreme revolutionary or democratic art, which makes the masses a true subject' (1989: 216). Heavily compromised by the rise of Nazism and Stalinism and the subsequent witch hunts of the Cold War era, in the shadow of the atom bomb the technologically subjected masses could no longer relate to the multiplicitous melting pot of their origins or their role as the seeds of a people to come, so that, 'In short, if there were a modern political cinema, it would be on this basis: the people no longer exist, or not yet . . . *the people are missing*' (Deleuze 1989: 216). On the positive side, this loosening of ties of the collective to a binding signified of concrete identity creates a dystopia ripe for the creative Spinozan *re*-presentation (as opposed to representation) of indicative or constitutive signs which weakens both the signifier and signified in a playfully ironic ethics of infinite possibility, what Guattari's friend and political comrade, Franco 'Bifo' Berardi calls 'semiotic insolvency'. Thus, according to Berardi,

> Irony, the ethical form of the excessive power of language, is the infinite game that words play to create and to skip and to shuffle meaning. A social movement, at the end of the day, should use irony as semiotic insolvency, as a mechanism of disentangling language, behavior, and action from the limits of the symbolic order. (2012: 158–9)

This is Deleuze's jumping off point for an activist Third World Cinema which he ties, with Guattari, to his earlier analysis of Minor literature, which fulfils the collective tasks in the absence of a people:

> This acknowledgement of a people who are missing is not a renunciation of political cinema, but on the contrary the new basis on which it is founded, the third world and for minorities. Art, and especially cinematographic art, must take part in this

> task: not that of addressing a people, which is presupposed already there, but on contributing to the invention of a people. (Deleuze 1989: 217)

Whereas Major literatures always maintain a clear-cut border between the political and the private, Minor literatures make the private affair political. Thus any clear distinction between, say, the progressive intellectual, such as Paulo Martins in *Terra em Transe* (who attempts to forge a viable leftist poetics), and the myths of the people that he claims to speak for (which in Brazil are rooted in banditry and prophetism, the violent flip sides of capitalist oppression) are blurred due to what Deleuze calls a

> compenetration of the old and the new which 'makes up an absurdity', which assumes 'the form of the aberration'. What replaces the correlation of the political and the private is the coexistence, to the point of absurdity, of very different social stages. (1989: 218)

As we shall see, Rocha uses this strategy to reduce his characters not only to 'types' (in the Brechtian sense) but also to singularities that can form new social and political aggregates through deterritorialising vectors. 'Was this not already Rocha's way of operating on the myths of Brazil?' posits Deleuze:

> His internal critique would first isolate a lived present beneath the myth, which could be intolerable, the unbelievable, the impossibility of living now in 'this' society (*Black God and White Devil*) (*Earth Entranced*); then he had to seize from the unloving a speech-act which could not be forced into silence, an act of story-telling which would not be a return to myth but a production of collective utterances capable of raising misery to a strange positivity, the invention of a people (*Antonio das Mortes, The Lion Has Seven Heads, Severed Heads*). (1989: 222)

In what way, then, is Deleuze's 'people to come' as virtual 'collective utterance' expressed in Rocha's films? Answer: through the silences! In each film the people are compromised, entranced, blinded by the rhetoric of demagogues, populists and the Marxist Left with little or no voice of their own. Catholicism is no better, for as Father Gil (Joffre Soares) emotes with religious fervour at the populist leader Vieira's political rally in *Terra em Transe*: 'What would have become of the Americas without priests? What about the Aztecs and the Mayas? What about the Tupis, Tamoios and all the Amerindians? What about the Faith?' Moreover, Rocha also discloses an inherent racism in Brazil's political hierarchy, whereby all the leaders are white and the underclass are almost always black or native. It is through the combination of a non-systematic, hybrid syncretism – the concordance of eclectic sources such as cannibalism, carnival, African-Latin Candomblé religious chants, jazz and opera – and silence that Rocha breaks down this colonial totalitarianism and opens up a vector for possible change. As in Fritz Lang's *M*, the sound drop-outs trigger a machinic phylum forging a possible 'people to come' that can't yet be imagined or concretised by a prevailing *dispositif*.

One would have hoped that over the course of the three films under discussion in this chapter (which span thirteen years) that we would gain an idea of continuity between the films, as if we were building towards a viable 'people to come' that would be fully manifest at the 'end of the line'. However, this is far from the case, as the silences in each film constitute a 'return to zero' as Rocha is forced to rebuild the people from scratch. They are still missing, still 'elsewhere'. This is all the more relevant today – those who elected Bolsonaro are the 'people who came' between 1980 and 2018, and obviously major lessons have still to be learned in order to project a new, egalitarian and ecosophically-minded political collective for the future. The fact that Rocha returned to zero three times with no definitive outcome suggests that it will be a long, hard process compared to, say, Cuba where Tomás Gutiérrez Alea's *Memories of Underdevelopment* (1968) demonstrated how the Cold War Missile Crisis could act as a catalyst for a new national identity. Obviously, in Brazil the 1964 military coup had the opposite effect.

Terra em Transe allegorically examines the tragic odyssey of the Hamlet-like idealist poet, journalist and film-maker, Paulo Martins (Jardel Filho) in the fictitious state of El Dorado (which evokes the Spanish conquistadores' dream of a gold-laden promised land). The film opens during a political crisis on the rooftop veranda of the Governor's palace in the province of Alecrim, where a group of politicians – ranging from populists to Marxists – and military officers argue with the governor, Felipe Vieira (José Lewgoy), who refuses to resist a coup d'état led by the right-wing demagogue Porfirio Díaz (Paulo Autran), a character appropriately named after the Mexican dictator who ruled from 1876 to 1880 and again from 1884 to 1911. In contrast, Paulo Martins is inspired by a Fanon-like love of violence as liberating catharsis in his desire to use any means necessary to overthrow Díaz, and after an angry confrontation with Vieira, the two go their separate ways. Accompanied by his lover Sara (Glauce Rocha), who is both Vieira's secretary and a loyal Communist, they flee the governor's palace by car. As they argue over the political efficacy of Vieira's highly compromised position, they drive recklessly through a motorcycle police cordon and Paulo is mortally wounded in the ensuing chase. As he dies – Rocha frames him in silhouette against the bright sky, holding his rifle in the air to the sound of dramatic orchestral crescendos and crashing piano chords (Heitor Villa-Lobos's *Bacchianas*) – he resembles Robert Capa's 1936 Spanish Civil War photograph of the *Loyalist Militiaman at the Moment of Death* at the Battle of Cerro Muriano.

We then begin a lengthy flashback to four years earlier as Paulo recalls the interconnection of both his personal and his political defeat, narrated through a combination of poetry and prose. Because the film is focalised through his death throes, as Ella Shohat and Robert Stam argue,

> The narrative is constantly derailed, deconstructed, reelaborated, while spatio-temporal discontinuity is exacerbated by dizzying camera movements, jump-cuts, and an autonomous discontinuous soundtrack. The film stages a conflictual dialog of styles and rhetorics, so that the meaning partly emerges from the creative tension among diverse modalities of filmic *écriture*. (1994: 274)

In his formative years as an aspiring poet, Paulo had been Díaz's protégé, forming a *ménage à trois* with the latter's socialite mistress, Silvia (Danuza Leão) until Díaz is elected senator and Paulo decides to move to the province of Alecrim, where he hopes to develop a unique form of political poetry. There he meets and forms a romantic relationship with Sara and links up with the liberal populist Vieira's gubernatorial campaign for progressive social change. After winning the election, Vieira fails to deliver on his promises and it becomes readily apparent that he is in the pocket of absentee landlords who ruthlessly exploit the peasants and underclass. When the latter protest, Vieira unleashes the police and army against them, and refuses to hold his chief military ally, Colonel Moreira, responsible when a peasant is murdered. A disillusioned Paulo leaves Sara and denounces Vieira, returning to the capital where he again meets up with Silvia and indulges in a life of orgies and existential excess.

Paulo then forms an alliance with Júlio Fuentes (Paulo Gracindo), a self-declared 'progressive' industrialist and media magnate who owns all of Eldorado's mineral resources, radio stations, TV networks and newspapers. As Randal Johnson argues, 'Fuentes recalls such historical figures as Assis Chateaubriand (owner of the *Diários Associados*) and Júlio Mesquita (owner of *O Estado de São Paulo*), both of whom supported the military overthrow of João Goulart in 1964' (Johnson 1984: 137). Paulo tells him that President Fernandez is using the economic support of an extremely powerful multinational named EXPLINT (Company of International Exploitation) that wants to take control of the capital. With Fuentes committed to supporting Vieira against Díaz (using the full powers of his media empire), Paulo (inspired in part by his love for Sara but also his friendship with his fellow journalist, Alvaro, played by Hugo Carvana), agrees to make a campaign documentary film – 'Biography of an Adventurer' – that shows the shameful history of all of Díaz's political betrayals. After Díaz denounces him as a traitor, Paulo officially throws in his lot with Vieira in the presidential race. We then see the appalling excesses of Vieira's populist campaign as the carnivalesque bandwagon – with its combination of samba, dancing and excessive rhetoric – is accompanied by brutal repression of authentic working-class voices. Scared of their incipient electoral defeat, Díaz and the multinational corporations prepare a coup d'état, this time with the full support of the traitorous Fuentes, who has betrayed Paulo and Vieira by making a deal with Díaz. Back on the Governor's palace veranda, Paulo offers Vieira a gun – both literal and symbolic – to initiate armed resistance, but he is rebuffed. The film ends with a more extended version of his final moments – rifle raised to the skies – but this time cross-cut with Díaz's Shakespearean 'coronation' in the grand palace, his words intermingled with Paulo's own political poetry, as if to merge the 'father' and 'son' into one syncretic delirium. As Xavier argues, the film's conclusion depicts a trance-like state of mind rather than the post-coup political and economic reality, so that

> We go beyond the sheer denunciation of the forces that carried out the coup or the elucidation of its immediate mechanism. The film places itself as a blunt expression of a state of mind and conveys a totalizing feeling of the crisis. (Xavier 1997: 82)

Ultimately, then, Paulo's role is not that of an active political leader but of a (virtual) intellectual instrument, the classic example of Deleuze's statement that

> The author can be marginalized or separate from his more or less illiterate community as much as you like; this condition puts him all the more in a position to express potential forces and, in his very solitude, to be a true collective agent, a collective leaven, a catalyst [for the people to come]. (Deleuze 1989: 221–2)

This agency is perfectly exemplified in Alea's *Memories of Underdevelopment* where the film's bourgeois intellectual protagonist, Sergio (Sergio Corrieri) grounds the narrative through his subjective focalisation but is ultimately found to be politically irrelevant as Havana (and by extension Alea's camera) mobilises itself collectively to face the Cold War threat of the Cuban missile crisis. The film's key question then becomes, 'As I look at the cityscape from Sergio's vantage point, will I remain a spectator like Sergio, or will I become a participant in the evolution from alienated individualism to committed socialism?' (Gardner 2013: 89). The same is true of Rocha's protagonist, who stands in (with inevitable bourgeois contempt for the working class and non-whites) for a potential collective that is still in the act of formation. As a result we never identify with him, either politically or emotionally.

So, given Paulo's political and artistic *aporia*, what is Rocha's achievement in *Earth Entranced*? For Deleuze, the result is the greatest 'agitprop' cinema ever made, for

> the agitprop is no longer a result of a becoming conscious, but consists of *putting everything in a trance*, the people and its masters, and the camera itself, pushing everything into a state of aberration, in order to communicate violences as well as to make private business pass into the political, and political affairs into the private. (Deleuze 1989: 219)

For Rocha, the main objective is to use *trance* to reduce the world (as opposed to the diegetic hero) to non-hierarchical, intersecting singularities (as Robert Stam points out, the film is not entitled *Paulo Entranced*, which would enfold all events into his own hallucinatory subjective flashback, but *Earth Entranced*, uniting the poet to a larger immanent Life-as-Becoming (Stam 1976: 50)). This allows Rocha to deconstruct the myths that bind the masses to controlling political figures like the dictator Díaz (and by extension, Bolsonaro) and his insidious ties to EXPLINT, the liberal Vieira (modelled on several Brazilian populist leaders such as Getulio Vargas, Janio Quadros, Miguel Arraes, Leonel Brizola and João Goulart himself) and the media baron Fuentes. 'Hence,' notes Deleuze,

> the very specific aspect assumed by the critique of myth in Rocha: it is not a matter of analyzing myth in order to discover its archaic meaning or structure, but of connecting archaic myth to the state of the drives in an absolutely contemporary society, hunger, thirst, sexuality, power, death, worship. (1989: 219)

In the case of Paulo, however, this leads to another impasse, a double impossibility: that of forming a viable political group and that of not forming a group, because if the people are missing there is no longer the consciousness of either revolution or evolution. Deleuze argues,

> The death-knell for becoming conscious was precisely the consciousness that there were no people, but always several peoples, an infinity of peoples, who remained to be united, or should not be united, in order for the problem to change. It is in this way that third world cinema is a cinema of minorities, because the people exist only in the condition of minority, which is why they are missing. It is in minorities that private business is immediately political. (1989: 220)

Memory in Third World Cinema should not be seen as psychological, as a means of summoning up recollections or even a collective memory of an existing people built on concrete myths, but rather as the contact between outside and inside, the people's business and private business, the people who are missing and the I who is absent: in short a double *becoming*.

Paulo plays this double role as the medium of exchange between the fragmented world and the fragmented subject, the included middle between singularities. However, Deleuze raises an important caveat when he asks the question:

> But is this I not the I of the third world intellectual, whose portrait Rocha and [Youssef] Chahine among others have often sketched, and who has to break with the condition of the colonized, but can do so only by going over to the colonizer's side, even if only aesthetically, through artistic influences? (1989: 221)

We noted earlier that Paulo potentially represents an alternative path to this impasse by acting as a collective catalyst or leaven between the major and the minor (both in terms of people and speech-acts). However, Paulo as a *diegetic* character fails in this task as he is unable to reconcile his poetry with his politics. Although Vieira proclaims that 'The country needs poets. The good ones, the revolutionaries, like the old romantics . . . Voices that stirred the crowds,' Paulo realises that this must be harnessed to express the 'hunger of the absolute', through violence-as-love, for as Rocha himself declared in 'An Aesthetics of Hunger',

> From a moral point of view, such violence [. . .] is not subsumed in hatred. Nor can we say that it's linked to the old colonizing humanism. The love that encompasses this violence is as brutal as violence itself, because it's not a love of complacency or of contemplation, but one of action and transformation. ([1965] 2019a: 45)

Yet Sara refuses to accept this Fanon-inspired solution, telling Paulo that 'You don't understand. A man can't be divided this way [. . .] Politics and poetry are too much for only one man.' It's no accident that Paulo's pre-flashback last moments are accompanied by superimposed written extracts from 'Epitaph of a Poet' by Mário Faustino which state: 'He could not seal the noble pact / Between the bleeding cosmos and the pure soul / A dead but intact gladiator / What violence but what tenderness' (Xavier 1997: 61). Significantly, in the reprise of this sequence at film's end, Faustino's poem is omitted and replaced instead by the superimposition of machine-gun fire over Villa-Lobos's dramatic score, which continue over the closing credits, suggesting that the only true political poetry is that of a violent catharsis-without-end. Diegetically then, a post-media poetics is unthinkable given the rigid dialectics of the Díaz-Vieira/Paulo-Sara opposition between violence and optimism, an *aporia* which may be broken only through the birth of a people that is always still-to-come.

It turns out that the latter – as a virtual collective – is constructed not within the diegetic story itself but from the outside, through Rocha's Brechtian distanciation devices which will reach their apotheosis in *A Idada da Terra*. Rocha draws attention to the cinematic device throughout the film, specifically through the repetition of lines of dialogue within the same scene, sequences repeated from different angles, and, most importantly, sound drop-outs, which set up jarring interstices and bifurcations within the narrative, sparking vectors from the film's diegetic plane of composition (for all its chaos it does, through populism, have at least the binding 'cement' of corruption) to a seemingly subterranean plane of immanence or body without organs which threatens to break out and smash the established order through a disjunctive act of violence.

There are six significant sound drop-outs in *Terra em Transe*, but given the double representation that structures the film, it is unclear at any time whether they are connected directly to Paulo's subjective flashbacks or to an omniscient narration. As Xavier argues, there is no clear separation (or alternation) between inner thought and outer reality, whereby subjective images are interpolated into a linear sequence of objective events (1997: 65). Thus, certain repetitions of shots and actions are not just the result of Paulo's disturbed state of mind but are Rocha's method of expressing a form of Brechtian didacticism. This is fully in line with the syncretic enfolding of Paulo's poetic lyricism and the film's more organised expression of his social engagement. We see this dialectic in the first drop-out which occurs at the moment when, during the flashback, Paulo breaks with Díaz in order to pursue his own poetic/political path. Because this also entails leaving Silvia, Rocha shows them having one last waltz, drinking and smooching before smashing their cocktail glasses on the floor. Suddenly we have silence for three seconds, as if to set up a vector of an alternative future that Paulo might have taken – marrying Silvia, becoming Díaz's epigone – that would have determined his political destiny and shaped his 'poetry to come'. On the other hand, just after we see a long shot down on Paulo and Silvia from an upper floor overlooking the central lobby, Paulo sweeps his arm in a grandiloquent gesture and breaks the silence: 'I see fields of agony, I sail seas of denial [. . .] On my sword, I bring remnants of passion, born in those wars, some more, some less, cloistered witnesses of the blood that sustains us.' Then, as he sits at the bottom of the stairs his voice-over proclaims: 'Death growing, flowing and devouring. We live with death. Inside us, death becomes the failure of our daily employment, as we advance, we retreat.' The vector of an alternative life is thus negated (or perhaps complemented, as this is not a dialectical film) by the life that Paulo actually chooses – that of politics and its inevitable corollaries: violence, death, oblivion.

The next two drop-outs are directly connected to this vector insofar as they express Paulo's concerns whether Vieira is willing to go all the way in pursuit of a true, Fanon-inspired revolution. On one hand Vieira has already shown his support of Paulo's vision of a political poetics, declaring that, 'The country needs poets [. . .] Voices that stirred the crowds.' As if to demonstrate the truth of this statement, Sara quotes the Brazilian Romantic poet Castro Alves (1847–71) from his poem, *The People in Power*: 'The street belongs to the people, as the sky belongs to the condor.' Paulo laughs and applauds, filled with optimism: 'We'll hold big rallies throughout Alecrim. Magnificent!' However, after Vieira's election victory we see a close-up of Paulo and Sara hugging at a political rally, as Vieira soaks up the crowd's adulation. The resulting silence suggests that they are more absorbed in each other than the campaign but Paulo's subsequent voice-over, as they sit together on the palace veranda, suggests that he is also concerned with future political policy:

> And we won! What I saw in that campaign [. . .] A tragedy, bigger than our strength. There, on that calm veranda where we've planned our struggle joyously, and then, at your side, I thought about possible problems and asked myself, 'How could an elected Governor answer to the candidate's promises?' Mainly, I asked myself and the others, 'How could we react to that?'

As if in response, Rocha gives us a twelve second silence over a shot of the gathered masses behind a barrier, waiting for Vieira to give his victory speech, a Mercedes logo prominent on a building in background (suggesting a multinational and global nexus far bigger than local Alecrim politics). We then pan left across the crowd and their banners, taking in a high-rise apartment building in the background. The silence is clearly a vector of response to these problems – how to live up to election promises, how to create a real people to come, not a retread of what has gone before?

In the scene that follows, Paulo shows his true colours and proves that he is less a real 'man of the people' than an elitist intellectual living a white man's revolutionary dream. Thus when Felicio (Emanuel Cavalcanti) and his wife (Telma Reston) approach Vieira surrounded by a group of black supporters, we see a clear divide between Vieira's idea of populism and true multi-racial class resistance to exploitative landowners. Felicio explains his desire to speak to Vieira as follows:

> our families arrived in these lands, over twenty years ago. And we worked the land, we planted them and our wives gave birth in these lands. Now we can't leave just

because some 'men' appeared from nowhere showing papers and saying they're the owners. That's what I wanted to tell you, Sir. We trust you, but [. . .] If Justice says we have to leave the land, we'll die, but we won't!

Suddenly an enraged Paulo moves aggressively towards Felicio: 'Be quiet, Felicio, show some respect for the governor.' Felicio steps back physically but holds his political ground: 'Mr Paulo, Mr Paulo . . . We must shout! [. . .] With whatever we have, bones, everything!' Although Felicio claims that Paulo was his friend and comrade in arms, Paulo denies it, calling him a wretch, a weak chatterbox, a coward. Afterwards we see Paulo and Sara on the staircase of their elaborate Modernist house and after another sound drop-out, Paulo conveniently 'rewrites' the incident to suit his own myopic prejudices:

> I went there. I beat a poor peasant because he threatened me [. . .] He could have cut my head off with a hoe, but he was so cowardly and servile! And I wanted to show he was a coward and servile. Weakness! Weak people! Always feeble and terrified!

Paulo reiterates this position at the post-election victory celebration but sees its cure not in party politics but in violence and death. Thus in a poetic voice-over he states that,

> I wander through the streets and see the people
> Skinny, apathetic, defeated
> This people can believe in no party
> This exhausted people with its lifeless blood
> This people needs death
> More than one could possibly think
> The blood that stimulates a brother pain
> The feeling of nothingness that generates love
> Death as faith rather than fear. (Xavier 1997: 84)

Sara then takes him to task, asking him why he wallows in such chaos, because it's reached a point where Vieira can't even make a coherent speech: 'You've thrown Vieira into an abyss.'

Paulo refuses to bend: 'For a century nobody will be able to speak [. . .] the abyss is out there and we all march toward it' (Xavier 1997: 85). She grabs him, arguing that it's not the people's fault but he replies that they're always willing to 'go after the first who shows them a sword or a cross'. We then slam cut to a man who cuts in front of Sara, arm raised. She takes the opportunity to introduce him – Jerônimo (José Marinho), a Union official – as a prototypical man of the people: 'Speak, Jerônimo. Speak, Jerônimo. Speak!' However, before he can address the crowd we cut to a close-up of a stern-looking Aldo (Francisco Milani), Sara's Communist comrade who, like all Marxists, sees populism as a defective but necessary stepping stone to a true proletarian revolution. To the sound of orchestral music Aldo raises a machine gun into the air and mimics the act of shooting it. Although the soundtrack drops out, the crowd react as if they have heard the sound of gunfire, yet we hear nothing but silence, as if no amount of theatricalised 'violence' on the artificial, carnivalesque stage of Brazilian political life can possibly express the repressed violence lurking beneath the surface.

Rocha demonstrates this by having an old senator (Modesto de Souza) encourage Jerônimo to speak – after all, he is a man of the people – and he directly addresses the camera:

> I'm a humble man, a worker. I'm the leader of my Union. I've been in the class struggle. Everything is wrong. I really don't know what to do. The country is in crisis and the best thing is to await the President's commands.

Once again, as in the case of Felicio, Paulo jumps forward to intercede, roughly putting his hand over Jerônimo's mouth as if to silence him: 'Now you can see how the people really are – illiterate, idiotic, depoliticized; can you imagine Jerônimo in power?' (Xavier 1997: 76). At this point we see a 'bona-fide' Representative of the People in a white shirt crawling on all fours through the crowd. He reaches Jerônimo and Paulo and reaches up to the former as he gets ready to appeal to the crowd: 'Excuse me, sirs! Jerônimo carries out our supposed goals, but he is not the people; the people is me, with seven children and nowhere to live' (Xavier 1997: 76). Suddenly one of Vieira's bodyguards grabs him, yelling 'Extremist!' multiple times as the crowd joins in. He punches the Representative of the People in the stomach and puts a rope around his neck, eventually leading him to his execution by a gunshot.

Meanwhile the old senator shows his true reactionary colours, stating that 'Hunger . . . And illiteracy are extremist propaganda. Extremism is a virus that infects actions, infects the air, the blood, infects the water and morals . . .' He continues that 'In El Dorado there is no hunger, or unemployment, or misery, or violence, or ugliness. We are a beautiful people, strong and virile like the Indians' (Johnson 1984: 139). It's at this point that we see a gun in the mouth of the Representative of the People and hear the post-synched sound effects of machine-gun fire and explosions (as if to extend an individual execution to the military repression of the people as a whole). Once again the sound drops out as we cut to an angle down on the dead man (or is he just symbolically dead as the sound was discrepant?), cradled by his wife. We angle up to the senator examining his face with his pince-nez, thereby recalling the scene from Eisenstein's *Potemkin* (1925) when Doctor Smirnov uses his glasses as a makeshift magnifying glass to examine maggot-covered meat, which, despite the sailors' complaints, he declares to be 'perfectly healthy and ready to be eaten'. Just as Smirnov dismisses the sailors, so the senator, having praised El Dorado as an ideal society, is obviously using his own glasses to examine (and ideologically justify) the corpse of the murdered 'man of the people'. As Stam argues,

> The analogy is clear – in both cases the corrupt representatives of established power deny the most glaring evidence of social ills. The senator's empty and swollen phrases mask sordid political realities. He too pronounces a visibly sick society, a maggot-ridden corpse, 'perfectly healthy'. (1976: 51)

When the sound returns, Paulo is also implicated in this critique, for Aldo repeatedly berates him for 'political irresponsibility' and another bearded man insistently puts it down to 'your anarchism' until Paulo shouts 'Enough!' Clearly they represent the Communist Party line of alliance with both the unions and the peasant underclass but it has to be done in a systematic way through the party itself. The silence and its corresponding vector generates a 'people to come' outside of traditional party politics. Thus an appalled Vieira says to Paulo: 'I'm almost fifty and I haven't lost my dignity. Tell me what you, Fuentes, and the others want? I'm not here to be a political clown.' Significantly, Paolo doesn't face him directly but turns away, à la Brecht, to directly face the camera: 'If you want power, you have to bite into the struggle. I've told you, inside the masses, there's man. The Man is hard to control . . . Harder than the masses.' When Aldo cuts in, urging 'No more reactionary theories', Paulo turns to Sara in response: 'The trance of the mystics. Look in our eyes, our skin. If we observe it clearly, or only through violence.'

This trance reaches its apotheosis at the end of the film when Rocha cross-cuts between Paulo in his last moments and Díaz's 'coronation'. Early in the film, Rocha had satirically re-enacted the arrival of Pedro Cabral, the Brazilian equivalent of Columbus, on the shores of the New World in 1500. Díaz 'plays' Cabral, emerging from the ocean carrying a huge cross, thereby constructing a myth of national origins rooted in Eurocentrism and Catholicism. However, unlike the accompanying priest and sixteenth-century conquistador (as well as the welcoming indigenous Indian who is bedecked in feathers and wears a carnival mask) he is not dressed in period costume but is presented as Díaz himself in a smart business suit. As he thrusts the cross into the sand and the others watch solemnly, we notice Paulo in the background, turning away and looking down as if he were witnessing a terrible taboo. And indeed he is, for Díaz drinks from a chalice – enacting, in effect, the 'first Mass' in the newly 'discovered' land – but in such a way as to enfold the Eucharist, colonialism and contemporary right-wing politics into a syncretic hybrid. This is reinforced by the Yoruba religious chants that dominate the soundtrack, which not only suggest that African tribal cultures precede the European invasion (i.e. they are the 'First Nation'), but also expand the film's trance-like expressionism to include Díaz and his fellow oppressors – as if so-called 'primitivism' were a better description of the 1964 coup than a condescending view of pre-colonial cultures.

It's no accident that the participants in this Cabral-like ritual are also present at Díaz's coronation, thereby tying together colonialism with contemporary oppression, but also enfolding it within a samba-like trance, for as Stam reminds us 'the actor who plays the conquistador is Clovis Bornay, a well-known figure from Rio's carnival' (1997a: 335) and it is he who 'crowns' Díaz in the palace. However, the cross-cutting between Díaz's coronation – where he proclaims his future policies – and Paulo's last moments are easily confused, not only in terms of focalisation (Paulo is present on the stairs in Díaz's palace and makes a last-second attempt to assassinate him, but he is also on the road with Sara and dying on the hilltop) but it's unclear who is speaking for whom. On one level Paulo seems to be putting words into Díaz's mouth but the voice-over sounds as much like that of Paulo Autran (Díaz) as it does Jardel Filho (Paulo). The confusion seems to be deliberate on Rocha's part as Díaz's proclamations seem to endorse Paulo's calls for violence rather than project an alternative. While Paulo calls for 'The triumph of beauty and justice!' the sound drop-out that follows links back to the vector of violence that Paulo advocated during the post-election celebration. As if picking up the baton, Díaz proclaims (in non-synched voice-over): 'They shall learn! I shall subdue this land and impose order on all its hysterical traditions. By force, by the passion of force, by the universal harmony of hells we shall attain Civilization!' (Xavier 1997: 61). The film then ends with the shot of Paulo silhouetted against the skyline, the accompanying machine-gun fire once again cementing together the poet with his father figure through a common advocacy of violence.

One should also mention that music, especially opera, plays a similar role to silence in reinforcing this vector of death/violence (as it will in *A Idada da Terra*). In his *Cinéaste* interview Rocha admitted that,

> I've had no experience in opera or theater but I've tried to make all my films, from the first to the last, very operatic. I'm not interested in theater per se but in cinematic

theater, a new vision of theater. I'm also very interested in music as a cinematic element of expression. (Rocha, Crowdus et al. 1970: 3)

Indeed, he took particular note of the significance of a revitalised opera for the creation of Epic Theatre, particularly its irrationality, for the rational is irrelevant to the creation of an aesthetics of hunger. As Brecht put it,

> The irrationality of opera lies in the fact that rational elements are employed, solid reality is aimed at, but at the same time it is all washed out by the music. A dying man is real. If at the same time he sings we are translated to the sphere of the irrational. (1964: 35–6)

Thus excerpts from Verdi's *Otello* highlight Díaz's confrontation with Paulo over his political betrayal, while Verdi's Brazilian counterpart, Carlos Gomes, accompanies many scenes featuring the dictator. Also, as Robert Stam points out,

> Paulo's death, coextensive with the film, recalls the protracted agonies of opera, where people die eloquently, interminably, and with poetry on their lips. As if to call attention to the operatic reference, the wounded Paulo twice declaims: 'Eu preciso cantar!' (I must sing!). Paulo does not try to escape or locate a doctor. Sara does not bind his wounds. (1976: 50)

Deleuze calls this a 'cinema of the speech-act', which avoids fiction and ethnology, an act of collective story-telling which resists a return to myth and instead, through a form of operatic trance, creates collective utterances capable of inventing the people-in-waiting. As Deleuze argues,

> The trance, the putting into trances, are a transition, a passage, or a becoming; it is the trance which makes the speech-act possible, through the ideology of the colonizer, the myths of the colonized and the discourse of the intellectual. The author puts the parties in trances in order to contribute to the invention of his people who, alone, can constitute the whole. The parties are again not exactly real in Rocha, but reconstructed . . . (1989: 223)

Rocha's recipe here is a combination of music and silence but also machine guns (thus the importance of Aldo's 'firing' of his gun 'in silence' as part of the creation of new singularities). As Rocha put it in a 1967 interview with Michel Ciment for *Positif*, while *Black God, White Devil* is a narrative film, a discourse, '*Entranced Earth* is more anti-dramatic; it's a film that destroys itself, with an editing full of repetitions' (2019c: 67). He also, as we suspected, sees it as a political dead end, for he admits that:

> At the moment I would like to change, because I think that there is a political way out which really is current and valid, and which responds to all the theoretical

insufficiencies of the traditional Communist Parties in Latin America. Characters like Paulo Martins or Antônio das Mortes no longer interest me. I think, for example, that Che Guevara is the genuine modern character. He is the real epic hero, neither an intellectual like Paulo, nor a primitive like Antônio. (Rocha 2019c: 67)

Because the alliance between the intellectual and the bourgeoisie is doomed to fail (exemplified by Paulo), Rocha saw Che as a viable alternative, 'a bourgeois who disconnects himself from his culture and makes a revolution. He articulates an answer through his own existence, and now with his legend he brings an answer to a series of problems in Latin America' (2019c: 67). Unlike the end of *Black God, White Devil*, where 'the sea will turn into the backlands (*sertão*)', *Terra em Transe* ends up in the desert, with the sound of machine guns in counterpoint to the Villa-Lobos soundtrack. Then, in what will become a recipe for *Der Leone Have Sept Cabeças* (*The Lion Has Seven Heads*, 1970), he states:

> Music and machine guns, and soon afterwards the sounds of war, that is, a song of hope. It's not a song in the *socialist realism* style, it's not the feeling of revolution, it's something harder and graver. I was happy to have included this in the film because a month later I read Che's essay in the *Tricontinental* [April 1967] which said: 'The place I should meet my death is of little importance. May it be welcome if our plea is heard [...] and that other men rise up to the rattling of machine guns, to intone funeral songs and to launch new cries of war and "victory".' (2019c: 68)

Rocha's reference to Che Guevara's essay – 'Create Two, Three, Many Vietnams, That is the Slogan' – in the *Tricontinental* is extremely important as it shows his early allegiance to Che's advocacy of a simultaneous revolutionary war on three continents: Asia, Africa and Latin America, a strategy that is central to the idea of a de-centred, trans-global 'people to come' in *Der Leone*. Believed to have been written at a training camp in Pinar del Rio in Cuba before Che set off for Bolivia in 1966, the tract was aimed at the 'Organization of Solidarity with the Peoples of Asia, Africa and Latin America' (OSPAAAL, also referred to as the Tricontinental), which held a conference in January 1966 in Cuba. They subsequently published Che's 'message' on 16 April 1967 in a special issue of their magazine – *Tricontinental*. It is thus often known as the 'Tricontinental Manifesto'. After arguing that imperialist countries like the United States are starting to feel the economic strain of conducting a perpetual war in South-East Asia, but still show no signs of pursuing peace, Che takes up a Fanon-like position of fighting fire with fire:

> The peoples of three continents are watching and learning a lesson for themselves in Vietnam. Since the imperialists are using the threat of war to blackmail humanity,

the correct response is not to fear war. Attack hard and without let-up at every point of confrontation – that must be the general tactic of the peoples. But in those places where this miserable peace that we endure has not been broken, what should our task be? To liberate ourselves at any price. (Guevara 2003: 353)

Che's basic strategy is to force the imperialist powers to send increasing numbers of troops and weapons across the globe in order to support their puppet regimes whose armies are rapidly disintegrating in the face of incessant guerrilla attacks. Slowly but surely the oppressors' resources will drain away. As Che argues,

> This is the road of Vietnam. It is the road that the peoples must follow. It is the road that Latin America will follow, with the special feature that the armed groups might establish something such as coordinating committees to make the repressive tasks of Yankee imperialism more difficult and to help their own cause. (Guevara 2003: 358)

For Rocha, the inclusion of Latin America in this tricontinental strategy is obviously paramount, for according to Che:

> Latin America, a continent forgotten in the recent political struggles for liberation, is beginning to make itself heard through the Tricontinental in the voice of the vanguard of its peoples: the Cuban Revolution. Latin America will have a much more important task: the creation of the world's second or third Vietnam, or second *and* third Vietnam. We must definitely keep in mind that imperialism is a world system, the final stage of capitalism, and that it must be beaten in a great worldwide confrontation. The strategic objective of that struggle must be the destruction of imperialism. (Guevara 2003: 358)

In his groundbreaking book – *Cinema Against Doublethink* (2019) – David Martin-Jones relates this 'decentralisation' of the global revolutionary struggle to the 'world systems analysis' of theorists such as Immanuel Wallerstein and Enrique Dussel, who see modernity's roots not in the Industrial Revolution or late nineteenth-century artistic movements such as Impressionism or Symbolism but in colonialism and slavery, the overall product of Europe's expansion from the Atlantic enclave to complete global domination from the fifteenth century onwards. All this was fuelled by the North Atlantic trade circuit – specifically the slave triangle that sent: 1) European cargo to Africa; 2) slaves to the Americas (where they were sold for silver, cotton and tobacco); and finally 3) trade goods back to Europe where the imports were processed into products for domestic and foreign sales. As Martin-Jones argues,

> The most important points to take from Wallerstein, and the use of world systems analysis by Dussel, are: firstly, that modernity is not exclusively the domain of the

Enlightenment, democracy, the Industrial Revolution, and so on, but commenced several centuries earlier in the Fifteenth Century; and secondly, that in the world system everything is related – centre and periphery develop together in a dynamic inter-related system, typically with centre growing at the expense of periphery. (2019: 39)

The upshot of Che's manifesto and 'world systems analysis' in any discussion of Rocha's work from 1970 onwards is clear: 'It is not solely the "limiting imagination" of national cinema that is being rejected by the transnational turn, but also the imperialism of the nation as a historical construct' (Martin-Jones 2019: 40). As a result, Rocha realised that he could no longer hold on to a specifically Brazilian, Afro-American national identity, however syncretic, but had to expand his horizons on a global level, whereby Brazil is both periphery (in relation to the history of European Modernism) *and* centre (via the vanguard of Che and Cuba's Latin American 'Third Way' achievements) in relation to worldwide revolutionary struggles. Thus it's no accident that in April 1965 Che, along with his second-in-command Victor Dreke, attempted to link up his Cuban forces with the Simba ('big lion' in Swahili) rebellion in the Democratic Republic of Congo (formerly Belgian Congo) in their unsuccessful attempt to avenge the assassination of the left-leaning prime minister, Patrice Lumumba, who had been ousted from power in 1960 by the US-supported anti-Communists, Joseph Kasavubu and Mobutu Sese Seko (aka Joseph Désiré Mobutu). One could make a strong argument that Pablo, the Latin revolutionary in Rocha's *Der Leone*, is loosely based on Che, although the film was actually shot in the former French colony, Congo-Brazzaville, which had already become a Marxist-Leninist state – The People's Republic of the Congo – the year before (the regime lasted from 1969 to 1992).

Rocha outlines his own debt to Che's manifesto in an essay of his own, also titled 'Tricontinental', in which he argues that 'any camera switched on to the evidence of the Third World is a revolutionary act' (2019d: 51). The latter, in turn, is the product of any action that reflects the process of struggle and for the film-maker this is both a question of capturing material reality – i.e. that which is placed in front of the camera lens – but also, and more importantly, creating a discourse against that material through dialectical montage (thus the importance of Eisenstein and Brechtian distanciation). Of course, tricontinental film-makers are as much hampered by the 'aesthetics of hunger' as they are guided by it, for as Rocha poses the main issue:

> What's a tricontinental film? Here, a producer is like a general. The instructors are in Hollywood just as they are in the Pentagon. No tricontinental filmmaker is free.

I don't mean *free* from imprisonment, or from censorship, or from financial obligations. I mean free from realizing that he's a *man of three continents*; but he's not imprisoned by this concept: rather, he finds freedom within it. The perspective of individual failure is diluted in History. In the words of Che Guevara: *Notre sacrifice est conscient, c'est le prix de la liberté* . . . [Ours is a conscious sacrifice, it is the price of freedom . . .] (2019d: 52).

A Brazilian, French and Italian co-production, *Der Leone* was shot in French Congo while Rocha was in self-imposed exile and applies Che's tricontinental revolutionary ideal to a fictitious African country still under colonial rule. The film's title, as well as its diegetic dialogue (almost none of the actors – mostly French and Italian – speak in the language of their characters), is deliberately multilingual, reflecting five different colonising powers on the continent – Germany, Italy, England, France and Portugal. Rather than opt for a neo-realist style with a coherent linear narrative, Rocha continues his Brechtian approach in *Terra em Transe* by reverting all characters to types or synthetic abstractions and shooting each scene like a form of non-chronological marionette theatre – filling each shot with an excess of information so that it can be read in isolation or in a dialectical relation to other autonomous shots. The film also follows a musical structure driven by pulse and rhythm (thus it's easy to retroactively apply the African chants of *Der Leone* back to Vieira's trance-like populist samba scenes in *Terra*). As Rocha put it during the pre-production of the film,

> My imagination astounds me but I know that it's not enough. Yesterday, sitting on the lavatory, I was writing the shots for *The Seven-Headed Lion* and I realized I was writing shots like a composer writes a score. I felt closer to cinema. [. . .] Montage is a dialectics whose structure is comparable to poetry. It's not atmosphere, but the editing of the words which creates a 'superstructure' of the atmosphere. (2019e: 108)

The lion with seven heads – i.e. imperialism – constitutes seven different interconnected character 'types' who work together – as well as in competition – to ensure the subjugation of the native population. The apparent 'head of state', is, as Stam colourfully puts it, 'a whore-of-Babylon Hollywoodish figure named Marlene, doubtless after Marlene Dietrich' (1997b: 254), an alluring blonde played by the Italian actress, Rada Rassimov, who had earlier co-starred in Sergio Leone's *The Good, the Bad and the Ugly*. In many ways Marlene is an exaggerated extension of Silvia in *Terra em Transe*, a courtesan-like woman-of-the-world whose sexual allure is allegorically tied to the colonial riches and spoils desired by the imperialist 'rapists' who attempt to court and seduce her. The latter include the regional governor (Reinhard Kolldehoff), a German ex-mercenary with ties to Hitler and the Third Reich who is an ardent militarist.

At one point he declares his prejudices, stating (in English) directly at the camera:

> I hate negroes, I hate Jews, I hate Commies, I hate hippies [sings] but I love sex and gold. [Speaks.] When I was a young man I thought that the world was marvellous. Dreams of my youth [. . .] and soon came the day of my first adventure. I discovered a dirty, dirty world. And I asked the Lord. And the King has the answer: This is a dirty, dirty, dirty world.

Then after lamenting the failures of Lincoln, Lenin and Hitler in dealing with blacks, *muzhiks* (peasants) and Jews respectively, he starts to sing *O Tannenbaum* before lamenting: 'There will never again be a day for the Hitler's sons' (*sic*).

The governor's two main allies are a Portuguese businessman/administrator (Hugo Carvana – Alvaro in *Terra em Transe*) and an American CIA agent (Gabriele Tinti) who work together to forestall a radical revolution by installing a comprador head of state, Dr Xobu (Andre Segolo), a Mobutu-style black bourgeois puppet who prepares for his inauguration by dressing in a French (and American) Revolution-era frock coat and white wig, a typical example of Homi Bhabha's 'mimic man', who recites Corneille and sings 'La Marseillaise' as if to showcase his European cultural credentials. As in Ousmane Sembene's *Xala*, the comprador bourgeoisie can only remain in power with the consensus of the native population, who insist that the time for a revolution is not yet ripe. At the beginning of the film two such advocates argue with one of the revolutionaries, stating that, 'To dispense with imperialism we must make sacrifices. But not at the cost of human life. [. . .] We can't win! [. . .] We need absolute calmness. [. . .] Sensibility must triumph!' For both Che and Rocha, they constitute the sixth head of the lion.

Finally we have an eccentric preacher (Jean-Pierre Léaud, one year after co-starring as Émile Rousseau in Godard's *Le Gai Savoir*), who represents the Catholic Church's attempts to convert the native population away from their indigenous religious practices and embrace the 'true church'. As we shall see in our discussion of *A Idada da Terra*, Rocha has an ambivalent relationship to organised religion, for as Randal Johnson rightly points out,

> Rocha has said that his personages are 'the beasts of the Apocalypse as projected by the powerful, for whom Christianity is completely bankrupt within the nature and the mysticism of Africa'. Implicit in Rocha's statement is his view of Christianity as a liberating force, especially in its 'liberation theology'. This is seen most clearly in the figure of the priest, who represents the revolutionary work of the 'new' church in Africa. The religious aspect of the film is emphasized even further, and with a

good deal of humor, when Rocha declares that, 'as I am Protestant by formation and African by alimentary education, I preferred to be inspired by "The Apocalypse of St. John"'. (1984: 150 – from the press book to *Der Leone Have Sept Cabeças*)

Thus Léaud's preacher turns out to be an unpredictable figure, capturing and handing over the Latin American, Che-like revolutionary Pablo (Giulio Brogli) to the colonial faction, but then joining the resistance by crucifying a naked Marlene before a group of tribal women as she lies helpless on the ground.

Apart from Pablo, who is clearly the catalyst for a tricontinental rather than a strictly nationalist revolution, the indigenous resistance is led by Zumbi (Baiack), who tells us that while the white man lives a life of luxury, cynically exploiting the natives' resources, his wife died for want of a medical remedy and his daughter was raped by a white mercenary. Zumbi is actually named after Zumbi dos Palmares (1655–95), the last of the kings of the Afro-Brazilian settlement, Quilombo dos Palmares, who led the local resistance against the Portuguese enslavement of Africans in Brazil and is today revered as a national hero and symbol of freedom against colonial oppression. Rocha deliberately extends Zumbi's Brazilian fame to the African context by making him a catalyst for a modern revolution. In an early address to the camera he says:

> We have been struggling for three centuries against the Europeans who never stopped decimating us with unprecedented barbarism. But the whites can never kill me, Zumbi, because I am here to reincarnate all the massacred leaders. My sword will cleave the earth in two, leaving the executioners on one side and a free Africa on the other. Here and everywhere, blacks will carry Africa in their hearts. We will no longer confront European arms only with swords and magic. Against hatred, hatred. Against fire, fire. (Stam 1997b: 255)

The key to understanding the film's overall message is that the preacher, Zumbi, and his fellow freedom fighter Samba (Miguel Samba) ally with Pablo to unite the black Africans against the colonising powers – Pablo eventually executes the CIA agent and Portuguese businessman after parading them through the streets tied to a jeep in order to rile up the observing crowds into a frenzy of anti-colonial anger – but as part of a tricontinental as opposed to a national alliance (epitomised by the exclusively nationalist Marxist-Leninist state of the Congo itself). Thus the final extended shot of the film consists of an allegorical recreation of Mao's 'Long March' as we hear the faint sounds of an 'O Africa' chant over a long line of revolutionaries emerging from a gully in the far distance, Zumbi's white suit prominently displayed against the undergrowth. Against the sounds of rolling thunder, the chant increases in volume as the troops eventually reach the camera before marching past us to the right, their voices loud and victorious. Significantly, Pablo is one of the last to reach us, his Che-like demeanour oozing confidence but also a sense of deferral to his African comrades-in-arms. As the chant continues, the final shot is of the number '7' in black on a white ground, as if to signify the 'decapitation' of the seven heads by a consolidated, transnational solidarity. One wonders what Patrice Lumumba would have thought of such an image.

However, there is one down-side to this ending: it smacks far too much of a pre-staged political allegory and, even worse, the revolution-as-spectacle (in Guy Debord's sense). As Che argues in his message to the Tricontinental Conference,

> The solidarity of the progressive world with the Vietnamese people has something of the bitter irony of the plebeians cheering on the gladiators in the Roman Circus. To wish the victim success is not enough; one must share his or her fate. One must join that victim in death or in victory. (2003: 352)

To his credit, Rocha undercuts this reading through the film's silences, creating an underground vector that forces us to share (and eventually take part in) both the defeats and the victories as a common phylum of death and violence. There are seven drop-outs in all, the first five inciting various forms of 'violence' or 'manipulation' against the colonised, the last two drawing us in to armed resistance (that will eventually take place, off-screen, once the collective has been formed).

The first bifurcation begins during the opening sex scene, where a semi-naked Marlene and the CIA agent are engaged in sensuous foreplay in a field accompanied by encouraging crowd noises off-screen, as if the natives were egging them on as a form of colonial pornography. The latter is an awkward mixture of wrestling, stroking, gasping and strange contortions. It's unclear what Rocha intends here if we take the scene in isolation, but it takes on a more concrete meaning when the sound drops out for thirty-two seconds and we suddenly hear the preacher's voice-over break the silence: 'It opened its mouth . . . and blasphemed . . . against God . . . Heaven and all its inhabitants . . .' As Marlene and the agent continue to grope erotically, the preacher continues: 'It received the power to make war among saints . . . and kill them . . .' Then shouting: 'It received the power to reign over any tribe, People, language or nation . . . All of Earth's inhabitants shall venerate it . . . All those whose name is not inscribed in the book of the Lion . . . Explored since the beginning of the World!' As the scene ends with Marlene reaching orgasm, Rocha seems to be creating a parallel between colonialism and the Devil's work, including sex, and man's ability to 'rape' native cultures for both sex and profit, a didactic view foregrounded by the Brechtian use of the silence as an analytical *V-Effekt*.

The preacher's response is to fight violence with violence (in this case using the hammer of God), for we soon see him approaching the camera through a group of natives gathered along the waterfront. The camera tracks back as he walks towards us in a tight shot, African music playing throughout. Suddenly, he raises his hammer as he walks, the crowd following him with their hands on their heads as if in surrender. Just as he steadies himself to strike us/the camera, the sound drops out as we slam cut to a group of camouflaged soldiers who are trying to keep a different crowd under control. We zoom in on a bearded mercenary as he attempts to subdue someone off-screen to the left. In this case, the preacher's vengeance of God is directly linked by the silence to mercenary violence. When the sound returns, we finally discover the context: the governor and the Portuguese businessman are hawking Marlene's new colonial policies as if they were at a political husting: 'Come and see, come and see. Marlene's new programme! Come and see, come and see. Marlene's new programme! Marlene only cares for your happiness!' After extolling their credentials as Christians who love their neighbour, they reduce Marlene's new reformism to a series of clichéd psychosomatic treatments, as if overthrowing colonialism were simply a case of going to see the local shrink: 'Come and see. Come and see Marlene's new programme! Against stomach aches! Marlene! Against heartaches! Against spirit aches! Marlene! [Dancing and clapping.] Marlene forever, yes! Marlene forever, yes! Marlene forever, yes!' And so on, and so on.

Unfortunately the reality is far more serious, for the real tactic of colonialism in this case is not hegemony, in Antonio Gramsci's sense, where the ruling powers use ideological state apparatuses to maintain governance by consent, but rather oppressive military coercion. We see this played out in two key scenes, the first during a street demonstration where a large crowd of natives chant 'Death to colonialism!' as the camera pans right across a large banner: INDEPENDENCE: YES; COLONIALISM: NO. Rocha then pans to a new banner – UNITY – but our view is immediately blocked by the arrival of a military truck. Our immediate response is to read this shot allegorically, a case of foreign mercenaries 'blocking out' the true collectivity of the people, but the truck door opens to reveal Pablo holding a machine gun (he had commandeered the truck in an earlier scene). He then sets up a call and response with the crowd, shouting 'Resistance!' in counterpoint to their 'Death to colonialism!' Rocha then zooms out to unify them all within the frame. However, this is immediately subverted by a two-and-a-half-minute sound drop-out as we cut to two lines of mercenaries pointing guns at camera level as they simultaneously move left and right across the frame (as if demonstrating their own form of military counterpoint) in front of a group of passive villagers: men, women and children. In Deleuzean terms they behave almost like a machinic phylum of oppression, in constant movement like two Taylorist conveyor belts moving in opposite directions. We slowly zoom in closer to isolate a young boy in a pale blue T-shirt, his face (and identity) almost erased by the soldiers' movement. The shot ends as the sound is restored and we see a close-up of Pablo continuing his cry of 'Resistance' before he is bludgeoned to the ground by the preacher.[1]

Temporality plays a key role here, because the sound of the demonstration and Pablo's active involvement draws us in as spectators – we tap our feet or nod our head to the rhythm – so that we are progressively 'in tune' with the collective expression of resistance. In contrast, the silence (and its accompanying symbol of oppression) seems to go on interminably, as if to express the insurmountable task of tearing down an inexorable machine. Interestingly, the opposite is true of the last major use of silence connected to the mercenaries because in this case death itself is connected to a repetitive staccato rhythm (both sonic and visual), not resistance. Rocha begins the sequence with an angle up to a group of natives chanting in a tree. The camera accentuates their sense of collective unity by circling around to the right but in the far background we spot a jeep approaching along a dirt road. As it nears the camera we see a gunman dressed in battle fatigues and a cowboy hat hanging on to the front grille. It too circles around the tree before parking. The governor gets out and starts to exhort the singers, before politely helping them down, one by one, from the tree, shaking hands with each as the singing continues. Suddenly the sound drops out and after one last look up into the branches of the tree he moves to the right where all the natives – again, men, women and children – wait for him in a long line as if they were privates on parade. Sure enough, he walks down the line from left to right as if inspecting the troops. After he reaches the end of the line he stamps his foot and the sound returns as the 'cowboy' moves to the back of the line and proceeds to shoot them all in the back, one by one, as they stand passively. The sound drops out again briefly as he surveys his actions, as if to reinforce the mechanical efficiency of colonial administration as a form of premeditated genocide.

---

[1] The preacher will repeat this scene (clearly faked and against a soundtrack of silence) in a subsequent scene as he parades Pablo through a village (a rope tied around his neck) as the crowd chant 'Come on towards the unexpected beast.'

Given this undercurrent of inexorable violence, the audience is primed for a Fanon/Che response – to fight such organised oppression with an even greater violence. However, Rocha seems to realise that this is ultimately unrepresentable – we can only imagine it as the catalyst for the creation of a 'people to come'. Instead, he uses the figures of Pablo, Samba and Zumbi as the allegorical representatives of that people, as a *latent* force working to unite a tricontinental revolution that will inevitably be some time in the making. We see the first example of this latency in a funeral sequence (a dead native is covered in fruit as Marlene and her cohorts sacrilegiously mimic the act of group sex over the body) where Xovu, after recounting all the profits and benefits of his pact with global capitalism – uranium, manganese, tin, salt, diamonds, bananas, cocoa – holds up a totemic bone (presumably the symbol of his country's natural resources) and offers it to a grateful Marlene. Led by the Portuguese businessman, the others – the governor and the CIA agent – are furious and all hell breaks loose as they fight her for the spoils. Marlene runs out of frame to the right and they all chase her, except for Pablo, who is revealed standing silhouetted against a lake in the far background, the preacher's rope still tied around his neck. The sound drops out for almost a minute as he faces the camera, then walks off slowly in the opposite direction to Marlene (i.e. to the left). We pan with him to take in a small canoe arriving from across the lake. The sound is restored as Samba steps ashore. Silence is thus used to link the two revolutionary causes via two Continentals – in this case Africa and Latin America – neither of which is seduced by Xovu's ideal of material goods and profit margins but rather true liberation from the yoke of colonialism. After Samba unties Pablo's rope, the two men shake hands and cement their pact:

> Samba: See you later, brother. I will find men.
> Pablo: See you later, brother. I will find weapons.

They head off in opposite directions as the camera holds on the dead man and the fruit: all the native deaths will eventually be avenged.

In an almost identical repeat of the latter part of this sequence, Rocha furthers the revolutionary mobilisation by focusing on a 'native' standing against tree (as if he were a collective stand-in for Pablo), once again with the lake in background. Just after we hear the faint sound of a siren, the sound drops out and we pan left to take in another group of natives in a clearing in the woods. We then pan back to the solo 'native' before the sound returns with an overdubbed local chant. In the background, Samba and his boatman cruise by on the lake and make a left turn to shore. Samba leaves the canoe and gives his spear to the Tribesman and exits right. The latter joins a group of his comrades and thrusts the spear into the ground in solidarity. Suddenly we see Zumbi in his white suit, back to the camera. He takes the spear, then turns around to face us, ready for action. In this way, Rocha lays a practical and visceral foundation, through the silences, for the symbolic 'Long March' that ends the film. A lot of blood will be shed – probably including that of our main characters – but the overall cost is both inevitable and necessary, for as Che argues,

> We cannot predict the future, but we must never give way to the cowardly temptation to be the standard-bearers of a people who yearn for freedom but renounce the struggle that goes with it, and who wait as if expecting it to come as a crumb of victory. (Guevara 2003: 359)

A decade later, in his last film, *A Idada da Terra*, instead of consolidating Paulo Martins' idealised collective revolutionary class as a viable political agency or *Der Leone*'s tricontinental resistance as a trans-global populism spawned by violence, Rocha produces an unlikely ecosophical solution, coloured by the intertextual Tropicalist and Cannibalist tendencies (dating back to Oswald de Andrade's 1928 *Manifesto Antropófago*) that dominated Brazilian cinema at the time (most notably Joaquim Pedro de Andrade's *Macunaíma* (1969) and Nelson Pereira dos Santos's *How Tasty Was My Little Frenchman*, 1971). In this case the devouring of metropolitan culture and science and their subsequent reprocessing as a combination of vomit and humus led to an unlikely fusion of aesthetic internationalism with political nationalism, the folkloric with the industrial, the *sertão* (hinterland) and the city, the collective with the subjective 'I' as a series of fragmented, multiplicitous becomings. In traditional western culture cannibalism was a watchword for 'the name of the other' as the denigrated half of a binary opposition – light vs dark, rational vs irrational, civilised vs savage. But as Stam points out,

> even within that tradition, a number of writers have turned the cannibalist trope against Europe. Montaigne, in 'Des Cannibales' (based, ironically, on interviews with Brazilian Indians), argued that civilized Europeans were ultimately more barbarous than cannibals, since cannibals ate the flesh of the dead only to appropriate the strength of their enemies, while Europeans tortured and slaughtered in the name of a religion of love. (1997b: 238)

Under the aegis of this revitalised tropicalism, in *A Idada da Terra* US imperialism (represented by the grotesque, Falstaffian buffoon, Brahms), is now challenged not by a disillusioned Marxist intellectual or a 'long march' of tricontinental solidarity, but by four different Christs (the film is an homage to Pasolini's 1964 *Gospel According to St. Matthew*) and their hybridised followers – Indigenous, Black, Guerrilla and Military. Similarly, the female characters are also reduced to types: an Amazon Queen (Norma Bengell); Aurora Madelena (Ana Maria Magalhães), representing the Indigenous Nations; and the 'New Woman' (Brahms's unfaithful wife), who seems to be playing all sides against the middle (Danuza Leão, who portrayed Silvia in *Terra em Transe*). In addition, Rocha decentres the geographical location of *A Idada da Terra* to include a number of diverse regions and sub-cultures, 'a choice', as Xavier argues, 'that enforces the idea of a national mythopoesis, also suggested by the use of the three major symbolic cities as locations: Salvador, Rio de Janeiro, and Brasilia, the successive capitals of Brazil from the colonial times to the present' (1997: 258). Each region – from *sertão* to ocean – is also represented by its specific festival or rite as a means of spectacularising ethnic and cultural difference as well as forging a new solidarity: Afro-Brazilian festivals in Bahia, the Carnival in Rio, evangelical preaching in Brasilia, an Umbanda ritual (based on the supreme deity, Olorum or Zambi), the Feast of Iemanjá (The Sea Goddess in Afro-Brazilian religion), and various open-air dances and celebrations that combine ballerinas from a local nunnery with the revolutionary exhortations and singing of Norma Bengell as the Queen of the Amazons. Together, all these elements forge a syncretic mash-up of political opposition and cultural solidarity that is by turns regressive and progressive, rural and urban, indigenous and global, but at the same time ecosophically united with the Earth as a fluid machinic assemblage rather than harnessed to a falsely optimistic isolationism, triggering what Guattari, in *Schizoanalytic Cartographies*, calls a 'post-media' poetics and a '*fundamental right to singularity*', 'an ethics of finitude that is all the more demanding with regard to individuals and social entities the less it can found its imperatives on transcendental principles' (Guattari 2013: 13).

Discussing anthropophagy and tropicalism in their essay, 'Transformation of National Allegory: Brazilian Cinema from Dictatorship to Redemocratization', Robert Stam and Ismail Xavier note that

> Inverting the binary pair civilization/barbarism in favor of barbarism, modernism articulated cannibalism as anti-colonialist metaphor in its 'Cannibalist Reviews' and 'Anthropophagic Manifestoes' and its famous slogan: 'Tupi or not Tupi, that is the question', that is whether Brazilian intellectuals should 'go native' by symbolically imitating the cannibalistic Tupi-Guarani tribes or alienate themselves into European domination. (1990: 289)

By the time he made *A Idada da Terra*, Rocha had come down firmly on the side of the former, recognising the need to

> overcome underdevelopment using the resources of underdevelopment. [...] Tropicalism, the anthropophagic discovery, was a revelation; it stimulated awareness, an attitude towards colonial culture which is not a rejection of western culture as it was initially (and that was madness because we have no methodology). We accept this *ricezione* [reception], the ingesting of the basic methods of a complete and complex culture, but also its transformation via *nostri succhi* [our juices] and via the use and elaboration of the correct policies. (Rocha [1969] 2019b: 101)

This hybridisation of both content and method – what Rocha calls 'ideographic cinema' – is evident from *A Idada da Terra*'s opening shot, which shows the sunrise over Brasilia's Alvorada Palace ('Palace of Dawn', the Modernist home of the Brazilian president, designed by Oscar Niemeyer in 1957) to the accompaniment of Afro-Brazilian rhythms and chants, punctuated by animal cries and bird refrains, as if to create an ironic reversal whereby the modern capital and its associations with global capitalism are 'cannibalised' by Brazil's Yoruba heritage. As Robert Stam and Ella Shohat argue in reference to a similar contrapuntal use of music and image in *Terra em Transe*, 'Although Europe posits African religion as irrational, hysterical, the film seems to suggest that in fact it is the European elite which is irrational, hysterical' (1994: 96 n.60). The scene also generates an ecosophical enfolding of Gregory Bateson's three ecological registers, the basis for Guattari's own taxonomy: the material (ecological and biophysical, through the brute reality of the sun as a natural force); the social (cultural and human: Brasilia as a modern, and more importantly, Modernist successor to Rio de Janeiro as the nation's capital); and the perceptual (the mind as an interactive system characterised by an exchange of information – images, sounds, looks and, in this case, tribal and animal refrains – which are transmitted within an extra-filmic world that is metacommunicative by its very nature: a case of 'difference that makes a difference').

In addition, this is an inherently Spinozist sequence, yet it moves far beyond his first principle, i.e. one substance for all the attributes, whether natural or man-made, human or ahuman. Instead, as Deleuze argues in *Spinoza: Practical Philosophy*, one might argue that Rocha's depiction of Brasilia typifies the principle of

> one Nature for all bodies, one Nature for all individuals, a Nature that is itself an individual varying in an infinite number of ways. What is involved is no longer the affirmation of a single substance, but rather the laying out of a *common plane of immanence* on which all bodies, all minds, and all individuals are situated.

> This plane of immanence or consistency is a plan, but not in the sense of a mental design, a project, a program; it is a plan in the geometric sense: a section, an intersection, a diagram. Thus, to be in the middle of Spinoza is to be on this modal plane, or rather to install oneself on this plane which implies a mode of living, a way of life. (Deleuze 1988b: 122)

In other words, Rocha's Tropicalism is Spinozist insofar as he defines bodies, architecture and natural forces in terms of their inherent capacities for affecting and being affected. For Deleuze:

> It should be clear that the plane of immanence, the plane of Nature that distributes affects, does not make any distinction at all between things that might be called natural and things that might be called artificial. Artifice is fully a part of Nature, since each thing, on the immanent plane of Nature, is defined by the arrangements of motions and affects into which it enters, whether these arrangements are artificial or natural. (1988b: 124)

Similarly, unlike Pasolini's Marxist Christ, who is a revolutionary man of the people fashioned just as Pope John XXIII was solving the ideological paralysis of the Catholic Church with regard to the problems of underdeveloped peoples, Rocha's four redeemers constitute an affective ecosophical multiplicity, representing indigenous, African, revolutionary and nationalistic positions in an increasingly complex, trance-like *chaosmosis*. As Rocha himself states in a voice-over during the last third of *A Idada da Terra*,

> Over Pasolini's dead body I saw Christ as a new, primitive phenomenon in a very primitive, very new civilisation. Twenty, thirty, forty, fifty million years. Science, physics, archaeology and anthropology [...] all the sciences that materialise desire [...] language itself is lost. Portuguese cannot adequately express our knowledge of a past devoid of memory.

This lack of a defining signified (a resurrected Christ in the Third World can re-present and 'consume' anything) means that all four Christs can best be seen as an immanent rather than a transcendental force, governed by irony, sensuality, animalism and play rather than acting as a force of spiritual redemption.

As Deleuze argues, paralleling Guattari and 'Bifo' Berardi's call for a post-media poetics:

> In modern thought irony and humour take on a new form: they are now directed at a subversion of the law. This leads us back to Sade and Masoch, who represent the two main attempts at subversion, at turning the law upside down. Irony is still in the process or movement which bypasses the law as a merely secondary power and aims at transcending it toward a higher principle. (Deleuze 1991a: 86)

Humour and irony are thus redefined: law is now seen in terms of the indeterminacy of its content and the guilt of the person who submits to it.

Thus it is perfectly apt, as well as ironical, that the film follows its ecosophical depiction of Brasilia with Rocha shouting 'Action' over a spinning disco mirror ball before we cut to an Afro-Brazilian festival in Bahia featuring a non-transcendental re-enactment of the original Creation (indeed this rite-cum-orgy is a syncretic mash-up of the earthly and the erotic, syncopated to a combination of Afro-Brazilian rhythms and freeform jazz) featuring Indigenous Christ (Jece Valadão), the Queen of the Amazons and an animalistic Brahms (Mauricio do Valle, who played Rocha's Cangaceiros killer, Antonio das Mortes) who has gone native in order to proclaim, 'My mission is to destroy this small, poor planet Earth!' As the manifestation of global capitalism – he looks like a strange, bloated hybrid of Donald Trump and Boris Johnson – Brahms is thus used to bridge the gap between late capitalism and creation myths. He is also later depicted as a latter-day pharaoh, building a giant pyramid that doubles as Oscar Niemeyer's Cláudio Santoro National Theatre, completed in 1966. Yet at the same time he is a comic Rabelaisian figure, naturally paranoid (if not guilty), breaking the fourth wall when he hurts his knee while filming on the beach, and it is on the building site that we also discover that both Indigenous Christ and Black Christ (Antonio Pitanga) work as his employees (again, like Paulo Martins, trapped in a double role of revolutionaries and unwilling servants to capitalism). Speaking of the latter, Guerilla Christ (Geraldo Del Rey) doubles as Brahms's son and heir while also having an affair with his father's wife. It is the son who finally puts Brahms on trial for his sins at the conclusion of yet another operatic 'family romance' but he is inevitably sidetracked when Brahms starts to parody a football commentator describing a Brazilian attack while celebrating national legends such as Pelé, Garrincha, Tostão and Gérson before ending with the inevitable Goooooal!!! As in the case of Émile in Godard's *Une femme est une femme*, 'footie' as a 'bread and circuses' form of national obsession – plus an increase in stock prices (which increases the son's eventual inheritance) – is far more important than Oedipal enmity or Guevara-like revolutionary aspirations in this Bakhtin-like carnival. Finally, Military Christ (Tarcisio Meira), who is based on the eighteenth-century national hero, Tiradentes, who led a revolutionary movement for independence against Portuguese colonial power, plays to the carnival crowd and also seduces Brahms's wife, that is when he is not monotonously spouting the usual rhetoric of defending the nation against impending cataclysm: 'Our structures, our foundations have been destroyed. At any moment we may be swallowed up by the abyss. We're doomed! We're doomed! Earth's core has imploded. Our foundations have been destroyed. We may be swallowed up at any moment.'

Significantly, the film ends with Indigenous Christ attending the Feast of Iemanjá in Salvador. As he walks amid the celebrants, we zoom out to a long shot as we see makeshift market stalls stretching into the far distance, framed by the hills and ocean. He exits to the left, engulfed by the throng, as if the 'I' and the collective were no longer defined by the linguistic law of the signifier or signified. As Guattari appropriately puts it,

> Rather than speak of the 'subject', we should perhaps speak of *components of subjectification*, each working more or less on its own. [. . .] Vectors of subjectification do not necessarily pass through the individual, which in reality appears to be something like a 'terminal' for processes that involve human groups, socio-economic ensembles, data-processing machines, etc. Therefore, interiority establishes itself at the crossroads of multiple components, each relatively autonomous in relation to the other, and, if need be, in open conflict. (2008: 24–5)

'I' as people, people as 'I', politics as poetics, poetics as politics, in short, a convulsive ecosophy that knows no boundaries.

As in the case of the other films discussed in this chapter, *A Idada da Terra* is full of Brechtian devices designed to draw attention to its own artificiality as well as Rocha's own complicit role in its syncretic construction. As Johnson points out, the film has no opening or closing credits, and therefore no specific beginning or end, so that its random syntagmatic non-ordering 'can be described as a great nonfilm made from fragments of possible films' (Johnson 1984: 157). Rocha himself drifts in and out of the film, discussing trivia with his actors ('Do you like coffee, Maurício?', hanging out with his friend, the writer João Ubaldo Ribeiro, and giving off-screen direction – 'Say that louder'; 'Look at the camera and say it like this [. . .] Ask her, Pitanga.' Similarly, non-fiction interjects with the diegesis when the Black Christ (dressed in modern clothing) interviews the political journalist Carlos Castello Branco about the military regime that took power in 1964. However, far from being a Godard-like dialectical injection of politics into the narrative fiction, Rocha, as Johnson points out,

> theatricalizes and cinematizes politics, and the accompanying Villa-Lobos music renders Castello Branco's interview dramatic, indeed epic; Brasilia, where the future of Brazil is being decided, is a 'stage', Rocha tells us [. . .] The Brazil that appears in the film is used as a dramatic and architectonic backdrop for the epic action taking place. Brazilian 'reality' has no place in the film, except on the level of abstraction. (Johnson 1984: 159)

Instead, the real subject of the film is outlined in Rocha's voice-over tribute to Pasolini as both the poetic and political source of the film:

> Here is the situation at the end of the twentieth century. There are rich capitalist countries and poor capitalist countries. And there are rich socialist countries and poor socialist countries. Actually, there is a rich world and a poor world.

On an international level, Rocha is recognising the shift from a Cold War dialectical conflict between capitalism and socialism (West vs East) to Dussel-like world systems, a transnational divide between rich and poor (i.e. the Global North vs the Global South). It is this recognition of the oblivion of hunger and Rocha's ambivalence towards its possible popular resistances that fuels the vectors generated by the film's silences. The first silence occurs immediately after the interview with Carlos Castello Branco where the writer expresses his doubts about the economic progress of the people:

> I believe our revolutionary governments have meant to improve the lives of the people as well as that of the country. However, we are experiencing a process in which this has not yet been possible. Economic growth and the battle against inflation continue to be priorities. Unfortunately, this is not true of higher salaries or the well-being of the people [. . .] both of which are mid- and long-term goals of projects currently in progress [. . .] the success of which we hope will be total although we cannot be certain of it.

We then zoom into a white dot in the middle of a black screen as the loud dissonance of orchestral music gives way to a pop-like ambient music with a male chorus. The sound then drops out as we cut to a long shot of the sunrise, as if to create a vector of hope and renewal – a new dawn – for a future egalitarian society. However, the sound returns as a jet lands on a runway and starts its taxi to the terminal, where we are introduced to Brahms for the first time, displaying the first of his many deadly symptoms (this time a heart attack). Obviously Castello Branco's insights are right on the mark: with Brahms and global capitalism in control of world markets, there is little hope for any remedy to Rocha's insight that

> We all know we are dying of hunger in the Third Worlds. We all know about the poor children [. . .] the forgotten elderly, the insane, the hungry so much poverty, so much ugliness, so much misfortune. We all know this . . .

Rocha reinforces this position in his scenes featuring Brahms's pyramid, where the great capitalist 'eggs on' his workers by proclaiming: 'For 500 years my slaves have been building the pyramid [. . .] that is to be my tomb.

My tomb shall be in the future!' Once again, however, he doubles over in agony from his heart condition but miraculously recovers in a matter of seconds. This comedic synthesis of Brahms the modern-day capitalist (who can barely go from one scene to another without keeling over) with an immortal Egyptian pharaoh undercuts the seriousness of an apocalyptic premonitory warning from a voice-over that sounds suspiciously like Military Christ:

> Brahms, the time has come for you to hear the voice of the Third World. You represent the pyramid. We are prisoners of that pyramid! Myself, my brothers, we, the slaves. Brahms, the time has come for you to hear the oppressed peoples of Latin America, Asia, of Africa. Humanity marches towards a Third World War. The world shall be destroyed by the atomic bomb!

Again, the sound drops out as we pan down the pyramid to Brahms and the workers in their yellow hard hats, including the Black Christ.

The workers disperse, as if to reinforce the hopelessness of instigating serious political and economic change under existing conditions. Even worse, after the sound returns with orchestral music choreographing the workers movements back towards Brahms and the pyramid, Rocha cuts the soundtrack again as they enter the structure, not unlike the Moloch-like nightmare fantasy from Fritz Lang's *Metropolis* that we mentioned in Chapter 1. The camera then swish pans back and forth across Brahms's construction site, taking in a wall covered in corporate logos, as if to underline the multinational corporate responsibility of the Global South's impoverishment. Significantly, as the sound returns, we then cut to Brahms's next heart attack outside the Metropolitan Cathedral. This time we hear Rocha himself feeding Brahms his lines via his off-screen direction, once again adding to the carnivalesque qualities of the scene:

> Brahms: 'John Brahms will never die!'
> Rocha VO: 'I shall return.'
> Brahms: 'I shall return . . .'
> Rocha VO: 'And you shall learn.'
> Braams: 'And you shall learn.'
> Rocha VO: 'Say that louder: "I shall return and you shall learn."'
> Brahms, shouting: 'I shall return and you shall learn!'

In *A Idada da Terra*, his Pasolini homage, Rocha directly states that,

> Underdevelopment is at the base of the pyramid. The underdeveloped are powerless. They all hope for peace. Everyone must seek peace. A dialectical synthesis of capitalism [. . .] and socialism shall come to pass, I am sure of it. And the Third World shall see the birth of a new true democracy. Democracy is neither socialist, communist

THE CONVULSIVE CARNIVAL OF A SYNCRETIC POPULISM   185

nor capitalist. Democracy has no adjectives. Democracy is the reign of the people. De-moc-ra-cy is the un-reign of the people.

Which isn't to say that Satan himself (Carlos Petrovicho), is depicted as a primordial figure of evil. Rocha sees him as a modern, immanent counterpoint to the syncretic role of the Christs as representatives of the people. Thus in a symbolic, choreographed 'duel' with Indigenous Christ in front of a static-filled TV screen, enveloped in a red-orange glow, Satan brandishes a human skull (alas poor Yorick?) in counterpoint to Indigenous Christ's globe as we see two rabbits and a bird eating on a table surrounded by baubles, as if to integrate the human and natural forces into an immanent whole. Then, accompanied by dreamy music and a military drum tattoo, we see Satan and Christ in left profile before Rocha cuts the soundtrack for almost two minutes. Satan picks up a small orb (a miniature version of Indigenous Christ's prop) lying in a dish as a flame envelops its surface (as if to symbolically unite the globe with the fires of Hell). Rather than being repulsed, Indigenous Christ leans in and they both examine it carefully. They seem to have come to some sort of spiritual accord as Satan carries the fire-covered globe towards the television as Indigenous Christ follows, both hands raised in a V-for-victory/peace sign. Johnson's overall summation of the film fits the scene perfectly, for as he argues:

> The driving force of this new order is *creation*: artistic, political, social, cultural. The film begins with a re-enactment of the creation of the world. Politics is theatre, thus it is an act of creation. *A Idade da Terra*, with its deconstruction of traditional cinematic structures, is itself an example of this creation. It is a moment of exultation and ecstasy, a moment of communion with the new order. *A Idade da Terra*, ultimately, is a moment of revelation, a moment of epiphany, a moment of the resurrection of the cinematic art itself based on the reinvention of its instruments. As Rocha wrote in 1970, 'Cinema Nôvo should provoke fiery indigestion, be devoured by its own fire, and be reborn from its own ashes.' (Johnson 1984: 161)

However, once again this silent mood of consensus is broken by the ubiquitous Brahms (a modern-day Satan), who shouts a loud incantation over a dissonant guitar and drums, as he takes the fiery bowl from Satan: 'I want your loyalty . . . [Laughs devilishly] your loyalty! Adore me and I shall give you the Earth.' As Brahms starts yelling, he also picks up the skull, causing a horrified Indigenous Christ to scream: 'No!' Rocha then choreographs Brahms's movements to physically envelop Satan and Indigenous Christ into his 'orbit' so that all three form a somatic whole (much like the film's opening Creation ritual where all the participants seem to meld together as one). As the camera holds on Brahms, Satan and Indigenous Christ yell, off-screen: 'The world is ours! The world is mine!' But of course it is not theirs in isolation, it is ruled by Brahms, who warns them both: 'If you do not adore me [. . .] you will be condemned to all Eternity!' Thus, for Rocha, the true pact with the Devil is a pact with Brahms, with Satan himself playing a subsidiary role.

In contrast the next four drop-outs accompany scenes of evangelical preaching in Brasilia, where the Black Christ 'resurrects' a dead 'Joseph' from the dead and performs a series of baptisms, preaching 'Blessed are the hungry. Blessed is poverty. For one day they shall be released.' Many of the silences connect his message to other Evangelists – a long-haired bearded man stares at camera and raises his arms – as well as the contemporary world, taking in aerial shots of a radio tower and the Brasilia skyline. These stand in marked contrast to the final drop-out which interrupts Military Christ's doom-laden tirade in front of Aurora Madalena: 'Our foundations have been destroyed. We may be swallowed up at any moment.' As in the case of all his speeches, this one is repeated word for word several times but Rocha deliberately interrupts it with a brief silence over a shot of swirling water and rocks, as if to suggest that natural forces will continue to replenish mankind provided humanity accepts its immanent ties to all matter.

It's clear from both the film's ostensible surface and its silent vectors that Rocha's 'people to come' is governed by a Spinozist virtual field-as-event. As Johnson stresses, Rocha's Christs are rarely the centre of audience attention or even of the camera's delimiting frame:

> If at one moment he walks through the crowd blessing the people, ultimately the camera leaves him and focuses instead on the immense crowd participating in the religious festivities. Finally the true key to Rocha's conception of this new Christ appears. The Christ of the Third World is the people themselves; their resurrection lies in their capacity for transformation. Carnival, Oswald de Andrade once wrote, is the religious rite of the race. From the people will come the creation of a new order. (Johnson 1984: 160–1)

In relation to Deleuze and Guattari's plane of immanence, Rocha's Christs represent conceptual personae on a transcendental field (as opposed to a pure transcendence), organising chaos into an activist plane of consistency. The transcendental field is immanent to Life itself, for as Deleuze argues,

> It can be distinguished from experience in that it doesn't refer to an object or belong to a subject (empirical representation). It appears therefore as a pure stream of a-subjective consciousness, a pre-reflexive impersonal consciousness, a qualitative duration of consciousness without a self.' (2001: 25)

Its relation to consciousness is purely conceptual for it cannot be defined by the consciousness that is coextensive with it. In other words the transcendent is not the transcendental:

> Were it not for consciousness, the transcendental field would be defined as a pure plane of immanence, because it eludes all transcendence of the subject and of the object. Absolute immanence is in itself: it is not in something, *to* something; it does not depend on an object or belong to a subject. (2001: 26)

In this sense, Deleuze and Spinoza's immanence acts as its own container, just as Rocha's Christs simultaneously 'contain' but are also immanent to, the people. 'We will say of pure immanence that it is A LIFE, and nothing else,' argues Deleuze. 'It is not immanence to life, but the immanent that is in nothing is itself a life. A life is the immanence of immanence, absolute immanence: it is complete power, complete bliss' (2001: 27). Or, to enfold it back into Rocha's cinematic oeuvre, pure trance.

CHAPTER 6

'See You at Mao': The '60s Left Returns to Zero with the Dziga Vertov Group

Having taken our tricontinental journey through Glauber Rocha's 'aesthetics of hunger', we our now ready to return to Europe and re-engage with Godard's 'return to zero' but with the added political baggage of a far more extensive global diaspora, impacted not only by the Vietnam War, the events of May '68 and the 1970 Black September Massacre but also Godard's Maoist turn, first expressed in *La Chinoise* (1967) but examined far more critically in his collaborative venture, the Dziga Vertov Group. The latter included the vitally important participation of Jean-Pierre Gorin (the editor, with Robert Linhart, Jacques-Alain Miller, and Jacques Rancière of the journal *Cahiers Marxistes-Léninistes*), Jean-Henri Roger, the cameramen Paul Burron and Armand Marco, Gérard Martin, Raphaël Sorin, Isabelle Pons and Godard's wife at the time, Anne Wiazemsky, who appeared in several of the films. *Ici et Ailleurs*, which began as a 1969 Group project with Gorin (as *Jusqu'a la victoire*), was eventually completed in collaboration with Godard's subsequent partner, Anne-Marie Miéville, and released in 1976.

Although Godard's politics and approach to film form evolves radically following his promised 'return to zero' in *Deux ou trois choses* it is still marked by a predilection for irrational cuts and interstices so that sound and image no longer unite to form a coherent narrative movement, marked by rational linkages and sensory-motor continuity, but exist independently in and of themselves. In certain cases, silences and black screen are used to make direct political statements. At one point in *Le Gai Savoir* Godard's voice-over announces: 'And now a minute of silence in sound to the memory of the Black Panthers killed in San Francisco by the FBI's hit men.' Although, as in the café scene in *Bande à part*, Godard doesn't give us the full minute (actually a mere ten seconds), the sonic interstice is enough to give us pause for (ideological) thought. He then cuts to a black screen, re-presenting a minute of silence in images, in particular, for the memory of the Afro-Asians and their friends, beaten by the police of Kimola and François Mitterand, who today are supposedly part of the opposition to the left. And, in general, a minute of silence in images, for all the absent images, censored images, prostituted images, machinated images, delinquent images, buggered images, images beaten up by all the governments, televisions, and Westernized cinemas that rhyme information and repression with trash and culture.

Jean-Pierre Léaud's character, Émile, had used a similar tactic earlier in the film by informing us, over a black screen: 'Here the image is missing. The Anglo-Canadian police gouged out the eyes of a cameraman who was filming the landscapes and faces of a free Quebec.'

In this way sound and image are reduced to extra-diegetic signs, where signifiers are split from their signifieds so that they can be reconstituted back into less orthodox (as in Barthes's *doxa*) sounds and images, both in terms of film content and, more importantly, film form. As Peter Wollen argues, 'Godard takes the idea of formal conflict and struggle and translates it into a concept of conflict, not between the content of images, but between different codes and between signifier and signified' (1982: 99). In Deleuzian terms, sound and image are deconstructed from their narrative role as aggregates of movement and action to pure singularities so that they can be constantly reconstituted as new aggregates, *ad infinitum*. According to Deleuze, narration always refers to a system of judgement. By adopting the more Nietzschean tactic of applying the 'powers of the false', narration frees itself from this limiting system, a process which affects the investigator (Godard) and the witness (the spectator) as much as the alleged semiotic guilty party (the contrived signifier-signified-sign system).

In this context silences and black screen act as interstitial agents for marking and facilitating the distance between sounds and images so that all components can act together *materially* in order to break down the structuralist relationship between Roman Jakobson's synchronic (*langue*) and diachronic (*parole*) axes in favour of the reconstruction of isolated, 'de-chronologised moments' and 'disconnected places'. As Deleuze explains:

> The point is that the elements themselves are constantly changing with the relations of time into which they enter, and the terms of their connections. Narration is constantly being completely modified, in each of its episodes, not according to subjective variations, but as a consequence of disconnected places and de-chronologised moments. There is a fundamental reason for this new situation: contrary to the form of the true which is unifying and tends to the identification of a character (his discovery or simply his coherence), the power of the false cannot be separated from an irreducible multiplicity. 'I is another' ['*J'est un autre*'] has replaced Ego = Ego. (1989: 133)

In the Dziga Vertov Group films, this 'degree zero of cinema' is harnessed as a source of positive and didactic meaning, so that the cinematic frame behaves less as a mimetic window on reality – in Bazin's sense – and more like a didactic blackboard in a classroom, an empty surface (both diegetically and exegetically) upon which the spectator can construct their own theory of film (and everyday language) on more radical lines. As Marcia Landy summarises the process,

> Godard's films are a metacritical and philosophical analysis of the image, taking as an object of reflection two important hypotheses often expressed in aphoristic fashion. The first hypothesis is that cinema is not a reflection of reality but the reality of a reflection, thus turning on its head traditional conceptions of mimesis and representation. The second hypothesis, also an aphorism and related to the first, is that there is no 'just image', there is only 'just an image'. (2001: 9)

Produced by the French national broadcast agency, ORTF (Office de Radiodiffusion Télévision Française) *Le Gai Savoir* (which, along with *Un film comme les autres*, predates the Dziga Vertov collaborations) was filmed in the latter's Joinville Studios from December 1967 to January 1968, but was edited after June 1968, which enabled Godard to insert a number of sounds and images from the May uprisings. Made specifically for TV, the original idea was to make a modern version of Jean-Jacques Rousseau's *Émile*, a novelistic 1762 treatise on the nature of education for the ideal citizen born of *The Social Contract*. Thus according to Godard, *Émile* was at first to be

> a modern film, the story of a boy who refuses to go to his high school because the classes are always overcrowded; he begins to learn outside of school, by looking at people, going to the movies, listening to the radio, or watching television. (Godard 1967: 70; cited in Brown 1972: 9)

However, with its complete lack of plot and less than subtle attacks on state media censorship, the ORTF refused to show it on TV and the French censor denied it a certificate for general release. The film was eventually released 12 July 1969 with a West German co-sponsor, Bavaria Atelier, and sporting a new title, *Le Gai Savoir*, an homage to Nietzsche's *Die Fröhliche Wissenschaft* or *The Gay Science/The Joyful Wisdom*, published in 1882, which contains his first reference to 'The Eternal Return'.

Set on a blacked-out television sound stage (which suggests that the context of the film's discourse extends beyond the film frame to an unrepresentable infinity, thus defying a confining exegesis), Émile Rousseau (Jean-Pierre Léaud), the great-great-grandson of Jean-Jacques (and the stand-in for the original Émile in the 1762 novel), and Patricia Lumumba (Juliet Berto), the daughter of Patrice Lumumba and the Cultural

Revolution (and also the former Third World delegate for the new Citroën factories in the North Atlantic), stumble across each other in the dark. After exchanging introductions (they are as much playing themselves – as actors – as they are their characters), they agree to spend seven nights developing a rigorous deconstruction of language and sound-image relations in order to analyse the correspondence between politics and film.

The first day – interrupted by countless extra-diegetical images and sounds such as news photos, advertisements, comic strips and moving shots of pedestrians and cars on Paris streets – is spent agreeing on a *modus operandi*. Thus a sequence begins with a photo still of a young man wearing a white coat sitting at a computer. Godard's handwritten text is scrawled over his body: 'l'homme unidimensional', a clear reference to Herbert Marcuse's *One Dimensional Man*. We then hear Godard's voice-over (unlike in *Deux ou trois choses*, where it is whispered conspiratorially, here it is accompanied by loud radio static, as if broadcast from another dimension): 'In the universities, we can meet.' We cut to a truck on a building site as Émile's voice cuts in (as if speaking for the film's frustrated audience): 'This disorder is really getting annoying.' We then cut back to the studio to a tight shot on Émile, in darkness, as Patricia explains her methodology: 'No, listen, we study links, relations, differences.' In other words, harnessing Saussure's semiology, we have to turn back against the enemy the very thing with which he attacks us: Language. Émile replies with his same complaint of annoyance but Godard himself cuts in to give us the bigger political picture: 'Organised like this, we can put into function the factories and universities for the profit of the national collectivity of all. The armed forces of the state can do nothing against them.' Émile seems to be won over to the cause: 'Well then, off to work. Might as well study that. Yes, we have to start again from zero.' However, as she is throughout the film, Patricia is far more conceptually precise: 'No, before we start again, we must first go *back* to zero.' Émile: 'And once we get there?' Patricia: 'Well . . . we'll look around . . . see if there are any traces.'

As Patricia fixes her hair (many commentators have mentioned that these scenes, with their chiaroscuro lighting, resemble a shampoo commercial), Émile sums up their strategy: 'Deep down, we're going to search for what's left. It's true, for social studies, it's not about composing man, but dissolving him. Is that it?' Patricia: 'Yes, of course.'

They then outline their order of analysis:

Émile: 'What will we do the first year?'
Patricia: 'We'll pick up images, we'll record sounds, like we said. It will create unorderly experiences.'

Émile: 'Actions, hypotheses.'
Patricia: 'Yes, and the second year, we'll criticise it all. We'll decompose . . . we'll reduce . . . we'll substitute . . . and we'll recompose.'
Émile: 'Okay. And afterwards, the third year, we'll create a few samples of sounds and images. My practice will not be blind, since you will have enlightened it with your revolutionary theory.'
Patricia: 'My theory will not be without object since it will be linked to your revolutionary practice.'

In this way theory enlightens practice which reconstructs theory on new lines. Adopting several of his Brechtian distanciation techniques from *Deux ou trois choses* – at one point Patricia/Juliet faces the camera in an ante-bellum costume garbling unintelligible poetry in front of a mural featuring cartoon images of Batman, Spider-Man and the Incredible Hulk in order to demonstrate a 'new' model of political film – Godard uses silence as a component part of his sound and image isolation and deconstruction but also as a critical vector pointing towards other modes of ideological interpellation: a strategy that he and Gorin will explore further in their more Althusserian-based collaborations in *Lotte in Italia* (1971) and *Vladimir and Rosa* (1971).

In 'Year 1', for example, where Émile and Patricia accumulate images and record sounds to create an assemblage of 'unorderly' experiences, Émile poses a very valid question: 'Images, do we *choose* them? Or do we encounter them by chance?' 'By chance,' responds Patricia, 'since we don't know exactly what they are. Any image.' Émile doesn't think that's very scientific but Patricia disagrees: 'Chance is structured just like unconsciousness.' Both agree that the secret to understanding images is to discover a method and then self-criticise afterwards. Then, as if to give the audience a test case, Émile announces 'The first image . . .' before Godard drops out the sound and then cuts to an insert of Nicéphore Niépce's *View from his Window at Le Gras* (1827). For the uninitiated, their immediate response might be to require more information via a documentary-style voice-over – the photo's author, context, year, etc., thus foregrounding the importance of art historical discourse in contextualising all photographic images. Of course Godard's intent here is to deny us that contextualisation so that we see the image on its own terms (but also make us aware that a sound-image dialectic is still crucial to all understanding).

However, we cannot help but bring some conceptual and historical baggage to the table, such as Charles Sanders Peirce's triadic classification of signs – the iconic (any representational image, including paintings, drawings, diagrams, graphs and cinema); the indexical (images with an existential connection to the object such as photographs, film, weathervanes and body language – e.g. the rolling gait of a sailor); and the symbolic (an arbitrary connection between image and object as in the case of all spoken and written languages). Thus in the case of the Niépce photograph, Émile doesn't clarify the image by saying 'The first *indexical* image', for he has no way of knowing what the first *iconic* image might have been. Furthermore he doesn't take into account the early eighteenth-century 'sun print' experiments of Johann Heinrich Schultze, who combined stencils of words and nitric acid to create primitive 'exposures'. Similarly there are strong arguments that Vermeer used the camera obscura and projected imagery as a template for many of his paintings, even going so far as to represent the light distortions rather than correct them: creating, in effect, the record of a mediation. As Svetlana Alpers lays out the prevailing theory,

> It would appear that those small globules of paint that we find in several works – the threads in the *Lace-maker*, the ship in the *View of Delft* – are painted equivalents of the circles of confusion, diffused circles of light, that form around unfocused specular highlights in the camera obscura image. (1983: 31–2)[1]

In other words, these gestures are both iconic and indexical, fusing the properties of painting and the photograph.

To his credit, Émile seems to be aware of these issues when he complains: 'You're only speaking of images. You've forgotten sound.' Patricia responds: 'No, I haven't forgotten. It's the same thing. But we can isolate them.' This is immediately followed by an extract from Mozart's Piano Sonata No. 8 in A minor, K. 310 (Movement 1. Allegro maestoso) as we see rapid cuts between a green-tinted portrait of a young Mao and a black and white photo of a nude female model lying on her back, her knees arched towards her chin. The montage slows down before the sound drops out and we cut to a black and white still of a demonstrator lying prone on the street as several CRS (Compagnies Républicaines de Sécurité) riot police, carrying shields, walk past him towards the background, as if to remind the audience that resistance to CRS oppression will take more than a fanciful alliance between Mao and eroticism (a blatant manufacture of the culture industry). In this respect Godard is continuing the discrepant editing experiments of Isidore Isou in *Traité* which privileged sound over image, a position stated repeatedly by Émile and Patricia throughout the film: 'Voices are the best expressions of freedom'; 'The eye must listen before looking'; 'In a film we always see people talking, never listening'; and in reference to Italian films, 'They refuse to show movies with the

---

[1] The most developed argument on these lines is by Daniel Fink (1971).

original soundtrack. From the beginning of the talking pictures they've never seen a spoken film. It's incredible, terrifying: they prefer an enslaved sound to a liberated sound.'

This 'liberated sound' is perhaps best illustrated in the sequence that follows, where Patricia states: 'What we need to discover are images and sounds that are free.' Thus, although the words 'Say' and 'Stalin' have no intrinsic connection, it may be possible to link them if we can 'Mark off in time and space, this silent word that separates them.' Again, silence becomes the space between word and images that creates a connection that avoids *doxa*, for as Patricia argues, 'And when we'll know, when we'll use those two sounds together, their connection will inevitably be correct.' Godard illustrates the point by inserting a black and white still of a young Stalin with an inked-in 'bloodstained' collar at the exact point that Émile says: 'In every image, we must know who speaks.' Godard's response, as one might expect, is to turn from Stalin to a combination of Mao and Che. He edits a sequence of shots that include a fashion model with a striped red scarf; a group of black GIs leading a group of Vietnamese children through the jungle; Vermeer's *Girl With the Pearl Earring* (how appropriate!), an elderly man on a Paris street approaching a red hoarding announcing a charcuterie/rotisserie; and a travelling colour shot featuring a suburban apartment complex (shades of the high-rise 'ensembles' of *Deux ou trois choses*). These are juxtaposed with two intertitles: 'Mao Sait TOUT' ('Mao knows everything') and the cover of the July/August issue of *Tricontinental* magazine featuring a camouflage-like break-up of a Third World face, with a yellow half circle against red. This obvious Che reference is reinforced at the end of the sequence when Godard inserts a 'flower power'-style poster advertising Cuba as a vacation option. The text reads, ironically: 'gai comme soleil' ('joyful as sunshine'). Throughout the sequence Émile and Patricia's joint voice-overs proclaim the following: 'It's the things and the phenomena as they exist objectively.' This is a paraphrase of an extract from Mao's 1941 text, 'Reform Our Study', which in many ways guides Godard's approach to image-sound relations throughout this period:

> To take such an attitude is to seek truth from facts. 'Facts' are all the things that exist objectively, 'truth' means their internal relations, that is, the laws governing them, and 'to seek' means to study. We should proceed from the actual conditions inside and outside the country, the province, county or district, and derive from them, as our guide to action, laws which are inherent in them and not imaginary, that is, we should find the internal relations of the events occurring around us. And in order to do that we must rely not on subjective imagination, not on momentary enthusiasm, not on lifeless books, but on facts that exist objectively; we must appropriate the

material in detail and, guided by the general principles of Marxism-Leninism, draw correct conclusions from it. (Mao Tse-tung 1941: 22–3)

As Patricia says, 'So that's what we said. The truth, it's the internal place of these things and phenomena, meaning the laws that govern them.' Given how the voice-overs link a disparate array of images through a consistent ideological text, these laws clearly entail a syncretic analysis of multiple levels of signification: everyday life in Paris, Vietnam, fashion and tricontinental globalism, through which a single voice speaks: not Stalin but Mao.

Significantly, it is sound rather than silence – the quote from 'Reform Our Study' – that accentuates the discrepancy of information in this case, but that isn't always the case. Thus an extended twenty-five-second sound drop-out accompanies a similar hodge-podge of twelve separate images – advertising spreads, sexy cartoons, photos of Fidel Castro, CRS (the general reserve of the French national police) violence on the streets of Paris, Third World guerrillas in the jungle, a boy and a girl washing the family car – but this time the discrepant text is not superimposed as a voice-over but inserted into the images themselves as script fragments (presumably handwritten by Godard himself). The full text reads: 'From now on, we will no longer accept any kind of blatant truths. We don't believe that there exist any blatant truths. Blatant truths belong to bourgeois philosophy.' ('Dorénavant nous n'acceptons plus aucune sorte de vérités évidentes. Nous ne croyons pas qu'il existe des vérités evidentes. Les vérités évidentes appartiennent à la philosophie bourgeoise.').

Although the continued silence throughout the sequence tends to unify and 'homogenise' a coherent reading from the spectator, the 'blatant truths' of each image are deconstructed by the word fragments themselves (obviously we can only assign them a coherent meaning retroactively, once the sequence is over). Thus the Castro portrait is accompanied by the fragment 'nous n'acceptons plus' ('we will no longer accept' – implying anti-imperialist resistance), while 'vérités évidentes' ('blatant truths'), repeated three times, is reserved for a cartoon image of the CRS; a split-screen photographic pairing of Jean-Paul Sartre on the left (+ 'vérités') and student leader Daniel Cohn-Bendit on the right (+ 'evidentes'); and a close-up of a bikini-clad blonde, her arms raised, displayed on the cover of *Cinémonde* (special issue: 'Au Cinéma l'Erotisme'). The final words: 'bourgeois philosophy' is scrawled on the windscreen of the red family car washed by the children, as if it were waiting to be scrubbed off, a radical shift from the car wash scene in *Deux ou trois choses* where the Jansons' Mini was used as a constructive meditation on phenomenology and Ponge's poetics of the object.

Once again the ideological subtext is Mao, this time his 'On the Correct Handling of Contradictions Among the People', a speech delivered on 27 February 1957 at the Eleventh Session (Enlarged) of the Supreme State Conference and eventually published in the *People's Daily* on 19 June of the same year. Godard inserts a close-up of the text as Image 7 in his sequence with the text fragment, 'that there exist any' ('qu'il existe des') that leads into 'blatant truths' (the *bête noir* of the statement). Perhaps the key statement in Mao's original speech is his analysis of contradictions:

> Marxist philosophy holds that the law of the unity of opposites is the fundamental law of the universe. This law operates universally, whether in the natural world, in human society, or in man's thinking. Between the opposites in a contradiction there is at once unity and struggle, and it is this that impels things to move and change. Contradictions exist everywhere, but their nature differs in accordance with the different nature of different things. In any given thing, the unity of opposites is conditional, temporary and transitory, and hence relative, whereas the struggle of opposites is absolute. (Mao Tse-tung 1957: unpaginated)

In this example the silence that binds the images to the text acts as an ideological vector, encouraging us to 'read' beyond the surface of language as a 'blatant truth' and take a much more Nietzschean approach: the constructive 'lie' as a 'power of the false', where 'I' is no longer a bourgeois subject but a *revolutionary* 'other'.

This by-play between sound and silence reaches its apotheosis in a fascinating sequence that opens Part 3 of the film that is almost a direct quotation of Godard's *Ciné-Tract #23* but with a significant formal change. It's generally agreed that the *Ciné-Tract* project was instigated by Chris Marker's film collective, SLON (Société pour le Lancement des Oeuvres Nouvelles) and also included the collaboration of the ARC Group (Atelier de recherche cinématographique) and Alain Resnais, as well as Godard. Although Godard rarely acknowledges the contribution and inspiration of others on his cinematic practice, in this case he generously credits Marker's *Ciné-Tracts* for providing the initial impetus and model for the Dziga Vertov Group:

> The *Ciné-Tracts* are Chris Marker's idea. The video camera and all these short films, it was a simple and cheap means to make political cinema for a *section d'entreprise* or an action-committee. [. . .] For, in the same way as in the classroom, we re-write the films with students, and likewise I believe we must make films with those who watch them. (Cited in Fargier and Sizaire 1969, reprinted in Godard 1985: 332)

Filmed at the Nanterre campus of the University of Paris in May–June 1968 at the time of the student-worker uprisings, the films were shot in black and white on 16mm. Each runs for approximately two minutes, fifty seconds (the length of 100 feet of 16mm film at twenty-four frames per second), although some ran for up to four minutes. Edited entirely in the camera, all the films were silent and were intended to be screened at student assemblies, factories during workers' strikes, and at political action committees as the May events unfolded. The films could be bought for fifty francs, at that time the overall cost of production. As Julia Lesage points out,

> In May 1968 *cinétracts* provided a kind of alternate 'information service' and an alternate aesthetic, formed in reaction to the mass media and the commercial cinema. To make *cinétracts* the filmmakers would often film a written message or a photo or some graffiti that appeared on the walls of Paris in those months. (1979: 93)

Also, as Phoebe Marshall informs us, 'According to Jean-François Dars, Marker kept a stockpile of photographs at *1 rue Littré*, in the studio *Dumage*, a stockpile that was already quite substantial by 15 May 1968' (2015: 7).

That raises an interesting question: are all of the images in Godard's *Ciné-Tracts* taken from this stockpile or did Godard film any footage of his own and convert it to stills? According to Colin MacCabe, 'It seems that Godard shot no footage of the riots. There is one famous image of him brandishing a super-8 camera but he told Chris Marker that it had no film inside' (2004: 399 n. 24). Nonetheless, Godard didn't stick exclusively to Marker's catalogue of images because, as one might expect, he also inserted a number of references expressing his own concerns at this time: the relation between aesthetics and politics, between sexual/personal liberation and political liberation, issues, let's face it, of little or no interest to the CGT (Confédération Générale du Travail – General Confederation of Labour – France's main trade union) or the French Communist Party which controls it. Of the forty-one surviving *Ciné-Tracts*, Godard is known to have made eleven of them (segments 7–10; 12–16; 23 and 40). They are recognisable by his consistent use of a title card which reads 'Eastman film Double X Type 7222', followed by the number of the Cine-Tract. Although his early efforts used text as intertitles on separate cards, the later tracts, including #23, included text written directly on the image.

It's interesting to analyse how the original tract, which is completely silent, compares conceptually to the modified extract used in *Le Gai Savoir*, which is accompanied by Cuban revolutionary chants and then a patriotic song that continues until the end of the sequence. Both feature an extract from Che – 'Le Socialisme et l'Homme à Cuba', an article originally written as a letter (dated 12 March 1965), to Carlos Quijano, director of the weekly *Marcha*, published in Montevideo, Uruguay – which reads: 'At the risk of seeming ridiculous, let me say that the true revolutionary is guided by a great feeling of love.' Godard cuts the subsequent line: 'It is impossible to think of a genuine revolutionary lacking this quality.'[2] In many ways this lays the foundation for Émile and Patricia's 'relationship', which is ruled as much by love and affection as it is by a common ideological desire to self-educate, but also their final methodological 'synthesis' at film's end. Bookmarked by another sound drop-out over the shot of an Express Services van passing a pedestrian crossing on a busy street, when Patricia asks Émile: 'What are you writing?' he responds: 'Mi so to di ment. Misotodiment.'

> Patricia: 'It sounds like the merging of "method" with "sentiment". Is that it?'
> Émile OS: 'Yes. [Mozart up.] I found this word, finally, to define images and sounds. And you?'
> Patricia: 'Me? This never was, never will be, because this is.'
> Émile OS: 'It's not bad either.'
> Patricia: 'Yeah. It's a bit vague, what we've discovered, no?'
> Émile: 'In other words, this film is a failure.'
> Patricia: 'Yes.'
> Émile: 'No, not really. In fact, not at all.'

Émile's dialogue then continues over a scrawled text in blue, red and black – 'Knowledge will be controlled by the imagination, representing class consciousness.' He then sums up their findings as follows: 'Listen, what better ideal to propose to the man of today, [than something] that is above and beyond themselves? Otherwise, regaining through knowledge of the void they themselves discovered.'

Both the original *Ciné-Tract* and the appropriation in *Le Gai Savoir* open with a black and white photograph of Che speaking in front of a bank of microphones. The script, 'laissez-moi vous dire' appears to be

---

[2] The original context for the quote, in French, is as follows: 'Permettez-moi de dire, au risque de paraître ridicule, que le vrai révolutionnaire est guidé par de grands sentiments d'amour. Il est impossible d'imaginer un révolutionnaire authentique sans cette qualité. Peut-être est-ce là un des grands drames du dirigeant. Il doit allier à un tempérament passionné une froide intelligence et prendre de douloureuses décisions sans que se contracte un seul de ses muscles. Nos révolutionnaires d'avant-garde doivent idéaliser cet amour des peuples, des causes les plus sacrées, et le rendre unique, indivisible. Ils ne peuvent descendre au niveau où l'homme ordinaire exerce sa petite dose *d'affection quotidienne.*' (*Marcha*, 12 March 1965).

coming out of his mouth then crossing his lower legs. In the *Ciné-Tract*, Godard then shows a student with makeshift weapons and an anti-tear gas rag across his nose and mouth with the text, 'au risqué'. In the new version he breaks with the exclusive May '68 context and turns to allegory: a painting of a naked, bearded Ulysses-like figure standing at the prow of sailing ship, a red and pink vertical striped sail billowing across the frame with 'au risque' scrawled across the boat, as if true revolution is a mythic adventure of Homeric proportions. The following shot in both versions is student demonstrators ('de paraître') but the *Ciné-Tract* follows with a black and white photo of de Gaulle with a split text – 'ridi e' + 'cul' (backside). Godard may have felt that this image was too specific to France and May '68 because the new version resorts to a fashion magazine layout featuring both a male and female model, as if to ally with Guy Debord's tirade against the spectacle.

Both versions then remain in synch with shared references to student revolutionaries waving flags or throwing Molotov cocktails, a book cover by Mélanie Klein and Joan Rivière – *L'amour et la haine (Étude psychanalytique)* – featuring two co-written lectures on love, hate and reparation, Vietnamese children getting a piggyback ride on a soldier, and finally, an interlocked nude couple to accompany the text, 'sentiments d'amour' ('feelings of love'). Interestingly, Godard eschews the opportunity to metacommunicate the filmic device because, unlike the *Ciné-Tract*, he ends the new sequence before showing a pair of black and white stills of Juliet Berto and Jean-Pierre Léaud from *La Chinoise* (with the accompanying text: 'dans notre ambition') and also another portrait and second quote from Che ('mais nous savons . . .'). More important is how the silence that ties the *Ciné-Tract* version exclusively to May '68 is expanded by the Cuban revolutionary songs to a more radical (and global) tricontinental *politique*. For those of us able to compare the two versions it shows the limitations of 'straight' silence as a potential vector of immanence – it is only when contrasted spatially and temporally to sound that we gain a full appreciation of its stratigraphic, deterritorialising power.

At this stage Godard seemed fully aware that such a task was beyond the scope of a single film, particularly a metacommunicative tract set ostensibly in a classroom rather than on the streets or in the jungles of real conflict. Patricia, for example, complains that 'half the shots are missing', only for Émile to remind her that they will be filmed by other directors: Bertolucci will give us the missing Marxist or Freudian analysis, Straub will feature the bourgeois family where 'everything is taboo', and of course the pillaging of the Third World will be shot by Rocha 'in Brazil' (actually in the Congo, co-starring Jean-Pierre himself!). Godard ends with a black screen (symbolising everything that is 'still to be done'), accompanied by his own static-laden voice-over:

> This film didn't want, cannot want to explain cinema, nor constitute its object. But, even more modestly, give an efficient method of achieving it. This film is not the film that needs to be made. But how, if we have a film to make, we necessarily have to go through the well-known paths of films.

Godard held pretty much the same view when interviewed three years later by Michael Goodwin, Tom Luddy and Naomi Wise in *Take One*, the Canadian Film Magazine.

> It was three years ago. It was done for French TV, which never showed it. It was an attempt to break with the ideology of making movies, to explain how movies are done, but since I was not politically aware it was still done in the same universalitarian style I was attacking. It was like a student booing his teacher – if booing is all he does, he is not acting politically. Maybe it is a step forward for him to be able to boo, as compared to just listening and writing what his boss tells him to write. (Cited in draft version of Goodwin et al. 1970: 63)

If the intellectual analysis of *Le Gai Savoir* never really left the safe confines of the TV studio/classroom, *Un film comme les autres* (*A Film Like Any Other*, 1968) constituted a brave expansion of Godard's 'return to zero' into the real world, even though on a formal level the films are very similar and Godard himself felt that 'It was a complete failure' (Carroll 1972: 53). Both films intercut scenes of theoretical discussion with documentation of the events of May '68, but the sound-image dialectic is radically different. Instead of Patricia and Émile as the discursive representatives of theory and practice, we now have colour footage of a small group of militant Sorbonne students meeting with Renault workers from the Flins factory, shot in either July or August 1968 in a grassy field at the foot of a tall HLM (moderate-rent housing) tower block in the western suburbs of Paris. Completely obscured by the tall grasses so that, apart from a few brief moments, we never see the participants' faces, they discuss radical politics, the successes and failures of the May uprisings, the divisive role of the CGT and the French Communist Party, as well as, in the language of Nikolái Chernyshevsky and Lenin, 'What Is To Be Done?' – i.e. what are the next practical steps that must be taken to further the revolution? Should these steps be idealist, violent or reformist? Replacing *Le Gai Savoir*'s hodge-podge of *Ciné-Tract* stills, cartoons, advertisements, book covers, black screen and silences, we now have actual black and white silent footage of the events of May themselves, probably provided by the

'États Généraux du Cinéma', a radical film collective led by Thierry Derocles, Michel Demoule, Claude Chabrol and Marin Karmitz (Brown 1972: 179).[3]

The latter images are overlaid by two separate and competing soundtracks: the animated and deliberately disjointed discussion of the students and workers in the field, which explicates the images after the fact, but is in turn illustrated by them; and the alternating voice-overs of a man and young woman, creating what Godard calls a 'sonorous image' (Serisuelo 2014: 302). The latter voice-overs are largely made up of quotations from revolutionary texts, fragmented Cubistically so that instead of expressing coherent ideological propositions for social change they are reduced to clichés and historical truisms, the kind of 'blatant truths' critiqued by Mao and Godard in *Le Gai Savoir*. Thus at one point, accompanied by a revolutionary song, the Female Narrator announces over the group of students and Flins workers:

> Wednesday, 5 June. Water, gas, electricity, petrol, supplies, price controls. In Nantes the inter-union committee is still sitting in the town hall and practically running the city. These six months of victory have seen strong coordination between the different zones of the People's Liberation Armed Forces, particularly the artillery, and all the South Vietnamese people. Previous revolutions needed historical memories to hide their content from themselves. The social revolution must let the dead bury the dead and liquidate all superstition about them. To realise its goals, it must take its poetry from the future. 'In the past form overwhelmed content. Now content overwhelms form.'

It's hard to know how much of this 'cut-up' statement Godard endorsed or opposed – which is true of most of the film's arguments – but it's clear that he is aligning its 'blatant truths' to bourgeois philosophy, with its combination of historiography and teleology, what Foucault calls an episteme, the historical *a priori* which,

> in a given period, delimits in the totality of experience a field of knowledge, defines the mode of being of the objects that appear in that field, provides man's everyday perception with theoretical powers, and defines the conditions in which he can sustain a discourse about things that is recognized to be true. (Foucault 1989: 172)

As if to avoid this charge against his own film, Godard introduces a number of de-centring and aleatory devices into both the film's *mise-en-scène*

---

[3] For the États Généraux du Cinéma's manifesto see Scott MacKenzie 2014: 162–5. (First published in French as 'États généraux du cinéma français', *Cahiers du Cinéma* 203 (1968): 42–60. First published in English in *Screen* 13, no. 4 (1972–3), pp. 58–89.)

and its mode of projection. According to most commentators, the film is composed of two 16mm reels of equal duration and Godard left it up to the projectionist to decide the order of their screening. This leaves us with an odd dilemma, for as we shall see, one of the reels has the strong suggestion of a climax as the camera pans along a gathering of demonstrators to the stirring sounds of the Italian Communist song, 'Bandiera Rossa'. This could, of course, be used as a fake climax in the middle of the film but, given its accompanying sound drop-out, it is a far more successful deconstruction of the revolution-as-spectacle when reserved for the end. Also, in the group discussion scenes, Godard deliberately plays around with the number of participants – at the beginning it seems to be five, towards the end, six – the consistency of their dress (they seem to change their shirts and jeans between takes, at one point appearing shirtless), but most importantly, the lack of synchronisation between voices and bodies. As Gary Elshaw points out:

> Significantly, as the film progresses, the spectator becomes increasingly aware that the voices Godard uses for the dialogue of the film are not necessarily those of the figures the spectator sees. By using multiple overlapping voices on the soundtrack, it is made apparent that many of the voices have been recorded in other locations, and not the outside environment of the field where we see the group. (2000: 104)

This argument is borne out by repeated viewings: although it's easy to diegetically align the single female student's voice-over to the one woman present in the group, the male voices are not necessarily consistent with the person whose lips are moving, so that a worker's political position may be ascribed visually to a student and vice versa. Again, Elshaw confirms this observation, arguing that,

> Particularly within the first reel, the spectator sees the characters gesticulate during parts of the debate to reinforce their points of view. The attendant sound goes some way to confirming what the spectator sees. However, in the second reel the sound heavily contradicts the images and undermines the spectator's belief that the voices heard on the soundtrack belong to any of the individuals seen speaking in the first reel. It is as if Godard were attempting to present a cautionary message telling the audience to question both what it sees and what it hears. (2000: 107)

The result is not unlike the radio-style aesthetic that we explored in Fritz Lang's *M*, where sound is the main carrier of information over image, particularly in the dissemination of state propaganda as a means of extending the power of the *dispositif*. By spilling the asynchronous Flins conversations over the May '68 footage we become highly aware that the ingrained political discrepancy between the workers and the students is somehow at the heart of the failure of the May events. In this sense, there seems to be a missing component that can link the two sides together, much like Émile and Patricia's discussion in *Le Gai Savoir*, whereby, although the words 'Say' and 'Stalin' have no intrinsic connection, it may be possible to link them if we can 'Mark off in time and space, this silent word that separates them'.

It turns out, that this silent word may be a young man's name: Gilles (no, not Deleuze – Tautin!). According to David Sterritt,

> In part, *Un film comme les autres* is Godard's response to the death of a young protester in a recent political action, and like other works by the Dziga Vertov Group, it would surely have acquired more viewers if the filmmakers had set forth that real-life backstory somewhere in the movie itself. Godard has always had a hankering for the cryptic, however, and people watching his films – apart from his earliest, most self-contained features, from *Breathless* in 1960 to *Weekend* in 1967 – are pretty much on their own when it comes to social, historical, and interpretive context. (2018: 419).

There's an excellent chance that this young protester was in fact Gilles Tautin (1950–68), a Maoist high school student who drowned while fleeing the riot police just outside the same Flins Renault factory featured in the film.

That this tragedy was important to Godard and Gorin is clear from their last feature as the Dziga Vertov Group, *Tout va bien* (1972), where Him/Jacques (Yves Montand), a radical film-maker and intellectual, looks back on the events of May '68 from the vantage point of four years later. 'I left the party without realising that I'd borrowed from them a way of understanding my role as an intellectual,' he opines. 'My job is to make films, to find new forms for new content.' Then, to the sound of a gunshot, we cut back in time to a man dragging a young teenager's body from a river as a group of onlookers witness the tragedy from a bridge and the muddy bank. A female student's voice-over gives us the context that *Un film comme les autres* denies us: 'His name is Gilles. He was born on April 17, 1951. He's a student at the Lycée Thiers. Gilles, they'll say you deserved to die as an "agitator".' As we cut to a side view of six students looking down to the right, she continues:

> I who fought beside you can find no more beautiful name to give you. [Insert frontal shot of what may be his family]. Gilles. They'll say that all you knew was family and school, and that you learned about the world from books. I say your books thrust you into life, [side angle on young woman and man in cloth cap] because from them you learned to unlearn. Gilles. At 4:00 on May 3, you joined forces with life and carried on your struggle in the light of day. [On Montand, as a photographer holds a camera in front of him.] At 4:00 today, June 10, you joined forces with history . . . [Intertitle: MAI 68 . . . LUTTE] . . . and met your death, leaving us behind. Don't cry, brother. We'll carry on!

So why wasn't Tautin strongly featured in *Un film comme les autres*? The answer is that he was, but only obliquely and through the film's two overt silences. In an extremely insightful article in the 5 May 2018 issue of *The New York Times*, Mitchell Abidor, author of *May Made Me: An Oral History of the 1968 Uprising in France*, questions the idealistic received wisdom of a collective rebellion against the repressive Gaullist state after conducting dozens of interviews with participants in the actual events. Despite evidence of clear fraternisation between the workers and students, as Abidor argues,

> the students and the workers were fighting for radically different things. Bernard Vauselle, who worked at Sud Aviation in St-Nazaire, made clear to me that 'in '67 and '68 it was really the bread-and-butter demands we were interested in, not the political demands'. Seemingly small issues mattered enormously to the workers, according to Mr. Vauselle, such as an official recognition of their unions. Before the uprising, he told me, union supporters 'had to distribute our tracts outside the factory', but afterward 'we entered the factory and had our own office'. (2018: unpaginated)

There was also evidence of a major division over tactics: most workers opposed students using violence – brandishing paving stones and setting cars on fire – because it not only scared them but also showed complete disregard for everything they had saved up to buy.

However, the key contrast between the very different worker and student solidarities lay in the form of two separate funerals in June 1968. The day after Gilles Tautin was drowned – 11 June – Pierre Beylot, a worker at the Sochaux Peugeot factory was shot and killed by the police. Instead of firing up a mutual solidarity, the opposite was true. As Abidor states:

> If you watch footage of the funeral of Mr. Beylot, no students appear to be in attendance. Likewise, if you watch footage of Mr. Tautin's funeral, there appear to be no workers. Indeed, the General Confederation of Labor, a Communist-led trade union, had issued orders that its members not attend the Tautin funeral, wanting to end the strikes and not risk any further disturbance. That workers followed this order, including those not in the union, speaks volumes about the distance between the two groups. (2018: unpaginated)

We have clear evidence of the lack of workers at Tautin's funeral because *Cine-Tract #3* (possibly directed by Chris Marker) consists entirely of still shots of the funeral and a commemorative march through the streets and almost every participant is of student age.

Abidor also points out the strength of the 30 May counter-march when half a million people paraded on the Champs-Élysées in support of

President de Gaulle, probably the largest demonstration of the period and heavily featured towards the end of the documentary footage in *Un film comme les autres*.

It seems far from coincidental then that Godard should stage his very artificial and contrived outdoor meeting between the students and workers – it's very unlikely that they would have instigated this themselves – in Flins, the location of Tautin's death, as if to metonymically construct the very camaraderie that Gilles's and Beylot's funerals failed to generate, one of the key strategic reasons why May '68 ended in the Gaullists' triumphant success in the June elections. Tautin's presence-as-absence thus haunts the film as a provocation to the audience to pursue a line of flight that would reconstitute the revolution on radically different lines. Thus, following the Female Narrator's dictum that 'The filmed image belongs to those who watch it as well as to those who make it', we should examine the placement of the sound drop-outs as conceptual counterpoints to both historicism and spectacle.

Against images of marching gendarmes and countless fires on Paris streets, the Male Narrator informs us that

> Shakespeare says men get involved in history in three ways. Some create it and fall victim to it. Others think they create it, but also fall victim to it. The rest don't create history, but they, too, fall victim to it. The first group are kings, the next are kings' confidants who execute kings' orders and the last are simply citizens of the kingdom.

This extremely negative and fatalistic view of history as an inevitable exercise in futility may have been appropriate to Shakespeare's time when the 'Divine Right of Kings' guaranteed a metaphysical act of humility before God, but it's absolutely not relevant to a secular republic and the events of May '68. As if to underline this point, Godard gives us thirty seconds of silence over a series of twelve short night scenes that accentuate the burning light of car fires and glowing street lamps, as if the rebellion had become cloaked in a film noir-like *chiaroscuro*. Thus we see a firemen hosing down a car, a helmeted CRS cop standing by a van, a flashing police car light as it drives down a street, four students, backs to the camera, looking at tear gas smoke, people walking past a *Le Mondial* shop sign, and finally, a CRS trooper approaching a man who is backing away defensively, using a dustbin lid as a shield to protect his face. As we see the flash of the cop's gun, we cut back to the group in the field as they continue their discussion of worker–student relations. The female student seems to represent Godard's own views when she says, 'It's in your own sphere, in whatever activity you do that you must first be revolutionary. For the students [. . .]

It means contesting a certain type of class and no longer putting up with it...'

The silent footage seems to serve a number of objectives in this context: negating Shakespeare's view of history to show that the public can take events into their own hands, even if it means succumbing to a violent reaction on the part of the status quo, but more importantly showing the need for a collective solidarity of workers and students, symbolised by the deaths and funerals of Gilles Tautin and Pierre Beylot. Godard achieves this by homogenising the two groups sonically (via the all-encompassing silence) and visually (by showing the 'struggles' at night, so that we can't distinguish between workers and students in the same way that the daytime scenes clearly contextualise the factories and the university). Also, the sequence uses silence to foreground (through Brechtian *V-Effekt*) the documentary film medium's tendency to spectacularise the events into a seductive visual display. Godard had already quoted Guy Debord on this subject earlier in the film, when the Male Narrator delivers an extract from *The Society of the Spectacle* which states:

> The spectacle grasped in its totality is both the result and the project of the existing mode of production. It is not a supplement to the real world, an additional decoration. It is the heart of the unrealism of the real society. (Debord 1983: parag. 6)

However, more pertinent is Godard's subsequent citation from Debord's Situationist comrade, Raoul Vaneigem, which reads in full as follows:

> Any analysis of revolutions past or present that does not presuppose a determination to resume the struggle more coherently and more effectively plays fatally into the hands of the enemy: it is incorporated into the dominant culture. The only time to talk about revolutionary moments is when you are ready to live them at short notice. Would that as much be said of all our mandarin Marxists of the 'totality' and the 'planetary'. (Vaneigem 1983: 74)

Godard applies the tenor of Vaneigem's critique at the very end of the film (or at least, the end of one of the two 16mm reels). The Female Narrator sets the scene, stating over footage of demonstrators with fists raised and CGT posters on the wall in the background: 'There were meetings in every factory, every school, every college, every administration, every station, and every neighbourhood. The police, however, fierce, were powerless.' Godard 'piles on' on the revolutionary rhetoric by fading up the 'Bandiera Rossa' anthem ['Forward people, to the rescue / Red flag, red flag / Forward people, to the rescue / Red flag will triumph'] as the documentary footage pans right to include banners – 'LA LUTTE

CONTINUE' – then past the celebrants on the pavement as they sing along in unity. Suddenly, there is a seven-second silence as we continue to pick out faces in the crowd (thereby breaking the unity of the spectacle) before the Male Narrator concludes with a massively deflating platitude: 'It all comes down to aesthetics and the political economy.' The 'Bandiera Rossa' fades back up as Godard ends with an abstracted reduction of the Tricolore to eight scripted rows of 'blue blue blue' [blank space], 'rouge rouge rouge'. One is reminded of Vaneigem's famous line that, 'Ideology is the falsehood of language, radical theory the truth of language' (1983: 74), but in this case we're not really sure whether language on any level – scripted, filmic, sound-image dialectic – can ever break out of its own prison house, despite Godard's best efforts to 'return to zero'.

However, *British Sounds* (also known as *See You At Mao*, 1970), co-directed with Jean-Henri Roger and retroactively appropriated as the first official Dziga Vertov Group venture, makes some headway against this impasse by focusing specifically on competing and discrepant elements of the soundtrack itself as a means of deconstructing the 'blatant truths' of dogmatic political narratives, both left-wing and right-wing. Made for London Weekend Television (LWT), who, like the ORTF in the case of *Le Gai Savoir*, refused to air it, the film was produced by Kestrel Productions, which had been set up by Tony Garnett, Ken Loach, Dennis Potter and Kenith Trodd as a collaborative venture with left-wing filmmakers, using LWT as their TV outlet. Mo Teitelbaum, the wife of one of the partners, Irving Teitelbaum, planned to bring in six European directors to make documentaries on Britain and as she knew Godard from his work in London on *One Plus One*, he was obviously an ideal candidate.

Godard makes his intentions clear from the start of the film: an opening shot of the Union Jack with a text placed in the middle of the central horizontal red field:

BRITISH
IMAGES (crossed out)
SOUNDS

The camera then zooms into the text as a woman's voice-over proclaims: 'In a word, the bourgeoisie creates a world in its image. Comrades! We must destroy that image!' just as a fist smashes through the flag from behind. Clearly, this will be a film that privileges sound over image (although Godard continues his exploration of discrepancy between the two) in order to raise the key question – 'Can the subaltern speak?' (in

Gayatri Chakravorty Spivak's terminology) – and how is this affected by divisions based on gender, race, class, caste, religion and other narratives? More importantly, who controls these narratives and what role does the popular media play in their dissemination and perpetuating their inequalities?

The film is divided into six distinct sections, four of which are interrupted by the voice-overs of two teachers (male and female) who recite key dates from a 'revolutionary calendar' which are then repeated, fragment by fragment, by a young boy as if he were in a private tutorial – a kind of rote learning of socialism's greatest moments. Thus: 'In 1368, peasants led by Tyler and Ball rose against feudal oppression. In 1648, peasant soldiers called Levellers fought for the new cooperative commonwealth. In 1791, artisans formed a free association to forward the ideas of the French Revolution.' These recitations are occasionally accompanied by enigmatic texts (in Godard's usual cut-up style) that seem to have little to do with the subject at hand:

> MONDAY TUE$DAY
> WEDNE$DAY TH
> UR$DAY FRIDAY
> $ATURDAY $UNDAY

The real subject of these tutorials is a classic case of what Foucault calls the archive. As he puts it, 'The archive is the first law of what can be said, the system that governs the appearance of statements as unique events' (1972: 129). Although the archive is an historical *a priori* – it takes account of statements in their dispersion and harnesses them to a group of rules that characterise a discursive practice, a practice with a given history – it's transformable, not fixed, i.e. it's not a formal *a priori*. As Godard illustrates through its random fragments, it's impossible to describe in its totality – it emerges only in fragments, regions and levels:

> The analysis of the archive, then, involves a privileged region: at once close to us, and different from our present existence, it is the border of time that surrounds our presence, which overhangs it, and which indicates it in its otherness; it is that which, outside ourselves, delimits us. (Foucault 1972: 130)

In short, it establishes us as difference and as dispersion.

Godard reinforces the import of this archive by placing these 'lessons' in tandem with random quotations from *The Communist Manifesto* over a ten-minute tracking shot along the MG assembly line at the British Leyland/BMC car factory in Cowley, Oxford (which immediately conjures up the similar tracking shot depicting the traffic jam and bloody car accident in *Weekend*). Thus the lesson about the Levellers is immediately followed by a quote from Marx:

> Workers must understand that existing society, with all the misery it heaps upon them, also gives rise to the material conditions and social forms necessary to its economic transformation. They must replace the conservative slogan, 'A fair day's wage for a fair day's work', with the revolutionary slogan, 'Abolition of the wage system!'

On one level, Godard uses these quotations to stress that the subaltern (i.e. the worker) is still unable to speak for themselves, noting in a 1976 interview with Penelope Gilliatt that, 'It is not good that we are still obliged to use Marx quotations instead of the words of the worker' (Sterritt 1998: 82).

However, Godard almost drowns out these didactic statements by combining two noise tracks from the plant, one synchronous with the workers' voices, the sounds of hammering and whirring machines, and another much louder track of shrieking machine noise taken from another source. As Godard stated in an interview,

> *Mao* should be projected very loud, especially during the long tracking shot at the BMC factory that opens the film. The movie was originally made for TV and that terrible noise in it is important. For bourgeois people to be uncomfortable with that scene for only eleven minutes may make them think that those workers must deal with that screeching every day all their lives. (Carroll 1972: 62)

As James Roy MacBean argues in *Film and Revolution*, Godard deliberately eschews realism (which has, of course, already been appropriated by bourgeois aesthetics and, via Hollywood, capitalism) in order to show how the average factory worker would have little time or energy for reading political theory or organising action committees:

> If he's going to complain about anything, it's not capitalism; it's noise. He's going to demand better working conditions, or shorter hours, or higher wages, or medical plans, or all of these; but with all these immediate evils to lessen or eliminate, his attention will not be drawn to the greater evil – capitalism itself – which is the root of the problem. (MacBean 1975: 104–5)

In this sense the undermining of didactic texts by machine noise acts as a form of objective correlative for the workers' lack of political consciousness, opening up a space for the film's audience to analyse capitalism's internal relations as a deliberate form of alienation (on all levels – production, knowledge and somatic).

Godard extends this analysis to gender relations in the second segment, overlaying shots of a naked woman moving from her apartment to a staircase before going inside to take a phone call, with Sheila Rowbotham reading extracts from her groundbreaking feminist essay, 'Women: the struggle for freedom', first published in the leftist journal, *Black Dwarf*, 10 January 1969. According to Colin MacCabe, Godard was introduced to Rowbotham's text by Mo Teitelbaum. As Rowbotham recalls:

> His idea was to film me with nothing on reciting words of emancipation as I walked up and down a flight of stairs – the supposition being that eventually the voice would override the images of the body. This made me uneasy for two reasons. I was a 36C and considered my breasts too floppy for the sixties fashion. Being photographed lying down with nothing on was fine, but walking downstairs could be embarrassing. Moreover, while I didn't think nudity was a problem in itself, the early women's groups were against what we called 'objectification' [. . .] Why on earth did the pesky male mind jump so quickly from talk of liberation to nudity, I wondered . . . (MacCabe 2004: 219)

Although the use of nudity – including a close-up of the woman's pubic hair – could obviously be read as sexist and exploitative objectification, its overlay by a 'women's liberation' text highlighting such exploitation and confining gender categorisation might also set up a Brechtian distanciation, foregrounding the contradictions between text and image. As MacBean argues,

> what Godard is exploring in this entire sequence is not the ways of sexually titillating the film-goer, nor the beauty of the unadorned female body, but rather the complex and ambiguous relations among nudity, sex, and liberation – especially as these concern women. (1975: 106)

Rowbotham, however, is more ambivalent, recalling in her memoirs,

> As for Godard's intention of making a cunt boring, I cannot say except that a friend in International Socialism told me that his first thought had been 'crumpet' – until the shot went on and on and on, and he started to listen. (2000: 220–1)

The key issue here however is less the sound-image dialectic than the male voice-over that interjects and drowns out Rowbotham's text and reduces the complex particularities of her analysis to a rigid Marxist and Freudian party line (in this context, the twin shibboleths of patriarchal discourse). Thus, as she states that, 'Revolutions are about little things. It's here that the subordinated relates to the dominated. It's here that discontent focuses', the male voice-over narrowly reframes gender difference as a simple problem of labour relations: 'The problem of women. The problem of the farm labourers.' As Rowbotham continues: '. . . it's here the experience is felt, is expressed, articulated, resisted through the particular', the male voice chimes in with a banal binary opposition 'Man. City. Woman. Country.' Rowbotham then explains the problem as if drawing from personal experience: '. . . the particular pummels you gently into passivity, so that you can't even see beyond the little things, beyond the particular. We don't know how to find one another or ourselves.' The voice-over has a clever solution, switching the expected patriarchal associations: 'Freudian revolution. Marxist sexuality.' But Rowbotham has a far more complex class as well as gender analysis that necessarily includes family relations:

> Thus we are divided like all oppressed groups, divided by real situations and in our understanding and consciousness of our condition. We're in different classes, as we devour and use one another. Emancipation is often only the struggle of the privileged to improve and consolidate its superiority. The women of the working class remain the exploited of the exploited, oppressed as workers and oppressed as women. We're divided, too, because sometimes we're with families and sometimes we're without them. This makes us distrust one another, because the woman with a home and children is suspicious of the women with no ties; she sees her as a threat, a potential threat to her territorial security.

The voice-over's only response, echoing the calendar-like historicism of the little boy's history class, is that 'In 1919, Lenin refused four days of rest to women workers during their periods.' What Godard seems to be saying in this sequence is that unveiling the female body is truly liberating only if it also unveils the ideology that exploits women's nudity: capitalism/patriarchy on the one hand, but also the reifying dogma of Marx and Freud that reduces women to an object of analysis, not a viably active agent of their own liberation.

The third segment is the most important for our purposes because it uses silences (eighteen drop-outs during a nine-minute sequence) in combination with disjunctive images to undermine the political authority of a spoken text and its contextual corollary – the seeming impartiality of ruling class ideology conveyed through the liberal media. One of only two sections not interrupted by the young boy's lesson in socialism, the main speaker is a political news analyst, shot in black and white as if addressing the film audience while appearing on television. He seems to be inspired by broadcasters such as Sir Robin Day, who presented the news magazine show *Panorama* from 1966 to 2000, and also the current affairs programme *Tonight*, presented by Cliff Michelmore. However, unlike the latter examples, which represented the liberal mainstream, Godard's 'mouthpiece' is overtly fascist, almost Nazi in his hatred of the working class, students, long-haired youth and particularly immigrants. In that sense he's a hybrid amalgam of Enoch Powell and the National Front, hardly the kind of figure you would expect to see broadcasting regularly on nighttime television. Thus, commenting on the Third World, he states: 'If the people of India breed too fast, it's no concern of ours. We're supposed to feel sorry for them because they're starving. Well, some of us don't feel sorry: we feel glad. Let them starve, let them die.' But of course he has the usual caveat:

> Now, we're not racialists, but the way these people live is filthy, as you'd see if you went to look at the backstreets of Wolverhampton today. These people just don't accept our standards of civilisation. They live in filth and squalor. They breed like rabbits, and they suck our social services dry. Unless we put a stop to the influx of this horde, our cities will soon be so full of aliens that we won't recognise them . . .

It's hard to know if the speaker is a real ideologue stating his own beliefs or an extremely convincing actor reading Godard's text – according to MacBean, Godard's programme notes indicate that the words are excerpted from speeches by 'Wilson, Heath, Pompidou, Nixon, etc.' (MacBean 1975: 111), thus implicating the Labour Party, the Tories, Gaullists and the Republicans in a common crypto-fascist ideology. However, MacBean is correct to note that

> the main point of this sequence is that the dissemination of information is not in the service of the people, but in the service of the ruling class, which controls the mass media and utilizes these resources to impose bourgeois ideology on the masses as a means of perpetuating control over them. And if the views expressed in the media are not normally so overtly and crudely fascist, it is simply because a cool, calm veneer of objectivity serves far better to lull the audience and to inculcate bourgeois ideology than would an aggressive harangue. But the goals are the same: to perpetuate the power and privilege of the ruling class and the exploitation and fragmentation of the working class. (1975: 111)

With that in mind, the sound drop-outs are a deliberate attempt to subvert this inoculation and interpellation by interrupting the speaker's diatribe in order to highlight an alternative Britain. Instead of the conventional newscast's use of cutaway shots to illustrate the speaker's argument, here they deliberately undermine it. As the newscaster complains that productivity and trade are being sabotaged by unofficial strikes and work-to-rules, Godard cuts to a silent shot of a delivery man outside a café, as if to show 'business as usual', and also underline the opposition between productive workers and the mass-media lackeys of the ruling class. Similarly, a tirade against the nation's youth – 'Aren't they filling their heads with a lot of fancy ideas that only give them an exaggerated idea of their own importance? They behave as if the world belonged to them, as if the world owed them a living' – leads to another drop-out over two street workers digging up the pavement with cars parked in the background. In this case at the end of the drop-out we hear the whispered command – '*Organise!*' This is actually an important cue because all of the silent inserts – depictions of street and farm workers, cows grazing in a field, passengers at an airport – always show individual workers, not the working class *as a class*. In other words, they seem unable to act collectively. The urge to 'organise' (which accompanies several of the inserts) is thus the necessary tactic for these workers to successfully resist the broadcaster's (and by extension, the establishment's) right-wing views. And make no mistake, the newscaster makes it clear that it's more than just a class war – it's real war:

> War's a nasty business: people are going to be killed. But I believe we must take this risk. In this kind of game, it's necessary to shoot and bomb. Sometimes it is necessary to burn women and children. Sometimes, to torture people. Sometimes, to slice their stomachs open and cut women's breasts off. Let's not kid ourselves: you fight wars to win them, by whatever means are necessary.

Another important role of the inserts is to disrupt the continuity of the newscaster's monologue so that after we return to the studio he has often progressed to another topic and we are left playing catch-up, but at the same time he is also the victim of an external irrational cut. In a 1976 interview with *Cahiers du Cinéma* on the subject of Godard and Miéville's 1976 TV miniseries, *Six fois deux / Sur et sous la communication*, Deleuze applied Godard's dictum that 'it's not a *just* image, just an *image*', to philosophical thought as a kind of stammering, opening up a conceptual vector to the plane of immanence. Thus:

> Philosophers ought also to say 'not the just ideas, just ideas' and bear this out in their activity. Because the just ideas are always those that conform to accepted meanings or established precepts, they're always ideas that confirm something, even if it's something in the future, even if it's the future of the revolution. While 'just ideas' is a becoming-present, a stammering of ideas, and can only be expressed in the form of questions that tend to confound any answers. Or you can present some simple thing that disrupts all the arguments. (Deleuze [1976] 1995: 38–9)

Deleuze argues that language has become a system of instructions instead of a means of conveying information, much like the dogmatic, fascist rhetoric of Godard's newscaster. As a result we need to reverse the basic schema of information theory which advocates for a maximum of information at one extreme, with noise and interference relegated to the other. In the middle is redundancy which, while reducing information, at least provides a buffer against noise. It's at this point that Deleuze makes the case for Godard's silences, because

> we should actually start with redundancy as the transmission and relaying of orders or instructions; next, there's information – always the minimum needed for the satisfactory reception of orders; then what? Well, then there's something like silence, or like stammering, or screaming, something slipping through underneath the redundancies and information, letting language slip through, and making itself heard, in spite of everything. ([1976] 1995: 41)

In this way sounds and silences ('aural images') take over a series of perceived images (which are always pragmatic, subtracting from the larger aggregate of images everything that doesn't interest us) as part of their struggle against power. Aural images/silences constitute the other side of perception as concepts and affects and set up unexpected conjunctions and relations with other images (thus Godard links grazing cows with street workers and street markets through his cut-aways from the newscaster). This is the equation of 'and' as opposed to 'either/or', for as Deleuze puts it,

> there are as many relations as ANDS, AND doesn't just upset all relations, it upsets being, the verb ... and so on. AND, 'and ... and ... and ...' is precisely a creative stammering, a foreign use of language, as opposed to a conformist and dominant use based on the verb 'to be'. ([1976] 1995: 41)

By artificially forcing the fascist newscaster to 'stammer' against his will, Godard turns his diatribe (and our reception of it) into a multiplicity or potential line of flight, for

> AND is neither one thing nor the other, it's always in between, between two things; it's the borderline, there's always a border, a line of flight or flow, only we don't see it, because it's the least perceptible of things. And yet it's along this line of flight that things come to pass, becomings evolve, revolutions take shape. 'The strong people aren't the ones on one side or the other, power lies on the border.' (Deleuze [1976] 1995: 45)

– i.e. where images become too full and sounds too strident.

Segments four and five are closely related as they form a counterpoint between workers and students responding in turn to contemporary social problems. Thus segment four focuses on a group of politically aware workers (all men) from the Cowley plant as they discuss the dehumanising and alienating conditions of accelerated work quotas, the lack of scheduled break times, piecework, the strain of maintaining night time shifts and the complete ineptitude of the Labour Party to bring about viable change. As one worker puts it,

> You can never overcome industrial problems whilst they belong in the hands of the employing class. The only way that you can ever overcome any industrial problems, indeed, in this country is the question of the property relationship of the industries concerned.

Interestingly, the camera pans around the room but never shows us the face of the speaker at any given time, only his listening audience, perhaps in order to generalise the points made in order for the audience to apply them to all types of working conditions. Only towards the end does it single out a man with a West Country accent who summarises and consolidates the discussion by stating:

> Perhaps they're trying to solve this economic crisis at the expense of the working class as they always have done. Ramsay MacDonald done it: he cut the dole in 1931. You've got the Tory party that is swinging rapidly to the right, which will be under the leadership of Enoch Powell, which will be a right wing, racialist government of the type that Hitler had in Germany. So what's before the working class? Do we carry on supporting these tired old traitors? No, we can't. What is needed in this crisis is the building of a new political party for the working class. A political party that is committed to Marxism, that is committed to Communism, that is prepared to lead the working class in their struggles to overcome all these other parliamentarians.

This is the moment when *British Sounds* pulls all its threads together and points out the path to be taken through the worker who matches concrete experience of the situation at hand with a concrete analysis of the situation. Godard, perhaps inspired by Rocha, then has a woman's voice-over expand this localised conflict to a global level: 'Vietnamese people's struggle is the first wave in the tide of world revolution, the culminating point of the common struggle of all labouring men.'

This turned out to be Godard's favourite group of discussants in the film because the workers were finally able to speak for themselves rather than be spoken for through the words of Marx or Mao. Unfortunately the same cannot be said for the students, for as Gorin commented at the time:

> Take two sequences, the workers' discussion and the students' discussion; they are treated in exactly the same way. The idea was that from these confusing things, something progressive could be worked out. There is something which is really *pushing* in these discussions and it is going to change society. But the way we show it is very liberal and paternalistic, because the way these things are done among workers and students is absolutely not the same. You can't look at the students and say,

'This is bullshit, but these kids are nice and they're moving things.' It's absolutely disgusting from a political point of view, to say that. You have to say, 'This is bullshit. You should do something else, act some other way.' (Cited in draft version of Goodwin et al. 1970: 46)

By filming at the University of Essex (one of Britain's more activist colleges at that time), Godard probably expected a far more politically savvy group of student radicals than the 'People's Poster Brigade' that he filmed making posters and re-writing the lyrics of Beatles songs such as 'Hello, Goodbye', 'Honey Pie' and 'Revolution'. Although the latter activity could be seen as a playful example of Situationist *détournement* . . .

'You say Nixon, I say Mao. You say . . .'
'No, that doesn't go.'
'. . . say US, when I say Mao.'

. . . it never deconstructs the original songs' ties to the commercial music business and their iconic status as Beatles tunes. Why not perform, say, Gil Scott-Heron's 'The Revolution Will Not Be Televised' and actually broadcast it on TV, something that Godard and Gorin would no doubt have appreciated? Godard didn't necessarily blame the students' lack of political awareness but rather his own lack of foregrounding the reasons why:

It was [. . .] correct to include the man giving the speech on TV, representing the government voice – it was correct to put it in the middle of the picture, but we should have explained *why* it is placed in the center. We should have pointed out that the ruling class ideology organizes all of the other voices, and that if the students are speaking in such a way it is because of the relationship (economical and ideological) with this center. This is how society works. (Cited in draft version of Goodwin et al. 1970: 45)

Instead, the most important and acute political statements in this section come from a woman's voice-over as one of the female students paints a poster: 'The Party controls the gun. Production controls consumption and distribution. If a million prints are made of a Marxist-Leninist film, it becomes *Gone with the Wind*.' Then, as we see that the poster states, WHAT AM I DOING HERE?, she states the film's central message:

During the projection of an imperialist film, the screen sells the voice of the boss to the viewer. The voice caresses and beats into submission. During the projection of a revisionist film, the screen is the loudspeaker for a voice delegated by the people which is no longer the voice of the people. In silence, people see their own disfigured face. During the projection of a militant film, the screen is no more than a blackboard, the wall of a school offering concrete analysis of a concrete situation. In front of that screen, the living soul of Marxism, the students criticise, struggle, and transform.

As if to stress the fact that cinema and TV are social practices fully tied up with the class struggle (and thus must be analysed as such), segment six ends the film with a bloodied hand and arm (Godard's own), reaching to grasp a red flag lying against a field of snow-sprinkled mud. As he clutches and waves it triumphantly, the soundtrack is filled with revolutionary songs from several countries before we end with a reprise of the fist smashing through multiple Union Jacks as a male voice and a female voice jointly call for solidarity, especially in the universities: 'Solidarity with the struggle of the revolutionary students and teachers at the London School of Economics against the Gestapo of the humanist university.' Then, as a colour-tinted red flag waves over black and white footage of winter trees we hear the singing of *'We want our revolution now! We want our revolution now!'* (from Peter Brook's 1967 film adaptation of Peter Weiss's play, *Marat/Sade*) before ending with a rebel-rousing text on the Union Jack: NO END TO CLASS STRUGGLE.

What's been lacking so far in the Group's linguistic and class-based 'return to zero' has been an acknowledgement of the need to break away from its ingrained Eurocentrism and recognise the need to acknowledge the difference (but also the interconnectedness) between 'here' (Global North) and 'elsewhere' (Global South), the main topic, as the title suggests, of Godard and Miéville's *Ici et Ailleurs* (1976). As John Drabinski rightly argues,

> The film's title, always our first frame, is everything. It names not the theme, but the function of the cinematic language to follow. Image and sound, *the film is itself* 'here and elsewhere'. That is, the film is concerned with two competing issues clustered around its title: the *here and elsewhere* of the image *and* the *here and elsewhere* of a representation haunted by, yet never responsive to, death. (2008: 150)

Moreover, as Drabinski also points out, following Deleuze's stress on AND (as opposed to 'either/or') as the manifestation of the interstice or 'in-between' as the vector/movement of the multiplicity-as-becoming, it's the '*et*' of the title as creative stammer that holds the secret to the meaning of the film.

The project began in November 1969 when Godard and Gorin, along with cameraman Armand Marco, were approached by the Information Service Bureau of Fatah (at that time the most important political wing of the PLO, Palestine Liberation Organisation) to make a film about the Palestinian revolutionary movement, to be shot in refugee camps in Jordan, Lebanon and Syria during a three-month period in the spring of 1970. Antoine de Baecque's *Godard: biographie* recalls that,

> contacted by the Arab League via Hany Jawhariyya, Fatah's 'official' filmmaker, Godard received an order in November 1969, in the amount of $6000, as well as, in due time, the ability to film under the protection of Fatah, who put guides and interpreters at their disposal. (de Baecque 2010: 469, translated and cited in White 2013: 63)

The film was to be called *Jusqu'à la victoire* (*Until Victory*) with a subtitle – *Méthodes de pensée et de travail de la révolution palestinienne* (*Thinking and Working Methods of the Palestinian Revolution*) – and was originally designed as a film tract on the lines of the other Dziga Vertov Group polemics, which were based not on the idea of 'making a political film' but 'making a film politically', the concrete analysis of a concrete situation in order to show specific political struggles in order to actively transform them rather than simply represent them.

Unfortunately, before Godard and Gorin could show their incomplete footage to the *fedayeen* in order to include their feedback in the finished film, the Black September massacre perpetrated by King Hussein's Jordanian troops in Amman resulted in thousands of Palestinian deaths, including almost all the participants in the film. What had been planned as a work of great immediacy designed to herald an imminent and inevitable victory – the triumphant emergence of a 'people *that has come*' – was suddenly transformed into an obituary destined for the historical archives. In a 1973 interview with Christian Braad Thomsen in the American film journal *Jump Cut*, Gorin explained the difficulty of finalising the film by editing the incomplete footage into a viable statement:

> We've had this film on our backs for two years, and it has passed through four or five stages of cutting. One of the interesting things about the film is our impossibility to edit it, but I think we've found some kind of creative possibility to reflect on the impossibility of editing the material. We plan to make four or five films, each lasting one and one-half hours out of the ten hours of material we have. They will be struggling films in the sense that we will honestly speak about the problems we have been facing in trying to film an historical process. (Thomsen 1974: 19)

Although Thomsen's follow-up question was, 'So these films will really be about the impossibility of finishing the film?' it turned out that *Jusqu'à la victoire* would become the raw material for a subsequent Godard–Miéville project under the aegis of their new, Grenoble-based studio-laboratory, 'Sonimage', which they established in the winter of 1973–4. The resultant film was, of course, *Ici et ailleurs*, which combined the original 16mm footage with chroma-keyed video-mixing, multiple images from TV monitors, intertitles, videotext and numerous sound drop-outs to create not only a self-critical analysis of the original film project but turned the Dziga Vertov Group's own 'didactic blackboard' strategy against itself – most specifically its Marxist-Leninist dogma.

The film is divided into three sections, creating a progressive shift from an immediate focus on 'elsewhere' as presence (the original *fedayeen* footage as a march towards victory), to 'here' (Paris) as the new presence (with Fatah relegated to a 'dead' 'elsewhere'), culminating in 'and' as an immanent multiplicity in its own right, divorced from both 'here' and 'elsewhere' and a potent weapon against the western appropriation of other people's struggles as a compensation for their own political failures. Part 1, which lasts for about seven minutes, gives the impression that the march towards victory is going according to plan and in a given order, for as Godard's voice-over states:

> We go to the Middle East. 'We?' In February, July 1970, there's 'I', there's 'you', there's 'she', there's 'he' who go to the Middle East amongst the Palestinians to make a film. And we filmed things in this order. She, you, he, I organised the film that way. First, of course, the people.

We then see a series of images of political speeches, guerrillas undergoing training, children doing calisthenics, two women loading and firing a bazooka, three men in red and white fishnet *keffiyeh* sitting and reading political pamphlets, all summed up by Godard: 'The people's will, plus the armed struggle, equal the people's war. Plus the political work equals the people's education. Plus the people's logic equals the popular war extended. Extended. Extended until victory of the Palestinian people. Until victory.'

Despite this surface veneer of impending success – the cathexis of weaponisation and ritual as certain signs of *intifadas* to come – there's an inevitable sense that all is not quite right. First we have a number of silences over intertitles proclaiming victory that culminate in another drop-out accompanying a green-tinted still photo of a dead Arab's face, eyes open, with a flashing digital text that reads: AMMAN SEPTEMBRE 1970.

Underneath is a smaller, fainter text, rendered upside down, that states:

UN SILENCE (flashing)
QUI DEVIENT
MORTEL (flashing)
PARCE QU'ON
L'EMPÊCHE

DE S'EN
SORTIR VIVANT (flashing)
(A SILENCE THAT BECOMES DEADLY BECAUSE IT'S PREVENTED
FROM BREAKING OUT).

The fact that 'silence', 'mortel' and 'vivant' are all flashing would seem to indicate that the silences will subsequently provide an index to the corpse (and by extension, the failed revolution) that haunts the rest of the film. Making this key subtext hard to read suggests that Godard and Miéville also want us to pay close attention to the images rather than take them at surface value. Thus, even though a subsequent flashing digital text (also in silence) tells us that ALMOST ALL THE ACTORS ARE DEAD another silent text proclaims DEATH IS REPRESENTED IN THIS FILM BY A FLOW OF IMAGES while another adds: A FLOW OF IMAGES AND SOUNDS THAT HIDE SILENCE, as if to argue that the true nature of death-as-abyss lies in the silences-as-interstices.

These texts are the core of the second part of the film, which transfers the 'here' to the daily life of a French family who witness the 'elsewhere' of the Palestinian struggle through western media – especially TV – and the constraints of typical working-class family problems as the father struggles to find work (while also attending political gatherings) while his resentful wife stays at home caring for their two daughters and doing the chores. As Irmgard Emmelhainz argues:

> The juxtaposition between France and Palestine creates a cartographic cognitive map of Palestine *seen from* the point of view of 'France'. The French family is depicted as a domestic gathering watching television in the living room, becoming the allegory of the *mediatised social space*, the site for the shared sensible, portraying the French as a community of viewers constituted by the television screen. It must be noted that the French family's living room is decorated with Palestinian *tatris* (embroidered tapestries and rugs). The shared sensible present in the artisanal souvenirs and in the televisual screen is the only dispositif available to access the Palestinian state of affairs from 'here' (France). (2009: 651)

On this limited level, the family thus represent a form of 'revolutionary tourism' via mediated TV imagery, whereby the Palestinian cause is a mere object of consumption by France's revolutionary left, in much the same way that Algeria had been France's political Other right up to the events of May '68 when the Charonne Métro massacre of 1962 was still prominently featured on posters and placards.[4] In all these cases, empathy (as opposed

---

[4] The Paris chief of police, Maurice Papon, ordered his troops to attack demonstrators in the station stairwells, crushing and killing nine demonstrators with heavy iron plates.

to direct action) is a passive case of seeing ourselves in the image of the Other. More importantly, however, the family also allegorises the filmmakers, who implicate themselves in the critique, especially when we see the husband and wife watching TV and Godard says in voice-over: 'Poor revolutionary fool.' We then cut to gun-wielding Palestinians on manoeuvres in the woods moving towards the camera (it's unclear whether this is a diegetic image that the couple are watching on TV or a non-diegetic insert in the form of a distancing device) and then back to the wife as Godard continues: 'Poor revolutionary fool. Millionaire . . . [Rear shot of three Palestinians manning a machine gun. Sounds of gunfire]. . . . in images of revolution.' He repeats the line over a shot of the husband before cutting to a flashing digital text – THINKING OF THAT AGAIN, HERE AND ELSEWHERE – which applies just as much to Godard and Miéville as it does to the couple and the film's audience.

Serge Daney sees the family sequences and the TV images as the main 'classroom' of the film, where the problematics of its politics and formal structure are both discussed and demonstrated, 'the "good place", the place that gets you away from the cinema and closer to the "real" (a real awaiting transformation, of course)' (Daney [1976] 2000: 116). Thus, in '*Ici et ailleurs* the family apartment has replaced the classroom (and television had taken the place of the cinema), but the essential remains. The essential: people giving each other lessons' ([1976] 2000: 117). As one might expect, in this case the lessons concern the relationship between images and sounds and consist of three key issues. The first is that film is a temporal medium that overrides the simultaneity of different spaces by turning everything – especially memory – into an uninterrupted chain of images – 'images à la chaîne' – an assembly line of images arranged for popular consumption much like the linear mechanics of the Cowley assembly line in *British Sounds*. Drabinski makes a key point here, noting that

> The production of memory as image means subjection to the logic and labor of the assembly line: a 'chain of images', 'arranging memories', 'chaining them in a certain order', all so that the *elsewhere* – in its cinematic, virtual *parousia* – becomes *here* as one 'rediscovers one's own image'. The filmmaker himself is the first betrayal of *elsewhere*; the spectator cannot but fall under the image's seduction. Seduction's pleasures obscure the Other's agreement or disagreement. (2008: 153)

Accompanied by three other workers, the husband and wife demonstrate this schema by pinning separate photographic images to a studio wall, each accompanied by a spoken title: 'The people's will'; 'Armed struggle'; 'Political work'; 'Extended war'; 'Until victory'. Godard's voice-over then explains the problem: 'Here, you see all the images together. At the movies you can't.' After cutting to a black screen, which gives us pause for thought, he continues: 'You see them separately, one after the other.' All five of the people then proceed to parade their image in front of a camera which then shows them as a linear temporal sequence. For Godard,

> All in all, time has replaced space and speaks for it. Or rather, space is recorded on the film in another form. And the film, which is a chain of images, gives a good account, through the images, of my double identity.
>
> Space and time. Each chained to the other like two production-line workers, where each is both the original and the copy of the other.

This Hollywood model is as true of Soviet film as Godard's own, so that all potential 'elsewheres' become harnessed to the controlling 'here' of the film auteur.

The second major issue is that 'the sound is too loud', which works on a number of levels throughout the film. The most obvious is when we see an extreme close-up of a Sony Integrated Amplifier as a hand reaches in to raise the volume of *The Internationale* from 0 to 10. Godard admits that, 'We did what many do, record the images with the sound too loud.' As the hand pushes the lever down to 0 everything goes silent as Godard gives us an example: 'Vietnam. Always the same sound, always too loud. Prague, Montevideo . . .' As *The Internationale* blasts up to 10: '. . . May 68 . . .' We then go from 0 to 10 several times as Godard recites a litany of political events – France, Italy, the Chinese Cultural Revolution, strikes in Poland, torture in Spain, Ireland, Portugal, Chile, Palestine. 'The sound so loud, it ends up drowning the voice it wanted to draw out of the image', an example of how sound is allied to doctrine just as silence acts as the interstice that shatters it. Another example is the emphasis Godard and Miéville place on Hitler's voice and image as they are laid over a series of video transitions from insert to full screen that cross-relate Golda Meir, Lenin and leaders of the 1936 French Popular Front via a sonic association with Hitler's rhetoric, encouraging us to jump to political conclusions that Godard sees all of these leaders as right-wing dictators instead of reading each individual image on its own terms. The subtext of this sequence would thus be that Israel treats the Palestinians in the same way that Hitler massacred the Jews. Godard and Miéville use a similar tactic using separate video monitors to link Richard Nixon, Moshe Dayan and Leonid Brezhnev as if to reveal a self-interested US/Israel/Soviet pact. As we shall see, the situation is far more complicated than that because Godard and Miéville extend this critique to their own practice. Firstly, their voice-overs indicate that the original Dziga Vertov Group footage wasn't authentically 'real' in the first place, that the Palestinian revolution is not only being staged for western viewers by Fatah but also aided and abetted by Godard and Gorin's superimposed rhetoric.

For example, as a young Palestinian girl starts to passionately recite a poem, Godard's voice-over gives the context, as if to give it documentary authenticity: 'In the ruins of the city of Karame, a little girl from Fatah recites a poem by Mahmoud Darwish: "I shall resist . . ."' However, as she recites, Miéville demythologises the scene, telling Godard (as if they were at the editing table together):

> First, you should talk about the set and the actor in the set. About the drama. Where does this drama come from? It comes from 1789, the French Revolution, and from the pleasure the Conventionnels of 1789 took in grand gestures and making their demands in public. That little girl is acting for the Palestinian Revolution, obviously. She is innocent, but perhaps this kind of drama is less so.

As if to reinforce the idea that it's all a staged spectacle, we hear a crowd roar with approval but we cut immediately to the French family watching a Germany vs Holland football match on TV, suggesting that the crowd noise is not from Palestine but overdubbed from the stadium.

Another example of pre-staging can be found in a sequence featuring a young Palestinian in a white *keffiyeh* who directly addresses the camera. Godard's voice-over informs us that she is a pregnant woman completely ready to give up her son to the revolution. However, Miéville's post-synched voice cuts in: 'That's not the most interesting thing in this shot. This is.' We cut briefly to a black screen as Godard says, 'Can you say it one more time?' We focus once again on the woman as Godard gives her instructions: 'Hold your head a little straighter. That's it.' Not only is the whole scene a contrived piece of theatre but, as Miéville points out,

> You always see the one who is directed and never the one directing. The one who commands and gives orders is never seen. Something else is wrong. You chose a young intellectual sympathizing with the Palestinian cause, who isn't pregnant but who agreed to play the part. Furthermore, she is young and beautiful and you remain silent about that. It's a short step from secrets of this kind to fascism.

The most important examples of the latter consist of two sequences featuring a small group of *fedayeen*. In the first, as the family watches TV, we have a brief sound drop-out as we cut to five men huddled together by the river. Godard's voice-over tells us the subject of their discussion: 'Near the Jordan, a small group of Fedayeen are trying to use debate to bind revolutionary theory and practice.' Then we hear a voice in French say: 'Speak more simply', as if guiding the discussion according to a pre-scripted model. However, as usual, Miéville tells us the truth:

> What are those Fedayeen saying? They are speaking about their links to the earth, using the example of digging a trench. And they're saying just this: 'In digging our soil, we bind ourselves to it more. And when the earth defends you, you become its lover.' So don't talk about practice and theory. They said: 'Make love to their earth.'

Then, as we cut back to the French family watching TV: 'They say: "Love" and say "Make".' In other words, instead of talking about theory and practice, they were talking about something far more ecosophical: the tying of their national liberation to an existential love of the land as a new singularity. As Guattari puts it in *The Three Ecologies*:

> Ecological praxes strive to scout out the potential vectors of subjectification and singularization at each partial existential locus. They generally seek something that runs counter to the 'normal' order of things, a counter-repetition, an intensive given which invokes other intensities to form new existential configurations. These dissident vectors have become relatively detached from their denotative and significative functions and operate as decorporealized existential materials. (2008: 30)

The sequences also include a group discussion, this time in the woods. Godard's voice-over immediately asks Miéville what they are saying and she informs him that their conversation focuses implicitly on their impending death:

> They say: 'In crossing the river, did you have difficulty or make mistakes?' 'There's one serious mistake. Since we always cross at the same place, we'll end up being spotted by the enemy guns and thus cause the end of the whole group.'

As their conversation continues in Arabic, Godard cuts in:

> I remember when we shot this. It was three months before the September massacres. It was in June 1970 and in three months, the whole little group will be dead. What's tragic, in fact, is that, here, they're talking about their own death. But nobody said that.

Ah, but they did: Godard never bothered to get it translated, for as Miéville states: 'No, because it was up to you to say it. And the tragic thing is, you didn't.' The scene then continues with Miéville giving further translations of their discussion: their fear that the enemy has spotted their entry point and that their lives are now at risk: 'That's why this kind of mistake should be avoided. That's why we shouldn't gather at one point. We don't want these passages to be individual, we want them big enough for two or three of our group to pass.'

Godard finally gets the point: 'It's true we never listened in silence to silence. We wanted to crow victory right away. Instead of them.' Miéville pushes the point home: 'We wanted to make the Revolution for them, because at that time, we didn't really want to make it where we are. Rather where we're not.' According to Michael Witt (2014: 321), when Godard revisited the original 1970 Dziga Vertov material with Miéville in 1973, he remixed the sound so that his own exegetic discourse was toned down so that he could hear the *fedayeen*'s dialogue. He then asked Elias Sanbar, his original interpreter in Jordan and Lebanon, to translate their conversation. According to Sanbar:

> We were stunned. He, because he hadn't asked me at the time to translate what these men were saying. And I, whose mother tongue it was, felt profoundly guilty that I hadn't heard a word, the theories and convictions having struck me deaf. It's by using this scene, and this discovery, that Godard constructed what for me is the strongest and most tragic sequence in *Ici et ailleurs*: the moving one in which Godard shows this scene and recounts in a broken voice how our voices had obscured those of the men that we were listening to, to the extent of wiping them out completely. (Sanbar 1991: 116)

This leads us directly to issue number three, which is, as Sanbar's testimony illustrates, the absolute necessity of placing one's trust in the revelatory potential of silence. Godard and Miéville are telling us that we must learn to see 'here', in order to hear 'elsewhere' and this necessitates turning down the sound of political dogma so that the Other can be heard. This is not possible through a binary 'either/or' system but through the autonomy of the AND between 'here' and 'elsewhere' that serves as an incommensurable death-as-abyss that destroys association between images in favour of differentiation, singularity and multiplicity. In *Cinema 2*, for example, Deleuze discusses *Ici et ailleurs* as the perfect example of this method but we have to be wary of misreading Godard's use of silences and interstices as strategies of *association*. Thus, as Deleuze points out,

> images like those which bring together Golda Meir and Hitler in *Ici et ailleurs* would be intolerable. But this is perhaps proof that we are not yet ready for a true 'reading' of the visual image. For, in Godard's method, it is not a question of association. Given one image, another image has to be chosen which will induce an interstice *between* the two. This is not an operation of association, but of differentiation, as mathematicians say, or of disappearance, as physicists say: given one potential, another one has to be chosen, not any whatever, but in such a way that a difference of potential is established between the two, which will be productive of a third or of something new. (1989: 179–80)

As the interstice/silence grows in autonomy, it allows us to get out of the chain of images (i.e. association) altogether: 'It is the method of BETWEEN, "between two images", which does away with all cinema of the One. It is the method of AND, "this and then that", which does away with all the cinema of Being = is' (Deleuze 1989: 180). The interstice-as-abyss is no longer a motor part of the movement-image, which the vector of action or sound leaps across, but instead

> the radical calling into question of the image (just as there is a silence which is no longer the motor-part or the breathing-space of discourse but its radical calling into question). False continuity, then, takes on a new meaning, at the same time as it becomes the law. (Deleuze 1989: 180)

In this sense, silences as AND in *Ici et ailleurs* work differently from the enforced stutters that interrupt the fascist newscaster in *British Sounds*, which simply challenge a right-wing political rhetoric with an alternative *spatialised* presence (the contemporary class role of domestic and immigrant workers). Here, the AND links images of death – epitomised by an 'abyssal' image of a burned Palestinian corpse that recurs throughout the film – with an unregainable time lost that serves to destroy all spatiality. It creates a distance without a relationship or identity, for there is literally no there 'there'. Instead, to compensate, we tend to over-focus on the specific image of the corpse, or images and references to Auschwitz and the holocaust as a means of historicising death as something locatable and localisable. However, the AND-as-silence is, in Deleuze's terms, a 'return to zero' as a pure time-image, a non-spatial haunting akin to what he calls the 'DREAM-IMAGE OR ONIROSIGN: an image where a movement of world replaces action' (1989: 335). Deleuze argues that this image has two poles: 1) Rich, overloaded images, like Godard and Miéville's video experiments which superimpose or fuse Hitler, Lenin and Golda Meir; or 2) Restrained, clear montage cuts – the 'images à la chaîne' that turn all spatiality into linear time. 'But,' argues Deleuze, 'whichever pole is chosen, the dream-image obeys the same law: a large circuit where each image actualizes the preceding one and is actualized in the subsequent one, to return in the end to the situation which set it off' (1989: 58). And so, once again, we return to topology, Brian Massumi's model of self-varying deformation, that Moebius strip-like biogram that constantly folds back into its starting point, only in this case difference as de-location isn't centred on coffee cups or the coffee itself but the bloodied corpse, seared by its own ghostly self-haunting.

CHAPTER 7

Silencing Interpellation: Gorin, Althusser and the Ideological State Apparatus

In his 1974 *Jump Cut* interview with Christian Braad Thomsen, Jean-Pierre Gorin discusses the circumstances of his fortuitous coming-together as Godard's collaborator in the Dziga Vertov Group: that just as the well-known auteur was leaving the world of cinema in order to become a political activist, the Maoist factory worker and former literary critic for *Le Monde* (he helped create its weekly literary supplement, 'Le Monde des livres') was looking to get involved in non-traditional film-making. As Gorin explains the situation as it was in 1968:

> Jean-Luc wanted to do a film with all the various groups in which people tried to live in new ways: groups involved with politics, music, theatre, etc. It was going to be a 24-hour film called 'Communications', and he asked me to make the Maoist part of it. So I started writing a script called 'A French Movie', based on the experience I had had for two years organizing political groups. I gave the script to Jean-Luc. It was an attempt to put political points into an aesthetic form, and it was never filmed. But all the films we made after '68 are in some way a transformation of this original script: *British Sounds*, *Pravda*, *Tout va bien*, etc. Jean-Luc brought a lot of reflections to the script and my own evolution with him also added things. (Cited in Thomsen 1974: 17)

Although the script for 'A French Movie' was the ostensible start of the Dziga Vertov Group, Godard actually directed the first films himself – *Un film comme les autres*, *British Sounds* and *Pravda* – but as Gorin points out, 'afterwards they were credited by the Dziga Vertov Group in order to point out that although the films are Jean-Luc's work, they were also a result of the theoretical discussions between the two of us' (cited in Thomsen 1974: 17).

These discussion were heavily grounded in Gorin's philosophical as well as political training. After receiving his baccalaureate in Philosophy in 1960, Gorin then enrolled at the Sorbonne, where he took part in the seminars led by a roll-call of philosophical giants: Louis Althusser, Jacques

Lacan and Michel Foucault (Ulman 2005: 35). It was through his studies with Althusser that he became well versed in the theory of 'The Ideological State Apparatus' (ISA) and its linguistic and cultural accessory, interpellation, both of which became central structural and ideological currents running through four important Group films: *Pravda* (1970), *Le vent d'est (Wind from the East*, 1970), *Lotte in Italia* (*Struggle in Italy*, 1971) and *Vladimir and Rosa* (1971). In all four cases, the use of silence acts as an intrusive stutter or multiplicitous AND that creates an epistemological rupture in the seeming uniformity of the ISA, sparking a deterritorialising vector into alternative modes of thinking and production.

As is well known, Althusser returns to Antonio Gramsci's theory of hegemony to rework Marx's fundamental Base/Superstructure definition of ideology, which argued that cultural phenomena – legal, political, religious, aesthetic, philosophic, and ideological forms – are determined by contradictions in the economic base – i.e. iniquitous class relations reinforced by the division of labour. For Marx, ideology is a *false consciousness* of these relations so that once economic production is revolutionised, a real consciousness of superstructural relations will be made apparent. Althusser reworked this dualism in favour of restructuring the ideological as a complex of practices and representations, whereby it has its own material existence in an *apparatus* (what Foucault would subsequently expand into the *dispositif*). Its main objective is to turn individuals into subjects so that any given subject's ideas exist only in his/her actions. These are in turn inscribed within social institutions, so that social being determines consciousness. Ideology is an *autonomous* level of production with an autonomous product: the consciousness of human subjects. Ideology (which has no history as it's an unchanging structure) therefore functions to secure the reproduction of the relations of production as a self-fulfilling prophecy:

> Ideology is conceived as a pure illusion, a pure dream, i.e. as nothingness. All its reality is external to it. Ideology is thus thought as an imaginary construction whose status is exactly like the theoretical status of the dream among writers before Freud. (Althusser [1969] 1971a: 159)

This reference to Freud and the dream-work is crucial, for as Althusser argues in *Pour Marx* (1965):

> It is customary to suggest that ideology belongs to the region of 'consciousness'. We must not be misled by this appellation which is still contaminated by the idealist problematic that preceded Marx. In truth, ideology has very little to do with 'consciousness', even supposing this term to have an unambiguous meaning. It is

> profoundly unconscious, even when it presents itself in a reflected form (as in pre-Marxist 'philosophy'). Ideology is indeed a system of representations, but in the majority of cases these representations have nothing to do with 'consciousness': they are usually images and occasionally concepts, but it is above all as structures that they impose on the vast majority of men, not via their 'consciousness'. (1990: 232–3)

Althusser's superstructure is overseen by two complementary forces, the Repressive State Apparatus (RSA) and the Ideological State Apparatus (ISA). The former is politico-legal, exercised through the judiciary system and state power, enforced via the police, courts, prisons and, if necessary, the military. The ISAs, which are fundamental to Gramsci's idea of hegemony or rule by consent, are furthered through religious practices, education, the family, trade unions, popular media and cultural institutions such as museums and archives. It is the ISA which is the *site* of class struggle because ideology functions through the 'representation' of the imaginary relationship of individuals to the real conditions of their existence. This is an effect of *misrecognition*, an inherently false relationship to the real conditions of social existence based on a false logic of one's social role and class. Thus the bourgeoisie see themselves not as exploiting capitalists but as an instrument of History. Ideology is thus a product of representations but it tries to hide this fact behind notions of common sense and self-evidence (Barthes's *doxa*). In other words, it's the sum total of taken-for-granted realities of everyday life: pre-given determinations of individual consciousness and the common frame of reference for the projection of individual actions. Although ideology takes an infinite variety of forms, it's important to understand that it is always contingent and that this contingency is always suppressed.

The latter is hidden behind ideology's main vehicle for spreading false representations, namely interpellation. The latter is a form of 'hailing', which absorbs us into the structures of language without our being consciously aware of it. Thus, say we are walking down a city street and someone shouts, 'Hey you!' We stop, turn around and call back, 'Are you talking to me?' 'Yes you!' In this way we are instantly drawn in to the structure of 'I = another', whereby we move from being the 'you' of the hailer's communicating 'I' to a reversal (but also a reinforcement) of that structure, whereby we are now the 'I' and the hailer is our 'you/Other'. Thus, although we imagine ourselves as being outside, even as originating, the ideological representations into which we are inserted we are actually 'misrecognising' ourselves as we are forever trapped within the prison-house of language. This is particularly prevalent in the case of revisionism (the main subject of *Pravda*), where the prison is constantly being repainted in new colours in order to camouflage its ideological cracks.

Althusser sees two possible resistances to this ideological 'fait accompli'. The first is Science, which he sees as an 'already there' containing no end point and no ostensible subject. Instead it imposes a subjectless system of representation on the world and opens up a new continent of knowledge – it *produces* problems rather than reduces them to a hegemonic status quo like ideology. The second, and obviously essential for Gorin and Godard's filmic strategies, is art. Placed midway between science and ideology as a kind of included middle (Deleuze and Guattari's plateau) art (at least before it is co-opted by the system) is not a relationship of identity but of difference, grounded, like Spinoza's ethics, in the body as much as the mind. As Althusser explains it in a famous passage:

> I believe that the peculiarity of art is to 'make us see' (*nous donner à voir*), 'make us perceive', 'make us feel' something which *alludes* to reality. [. . .] What art makes us *see*, and therefore gives to us in the form of '*seeing*', '*perceiving*' and '*feeling*' (which is not the form of *knowing*), is the *ideology* from which it is born, in which it bathes, from which it detaches itself as art, and to which it *alludes*. (Althusser 1971b: 222)

This has obvious Brechtian connections, because in an ideal world art makes visible, through alienation, distancing and foregrounding operations, the reality of existing ideology, allowing the artist to rupture it from within, to make films politically by applying montage at every level of the production process, not, like Eisenstein, ex post facto in the comforts of the editing room. As Althusser's pupil, Pierre Macherey, sums it up in relation to literature:

> By means of the text it becomes possible to escape from the domain of spontaneous ideology, to escape from the false consciousness of self, of history, and of time. The text constructs a determinate image of the ideological, revealing it as an object rather than living it from within as though it were an inner conscience. (Macherey 1978: 132)

Art, then, is seen by Althusser as a form of halfway house on the road from the misrecognition of ideology to the knowledge of science. However, as we shall see, Gorin and Godard are far more wary of art's seeming incorruptibility in this role, seeing it as an unreliable ally in their search for a viable political philosophy, for following the position of late Althusser, 'Philosophy is, in the last instance, class struggle in the field of theory' (1976: 37). In all four films discussed in this chapter, the sound drop-outs and extensive use of black screen act as interstices so that we can move from art to philosophy, or in the language of chaoids, from the plane of composition to the plane of immanence where knowledge is used to *transform* the world, not merely to understand it.

However, one should also point out that the Althusserian connection becomes highly problematised in the wake of May '68 when his brand of structural Marxism was attacked by a number of young leftist intellectuals due to his alliance with the PCF (French Communist Party) and its control over the trade union movement via the CGT. As a result, he was criticised by his Maoist disciples – Jacques Rancière in particular – at the École normale supérieure for being a revisionist and betraying the cause. In a letter to Maria Antonietta Macciocchi, dated 15 March 1969, Althusser defended himself, arguing that,

> This is simplistic because it is not a Marxist-Leninist explanation to believe in *the determining role of leaders* when a mass movement of these proportions is involved. The truth is that the entire working class, and not just its leadership, was not, in general, at all disposed to 'follow' the suggestions of the students, which were based more on a dream-experience than on an understanding of reality. (Macciocchi 1973: 309)

Although *Pravda* is a fairly straightforward (and uncritical) application of Althusser's principles to the Czechoslovakian context, we will see Godard and Gorin's ambivalent approach to the philosopher play out in *Le vent d'est* in the form of Anne Wiazemsky as a radical university lecturer, appropriately named 'Miss Althusser'. Wiazemsky's character teaches Marxism-Leninism to radical students and workers but is caught in a double bind between the controlling hand of a revisionist union official (who intervenes in the dissemination of her set texts by privileging specific books and chapters), and radical Maoist students (played off-screen by the cantankerous film crew) who berate their instructor for her lack of self-criticism. As a result, the prime analyst of the ISA and interpellation is symbolically accused of the exact same revisionism that structural Marxism professed to attack.

Filmed in Czechoslovakia seven months after the Warsaw Pact invasion (20–21 August 1968) overthrew Alexander Dubček's 'Prague Spring' reformist government and installed Gustáv Husák's hardline regime of 'Normalisation', *Pravda* is both an attack on reformism (not only Dubček's 'Socialism with a human face' but also US and Soviet imperialism), as well as a trenchant critique of contemporary documentary film practice as a whole. As Colin MacCabe argues, 'Every element of the film's construction denies the possibility of cinematic technology's privileged access to reality' (MacCabe et al. 1980: 114). Intended for West German television, it was a collaborative effort between Godard and Jean-Henri Roger as well as their cinematographer, Paul Burron, who surreptitiously filmed on the streets of Prague as well as directly off TV broadcasts from the Czech

National Television in Godard's hotel room. Roger left the project as the filmed footage was set aside in order to work on *Le vent d'est*, so that Gorin was able to join Godard to complete the editing.

The key to understanding *Pravda* is the fact that it failed to follow Dziga Vertov's expanded concept of film montage and was itself a grievous example of revisionism in both film form and content. As Colin MacCabe, Mick Eaton and Laura Mulvey point out,

> Whereas Eisenstein's theoretical writing suggested that montage was an operation limited to the moments of shooting and editing, for Vertov montage was a principle which had primacy in every moment of filming – the Dziga-Vertov group formulated this principle in the slogan: *Montage before shooting, montage during shooting and montage after the shooting*. (MacCabe et al. 1980: 42–3)

In this schema, there is no unified subject or object that precedes the camera's view of the world, no self-sufficiency that predetermines a political reading. While this has obvious connections to André Bazin's advocacy of deep focus (which highlights divisions that are internal to the image), Godard takes this a step further by dividing the image itself and enfolding it back into a dislocated mode of production. The latter reaches its apotheosis in *Tout va bien* where the factory workers at the Salumi plant were played by unknown, unemployed actors, not actual factory workers, in order to exacerbate the real-life economic contrast with the highly paid stars of the film, Yves Montand and Jane Fonda, whose characters are held 'prisoner' in the factory for a period of twenty-four hours:

> By employing actors on the economic breadline, relations of envy, jealousy and guilt were established between them and Fonda and Montand which provided some of the raw material of the film in a way that escaped any unification by the script and which, at the same time, would reproduce some of the features of the relations between militant workers and radical intellectuals. (MacCabe et al. 1980: 43)

The basic structure of *Pravda* is thus an application of this more radical dialectical method to its own inadequacies through a three-part critique of both film form and Czech revisionism. Even then, Godard didn't think much of it, stating in an interview that 'This is a garbage Marxist/Leninist movie, which is a good way of titling it. At least now we know what not to do anymore' (Carroll 1972: 54).

Drawing on writings by Mao and Brecht, the (failed) critique takes the form of a voice-over exchange of letters between the political tourist, Vladimir (Lenin) (which seems to be voiced by Gorin, although Wheeler Winston Dixon (1997) thinks that it's Godard himself) and his friend back home, Rosa (Luxemburg) (actress uncredited), based on a real-life correspondence between the two, although, as we shall see, Rosa isn't always politically coincident with her historical namesake. Part 1 of the film takes the form of a travelogue or tourist documentary shot in 'poor colour, West German film developed in Bulgaria', as Vladimir and Rosa's voice-overs reinforce, often to the point of redundancy, what we already see on-screen, albeit with an ideological layer. The revisionist reality of the situation is palpable from the beginning, for as Vladimir says, 'You often hear rearranged American tunes. They produce tooling, weapons, uranium, a lot of steel, trucks, locomotives, trams. A country that has joined the modern economy, then, a Western country.' Thus we hear a rearranged foreign language version of O. C. Smith's hit song, 'Hickory Holler's Tramp' (itself about prostitution) that is superimposed over shots of workers and factories; a billboard out in the sticks advertising 'Honeywell: Take the world by the tail'; shots of TV presenters 'wearing cashmere sweaters'; shots of suburban high-rise apartments similar to the HLMs in *Deux ou trois choses*; Vladimir's outraged observation that 'There are tanks – you hear me? – tanks watching the farmers!' and brightly coloured magazine covers on newsstands, including the *Tricontinental*, 'a magazine mailed from Prague by Cubans for militants in countries where it's banned'. Then, over a black and white still from the Terrytoons animation, we see the identical magpies, Heckle and Jeckle as the 'Ghosts of the Second International. They swoop like vampires on the Czech working class' (represented throughout the film by a red rose). Vladimir makes it clear that these crows have historical names: 'Yesterday, Bernstein and Kautsky; today Brezhnev and Kosygin. They shoot the people with their James Bond gun, painted red to cloud the waters for honest communists.'

Sound drop-outs are sparingly used in Part 1 because the sound-image dialectic does most of the foregrounding of revisionism on a very obvious level. However, there is a key moment of silence that effectively points the finger at the political unawareness of Prague's youth. Following shots of executive secretaries working in an office and a daytime shot of snowed-in country houses, we cut to an overhead angle down on a disco with teenagers dancing. Vladimir cynically says, 'These are students. In 1968, they danced all spring', before we cut to a silent outdoor shot of kids playing football in a fenced-in playground. As we pan left beyond the fence to take in a man walking on the adjacent suburban street, Vladimir's voice-over continues, 'This is fencing. The government use it to surround the people's property', as if to indicate that sports and leisure are just inoculations for the furtherance of the ever-confining status quo.

Vladimir then sums up their findings at the end of Part 1:

> What we've just seen, Rosa [animated footage of the crows in a tree, one waggling his 'ears'] is just the concrete situation in Czechoslovakia. [On two crushed roses in a puddle, i.e. the crushed proletariat.] Just impressions of a journey. Like Delacroix in Algiers or Chris Marker in the strike-torn factories of Rhodiaceta. *The New York Times* and *Le Monde* call it news. And I agree with you, Rosa, it's not enough. Why? Because it's only the knowledge perceived by our senses. Now one has to make the effort to rise above this perceptual knowledge. One needs to struggle to transform it into rational knowledge.

It's clear from this statement that Godard and Gorin are challenging Althusser's advocacy of art and perception as an antidote to the interpellating circumventions of the Ideological State Apparatus and instead see it as equally complicit in perpetuating revisionism. Instead, Rosa poses the question differently: 'What does the effort involved in fighting mean to us?' Over another insert of the crushed red rose in a puddle, Vladimir responds: 'It means analyzing this concrete situation. We're dealing with sick people. It's obvious. But what sickness is it?' Vladimir argues that it's a sickness linked to betrayal, 'the revision of Marxism by pseudo-communists. [. . .] To fight the revisionist traitors, we must unmask them. [BLACK SCREEN.] Learn their story. Know them. Going from "feel" to "know", what does it mean to us?' In other words, Vladimir declares the next logical step required to build on Althusser's resistant role for art. Deleuze would see this as the need to shift from the plane of composition (affect, sensation) to the plane of immanence (concepts). In short, as Rosa puts it, 'It means: start editing the film', except it also means editing the sounds and images differently in order to see them for what they really are:

> *External* manifestations of communist reality [on the crushed red roses in puddle] and unreality in Czechoslovakia. [. . .] Show these images and sound on an anti-revisionist line. Establishing a new contradictory relationship. Stripping bare the internal causes, getting to know the substance of things which is called 'the current situation in the Czech Socialist Republic'.

This is of course the basic role of Part 2, which is not only a critique of revisionism and interpellation but also Occidentalism (especially humanist cinema) as equally complicit. Perhaps the best example of this 'concrete analysis of a concrete situation' is the opening sequence of this section, which focuses on a Skoda car parked at, or driven through, various locations as a specific case of practical revisionism. The crew rented the car at Prague airport and it is supposed to symbolise the idea of 'the people's car', for the company was nationalised in 1945 immediately after the defeat of the Nazis. However, as one might expect, the car was rented from an American company – Hertz – who exploit the people's product for western profits. As Vladimir explains it:

> This Skoda now belongs to Skoda workers. And the Czech people who seized the means to produce it. Hertz and Avis, firms on the imperialists' side, don't rent cars for charitable reasons. Hertz and Avis do it for a profit. Hertz and Avis profit indirectly, with the complicity of Czech leaders, from the overwork of Skoda workers demanded by leaders. [...] In practice, the more socialist Skoda workers work, the more imperialist shareholders of Hertz and Avis earn. Revisionism has worked. The theories of Ota Šik and Liberman have become those of Galbraith and Servan-Schreiber. The market needs slaves and those of revisionist countries [BLACK SCREEN] are better trained.

Vladimir and Rosa extend this revisionism to basic modes of production, equating Taylorism (aka Fordism) with Stakhanov, both serving to automatise the workplace to maximise profits. The result: 'at the Northern European bank, Paris, the golden rouble morphed into the Euro-dollar, supreme stage of financial imperialism. The rouble had the idea before the dollar. Result: Novotný or Dubček, whichever, worker or student, are like slot machines.'

Vladimir and Rosa's critique of revisionism includes cinema, specifically what they call the 'suicidal humanism' (as opposed to 'revolutionary will') of film-makers like Vera Chytilova who reduces issues of freedom and non-freedom to individual will (while comfortably working within the state system). Meanwhile, Milos Forman is making a film for Paramount (presumably *Taking Off* with Buck Henry, although it was actually released by Universal), and for Vladimir, 'Paramount is Novotný' (the anti-Dubček hardliner). Western culture is clearly the weapon of modern revisionism and because Czechoslovakia is now a 'people's democracy' they inevitably serve up cinematic pulp in the form of Bernard Borderie's popular *Angélique* (1964), currently playing at the Orlik Cinema. As Vladimir states, even though it's doubtful that the working class want to see *Angélique*, 'here, as in Hollywood, they make films for the masses. The people are the target, not the source. We criticise their faults, but never from their standpoint. We make the same films as the people's enemy.'

Part 2's single sound drop-out illustrates this point by drawing a clear distinction between class *being* and class *position* and the need to be aware of the difference. The sequence opens with a factory worker in a machine shop accompanied by a loud, alienating machine noise, intercut with an aerial shot of a street car terminus circle, as if to underline the Hegelian circularity of practice and knowledge as it reaches higher levels of overcoming. Vladmir acknowledges the effects of reform on working conditions:

> Here the demands of the French CGT, English shop-stewards and Italian activists have been met. No infernal rates here. Crèches, the same housing for all, but every day, as in Paris, New York, Stockholm every day, but every day, as in Paris, New York, Stockholm, Madrid, every day is work-travel-sleep.

We end on the street car circle as if to underline the shift from Hegel's transforming synthesis to a return of the same. Suddenly, the machinist turns off the machine and the loud sound cuts out, triggering an alternative vector in the fight against revisionism. The worker makes an adjustment to his machine as Vladimir continues:

> Class being, class position. To be a revisionist is to become a class being again. How does one become a class being? By refusing to fight about class positions. By refusing fight-criticism-transformation. By refusing to fight right-wing red deviationism in the name of left-wing red proletariat. Moreover, Rosa, there's the concrete evidence

– as interviews with workers and peasants will show.

So what is the solution? The answer is to create a radical discrepancy between sound and image. Intercutting a shot of Paul Burron pointing his camera at the audience as he holds up a copy of Mao's 'Little Red Book' with intermittent black screens, Vladimir lays out the plan for the film's last section: 'On a sick image [in this case Burron] put a sound that is not sick. Part 3: put a right sound with a wrong image to first find a right image.' We cut to the close-up of the red rose: the 'right image'. 'That's what we'll do now, Rosa.' Rosa then puts it in concrete Maoist terms: 'Use the Marxist-Leninist law of the unity of opposites to observe a socialist society.' The sound immediately cuts out as we see a cartoon of a revolutionary worker against a red flag with a superimposed text – REVOLUTION VIVE. He holds a hammer (his arm bearing the word 'Mao') and sickle (bearing 'Tse Toung'), as if, via adherence to Marxism-Leninism, they will now be used as weapons for revolution, not revisionist attacks on the worker. On a superficial level, silence is thus used to highlight the contrast between revolutionary praxis and reactionary revisionism but is this massive statement of the obvious not a case of still more revisionism in the guise of a self-conscious political film, not a film made politically?

This argument is at least borne out when we quickly realise that these so-called 'right' sounds are merely a series of Maoist texts applied to issues such as the re-education of the intellectuals, for as Rosa argues,

> The proletariat, after seizing power, must remake intellectuals in its image and train a contingent of intellectuals in its service. This is key to the establishment of the proletarian dictatorship, key to keeping the proletariat dominant in ideology and culture. This task involves a radical revolution in teaching. [...] We must take big steps. Send students and teachers into production. Condemn bourgeois theory of abstract knowledge. Systematically ask the question: for whom and against whom? Denounce all academic leading lights committed to revisionism. Spread propaganda groups throughout universities.

Significantly, this re-education includes a didactic sequence related by Rosa on Lenin's land reform lifted almost word for word from the subsection, 'Do your own thing and let nature do the same', from Brecht's *Me-ti: Book of Interventions in the Flow of Things*, a collection of essay fragments on a wide variety of topics. Lenin's introduction of new iron ploughs to replace inefficient wooden ones led to an increase in food production – therefore benefiting all farmers, rich and poor – but at the expense of the poor farmers' ability to sustain their small plots, even though they were encouraged to keep them functioning. In Brecht's account Lenin is now called Mi-en-leh, whose message was:

> You want the land because of the corn; now give up the land because of the corn! In other words: If you give up your own little strips of land, you'll get more corn. That was the truth. Soon huge farms were formed, bigger than the former estates. After a while, the more prosperous farmers also had to join these farms, since they couldn't get workers any more for wages and their fields delivered little corn, because the old wooden ploughs didn't turn over enough earth. Thus Mi-en-leh realized his programme by doing his own thing and letting nature do the same. (Brecht 2016: 121)

This discourse is overlaid on several images of Czech farmers, including a night shot of two men standing on a hayrick, but the shots themselves reveal little or nothing about the concrete nature of Czech agriculture at that time. Instead, the text is everything, and even then it is riddled with contradictions, because Rosa the narrator is forced to admit that her namesake, Rosa Luxemburg, was highly critical of Lenin's policy: 'She said: Lenin is just the same. Power weakens the memory. He who arrives, forgets a lot. Lenin replied: I taught, now they are learning.' However, this isn't the whole story for, as Brecht reminds us, Rosa Luxemburg (aka 'Sa'),

> objected to Lenin's handling of land reform since, by allowing the small farmers to retain their small holdings, their misery increased as they discovered by themselves

how they could not compete with larger holdings, which could afford to mechanize on their own. Lenin argued that those who opposed land reform must discover for themselves the disadvantages of not enabling it under the new developing circumstances. (2016: 121)

Although *Pravda* separates the two 'Rosas', it tends to privilege the truth claims of its own characters because their discourse is presented in the context of a counter-revisionism, when an objective observer could accuse it of the same crimes of party line interpellation.

To their credit, Godard and Gorin know this, for the sequence ends with Vladimir declaring: 'Re-education of intellectuals. Do not say: nature. Say: dialectics of nature, cf. Friedrich Engels', accompanied by a long silence as we hold on a shot of the hayrick workers, as if to retroactively question the efficacy of Brecht's account of Lenin letting 'nature do its own thing' and instead read it dialectically according to specific circumstances. Vladimir seems to understand the problem towards the end of the film when he accuses Rosa of the same degree of dogmatism as revisionism itself:

Look, you're going too far, Rosa. You quote accurately, but with what? With half-fake images. [We zoom in on Paul Burron holding up his 'red book'.] You thought we'd grasp, by chance, the production links between image and sound. You were acting dogmatically, in fact, and in the end adopted a sloganeering style. You went one step forward. We ended up two steps back. Now we're here, let's look back. Czechoslovakia. We saw practically: 1: The sick man. We showed theoretically: 2: The sickness, revisionism. Concrete analysis of a concrete situation. We showed, without managing to go from theory to practice: 3: Marxism-Leninism. How to fight revisionism.

Because all three stages have resulted in failure, just as a red street car enters from the left and stops, its red paint filling the screen, Vladimir advocates for a Part 4: a new concrete situation: 'Class struggle. Fight between old and new. Between red revisionists and red Marxist-Leninists. The red of the proletariat.'

The essence of this new dialectic is the colour red, but as the accompanying use of silence shows, it's no longer a red associated with the blood shed by the workers' struggle, but red as a category that links up with other categories in much the same way that Deleuze's AND forms a vector with other multiplicities. This is actually an old gambit of Godard's for when critics from *Cahiers du Cinéma* noted that 'There is a good deal of blood in *Pierrot*', Godard famously replied, 'Not blood, red' (Godard [1965] 1972d: 217). Deleuze agrees, noting that

The formula in *Weekend*, 'It's not blood, it's red', signifies that blood has ceased to be a harmonic of red, and that this red is the unique tone of blood. One must speak and show literally, or else not show and speak at all. (1989: 182–3)

This is neatly illustrated by the recurring close-ups of the bright red livery of the Prague streetcars as they pull in and out of the station, filling the screen but also drawing attention to their flaking paint and fragments of graffiti, the 'sick' qualities of revisionism. As one might expect, some of the cars exit to the left (progressive radicalism); others to the right (revisionism), for as MacBean points out,

> Instead of merely using the red streetcar shot for its combination of 'local color' and abstract beauty (which is how Chris Marker uses an almost identical shot in his *Sunday in Peking*), Godard takes these elements as starting points – eminently cinematic ones – and links the abstract to the concrete while transforming the superficial aspects of local color into conceptual tools for probing deeper into the 'red of socialism' in Czechoslovakia. (1975: 153–4)

In this way, Vladimir's earlier statement that, 'We're in a socialist country. Socialist means red. Red for the blood of workers killed in its liberation' is superseded by 'There were fights between reds, red from the left and red heading right', the latter accompanied by a sound drop-out over the side of the street car, as if to replace the earlier revisionist discussion with the new focus on categories as themselves a form of social practice.

Between alternating sound drop-outs and images of Burron behind his camera and workers at their machines (effectively equating film itself with material forms of production), Vladimir's voice-over tells us that right ideas come from three forms of social practice: struggle for production, class struggle, and scientific experimentation. Rosa agrees: 'Man's social existence determines his thoughts' and over a shot of a factory worker Vladimir sums it up: 'Shed your illusions and prepare to fight revisionism.' The film then cuts to a close-up of its only 'true' image, the red rose, as Rosa engages in yet another Marxist-Leninist interpellation by proclaiming: 'Long live the thoughts of Mao Tse-tung!'

Fortunately, the film doesn't end there for the closing image is an angle on a red flag fluttering in the breeze on the driver's side of a car as it speeds through the countryside. On the soundtrack we hear a French rendition of *The Internationale* in competition with a loud Soviet revolutionary hymn. The French singer seems to be winning out as the hymn fades but suddenly the sound drops out entirely and we are jolted out of our identification with the red flag as a revolutionary symbol. It's then that we notice, like the red flag at the end of *British Sounds*, that the banner has no yellow hammer and sickle embellishment so it is untainted by Soviet or Chinese ideological dogma, setting us up for a future people 'yet to come', ready to challenge both interpellation or its corollary, revisionism. Instead, we have pure categories, pure ideas, pure philosophy, but not at the expense of social practice. Maybe *Pravda* isn't a garbage Marxist-Leninist movie after all, largely because it's not really a Marxist/Leninist movie *per se* but a subtle critique of one.

In his *Godard: A Portrait of the Artist at Seventy*, Colin MacCabe argues that *Le vent d'est* 'is the most experimental of the series of Maoist films; it is also the most coherent in its application of Althusserian politics' (2004: 225). As we shall see, this is true on multiple levels, ranging from the film's attack on bourgeois (read: Hollywood) and revisionist cinema as well as its own self-deconstruction as a film 'made politically', expressed, as usual, by a combination of silences and intertitles. Based on a script by student leader Daniel Cohn-Bendit and developed by Sergio Bazzini and Gianni Barcelloni, *Le vent d'est* was filmed on location and at Elios Studios's far western town setting with interiors shot at De Paoli Studios between May and June 1969 (Lesage 1979: 104). It was originally intended to be a Marxist spaghetti western whose main plot focused on a mining strike. The casting of Gian Maria Volonté – Clint Eastwood's co-star in Sergio Leone's *A Fistful of Dollars* (1964) and *For a Few Dollars More* (1965) – would not only guarantee the film a modicum of box office success but also give it some credibility within the revisionist western genre. However, Godard and his original collaborators – Gérard Martin and cinematographer Mario Vulpiani – feared that the subject matter would be easily co-opted by Hollywood narrative conventions, as if John Ford's 'Cavalry Trilogy' – *My Darling Clementine* (1946), *Fort Apache* (1948) and *She Wore a Yellow Ribbon* (1949) – were allowed to colonise the content of a radical film like Octavio Getino and Fernando E. Solanas's *Hour of the Furnaces* (1968). As MacCabe and his collaborators argue,

> Insofar as the film would preserve the same relationship with the audience as traditional Hollywood cinema, it little mattered what the content of the film would be. What was necessary was the disruption of the traditional organization of Hollywood cinema so as to investigate how images found their meaning within specific articulations determined by ideological and political struggles *and* to engage the film viewer in that investigation. Only through such an engagement could there be a possibility of making a political film. (MacCabe et al. 1980: 61)

Although Godard was the film's ostensible director, according to Dixon 'shooting was hindered by political and artistic differences between the various collaborators' (1997: 114). This was largely the legacy of the student uprisings of May '68, which had led to a rabid distrust of representative bodies and any kind of artistic production determined by hierarchical decision-making. The latter controlling mechanisms were replaced by direct democracy, whereby all decisions were made through unwieldy and completely unmanageable mass meetings that tended to be dominated by a 'more leftist than thou' (or, more accurately, 'more Maoist than thou') self-righteousness. As MacCabe argues,

> Whatever their disbelief in institutions of representative democracy, the anarchists did not have a problem with representation as such; they wanted a left-wing Western which would be able to represent the class struggle in the most popular of genres. The Maoists, schooled in Althusser and Brecht, wanted none of this. To repeat the declaration from *British Sounds*, 'If you make a million prints of a Marxist-Leninist film then you get *Gone with the Wind*'. (MacCabe 2004: 224)

Godard restored order by bringing in Gorin and the two completed the shoot and collaborated on the editing, which sarcastically included a scene depicting the unruly crew 'scratched out' by a *pellicule brossé* that would have made Maurice Lemaître proud.

In the final version, the original 'content' – the strike as political action – is referenced solely through voice-overs (along with a number of other subjects, such as how to understand the meaning of an image) while the actual diegesis is reduced to an absolute minimum (often unrelated to the subject of the voice-overs) with almost no synchronous dialogue except for direct addresses to the camera through the readings of political texts. Thus Cohn-Bendit's original strike is relegated to the film's opening scene where, in typical Brechtian fashion, Godard has the story briefly narrated in the third person by an anonymous woman and the Union Delegate while the camera lingers for almost eight minutes on Wiazemsky and her lover, their hands chained together, lying in a field. The female voice informs us about a strike that took place in her childhood at an aluminium mine owned by the Alcoa Company near Dodge City, during which the workers locked up her uncle in his office. The Union Delegate protests: 'Listen, you're jumping to conclusions. Think it over. Things don't just happen. There was already general discontent about the bad working conditions.' For anyone not used to a Godard film, the overlaying of the voices on the two lovers would suggest that they express their inner thoughts and reminiscences, as befits a typical psychological representation of characters. Of course, we know better and immediately suspect that the sound and image are truly discrepant, setting the tone for the rest of the film where another woman's authoritative voice-over represents the voice of truth (i.e. a somewhat bullying Maoist political correctness), a clear development from Vladimir and Rosa's amateurish attempts in *Pravda*.

Cohn-Bendit's original western characters are now mixed and matched to create six different class and cultural stereotypes taken from different historical periods. Volonté's Cavalryman clearly represents the ruling class and it is he who guides the group single-file through the woods and across fields, leading either on foot or on horseback, to an unnamed destination referred to cryptically as 'the camp', with the sinister allusion to concentration camps. The main villain of the piece, because he is a revisionist ally of the ruling class, is the well-dressed Union Delegate (Paolo Pozzesi), who not only sells out the unions and the Communist Party but also corrupts all dialogue and communication for his own ends – in other words he is the absolute essence of interpellation. Thus at one point he reads aloud from *L'avenir du parti communiste français*, by Waldeck Rochet, the PCF leader who denounced the May '68 uprisings while at the same time supporting Dubček's Prague Spring. The text sums up the revisionist line that the film attacks so vehemently:

> The task of the new political power of the working class and its allies is to create a new economy and a new way of life, a socialist way of life. The realization of this gigantic and exciting task requires the broadest and most active participation of the masses in the management of public affairs. Socialism does not only mean the liberation of the worker from capitalist exploitation. It represents, and it must create, a democracy superior to all bourgeois democracies. Encouraged by the results achieved so far, and knowing the road which is still left to travel, we shall put all our energy into the fight and bring to a victorious end the work of uniting the lifeblood of the nation.

As one might expect, the last line is almost drowned out by an off-screen voice shouting, 'That's wrong.'

The bourgeoisie are represented by a young woman in a flounced petticote (Cristiana Tullio-Altan, the future star of *Lotte in Italia*), who seems to have stepped right out of a Monet painting. She is the epitome of restrained good manners and elegant decorum but is also featured at the beginning as Tullio-Altan the actress being made up for her role, as if to deliberately defamiliarise her character as an elegant bourgeois *type* that one would find in a Hollywood period film. The same is true of the representative of the oppressed Third World, the film's ostensible Native American played by the Andy Warhol impersonator, Allen Midgette, who is also getting made up alongside Tullio-Altan, only this time his thick, brightly coloured 'warpaint' would be more at home on a Jackson Pollock canvas than on a film set. Finally, in addition to playing 'Miss Althusser', Anne Wiazemsky plays a young *révolutionnaire* in a white petticoat whose lover – a dapper young man in green jacket and magenta trousers – ends up allying politically with Midgette's 'Indian'.

Although *Le vent d'est* creates an intricate weave between sound and image, diegetic action and authoritative voice-overs (it would probably take a whole book to do the film full justice), it does have a fairly concrete structure (with accompanying vignettes) announced through silent intertitles. Part 1 is entitled 'Mechanism' and is sub-divided into seven sections: 'La Grève' (The Strike); 'Le Délégué' (The Union Delegate); 'Les Minorités Agissantes' (The Active Minorities); 'L'Assemblie Générale' (The Mass Meeting); 'La Répression' (The Repression); 'La Grève Active' (The Active Strike), and 'L'État Policier' (The Police State). Around the fifty-minute mark, the authoritative woman's voice-over announces the beginning of Part 2:

> You have made a film. How did you make it? Now criticise, now fight, now transform. Don't forget it's difficult for any individual to avoid mistakes. To correct them we must move towards a Marxist education. Start again from the beginning, with the people. Be critical of your lack of liaison with the masses.

Let's examine two sequences from each of the two parts in order to illustrate the difference between the presentation of mechanisms and the concrete analysis of concrete situations. Following the opening sequence – the verbal description of the strike in counterpoint to shots of Wiazemsky and her lover lying in a field – we transition to the cavalryman keeping watch on the roof of a run-down building as the female voice-over announces the next phase of the film – self-criticism:

> Today the question of what is to be done is one the militant filmmaker cannot ignore. For them it is no longer a question of choosing a path, but of determining what must be done practically, practically, on a path the history of revolutionary struggles has taught them to recognise. Yes, what is to be done? Make a film, for example. That means asking oneself, 'Where are we at?' What does asking where we are at mean for a militant filmmaker? It means first of all opening a parenthesis and finding out about the history of revolutionary cinema.

As if to encourage a vector of critical analysis, the sound drops out for fourteen seconds as we cut to Tullio-Altan and Midgette as they are being made up for their roles as the young bourgeoise and the 'Indian'. The voice-over then cuts in to announce:

> Victory of revolutionary cinema, 19 July 1920. After the speech by Comrade Lenin at the 2nd World Congress on the main stage of the Comintern, Comrade Dziga Vertov declares to the tribune, 'We Bolshevist filmmakers know cinema does not exist outside of the class system. We also know the act of filmmaking is secondary and our aims are quite simple: to see and show the world on behalf of the proletariat revolution.'

As the camera frames Tullio-Altan in a tight close-up, Vertov's statement continues: 'It is the people who make history. And yet the films of the western hemisphere only portray elegant ladies and gentlemen.' As if on cue, she smiles at the camera, knowingly representing both a bourgeoise persona and the passive actress following the auteur's directions. The voice-over continues,

> Demands are always placed on actors, under the pretext that they must focus on feelings and instincts, to show only the corrupt ideas held by the bourgeoisie and to unscrupulously represent a degenerate bourgeois way of life, under the cover of their makeup.

In this way Tullio-Altan is presented as both a self-fulfilling prophesy of the critique and a Brechtian distanciation for the audience's own self-critique as willing accomplices (after all, who doesn't like *Gone with the Wind?*).

If the first sound drop-out helped to conceptually introduce the 'Victory of revolutionary cinema', the second serves to frame two examples of defeat, once again over the actors being made up. The first example, often used by Godard, is that of Eisenstein who, deeply influenced by 'the American imperialist' D. W. Griffith's *Intolerance* (jokingly used by Maurice Lemaître as a seductive lure through which to drench his waiting audience in *Le film est déjà commence?*), made a retrospective film in 1925 about the sailors on the battleship *Potemkin* instead of glorifying current struggles. The voice-over argues that,

> As a result, in 1929 in *The General Line*, on the subject of agrarian reform, while Eisenstein uses new terms to describe tsarist oppression he still uses old concepts to talk about collectivism. In his films the old triumphs over the new. As a result, five years later, Hollywood paid for him to travel to Mexico to film the revolution while in Berlin Dr. Goebbels urged the directors of UFA to produce a Nazi *Potemkin*.

Then, following a shot of the Revisionist Union Delegate reading aloud Rochet's *L'avenir du parti communiste français*, we cut to a title – THE FUTURE OF THE FRENCH COMMUNIST PARTY – and the female voice proclaiming: 'The dialectic of history is such that the theoretical triumph of Marxism forces its enemies to pose as Marxists' (she repeats the last four words five times to emphasise the connection between the PCF and revisionism). The sound then drops out to give us further pause for thought, namely that all those radical formal innovations that Eisenstein was known for – the montage of attractions, discrepant sound, the Odessa Steps sequence, the maggot-covered meat and the lorgnette – are really just revisionist cosmetics (like actors' make-up) designed to cover up the film's lack of relevance to real proletarian problems.

Even Vertov himself doesn't escape unscathed, for the silence sets us up for the second 'defeat', this time dated 17 November 1935, marking a speech by Stalin at the first All-Union Stakhanovite Conference. 'Confused by the obscurity of this speech,' says the voice-over, just as Tullio-Altan narcissistically looks at herself in a hand mirror,

> Comrade Dziga Vertov forgot that politics commands the economy. His film, *The Eleventh Year* became a hymn to economic progress rather than to the 11-year dictatorship of the proletariat. [Pan right to Midgette.] The dictatorship of the proletariat. It was then that revisionism finally found its way into Soviet Cinema.

This is followed by a long, thirty-three-second drop-out as Midgette continues to apply his warpaint before the voice-over returns to sum up the critique:

> The revolution advances in disguise. False victory of revolutionary cinema, 29 August 1962. Renouncing all initiative the progressive states of Africa elect to rely on the West for their films, giving white Christians the right to talk about black people and Arabs. Algiers – Pontecorvo, Klein. Konakry – Société Comacico. Civil wars and mass movements brought the imperialists down, but they're clawing their way back with the help of the camera, thus endangering the revolution.

Given these examples and our developing critical awareness as spectators, it would be easy to include Godard and Gorin in this critique, specifically the extremely bourgeois narrative of *Weekend* and *La Chinoise*. Godard himself is refreshingly honest about *Weekend*'s shortcomings, for in the 1970 interview with *Take One* magazine, when asked what he thought of Costa-Gavras's film *Z*, he replied that it was 'An objective ally of Hollywood'. So, 'What do you consider *Weekend*?' Godard: 'The same. Maybe more fun, but the same' (Goodwin et al. 1970, draft version: 29). Similarly, discussing *La Chinoise* (which he contributed to as a student advisor), Gorin informed Thomsen in the 1974 *Jump Cut* interview that:

> At that time I found the form of the film highly satisfactory. But then we have seen it again after we started working together, and we found that the film is really very traditional in the narrative, and in a lot of aspects it seems to us to be obsolete today. It is less advanced than *Two or three things I know about her* or *Masculine feminine* or even *Made in U.S.A.* – which I didn't like at all when I first saw it, but which is still a very interesting film in its attempt to link together two words which have a lot more in common than the first two letters: politics and poetry. (Thomsen 1974: 17)

The second example of 'Mechanism' is a fascinating scene framed by the intertitles, 'L'Assemblie Générale' (The Mass Meeting) and 'La

Répression', introduced by Godard's own voice-over: 'During a general assembly the camera is at everyone's disposal.' We then see the film crew assembled in a clearing as they argue heatedly about a page cut from the Italian newspaper *Servire il popolo* featuring images of Stalin and Mao that is pinned to the door of a wooden shed under a Pepsi Cola advertisement (the children of Stalin and Pepsi Cola?). Scrawled across the newspaper is the text: WANTED FOR MURDER. Interspersed with sound drop-outs the camera cuts repeatedly between the images of Stalin (now with diagonal lines scored across his face as if to make him a 'marked man') and the 'clean' image of Mao as the film crew discuss the right approach to dealing with the nature of the image in-itself. While some object to having a picture of Stalin in the film at all others feel that another image would fit the 'wanted for murder' accusation more accurately.

The authoritative female voice contextualises the issue accurately: 'Why Stalin? Because for these comrades the issue known as the Stalin problem is part of the revolutionary movement whether they like it or not.' At this point another voice-over, which sounds like Godard himself, suggests that there is a discrepancy between the image and the reality: 'I'm not saying he is Stalin, but that others accept him as Stalin. We reject Stalin, but we are in a Stalinist situation. Precisely because—' Before he can finish we cut back to the newspaper image and the sound drops out to give us a chance to think through the problem of representation as a whole beyond the limited confines of the film itself. This is borne out when another male voice, following another silence, associates the image with 'The Party Secretary'. Taking this oblique reference to interpellation as a lead, another voice states: 'There, for instance, there is something that goes back to Stalin, something we are up to our necks in, and that's realism... What is it called?' Answer: 'Socialist realism.' The film explores this issue with the famous title card mentioned earlier by Marcia Landy: 'CE N'EST PAS UNE IMAGE JUSTE, C'EST JUSTE UNE IMAGE', or 'This isn't a *just* image, it's just an *image*'. As Colin MacCabe and his collaborators rightly assert, the statement

> insists on the fact that no image has a life of its own outside the institutions which exist to fix its meanings. Film does not exist as a neutral medium to convey messages which are independent, rather it finds its meanings in a series of social relations which place producer and consumer so that only certain meanings are possible. '*In every image we must know who speaks*' – thus Godard, and this imperative demands that we uncover the terms in which we are constructed as spectators. Godard's films pose, as the French philosopher Gilles Deleuze has said, '*questions which silence answers*', questions whose importance lies in the very fact that they disrupt and displace our routine ways of talking about the cinema. Questions which reveal that both

the cinematic technology and the discourses which surround it and support it are fundamentally and profoundly ideological. (MacCabe et al. 1980: 111)

The '*questions which silence answers*' are thus the interpellations of ideology broken by the deterritorialising interstices of AND, AND, AND that break the confining signifier-signified relationship. This view is completely endorsed by the authoritative female voice-over: 'The positive outcome of what has been done is proof that an image means nothing, that there is no image in itself, no image outside of the class struggle.' We then cut back to the poster where both Stalin and Mao are now clean and pristine as the voice-over continues:

> This was proved with an image of Stalin. The negative outcome is not having found the right image, one that was necessary and adequate. Stalin and Mao wanted for murder by capitalists was a necessary image of repression, but an inadequate one. We must find other images of repression, from there, here and now.

As we have seen, viewed through an Althusserian lens, it is the Union Delegate who represents the main repressive force (via the accusation of revisionism), throughout the film, to the point of corrupting Althusser's own Marxist legacy. The scene with Anne Wiazemsky as 'Miss Althusser' takes place in Part 2 of the film as part of the imperative to criticise and transform. Significantly, it is not interrupted by any sound drop-outs, as if to forestall an analytic audience response – via an application of Deleuze's multiplicitous AND – that might defend Althusser against the Maoist critique. It's worth pointing out, for example, that in *Anti-Oedipus* Deleuze and Guattari positively link Althusser to their own theory of desiring-production, arguing that

> Even in Louis Althusser we are witness to the following operation: the discovery of social production as 'machine' or 'machinery', irreducible to the world of objective representation (*Vorstellung*); but immediately the reduction of the machine to structure, the identification of production with a structural and theatrical representation (*Darstellung*). (1983: 306)

– i.e. to the confining *dispositif* of the ISA.

Deleuze and Guattari's analysis specifically references Althusser and Étienne Balibar's *Reading Capital*, which, significantly, is the book that the Revisionist Delegate appropriates from Miss Althusser in this key sequence where they are attempting to instruct the people of the Third World. As the authoritative female voice announces:

> Spell it out. Know how to learn. Knowing how to learn means first, for you, [on the Delegate once again reading from Waldeck Rochet] confronting the bitter, absurd,

sordid spectacle of the revisionist school teacher collaborating by reinforcing the ideological power of the bourgeoisie.

Miss Althusser invites her pupils to come forward and as Midgette's 'Indian' approaches she hands her preferred books to the Delegate, who rejects them with a curt 'No!'. Then with Wiazemsky conveniently out of frame (as if the Delegate as revisionist had completely co-opted Althusser's work) he selects *Reading Capital* and writes a dedication before handing it to Midgett: 'To the people of the Third World, with esteem and friendship' (as opposed to 'comradeship and solidarity').[1] As Lesage rightly points out, 'In Marxist-Leninist vocabulary, the difference is profound. It means that the PCF does not actively support Third World liberation struggles, but rather contents itself with gestures of humanistic concern' (1974: unpaginated).

Before Midgette leaves, the Delegate also tells him to start at Chapter 2, leading the voice-over to admonish him:

> What did the revisionist school teacher just say? He said, 'Read *Das Kapital*.' He did not say, 'Use it.' Use it. He criticised the defects of the people, but he did not do this from the people's point of view. By treating a comrade like an enemy, he has adopted the position of the enemy.

In a humorous aside, instead of leafing through the book, Midgette places a piece of meat between the pages and bites into it like a sandwich as he exits, as if to show that Rocha's 'aesthetics of hunger' are far more pertinent to Third World needs than abstract theory. Lesage puts it well when she comments: 'As Brecht was fond of saying, "Grub first, then ethics"' (1974: unpaginated).

It's significant that at film's end, following collective shouts of 'Death to the bourgeoisie!' over a black screen, we see Wiazemsky and her revolutionary lover shoving the Delegate along a dirt road towards the camera. The sound drops out as the group of revolutionaries and the 'Indian' form a firing squad and aim their guns not at the Cavalryman (the symbol of the ruling class) but at the revisionist. The female voice-over breaks the silence, declaring: 'Daring to rebel. For us, here and now, this means fighting on two fronts, against the bourgeoisie and against its ally, revisionism.' The sound drops out for one last time as we focus on the firing squad

---

[1] The original two-volume French version of *Lire le Capital* also contained essays by Étienne Balibar, Roger Establet, Jacques Rancière and Pierre Macherey.

(thus denying us the affective indulgence of hearing the shots and seeing the blood) before we cut to a closing title:

> THERE ARE TWO WINDS IN THE WORLD, THE EAST WIND AND THE WEST WIND. THE EAST WIND CURRENTLY PREVAILS OVER THE WEST WIND. THE REVOLUTIONARY FORCES HAVE ACHIEVED an overwhelming superiority over the imperialist forces.

If we learn anything from the critical vector triggered by the film's silences it's not to trust pat solutions to complex concrete situations and this convenient binary between East and West is far too steeped in the dialectics of the Cold War and eighteenth-century Orientalism to be relevant to the modern context of the Global South's transnational relationship to the Global North. We see this non-dialectical problem play out in a famous scene often called 'Glauber Rocha at the Crossroads', where the Brazilian director, playing himself, stands at the intersection of two forking paths, arms outstretched at the edge of a copse as he chants the ballad from *Antonio das Mortes* in Portuguese: '*Atenção: é preciso estar atento e forte. Nâo temos tempo de temer a morte*' ('Attention: we have to be alert and strong. There is no time to fear death') (Avellar 2005: 85). A pregnant woman (played by Gorin's then girlfriend, Isabel Pons), a film camera slung over her shoulder, approaches from the background as the woman's voice-over appears to speak both for her and the audience:

> You talked earlier about the path the history of revolutionary struggles has taught us to recognise. But where is it? In front? Behind? Left? Right? And how? You have changed your method. You have asked the cinema of the Third World where it is at.

Pons approaches Rocha and asks him if he knows the way to political cinema. He points to our left: 'That way leads to unknown cinema, the cinema of adventure.' He turns and points behind him to our right: 'And that way is Third World Cinema, a dangerous cinema, divine and marvellous.' She takes that path and casually kicks Rocha's football away from the camera as he continues: 'A cinema of the oppression of imperialist consumption, a dangerous cinema, a marvellous cinema, a cinema out to repress the fascist oppression of terrorism.' Unfortunately the authoritative female voice doesn't give her a chance to think through the situation critically, telling her: 'And there you discovered the complexities of the struggle. You discovered that you lack the means of analysing it.' Pons sets off on the path towards unknown cinema but quickly cuts to the right through a thicket, as if returning to her place of origin like a cinematic biogram.

Now alone, Rocha continues to make his case for a Tropicalist cinema that, even though it may be dependent on western capital and distribution, at least speaks for the Global South:

> It is a dangerous, divine marvelous cinema. It is a cinema that will build everything – technique, projection rooms, distribution, technicians, 300 movie makers to make 600 films a year for the entire Third World. It's the cinema of technology, it's for the people, to spell it out to the masses of the Third World. It is cinema. (Fry 1972: 165)

As in the case of the 'Miss Althusser' scene, there are no sound drop-outs to encourage the laying down of a new plane of immanence that can reconcile the dialectic between the two kinds of cinema – the conceptualists of the First World and the Tropicalists of the Third. That is the main reason why we interjected a chapter on Rocha between the different phases of Godard's career – so that the reader can be aware of the different layers that make up a cinema of resistance and to resist a general tendency towards Eurocentric historicity. Significantly, Gorin himself (a huge fan of Rocha), never saw the relationship as a strict dialectic but as a series of folds – an apt example of Laura Marks's enfolding and unfolding – for as he stated in an enlightening interview:

> The question was not the question of a 'true' path, but the question of the type of dialogue that could be knotted, folded from all this disparate questioning that was going on. Nobody could simply dream to adopt wholesale the experimentation of anybody else, precisely because these experimentations refracted the specificity of experience. That's why the guys of the Cinema Nôvo were so important: for how Brazilian they were determined to be, for their specificity and how it forced us to interrogate our own and sent us in a direction that had not been mapped out. Glauber's apparition in *Vent d'Est* is both an homage to the Cinema Nôvo and an affectionate piece of naïve theater that indicates that the works done in Brazil forced us to bushwhack our way out of the thicket (Hollywood, the New Wave, the Ice Age political cinema of the Cold War etc . . .) toward the specificity of our time and place. (de Almeida 2005: 50)

Or, to put it another way, cinema never consists of a single path: the path of cinema is all paths but their relationship to zero (in Rocha's case the 'aesthetics of hunger') is different in each case, for as Rocha put it in his light-hearted review of the film: 'Godard and co. are above zero. We are below zero' (Rocha 1970b: 53).

Having put Althusser's structural Marxism under a critical microscope in *Le vent d'est*, Gorin's script for *Lotte in Italia* (*Struggle in Italy*, 1971) is a direct (affirmative) application of his essay, 'Ideology and Ideological State Apparatuses (Notes towards an Investigation, 1969)' to a specific social situation, in this case the everyday life of a young Italian militant,

Paola Taviani (Cristiana Tullio-Altan) and her growing awareness of the unconscious forces that interpellate her into the prevailing bourgeois ideology. As Gorin explains the plot:

> *Struggle in Italy* is a film about the transformation of a girl who, in the beginning, says she is involved in the revolutionary movement and is a Marxist. The film has three parts. During the first part of the film, while she speaks, you discover bit by bit that she isn't really as Marxist as she has said. In various aspects of her life there is a victory of the bourgeois ideology. What we try to explain in the second and third parts is how things have happened. So the whole film is made of reflections of the few images in the first part. (Goodwin et al. 1970, original draft: 19)

Part 1 is thus a basic expression of Althusser's principle that ideology is a 'representation' of the imaginary relationship of individuals to the real conditions of existence, an effect of *misrecognition* and the false logic of social role and class designed to reproduce the relations of production through various 'vehicles'. We thus see Paola in a series of isolated vignettes that circumscribe her place within the prevailing ideology through the social apparatuses of her militancy (through the PCI or Italian Communist Party), family, education, fashion, housing, sex, health and identity. As MacBean rightly argues,

> What happens, according to Althusser, in each of these vehicles, is that the individual's real relations to the relations of production are distorted because they are short-circuited into a relation to an absolute: in the schools, Learning; in church, God; in the courts, Justice; in politics, The Party; in labor organization, The Union; in the communications media, The Facts; in art, Truth and Beauty; and in the family, Proper Behavior. (1975: 157)

One might also add that Paola's resistance to these absolutes – especially the family – still reinforces them as standards of authority.

These scenes are constantly disrupted by three main formal discrepancies. Firstly, although the film is set in Italy all the interiors were actually shot in Godard and Wiazemsky's Paris apartment on rue Saint-Jacques in December 1969, supplemented by a few factory scenes actually shot in Rome and Milan. While Paola's dialogue and monologues as well as the voices of the male characters (her pupil, boyfriend, father, lecturer, policeman and porter) were all recorded in Italian, a post-synchronous woman's voice-over (which sounds suspiciously like Wiazemsky) translates them into French. Significantly, the voice-over seems to be deliberately off-kilter with the diegetic dialogue, translating before or after the spoken Italian lines rather than simultaneously (reinforced by the similar timing of the English subtitles), as if every facet of the production were designed to interpellate, through language, the Italian context into a French ideological *reflection* of Paola's actual circumstances. As we shall see, given Part 3's detailed analysis of reflection's different relations to ideology, this was probably a deliberate foregrounding strategy designed to allow the audience to witness interpellation at first hand.

This tactic is reinforced by the film's other two discrepancies – the use of silences and black screens which seem to play very different structural roles. The former act as centrifugal lines of flight or unfoldings out of the hermetic confines of Paola's life to a deterritorialising vector of struggle/work/struggle/work in both Italy and capitalist ideology as a whole, while the latter act as a trigger in Parts 1 and 2 for a centripetal reinterpretation of images as they are connected to broader modes of production in Part 3. Thus as Gorin explains the strategy:

> In the first part, the most striking thing to the person seeing the film is the intrusion of the black leader in the speech of the girl. The second part asks, 'Why these black spaces?' 'What have they been taking the place of?' 'Who organized these black spaces?' 'Who put those black spaces in her speech?' Little by little, those black spaces will be replaced by other things, which are the real . . . I know the word in French . . . *rapport de production*. It means the real economical and social pattern which governs ideology, and the way it rules things. (Goodwin et al. 1970, original draft: 20–1)

In Part 2 Paola is still struggling to find the clues to solving these problems *practically*. However, as she tries on clothes in a boutique, helped by her shop assistant comrade (played by Wiazemsky herself) she at least begins to grasp the fundamentals of how ideology works: 'What's happening? Your life divided under headings, like a university subject, all part of a whole. You realise the whole is imaginary.' Then after a shot of her reading *PEKIN*, which blocks out her face, she suddenly breaks free of received wisdom and speaks directly at the camera to declare the real nature of the contradiction:

> The imaginary whole, the conditions of your existence, the relationship between them, what does it mean? What did I say at the start? I said, 'There is, there is.' There is Marxism, there is idealism. But I didn't say that Marxism was fighting idealism. What else did I say? A metaphysical conception and a dialectical conception have given rise to two opposing conceptions of the world. Opposing conceptions. They were opposing. That's what I had forgotten. So I called myself a Marxist but in fact I was still an idealist. There are two conceptions of the world. To find out why they are opposing you need to know how they work.

Unfortunately in Part 2 Paola still suffers from enough 'false consciousness' to believe that the solution lies in acts of lifestyle rebellion. Thus an obvious first step to replace her ingrained idealism with a practical experience of dialectical materialism would be to take a job in a factory but the inadequacies of this form of proletarian 'slumming' are quickly made evident when she is not only rejected by her co-workers as too bourgeois but fails to keep up with the strenuous workload demanded by the foreman. Her alternative outlet is to tutor the young male worker in mathematics as a means of 'serving the working class' but even then it is evident that she is too much of a know-it-all and has no time or patience to answer his questions. Finally, she decides to 'revolutionise' her sex life by making love in the afternoon instead of at night, obviously blind to the fact that this is a middle-class privilege because real factory workers have to work all day unless they're on nights.

Paola's real breakthrough occurs in Part 3 when she learns the basic principle of Marxism that people's social existence determines their thoughts and also understands the twin nature of reflection as a determinant part of different ideologies. Framed by a sound drop-out, as if to centrifugally stress the statement's universal value as a revolutionary insight, Paola faces the camera in a mirror shot (thus visually accentuating the idea of 'reflections') and we see her lips move but the only sound comes from the voice-over: 'Having criticised the notion of reflections at the start of the second part I later realised that notion didn't come from bourgeois ideology but that it was the mechanism central to all ideologies.' She then reads directly from Mao:

> The problem is not the problem of reflections in itself but of the struggle between a reflection which denies objective contradictions and a reflection which expresses them. The struggle between bourgeois ideology which wants the world to remain as it is and revolutionary ideology which wants to transform it.

Paola then metacommunicates that we are watching another form of reflection – cinema – as she announces the

> Third part of the film. With elements from the second part reconsidered through the mechanism of the ideology which is at work in the first and second parts of the film. Third part of the film. To repeat what I've just said but, since it's a film, to say it with images and sound. Third part of the film.

She then finishes with another quote from Mao: 'Research, work, struggle. Programme for the struggle.'

The strategy of Part 3 is to revisit the black screens of Parts 1 and 2 in order to illustrate where Paola's discourse comes from: i.e. with what precedes the blackness and also with what will come afterwards, namely direct images of the relations of production. Framed by two sound drop-outs, we see an exterior shot of the Zanoletti Metalli factory followed by a mirror shot of Paola singing *The Internationale*. The music continues over a darkened shot of factory workers as Paola explains not only the film's strategy but also her awakening into an understanding of the true nature of ideology:

> In the first part of the film there was a black screen. Now a workshop, an image of the relations of production. In the first part of the film after this black screen there was [cut to Paola trying on red sweater] a shot of me buying a sweater. And then another black screen. But now it's a factory that we see, [snowy exterior shot of a factory] showing the relations of production.

The framing silence completes the sequence by showing a car leaving the factory area and driving past the camera, as if to show the inherent connection of production to everyday life (including conspicuous consumption).

Paola repeats these demonstrations – replacing black screens with shots of workers and factories – using several other images from Part 1. These include her sipping from a bowl of soup during her argument with her family, a policeman asking to see her identity papers, and a university lecturer's voice calling her into an exam room and her ensuing rant against the education system:

> It talks of right and wrong ideas, ideas in themselves, without saying where they come from. This voice doesn't talk about the real conditions of existence and scientific practice. This voice confirms that people's thoughts are not determined by their social existence. It's the voice of idealism. It's fake. It lies. It leaves you in the dark.

Godard and Gorin then show how this self-analysis is intrinsically tied to sound and image relations. Paula summarises the process as follows: 'In the first part of the film my life was a conflict.' We see the back of her head, as if her turmoil were unexpressible through a facial expression.

> Here I oppose the teacher, the agent of the ideological state apparatus of the university. [Cut to the bowl of soup.] Here I oppose my father, also an agent of the ideological state apparatus of the family. [On Paola canvassing on the street as she is asked for her identity papers.] And here the police, the most obvious agent of the state apparatus. [The policeman demands to see her documents.] So, a conflict between various practices.

The film ends with a fourth practice: acting itself. Tullio-Altan breaks out of her character and addresses the camera directly as if she were appearing on Italian television. She tells how the main error of her character was to indulge in an account of her own militancy, 'A bourgeois girl grappling with her militancy, a bourgeois girl contradicting herself, a bourgeois girl who can't tell where right and wrong ideas come from, who can't resolve her contradictions and who does not know what to do.' She then realises that she has to stop talking about herself and analyse the external reality that produces her ideas: 'In other words, the reality of Italy. But what is to be done with that? Something transformative or nothing? I said, "People's social existence determines their thoughts."' However, even given that change of consciousness, another step forward is needed but of course it's a difficult path: 'What I said is at best an indication of the work, of the struggle, of the work, of the struggle, of the work, of the struggle, of the work, of the struggle of the work and of the struggle.'

If this closing line sounds like a reiteration of the Deleuzian stuttering AND that has been a running theme throughout this book it isn't by accident, because as we noted earlier, the film's seemingly random use of silences (apart from their repetitive use with intertitles) suggests a connective phylum with broader issues than the hermetic nature of the narrative might suggest. In most cases the silences accompany signifiers not only of capitalist and establishment ideology – especially conspicuous consumption – but also its institutional resistance: the front entrance to the PCI building with its accompanying hammer and sickle. Thus we see Fiat car signs, a Citroën passing a factory, bourgeois families posing with their children, Paola writing mathematical equations on a blackboard (Althusser's marker of Science as a process without a subject), Paola or her boyfriend closing the French windows of their apartment (a clear prelude to sexual activity), and the Zanoletti Metalli factory and its interior workshops.

Perhaps the most significant framing silence accompanies a sequence of Paola writing following an intertitle that reads 'Bleak Battipaglia', a likely reference to the 1969 popular uprising in the Campania town when sugar and tobacco plants were threatened with closure. Accompanied by other students and workers, protesters took to the streets, resulting in two deaths. Thus, even if the film fails to provide us with a documentary picture of contemporary Italy across a full spectrum of different classes, these image-based vectors point to a larger national and world picture and perhaps the prospect of an Italy-to-come. For, unknown to Godard and Gorin at the time, in a mere seven years it will witness the 1977 Bologna Uprisings, Italy's very own version of May '68, inspired by the Autonomia Movement and highlighted by the spectacle of the 'Metropolitan Indians' dressed in warpaint and the birth of Radio Alice, 'Bifo' Berardi's 'free radio' inspiration for Guattari's subsequent Radio Tomato that was broadcast from his Paris kitchen. The following year Aldo Moro was kidnapped and killed by the Red Brigades and the radical Lotta Continua collapsed in disarray. Meanwhile Christiana Tullio-Altan had retired from acting and was working as an assistant editor on two films by Jacques Rivette: *Duelle* and *Noroît*, fantasy thrillers that Godard and Gorin undoubtedly hated.

Filmed in the autumn of 1970 in Paris and financed by Munich Tele-Pool in Germany and Grove Press in the US, *Vladimir and Rosa* was made largely as a means to help finance the completion of *Jusqu'à la victoire*. Grove Press (who produced the English dubbed version) was obviously attracted to the film's subject matter, the Chicago Eight Conspiracy Trial which began on 20 March 1969. The defendants – Abbie Hoffman, Jerry Rubin, David Dellinger, Tom Hayden, Rennie Davis, John Froines, Lee Weiner and Bobby Seale – were charged under the anti-riot provisions of Title X of the Civil Rights Act of 1968, which made it a federal crime to cross state lines to incite a riot, or as Godard and Gorin pointedly argue in their film, to 'intend to incite a riot', or even to 'intend to intend'. The original eight defendants were reduced to seven when the Black Panther Bobby Seale was charged with contempt of court by the trial judge Julius Hoffman for a number of courtroom protests and interruptions, which led to his being bound and gagged by federal marshals before ultimately serving four years' imprisonment. He was subsequently put on trial again on an unrelated murder charge in 1970 but the jury was unable to reach a verdict and all charges were dropped.

Godard and Gorin see the ingrained class and race bias of the trial as a typical example of the judicial ISA at work, turning what amounts to an absurd piece of 'politics as theatre' into its critical reverse: 'theatre as revolution'. MacBean sees a direct correlation with Georges Méliès theatricalised reconstruction of the Alfred Dreyfus espionage trial in his *L'Affaire Dreyfus* (1899), a series of eleven one-minute instalments that recreate a single event from the trial (with its ingrained antisemitism), striving to get at the truth through the dialectical synthesis of the fictional and the real, a form of documentary *commedia dell'arte* (MacBean 1975: 161). Adopting a carefree and satirical Yippie tone throughout, as if the Marx Brothers had formed an unholy alliance with Antonin Artaud (who was himself a huge fan of *Animal Crackers* and *Monkey Business*, particularly their fusion of humour with nervous anxiety), Godard and Gorin recreate the political and racial bias of the trial but with a number of differences. Firstly, the eight now include two women, Anne Wiazemsky as a militant from the Women's Liberation Front, and Juliet Berto as a Maoist activist with connections to the Weather Underground. Secondly, Godard and Gorin, as well as filming and documenting the proceedings critically and self-analytically, are also on trial as Friedrich Vladimir (Godard), a friend of

Danny the Red 'back in the heyday of the Moscow Circus', and Karl Rosa (Gorin), thereby nominally reprising the two Maoist voices from *Pravda* but this time replacing the latter's spontaneity with a more measured criticality based on the concrete situation of a racist American legal system. Even then they are presented as figures of ridicule, walking up and down alongside a tennis court net holding a microphone and recorder while a mixed doubles game is in progress. They stutter inarticulately, trying to express that, 'We're in a situation of constant repression and we're going to show you some victims of that repression who are nonetheless trying to break free.' Finally, the remaining four defendants pay at least some lip service to the original Chicago Eight: Dave Dellinger (Claude Nedjar), a liberal doctor; Yves (Yves Alfonso), a revolutionary student at Vincennes and then Berkeley whose serious intellectual approach in the courtroom is perhaps intended to evoke Tom Hayden; Jacky Martin, a 'maladjusted' worker from the northern suburbs of Paris who plays a very loud guitar in order to 'wake up' the workers; and most importantly, Bobby X, a militant from the Black Panthers who is an obvious composite of Malcolm X and Bobby Seale.

While the original prosecutors – Richard Schultz and Tom Foran – are reduced to anonymous voice-overs in the trial scenes, William ('John' in the film) Kunstler, the defence attorney behaves in much the same way as Dellinger, what MacCabe calls a stuffy, traditional legal defence in terms of courtroom procedure – respect for at least *some* legal process, even if corrupt, for as Godard argued, 'they hadn't radicalized themselves yet' (Godard in MacBean 1975: 163). Thus in the film Vladimir's voice-over informs us that 'He's full of altruism. But he, too, must realise that he must [insert shot of Kunstler rehearsing] change his life. It's fine to want to change other people's lives, but you've got to start by changing your own.' The inadequacy of Dellinger's tactics is made all the more obvious when faced with the judicial centrepiece of the film, Judge Julius Himmler (Godard film veteran Ernest Menzer, who had played Arthur's uncle in *Bande à part* and the revolutionaries' cannibalistic butcher in *Weekend*). Himmler seems to be a composite of the Chicago trial's Judge Hoffman and the Nazi Judge Roland Freisler (1893–1945), the President of the People's Court from 1942–5 who was killed by an Allied bomb during an air raid on 3 February 1945. Like Judge Himmler, Freisler was a brutal presence in the courtroom, silencing and ridiculing witnesses with extreme right-wing bias and handing out the death penalty at whim (often a hanging by piano wire). Himmler's idiosyncratic authoritarianism is expressed by his constant interruption of witness testimonies as he bangs his gavel and yells 'Silence!!!', while jotting down his case notes on a series of *Playboy* centrefolds. Himmler also has a more contemporary French counterpart, for as Marc Serisuelo argues,

> It is imperative to point out that Godard was completely obsessed by Raymond Marcellin [France's Minister for the Interior, 30 May 1968 to 27 February 1974], and saw his hand in everything, and whom he portrayed – in addition to his multiple incarnations – as the symbol of Gaullist France. (2014: 311)

The aims of the film are stated right up front as Rosa's voice overlays shots of Chinese factory workers, shirtless revolutionaries and images of Lenin, informing us that we are about to see,

> a film aimed at a political analysis of charges currently being brought by the bourgeois justice system against radicals arrested by the police for so-called riots and conspiracy. [...] The voice is committed to a revolutionary movement fighting conservatism. The real title of the film should be, 'The Meaning of the Charges Brought'.

Vladimir then poses and answers the key question:

> Why and on what grounds is imperialism trying these Eight? We've just told you. The government's own violence forced it to arrest eight cops and indict them, in parenthesis, in the name of eternal justice, end of parenthesis. And so, to restore the balance, the government has decided to indict a representative of each type of radicalism, in parenthesis, class justice, end of parenthesis.

Bobby X, even though he wasn't even present at the Chicago demonstrations, was singled out because the government 'was hell-bent on putting a black man on trial'. Then, over a black screen, Godard continues: 'That's why Bobby's here. He's the only one of us who's not out on bail.' We cut to Bobby behind diagonal bars: 'He'd already been accused of killing a cop.'

This connection of a black screen to Bobby is important because after being bound and gagged for insubordination and then banned from the court proceedings by Himmler, Kunstler refuses to represent him and the judge won't let him defend himself. He is effectively silenced. Vladmir then tells us over several shots of revolutionaries intercut with a series of black screens that:

> This black section represents the disappearance of Bobby, the black radical. So for once this black screen really means something. It represents Bobby's absence. For us, Vladimir and Rosa, it's a great victory in filmmaking. [...] We've been trotting out these black frames for ages [...] At first, these black frames were shots we couldn't shoot. We were told that the images belonged to CBS or that the images belonged to Gaumont and we couldn't afford them so we'd leave the screen black instead. Then we realised that those black frames were shots we didn't know how to shoot, shots of

bourgeois ideology and imperialism [...] And so now, after shots of Yves or of the jury, of Vladimir and Rosa or Juliet, this black shot indicating that Bobby is gone at last has a meaning, so it's a victory. A real victory, not like Proust's pyrrhic victory but more, 'Until victory, always', with the Palestinians and all the rebels in the world.

On one hand the black screen (or black leader punningly standing in for a 'Black Leader') acts as a metaphor for Bobby's enforced (and illegal) silencing and represents a major break in the interpellative surface of the so-called 'equal' justice system in order to disclose its innate class and racial bias. On the other hand it is metonymically connected, through an active plane of consistency, to the similar examples that we noted in *Le Gai Savoir*: not just censored images but the specific memory of the Afro-Asians beaten by the police of Kimola and the cameraman whose eyes were gouged out by Québécois police.

Interestingly, Godard and Gorin never discuss their use of silence and sound drop-outs in the same way, either in the films themselves or in interviews. In this case, the silences tend to either reinforce the role of the black-outs or extend them centrifugally to other layers of hidden oppression. An obvious case of the former occurs an hour into the film when Vladimir and Rosa lead a press conference with a TV crew when all the defendants were out on bail except for Bobby who was interred on the murder charge. Godard and Gorin stammer their lines as they playfully toss a football around the studio and explain: 'The problem we faced during each press conference was this: while John was telling the reporters about our daily struggle against imperialist justice, Vladimir and Rosa forced the imperialist television cameras to shoot Bobby's absence instead of our presence.' This absence is symbolised by an empty red chair, marking both the colour of revolution and the bloodshed of racial oppression. The two directors continue:

> In other words, they forced the cameras, the enemy, to shoot politically a political fact that was more important than the faces of us radicals. If we fight all day long with the police we must also fight the police state's press. It's logical.

The sound then drops out for a full eight seconds as we hold on the red chair before the silence ends with a close-up of a struggling Bobby, a gun to his head as he is gagged by marshals. The silence thus represents more than the denial of civil rights to Bobby in particular but to all who resist the system and it makes a clear claim that this is done in league with the Repressive State Apparatus, not just the internal mechanisms of the ISA.

This point is underlined by the repeated use of silence in accompaniment with police violence throughout the film – the savage beatings of

Anne, Juliet and Jacky in the opening five minutes; Dellinger pinned to the floor at the hour mark as he is restrained and handcuffed by two marshals who handcuff him; Bobby gagged and a gun pointed at his head on Himmler's orders. In the wake of the police murders of George Floyd and Breonna Taylor in 2020, all these incidents can be linked by a centrifugal vector to the importance of the Black Lives Matter movement, indicating that the fight for civil rights and anti-racism is still far from over. Godard and Gorin seem to realise the importance of underlining this connection between civil rights and class war, for when Jacky is being particularly demonstrative in court, Himmler berates him: 'Will you be quiet? Do you understand French? [Jacky is silent.] Well? Do you understand French? [Silence.] Will you be quiet? [Silence.] Will you, yes or no? Yes or no?' Jacky then lets it all out: 'Yes, you motherfucking fascist, capitalist bastard!' We then cut to a black screen and brief sound drop-out before Godard informs us that,

> For this passage Vladimir and Rosa decided it would be a good chance to pan from Jacky to Bobby and back again. It would show the objective links between the wild revolt of young workers and the revolutionary movement of black people.

The film is careful to include Himmler directly in these racist accusations, for at one point the sound drop-out accompanies a pair of framing white screens (representing white hegemony) as the judge asks Vladimir, 'can you explain to me the meaning of the word "racist" which Mr Bobby X keeps throwing at me?' Black and white screens then alternate as Vladimir explains in voice-over:

> I'll explain to you with an image. Imagine a worker who is so poor he has to eat shit. [BLACK SCREEN]. Now ask him this: given that he has to eat shit would he rather eat shit from a white man's arse [WHITE SCREEN] or a black man's arse? [BLACK SCREEN]. If he prefers white man's shit then that worker is a damned racist.

Although funny in a rude, off-kilter way, it does make a key point that anti-racism, like all radical politics, entails far more than a transformation of the judicial system, it requires a complete integration of lifestyle with political action.

This issue is illustrated immediately after another combination of black screen and silence as we cut to a shot of Juliet Berto in a green helmet and goggles holding a billy club across her face. Rosa admits in voice-over that 'she's a fighter. She has courage. She's come to blows several times with the police. And then she uses a type of discourse which is often right.'

That's the political side. As music fades up we see Juliet sitting on a living room floor smoking with a group of radicals and Rosa continues,

> OK, but let's look at the practical side. How does she live? Here she's in a kind of collective. This group of friends got together and formed a collective. But they haven't really tried to think through the reasons for it and the practical aspects of it. And anyway, how is this collective any different from the way they lived before? It's still pretty obscure.

We then cut back to the militant Juliet in her helmet with the billy club. 'There's an awfully big difference between this shot and the shot that's meant to be political, the one where she's got her helmet and club. They just don't seem to go together.' The silence in this case thus sets up a discrepancy that Godard and Gorin attempt to at least partially resolve by film's end.

The first is attempted within the ISA itself through the increasing radicalisation of Kunstler who evolves from refusing to defend Bobby X and upholding the principles of Himmler's court procedure to actually practising class-based justice. 'The country's future and the solution to its problems must no longer depend on the interests of a handful of billionaires,' he tells Himmler. Two of the jurors nod in agreement as Himmler looks on, incredulous. Then Kunstler, intercut with shots of the defendants, really reads him the riot act:

> There is no justice in this courtroom. This trial is meaningless. Jailing these people is a legal lynching. The Declaration of Human Rights says that if a government violates people's rights [on Juliet, fist raised] insurrection is a sacred right, indeed it is an obligation. When an individual seizes absolute power they must be put to death by free men. We are free since we have nothing to lose but the chains you have laden us with. As free men, we sentence you to death.

This is followed by a heavy silence, allowing time for a horrified Himmler to take it all in, and for the audience to raise their fist in defiance.

Obviously all the defendants are found guilty and will do jail time, but the film ends on a complex racial and class analysis of the justice system by Bobby X and Juliet Berto. Bobby sums it up from the position of the Black Panthers:

> The bourgeoisie would have us believe that only hoodlums and gangsters use certain methods to free themselves, but the bourgeoisie reserves the 'right' to use force. If anyone else uses force to preserve his or her dignity, they are immediately vilified by the mass media who are under bourgeois control. The Black Panther party is going to send a letter to the Supreme Court, the gist of which will revolve around the fact

that the death penalty is applied only to the poor and to people of colour. This is very apparent on death row where they await the electric chair. There, the cells are occupied solely by poor white people, black people, Arabs and other people of colour. The death penalty is a class weapon. It's high time someone stepped in between the people and the bloodthirsty madmen.

Juliet, tugging desperately against vertical prison bars, switches the discussion from the courts and the law to the plight of the workers:

> Comrades! Comrades! We are all in a state of revolt. Against the bourgeoisie. The distinction between ordinary and political prisoners is artificial. It is meant to divide us. They don't want us to communicate with you. But bars cannot prevent revolutionary ideas. Why are you in prison, comrades? Because you refused to work for the bourgeoisie. Because you didn't want to be exploited, you didn't want to work for starvation wages while the boss lined his pockets at your expense. [. . .] It's always right to rebel against the powers of the bourgeoisie. You were right, in a way. But you have to understand, comrades. You have to understand. Trying to find a place in the sun for yourself doesn't change much in the long run. One petty theft, two break-ins, three hold-ups, four bank robberies and five murders won't stop the bourgeoisie from exploiting us. Comrades, we must unite.

The final image is of two shirts, one bearing the name Vladimir, the other Rosa, lying across a car engine. A voice-over concludes the film's discursive plane with

> The only way to get to the bottom of a situation is to investigate society and the reality of class differences. Those in charge should devote themselves to a few towns or villages, carrying out detailed investigations from the basic Marxist point of view of class analysis. This is the basic way to get to the bottom of a situation.

We then cut to a sign in the same engine as it starts to rev, ready to go: COMMUNISTS ARE BOTH THE DRIVING FORCE AND THE TARGET OF THE REVOLUTION. We then fade to black and complete silence as we await what the future might bring. Flash forward to 2020: Black Lives Matter, Extinction Rebellion and Donald Trump as US president.

CHAPTER 8

'We're Projectorists!': Concrete Duration and the Spectacle of Attractions in Malcolm Le Grice's *Little Dog for Roger* (1967), *Threshold* (1972) and *After Lumière – L'Arroseur Arrosé* (1974)

So far, our case studies in silence and sound drop-outs – whether acting as interstices or irrational cuts – have followed a very conventional Deleuzean line, either as interruptions in the smooth flow of action governed by the movement-image outlined in *Cinema 1*, or as multiplicitous vectors connecting to a different plane of immanence in relation to the direct time-image, detailed in *Cinema 2*. It thus seems timely and appropriate to introduce a different (and discrepant) analysis of silence that breaks open Deleuze's somewhat pat distinction between the two images, especially his focus on the immediate post-World War II period as the moment when the action-image begins to stall amid the bombed out, rubble-strewn streets of Italian Neorealism, where affected characters do not so much act on, but rather passively *experience* time and space. In short, they lack agency. This is the moment of the 'chronosign' as both a singular point and as an assemblage, 'an image where time ceases to be subordinate to movement and appears for itself' (Deleuze 1989: 335).

However, what Deleuze's schema fails to do is acknowledge that the time-image had already 'infected' the movement-image long before the Cold War era – indeed this hybridisation had been a fundamental characteristic of non-western film (especially in India) as well as so-called 'primitive' silent cinema (the 'pre-cinema' era of Méliès and the Lumière Brothers), a 'cinema of attractions' that Deleuze conveniently ignores. This is an important area of study for, as we shall see via the films of the British experimental film-maker Malcolm Le Grice, the bringing together of the materialist components of silent film with the formalist trappings of the 1960s and '70s avant-garde (epitomised not only by Le Grice but also the films and writings of Peter Gidal) produced a radical new paradigm that defies categorisation into either movement- or time-images, for instead of being active or passive viewers we instead become an embodied part of the apparatus itself. In short, we become 'projectorists'.[1]

As is well known, Deleuze bases his idea of the movement-image on Henri Bergson's rejection of Kant's distinction between the One and the multiple (where all difference returns to the totalising Whole of an all-encompassing Reason) in favour of two types of multiplicity. As Deleuze explains the difference in *Bergsonism*:

> One is represented by space [...] It is a multiplicity of exteriority, of simultaneity, of juxtaposition, or order, of quantitative differentiation, of *difference in degree*; it is a numerical multiplicity, *discontinuous and actual*. The other type of multiplicity appears in pure duration: it is an internal multiplicity of succession, of fusion, or organization, of heterogeneity, of qualitative discrimination, or of *difference in kind*; it is a *virtual and continuous* multiplicity that cannot be reduced to numbers. (1991b: 38)

Deleuze's cinematic schema redefines the nature of the cinematic image as equivalent to these different types of Bergsonian multiplicity. Thus, the movement-image is a quantitative multiplicity of space, actuality, externality and differences in degree, while the time-image is a qualitative multiplicity of duration, virtuality, internality and differences in kind. It's important to note that Deleuze re-theorises our understanding of the image by tying it to Bergsonian *intuition* instead of to the intellect or dialectics: 'The cinema seems to us to be a composition of images and of signs, that is, a pre-verbal intelligible content (*pure semiotics*), whilst semiology of a linguistic inspiration abolishes the image and tends to dispense with the sign' (1986: ix).

However, it's something of a contradictory situation because when Bergson actually discusses cinema in *Creative Evolution*, he disparages it for its tendency to spatialise duration, reducing an intrinsic intuitive flow to a series of artificial frames – at that time between sixteen and twenty-four frames per second, depending on the speed of the hand cranking – much like Zeno's paradox in the race between Achilles and the tortoise, whereby Achilles (obviously the faster runner) never overtakes his rival because his progress is always measured in *spatial* relation to the points that the tortoise has just left (and thus gained ground). Indeed, rather than appreciate the sensation of captured images as real movement the cinema

---

[1] If you'll excuse the pun: apologies to one of my favourite TV shows, Mackenzie Crook's brilliant *Detectorists*.

allowed Bergson to conflate the machine, the filmic apparatus, form, and the intellect with the *non*-intuitive:

> In reality the body is changing form at every moment; or rather, there is no form, since form is immobile and the reality is movement. What is real is the continual *change of* form: *form is only a snapshot view of a transition*. Therefore, here again, our perception manages to solidify into discontinuous images the fluid continuity of the real [. . .] Instead of attaching ourselves to the inner becoming of things, we place ourselves outside them in order to recompose their becoming artificially [. . .] Whether we would think becoming, or express it, or even perceive it, we hardly do anything else than set going a kind of cinematograph inside us. We may therefore sum up [. . .] that the *mechanism of our ordinary knowledge is of a cinematographical kind*. (Deleuze 1983: 306)

As we shall see, Le Grice celebrates this fusion of intellect and the apparatus via the body-as-projector, thus privileging the machinic qualities of the image itself. Deleuze, in contrast, because he privileges the perception-image as the ground zero of cinema, has to deflect attention away from Bergson's critique in *Creative Evolution* (1907) by turning to one of Bergson's earlier books, *Matter and Memory* (1896) which, although it doesn't mention film, allows Deleuze to argue that Bergson had invented the *concept* of cinema before it became a concrete media practice.

According to Deleuze, this 'invention' of cinema is grounded in Bergson's three main theses on movement, which actually contradict his later position outlined in *Creative Evolution*. The first is that

> Movement is distinct from the space covered. Space covered is past, movement is present, the act of covering. The space covered is divisible, indeed infinitely divisible, whilst movement is indivisible, or cannot be divided without changing qualitatively each time it is divided. (Deleuze 1986: 1)

While the spaces covered belong to a single homogeneous space, all movements are heterogeneous and are not reducible among themselves (i.e. they behave like a multiplicity). This first thesis triggers a second, that 'you cannot reconstitute movement with positions in space or instants in time: that is, with immobile sections [*coupes*]' (Deleuze 1986: 1). You can only reconstitute movement by adding new positions or instants as mechanical successions of time and space (thus providing the first hint of the necessary role of montage). However, no matter how much you subdivide time through 'edits', movement will always occur in the interval between the two (a nascent time-image) with its own qualitative duration. Thus, as Deleuze sums up thesis three, 'In short, cinema does not give us an image to which movement is added, it immediately gives us a movement-image. It does give us a section, but a section which is mobile, not an immobile section + abstract movement' (1986: 2). In her excellent essay on Deleuze and early cinema, Susana Viegas rightly argues that,

> We have to face Deleuze's anachronism, and the fact that even if it is highly probable that Bergson was indeed aware of the movement-images and the mobile sections, his ideas on the immobile sections and the spatialized time lead him to understand the cinematograph as false movement. It was not his ideas on the mobile sections or moving-images, as Deleuze (*Cinema 1*, p. 3) insists: 'The discovery of the movement-image, beyond the conditions of natural perception, was the extraordinary invention of the first chapter of *Matter and Memory*.' (2016: 240)

Instead, as Viegas argues, Bergson was adamant that you can't make images *of* real movement or real duration (*durée*) because he had already collapsed the difference between materialism and idealism through the agency of memory, which 'is just the intersection of mind and matter' (Bergson [1896] 1991: 13).

Deleuze's solution to the problem is to quash the material, spectacular aspects of early cinema, with its focus on the apparatus, projection and exhibition, and focus on montage as the logical expansion of movement into narrative sets and sequences. As he argues in *Cinema 1*,

> The evolution of the cinema, the conquest of its own essence or novelty, was to take place through montage, the mobile camera and the emancipation of the view point, which became *separate from projection* [my italics]. The shot would then stop being a spatial category and become a temporal one, and the section would no longer be immobile, but mobile. (1986: 3)

However as we have seen, Deleuze himself can be guilty of a reductive formalism that circumscribes his otherwise brilliant contributions to developing an ontology of the image through his tendency to tie it exclusively to historically specific European and American filmic paradigms.

Deleuze thus roots the movement-image in four main national schools of montage, roughly defined as: 1) The Organic Trend or The American School; 2) The Dialectic Trend or The Soviet School; 3) The Quantitative Trend or The Pre-War French School; and 4) The Intensive, Spiritual Trend or The German School. For Deleuze, montage is the defining characteristic of these aesthetic types and their corresponding narrative tropes, all of which attempt to reference an ontological whole (Bergson's aggregate of images) through varying organisations of parts and subsets. However, as David Martin-Jones argues, Deleuze reductively begins his story with D. W. Griffith and narrative-driven parallel montage, ignoring the 'pre-history' of Méliès and the Lumière Brothers, which is defined less by realist linearity than discontinuous *spectacle*, what Tom Gunning has called a 'cinema of attractions' (2006: 381–8). For Martin-Jones, 'Spectacle (and accordingly, context) is undervalued in Deleuze's conceptualization of the movement-image throughout *Cinema 1*, which primarily focuses on formal qualities, especially montage' (2011: 23). Further, 'Early silent films should not be understood as primitive attempts at narrative, but as deliberately eye-catching spectacles designed for an audience desirous of immediate distraction' (2011: 32–3).

According to Gunning in his seminal essay, 'The Cinema of Attraction(s): Early Film, Its Spectator and the Avant-Garde' (2006), early cinema deliberately broke the fourth wall by soliciting audience attention towards the film event itself (as opposed to drawing them passively into the narrative), whether through close-ups (often sexually titillating) or cinematic tricks such as slow and reverse motion or multiple exposures. Instead of fictional elements being geared towards psychological or action-based narrative, as in the early films of Griffith, these films privileged slapstick sight gags, vaudeville song and dance numbers and recreations of current events, often within the context of showing the films in a real vaudeville setting between live performances (i.e. as one part of a larger spectacle). Even Edwin S. Porter's *The Great Train Robbery* (1903), an otherwise straightforward western narrative, features an opening shot (or closing, depending on the print) of the leader of the outlaw gang emptying his gun at point-blank range at the audience, shocking them out of their seats while also seducing them into an unbelievable spectacle. As Gunning sums it up:

> It is the direct address of the audience, in which an attraction is offered to the spectator by a cinema showman, that defines this approach to filmmaking. Theatrical display dominates over narrative absorption, emphasizing the direct stimulation of shock or surprise at the expense of unfolding a story or creating a diegetic universe. The cinema of attractions expends little energy creating characters with psychological motivations or individual personality. Making use of both fictional and non-fictional attractions, its energy moves outward to an acknowledged spectator rather than inward towards the character-based situations essential to classical narrative. (2006: 384)

More importantly in relation to the work of Le Grice (or Hollis Frampton's *Gloria!*, as we saw in Chapter 2), this so-called 'attraction-image' resurfaces throughout cinema history, disrupting Deleuze's neat historical categorisation of movement- and time-images because it contains elements of both. Thus Martin-Jones notes the resurfacing of spectacle for its own sake – via repetition and narrative retardation as well as seemingly gratuitous fight scenes – in spaghetti westerns such as Sergio Corbucci's *Django* (1966) and Enzo G. Castellari's *Keoma* (1976). As Martin-Jones explains,

> in the attraction-image montage is not used to construct the continuous view of time that characterizes the movement-image. Yet nor does this structure correspond to the discontinuous linkages found in the time-image. Rather, montage is motivated primarily by the construction of non-continuous spectacles, for a viewpoint situated to facilitate appreciation of the 'display' of events taking place on screen. The attraction-image, then, takes the form of a series of spectacles through which a non-continuous movement of the whole can be perceived, even in the fixed shot, through non-continuous montage. (2011: 42)

– an excellent summary, as it turns out, of Le Grice's *Little Dog for Roger* and *After Lumière – L'Arroseur Arrosé*.

Closely linked with the London Film-Makers' Co-op (1966–99), which included key experimental film-makers such as Peter Gidal, Michael Attree, Roger Hammond, William Raban and Sally Potter, Le Grice's practice has moved from analogue to digital manipulation of both found and recreated footage and from cine-club single screenings to multiple projections in art galleries where the audience is as much in control of the film's projection as the art institution itself. His work tends to be defined by four main guiding principles: 1) Duration as a concrete dimension of conceptual and physical awareness (thus the Bergsonian import of his work); 2) A focus on the printer as both a reproductive *and* constructive tool; 3) The projector as both tool and spectacular event; and 4) The importance of real time/space, whereby all facets of the film's production and exhibition process, from pre-filming and the actual shoot to editing, printing and projection, are witnessed in the present and not retroactively. Each of these elements is key to understanding the role of silence in the three films under discussion, so let's deal with them in turn.

In terms of duration, Le Grice is largely concerned with matching the real-time experience of the film's spectator (which takes place within a finite time much like the spatial properties of a piece of sculpture) with the real-time properties of the film itself (as both narrative and material production). Unfortunately, within conventional narrative film (ruled by the exigencies of the action-image),

> time becomes irrevocably illusionistic. Not only is the duration of the film's represented action unrelatable to the duration of its presentation, but through subversion by illusionistic continuity between shots, the shots themselves lose their durational documentality. In other words, the material duration of the film's presentation, production and represented action becomes entirely dissociated; the spectator, with no

way of integrating the relations of present, retrospective record, and fiction, can only give in to the fictional duration which subsumes all others. (Le Grice 2001: 199)

Unlike the films of Béla Tarr, where a fifteen-minute diegetic sequence of a man walking across the windswept Hungarian plain is actually shown in one long fifteen-minute take (usually a close-up of his back, so that we actually feel the arduous nature of the action – a form of 'endurance-image') commercial film tends to compress durational experience for the sake of narrative convention. 'Furthermore,' adds Le Grice, 'the conventions of editing and montage obliterate any trace of the temporal relations in the production, and reinforce the spectator's condition as passive consumer' (2001: 199). However, it's important to note that when Le Grice uses an uninterrupted long take he is not striving for Bazinian realist authenticity but opening up a temporal space whereby

> the spectator can reflect on the conditions and relations of production as inscribed through, for example, the form of camera action, framing, surface qualities of image and printing. The long take then has no intrinsic privilege but served (and serves) to initiate consideration of certain cinematic issues. (2001: 199)

In this way, every facet of the pro-filmic – that which is placed in front of the camera – is integrated with the film's material process, from the real time of production to the real time of projection.

In his key 1972 essay 'Real Time/Space', in *Art and Artists* Magazine, Le Grice discusses the fact that in the earliest days of cinema history,

> the same piece of equipment was often used as camera, printer and projector. The similarities of functioning provide something of a 'mechanistic' basis for the 'equivalence' idea. Until recently, printing has been the area of retrospective TIME/SPACE (or content) which has involved me most. I have been interested by the way in which it allows physical aspects of the medium, the reality of the celluloid, emulsion, sprockets, the nature and capabilities of the machinery to become the basis of experience and content. (1972: 40)

In other words, instead of being a retrospective element in the film-going experience (i.e. we don't really think about how the print was produced or transported to the cinema), we now start to see it as part of the projection event in itself, overriding the hegemony of the filmic narrative as the driving force of its duration. As Le Grice argues,

> Historically (certainly for myself), the relationship between the printer and projector has helped to develop awareness of the components of the projection event. (Although I now see some of the involvement in this area as an inhibition to a more thorough concern with the projection event itself). (1972: 40)

This provides a useful segue to the third facet of Le Grice's practice: the projector as the key part of both the pro-filmic and the actual theatrical event. Although Le Grice makes no mention of Syncinema in his writings, there is obviously a strong connection to Debord and Lemaître's Lettrist and Situationist innovations in this area. We see this in Le Grice's emphasis on the active role of the individual viewer, whose

> point of access is through the projection event only, and that for him is the current confrontation. Certainly this factor has been a prime consideration for me, and I have given a great deal of thought to the kind of condition, role and behaviour which is available to the audience, to the 'credibility' of what is presented as some form of, or relation to 'reality'. I have considered the situation of the audience politically and ethically, and have reacted strongly against the passive, subjectivity to a prestructured substitute and illusory reality which is the normal situation for the audience of the commercial film. (1972: 39)

However, as we shall see in our analysis of *Little Dog for Roger* and *Threshold*, Le Grice moves beyond Lemaître and Debord's 'situational' focus on the seated audience facing the screen (or waiting to enter the theatre) and places them instead inside the projector itself, creating a machinic phylum that bodily *constructs* the film at the same time that it screens/perceives it.

This is the essence of the fourth factor of Le Grice's cinema, the importance of real (as opposed to illusory) time/space which can communicate every stage of the film's existence, from scripting, through shooting, editing, printing, promotion to projection, where all facets come together in the durational synthesis of the projection itself.

As Le Grice puts it,

> The direction of my thinking, and the tendencies in my films, keep returning me to an affirmation of the projection event as the primary reality. In other words, the Real TIME/SPACE event at projection, which is the current, tangible point of access for the audience, is to be considered as experiential base through which any retrospective record, reference or process is to be dealt with by the audience. This reverses the situation common to the cinematic language where experience of the real TIME/SPACE at projection is subsumed by various aspects of manipulated retrospective 'reality'. (1972: 39)

All four of these factors play a key role in Le Grice's short films, *Little Dog for Roger* (1967); *Threshold* (1972); and *After Lumière – L'Arroseur Arrosé* (1974), all three of which enfold silence into the larger matrix of time/space projection and its corollary, concrete duration.

There are several important precursors to materialist film, the most obvious being Dziga Vertov's Kino-Eye, less for his use of the dialectic at every stage of the film process (which was such an attraction to Godard and Gorin) than for his machinic conception of human perception, as a creator of singularities and assemblages, in Deleuze's sense. Thus his famous statement that:

> I am a kino-eye, I am a mechanical eye. I, a machine, show you the world as only I can see it. Now and forever, I free myself from human immobility, I am in constant motion, I draw near, then away from objects, I crawl under, I climb onto them. [. . .] Freed from the rule of sixteen-seventeen frames per second, freed of the limits of time and space, I put together any given points in the universe, no matter where I've recorded them. My path leads to the creation of a fresh perception of the world. I decipher in a new way a world unknown to you. (Vertov 1984: 17–18)

As Constance Penley argues in her seminal 1970s analysis of the avant-garde and the imaginary, Vertov's

> *Man with a Movie Camera* is seen as a forerunner of recent films which explore self-referential structures: seeing the camera, the projector, the screen, the roll of film itself in the film can recall to the spectator the fact that s/he is watching a film and thus of his or her own perceptual processes. (Penley 1977: 7)

Another key influence on materialist film is Man Ray's *Retour à la raison* (1923), a three-minute filmic version of his subsequent photographic 'Rayograms' which eschewed a pro-filmic placement of objects before the camera lens in favour of placing small objects such as nails, pins and springs on the film strip itself, exposing them to direct light without the use of a mediating camera lens. Laszlo Moholy-Nagy had worked in a similar fashion with his gelatin silver print photographs from the early 1920s onwards, one featuring an ethereal-looking scale model of the Eiffel Tower in seeming orbit around a navigator's compass. In the context of the late 1960s, Le Grice was well aware of these Bauhaus and Surrealist forebears but was more specifically influenced by Birgin and Wilhelm Hein's *Rohfilm* (*Raw Film*, 1968) and George Landow's *Film in which there appear Sprocket Holes, Edge Lettering, Dirt Particles etc.* (1966) – a six-minute loop in which a stalled, vertically-split double shot of a woman to the left of the frame is supplemented by the animated material 'debris' of the film process to the right. In this light, Le Grice's second film, *Little Dog for Roger* is a quintessentially materialist film but it adds significantly to the Heins and Landow formal inventory by including celluloid scratches, processing stains, splicing-tape marks, fingerprints and image slip. As Le Grice described the process in his book, *Abstract Film and Beyond*:

> Not only are the films concerned to include cinematic elements basic to it as a mechanism, like the sprocket-holes, the celluloid support, and the emulsion as material, but also to include elements which are usually considered as error, fault, or in cybernetic terms, noise. This is particularly true of *Little Dog for Roger* and *Roh Film*, which, as well as referring to the physical aspects of the film strip, also refer to material aspects like the act of splicing and to the functioning of the projector. For example, in *Little Dog for Roger* there is a long section of image slip, where the material is disengaged from the printer claw, deliberately simulating the skidding of film in the projector. (1977: 118)

However, there is a considerable difference between Le Grice's objectives and Landow's, for the latter had created a semantic/semiotic work whereby the visual 'noise' of the film refers to the film's materiality in the same way that a sign refers to a referent. Le Grice is far more concerned with film process as rhythm and repetition (it is no accident that his films are heavily influenced by jazz, especially the improvisational, free-form development of refrain-variation-transformed refrain) generated through tactility and process, whereby the

> traces of the films' handling are deliberately retained. [His films] attack the implicit alienation in the film process which loses contact with the vital stages of image transfer and chemical development, and [. . .] are the result of contact between the filmmaker and film at all stages. (Le Grice 1977: 118)

The source material for *Little Dog for Roger* was actually obtained from a box of damaged 9.5mm home movies that Le Grice discovered in the basement of his parents' home in Plymouth, Devon. The film was originally shot by Le Grice's father and features his mother, himself and his younger brother, with a central focus on their terrier, basically a 'Little Dog for Malcolm'. Although the home movie retains a considerable amount of nostalgia, its somewhat taken-for-granted familial subject matter from the 1950s now explodes into life as a resurrected memory. As Tim Cawkwell argues,

> Film of a little dog running is just matter with no public meaning, and it is only by reworking it, re-filming it, renewing it that it takes on a more than private significance and that connects it with the universal experience of remembering the past. (2016: unpaginated)

The key to Le Grice's reworking of the found footage is that he built his own printer (converted from a projector) to process the film, which, according to Cawkwell, allowed him to take a negative from filmed footage and to make a work print from the negative. As Le Grice explains a complicated process:

> In *Little Dog for Roger*, much of the material was produced on a primitive printer converted from a projector, and long sections were produced by direct contact printing of an original 9.5mm home movie onto 16mm in short strips under glass. Sometimes the resultant 16mm strips were similarly treated in a second generation, creating an image of film-strip on film-strip – the film edges and sprockets of both generations interacting. (1977: 118)

We see this process right from the start of the film, for as Noam Elcott argues,

> The film is first and foremost a self-reflexive and lyrical documentation of that transfer. For the first minute of the roughly ten-minute-long film, a flood of blurred images rushes down the screen, as if the shutter had been removed from the projector (instead Le Grice detached the film from the claw of the printer), and reminds the viewer that printers and projectors were once coupled with the camera as a single apparatus. (2008: 16)

Despite this tidal wave of discrepant images, the film does have a rough visual 'plot', linked by repetitive loops, as we progress from shots of Le Grice's mother running and playing with the dog, often twirling him in the air while holding his feet, shots of the dog running alone and then an image of one of the two brothers with the dog in the form of a frozen still moving vertically across the shutter. We then cut to a freeze frame of a nearby bridge over a river (also moving across the screen) as we end with the boy and his dog running along the river bank and a closing black screen. Eventually we also get used to the foregrounding of the filmic process itself – repetition of the narrow, 9.5mm film running along the middle of the 16mm aspect ratio which causes an intrusion of the narrower film's frame and sprocket holes; skipping frames that resemble a lantern slide show from the early days of pre-cinema; freeze-fames; upside down footage; interjecting black and white screens; water damage and scratches. Also, as Le Grice recalls the early screenings of the film, 'The projection slip printed on the film still causes projectionists to stop the film to correct the fault' (1972: 40).

For our purposes, the use of sound is equally complex, once again creating an improvisational jazz-like rhythm that stresses continuity (through repetition) and non-continuity (through arbitrary breaks and discordances). The main musical refrain that creates a modicum of coherence is the repeated fade-up of two songs that evoke the era of early synchronous sound film: Ray Henderson's '(Keep Your) Sunny Side Up', from the 1929 Movietone musical of the same name starring Janet Gaynor and Charles Farrell, and a difficult to recognise refrain with the appropriate (at least for the family and their dog) lyrics, 'Two in love, hand in hand, that's why I want to be with you all the day'. Both heighten the nostalgia by evoking the types of music that one might have heard on the BBC Light programme back in the late 1940s and early 1950s and linking them – as a montage of attractions – to the birth of the musical as a trail-blazing sound-image genre in the late 1920s.

However, Le Grice is also aware that the original home movie would have had no sound accompaniment (unlike commercial 'silent' films which were always screened with live music) and he is careful to foreground the different kinds of 'material' silence that serve to define the spectator's *active* relationship to machinic projection. The most obvious sonic layer that expresses audience-as-projector is the sound of the projector itself, a somewhat noisy 'flutter' as the film passes through the gate that connects the musical interludes and tends to express the various technical glitches through a variation in ambient 'noise'. In many ways this is Le Grice's variation on John Cage's dictum that 'there is no such thing as silence', for 'Not one sound fears the silence that extinguishes it. And no silence exists that is not pregnant with sound' (Cage 1973: 135).

In addition to projector noise (that serves to rhythmically and bodily connect us to the apparatus rather than to what we see *imagistically* on the screen), there are two bona-fide sound drop-outs, as if to suggest that this direct machinic identification also has its glitches and break-downs, a sonic equivalent of the 'projection slip' that is actually printed on the film. The first is introduced by a freeze frame on the dog as one of the two songs fades up briefly. We then cut to silence over a white screen before returning to the dog and cutting to a long shot that incorporates the film frame and sprocket holes. Orchestral flute music then fades up before we return to the original song. The relative framing symmetry of this sequence draws obvious attention to the mechanics of the apparatus itself, that 'dead' silence is different from projector noise and can be used to jolt us out of our new subjective mode of identification with the latter, as if to say, 'this is still just a film and you're not an actual machine'. This is reinforced by the film's closing shot of a black screen where the projector hum is finally replaced by dead air, bringing us back to the reality of *in situ* spectatorship.

However, this analysis is complicated by the fact that *Little Dog for Roger* was intended to be projected as loops on *two* screens from the start,

CONCRETE DURATION AND THE SPECTACLE OF ATTRACTIONS 275

then as a complete two-screen film in 1968. As Le Grice described his motives:

> In Warhol's *Chelsea Girls* (1966), the double projection was largely designed to present lengthy material in half the time: though it functioned like the simultaneous observation of two rooms, there is no deliberate formal interaction between the screens. In [...] my own two-screen films, on the other hand, visual interaction between the screens is essential. [...] In *Little Dog for Roger*, the two projectors run at different speeds, one at silent (sixteen frames per second), the other at sound speed (twenty-four frames per second) thus creating a gradual shift between the two screens. (1977: 122)

Twin projection not only creates a material shift in parallel (but different) temporalities – we see the same footage but at different speeds and non-synchronously – but the bifurcation also affects the impact of the silences: one film drowning out the other, as if one were playing John Cage's *4'33"* on an office computer while a family member is simultaneously blasting Motörhead in a neighbouring room. The silences are still there, materially, but become buried as hidden chaoids between two discrepant sonic spaces.

In light of this it's significant that according to Noam Elcott, *Little Dog for Roger* existed in multiple versions – sound and silent, single and double projection – so that the nature of the projection was always variable. However,

> In more definitive versions – the work has recently been standardized as a two-screen digital installation – Le Grice used a single sound track and edited the 16 fps version down so that the reels start and end at the same time and are repeatedly, if only fleetingly, aligned during the course of the film. Woven tightly into the many loops and edits, the temporal displacement is difficult to observe. Instead, the viewer struggles to ascertain the temporal filiations and frequently submits to their ever-modulating present' (2008: 15).

If this is the case, by putting an end to the overriding of silences by the 'noise' of the parallel projection (as well as the temporal displacement between the twin projection speeds), Le Grice creates a far more homogeneous affective experience whereby the role of the silences and projection hum is fixed in a set rhythm, not as a sonic jazz improvisational counterpoint between, say, John Coltrane's tenor sax and Miles Davis's trumpet as separate harmonic progressions. In addition, Le Grice has now downplayed the real-time contribution of the audience as part of a situational material event. This is perhaps an inevitable outcome of changing technologies, whereby old Syncinema tactics and their dependency on 16mm projection have been superseded, first by video, then by DVDs, and now by computer streaming. As the technology develops, the audience's role inevitably becomes more passive and every facet of film's materiality becomes retrospective and the presence of real time/space becomes increasingly impossible to establish.

All is not lost, however, because it is always possible to shift attention away from the uniformity of the sound-image-perception ensemble by changing the position of the projectors. This is exactly what Le Grice does in *Threshold* (1972), which, as he describes it,

> is based on a small number of component sequences. It begins with abstract colour fields filling the whole screen then develops through other simple abstract images created by accidental exposure of film stock – edge fogging. The main image of the film is of border guards at a frontier post. The film explores a range of film printing techniques using colour filtering, mattes and multiple superimpositions. It also includes a short section of computer generated abstract animation made at the Government Atomic Energy Laboratory in Britain in 1969. (Le Grice 2014: unpaginated)

The film's title not only suggests different forms of threshold or limit, such as the literal geographical border between two territories, but also perceptual and optical edges and frames, both computer-generated and analogue. In this way, Deleuze's perception-image – the 'set [ensemble] of elements which act on a centre, and which vary in relation to it' (1986: 217) – can be delimited but also transformed as the centre is deterritorialised and destabilised, whether through one colour melding into another or an abstract shape metamorphosing into another (much like Oskar Fischinger's non-representational short, *An Optical Poem* (1938), or, more materially, Stan Brakhage's *Mothlight* (1963)). In this case the film's scattershot silences act as both limits and bridges between sonic centres and help to shape the film's perceptual whole into an *internal* montage of disconnected attractions (as opposed to a narrative montage between *external* shots).

Thus the film moves from alternating black and green screens to the introduction of additional coloured filters – red, orange, yellow – and strips of celluloid that wobble and transform into 'buxom' anthropomorphic shapes with visible raster lines which muddy the colours together. Approximately halfway through the film we see the first glimpse of the border guards at the frontier post but instead of leading us into a potential linear narrative they too are eventually overwhelmed by strobing filters and abstract animated geometries that absorb them into the film's repetitive biogram of filtered loops. However, if the film's *images* keep us mesmerised as distanced observers, it's the eclectic *soundtrack* that absorbs us into a more 'projectorist subjectivity'. The dominant sound in the first half of the film is a short repetitive chord that seems to be electronically induced, interrupted at times by a crackling sound and loud rhythmic thudding as if the film had been caught in the projector, thus reinforcing our subjective identification with the apparatus. The latter is particularly apparent as we catch our first glimpse of the border guards at the frontier post (as if seen through a spy glass) for we get our only bona-fide sound drop-out in the entire film before the screen is once again filled with strobing filters of orange, blue/green and red. The second half of the film – dominated by the image of the border guards and computer animation – also features broken fragments of dialogue overlayed by short crescendos of sound chords as if someone were randomly scanning and tuning through different radio frequencies. Everything then drops out as we cut to the final credits.

When viewed as a single screen film, *Threshold* easily fits the category of what Patricia Pisters calls the Neuro-Image, in this case a kind of subjectivised schizoid delirium, for as she argues,

> If the cerebral model is an important reference to assess images, and all images are fundamentally related to the brain in the sense that brains are screens and screens operate like brains, then changes in the image are also connected to changed conceptions of the brain. (Pisters 2012: 37)

She then goes on to relate it to certain aspects of Deleuze's time-image, in particular the chapter in *Cinema 2* entitled 'Cinema, body and brain, thought', where he links synaptic skips and discontinuity between neurons to the unresolved narratives of directors like Godard, Resnais and Antonioni. As Deleuze argues,

> in the case of synapses with electrical transmission, we think that the cut or point may be called 'rational', in accord with the mathematical analogy. In contrast, in the case of chemical synapses, the point is 'irrational'; the cut is important in itself and belongs to neither of the two sets that it separates. (1989: 318 n. 32)

In this sense, Le Grice's digital works fit neatly into the latter category as subjective representations of synaptic 'cuts'. However, as in the case of *Little Dog for Roger*, Le Grice uses multiple screens – in this case three – so that, as he puts it, 'the performance version of the film is an improvisation – moving the projectors and superimposing the image as the projection takes place' (2014: unpaginated), so that the spectator is part of a much larger, hands-on manipulation of the screen 'as attraction', either by showing the images side-by-side and splitting them up, or more importantly, superimposing them to form a conglomerate image where the 'frontiers' between colours, sounds, lines and images are constantly broken and remade, forcing us to re-theorise where the film and its frame begin and end. This dialectic between absorption in the film AND awareness of one's surrounding environment calls to mind Roland Barthes's 1975 essay, 'Upon Leaving the Movie Theater', in which he describes himself as a split viewing subject, whereby

> ... it is by letting myself be *twice* fascinated by the image and by its surroundings, as if I had two bodies at once: a narcissistic body which is looking, lost in gazing into the nearby mirror, and a perverse body, ready to fetishize not the image, but precisely that which exceeds it: the sound's grain, the theater, the obscure mass of other bodies, the rays of light, the entrance, the exit: in short, in order to distance myself, to 'take off', I complicate a 'relationship' with a 'situation'. ([1975] 1980: 4)

Le Grice pulls all these deterritorialising threads together in perhaps the most successful of his films from this era, *After Lumière – L'Arroseur Arrosé* (1974). A direct return to the late nineteenth-century's 'cinema of attractions', it consists of four slightly different 'remakes' of the Lumière Brothers forty-five-second, single take 'gag film', *Arroseur et arrosé* in which a gardener, filmed watering the plants in a garden with a long hose, is the victim of a young boy's prank. The boy steps on the hose, blocking the water flow, causing the gardener to point the nozzle at his face to see if there is a malfunction. The boy then releases his foot, causing the gardener to be drenched, and the little scamp runs off. However, the gardener apprehends him and the naughty boy gets his appropriate comeuppance.

Interestingly, there is no definitive 'original version' of this film as it was remade several times, largely due to the film's degradation due to the delicacy of the film stock. Thus, the first known print dates from 1895 and was co-directed by Alice Guy and Louis Lumière, with François Clerc as the gardener and Benoît Duval as the young boy. In this version the gardener gets his revenge by hitting the boy several times on the backside before the latter exits sheepishly to the right. In a remake the following year, directed by Francis Doublier, the gardener grabs the boy (now a teenager), kicks him on the arse and then hoses him down as he runs off into the depth of the shot, a classic case of tit-for-tat. It's thus completely appropriate for Le Grice to add his own variation on these attractions because like a vaudeville act they are open to endless reinterpretations.

Part 1 of *After Lumière* is formally the closest to the original for it is shot in black and white and contains no accompanying soundtrack. Following a white screen we fade in to a small garden with a framing fence with a glimpse of a children's swing in the neighbouring garden. Unlike the original versions, the gardener (William Raban) isn't present in the opening shot but emerges into the frame from screen right, hosing the edge of the grass closest to the fence. Then Le Grice adds a new feature – a third character (Marilyn Halford), who is the woman of the house (the gardener's wife, lover, or simply his boss?) – who enters from the left wearing a large bonnet. They chat for twenty seconds before she returns to the house (off-screen), and he continues hosing. The Lumière Brothers' young boy is now a girl dressed as a boy (played by Le Grice's daughter, Judith) who steps on the hose and the film plays out exactly like the original except for the 'punishment' of the boy which now takes place off-screen to the right. The decision to exclude the comeuppance seems to be deliberately designed to reinforce the hermetic nature of the original *mise-en-scène* so that the audience not only craves a larger context for the events but also associates Part 1's silent soundtrack as a potential vector for discovering ever-broadening new sounds and spaces.

Indeed, this is borne out (albeit minimally) in Part 2 which is not only re-shot with slightly different camera angles, tighter framing (the gardener's head is occasionally cropped off) and a more mobile camera but also presented in negative with an accompanying solo piano soundtrack, Erik Satie's *Gnossienne # 1* (1890–93). The latter seems to be diegetic music because it stops when the woman of the house enters the garden and we hear ambient room tone, suggesting that it was she who was playing the piano inside the house. This assumption is reinforced when the music starts up again after she goes back inside, just as the gardener is soaked and the boy runs off. Le Grice adds a variation in this part by holding on the garden fence after the main protagonists have left the frame, zooming into a shrub and then wobbling the camera slightly as we zoom back out. This suggests a slightly larger *mise-en-scène* divorced from the diegetic action, as if the 'montage of attractions' included social setting (a wife who enjoys music, with its obvious class connotations) in addition to the entertainment provided by the sight gag.

Le Grice ends the section with a fade to black accompanied by scratch marks on the black emulsion (a clear metacommunication of the cinematic device) but also the sound of a gramophone stylus as it reaches the end of the vinyl platter. The latter raises two possibilities: that the Satie music was non-diegetic after all (as the audience of a 'silent' film would come to expect), or it was diegetic 'as a 78 rpm record', played inside the house by the wife and interrupted as she entered the garden. In this way Le Grice subtly opens up the confines of the film still further, not only drawing attention to issues of synchronous and non-synchronous sound but also the wider social ramifications of musical taste (owning a record collection) and prowess (being able to play the piano).

Part 3 once again begins with the *Gnossienen* but this time over fairly loud ambient garden sounds – children's shouts from next door, song birds, neighbourhood 'noise', and even the sound of the hose water hitting the grass – thereby providing the audience with an even wider sense of location, as if the microphone were 'zooming out' to a broader suburban setting even if the camera is still focused on the garden. As in Part 2 we fade up into a negative shot of the garden but this time it's orange 'tinted', the most common colour process during the silent era, which treats a filmstrip with a single dye. According to Tom Gunning, 'The process consisted of immersing sections of a black-and-white film print into a vat containing a single color. This tinting process would then color the areas of the image that were white with the hue of the dye' (2015: 17). In general, although the overall effect was obviously contrived and artificial, it was invariably used to create realistic effects so that red would often be used for scenes featuring fires blazing out of control, blue for nighttime sequences, yellow for electrically lit interiors. In Le Grice's case, the orange tint seems to be designed to evoke a bright sunny day. Part 3 is similar in narrative to the other parts although this time the Satie ends without the stylus scratching, creating confusion as to whether it's diegetic or non-diegetic. Also, ten seconds before the end we hear a rumbling sound as the image seems to be affected by water damage and deterioration, thus underlining the material nature of the film as an archive print, reinforced by a closing cut to a white screen and absolute silence.

This print 'damage' (or, more accurately, manipulation by Le Grice) continues over the opening shots of Part 4 as the *Gnossienne* fades up over shots of bubble shapes against the same white screen. We then see a yellow filter segue to orange as we fade to a close shot of the wife's hands playing piano in natural positive colour. So, we were right after all: the Satie was diegetic (as well as non-diegetic) for now we see it being played in real time. In addition, Le Grice's camera, although still static and shooting in a single take, has broadened its perspective still further by moving inside the house so that we now see the events in the garden through the French windows from the perspective of a domestic interior. As one might expect, the wife stops playing to converse with the gardener and resumes the *Gnossienne* as the film comes to a close in the deep shadow of the living room. However, Le Grice continues to accentuate the materiality of the film experience, inserting a red filter 'flare up' over the wife's sheet music and showing some water damage to the print before cutting to his trademark white screen.

Taken as a progression of four successive sequences one can read the film as the equivalent of a slow zoom-out to disclose a wider social context as we move from the site and action of the initial prank (i.e. the garden), to the broader (bourgeois) social context of the household based on the limited information given, or, as Le Grice puts it, 'It places the spectator into the role of cinema detective – philosophically it asks what can you know for sure from the evidence of the cinematic document' (2014: unpaginated). All variations exist both within the image itself – framing, *mise-en-scène*, camera movement – and also off-screen space expressed through diegetic and non-diegetic sound. In this sense the initial 'silent' film is merely a jumping off point for film as both a mechanical and phenomenological 'eye' in which the onus is on the spectator to structure and make sense of the filmic raw material.

However, as usual, Le Grice doesn't stop there because *After Lumière*'s four separate parts are screened simultaneously as a single concrete duration, so that the 'silent' segment's autonomy is 'drowned out', firstly by the diegetic sound of the children, the hose and the birds and then the three vibrant renditions of Satie's *Gnossienne* (probably non-synchronous) enfolding all mechanical aspects back into the performative. In *Matter and Memory*, Bergson defined the difference between the component parts of his book's title as follows: '*I call* matter *the aggregate of images, and* perception of matter *these same images referred to the eventual action of one particular image, my body.*' ([1896] 1991: 22). In the four-screen version, the progressive filling-in of the 'out-of-shot' (perception) is shown as a simultaneous aggregate of images (matter), so that our attentive recognition of the filmic performance is caught inextricably between the two, in effect stalling a clear phenomenological intentionality. As Deleuze describes it:

> attentive recognition informs us to a much greater degree when it fails than when it succeeds. When we cannot remember, sensory-motor extension remains suspended, and the actual image, the present optical perception, does not link up with either a motor image or a recollection-image which would re-establish contact. It rather enters into relation with genuinely virtual elements, feelings of *déjà vu* or past 'in general' [...], dream-images [...], fantasies or theatre scenes [...] In short, it is not the recollection-image or attentive recognition which gives us the proper equivalent of the optical-sound image, it is rather the disturbances of memory and the failures of recognition. (1989: 54–5)

If this is true, then the most successful projectorists are those with the greatest number of mechanical glitches, because it is only through some degree of perceptual and phenomenological breakdown – much like Heidegger's 'present-at-hand' broken hammer – that the audience can come to grips with the complexity of cinematic procedures and successfully restructure the material so that we become even more aware of our embodied relation to the apparatus. As Vivian Sobchack argues in her seminal book, *The Address of the Eye*,

> Not only is the cinema a visible paradigm of our inherence in the world and others, but its technology is joined to intentional consciousness and is predicated as an instrumentality of the latter. Indeed, technology is considered here as the means of a certain way of being-in-the-world. (1992: 165)

Maybe all cinema should follow Le Grice's lead and turn us all into projectorists, for as Heidegger says, 'Technology is a mode of revealing. Technology comes to presence in the realm where revealing and unconcealment take place, where alātheia, truth happens' (1993: 319). 'Unconcealment' is an extremely apt term for Le Grice's practice because it is in his desire to make present every phase of a film's process at the exact moment of its screening that being-in-the-world turns into pure becoming and phenomenology embraces the eternal return.

CHAPTER 9

On Truth and Lie in an Extra-Formal Sense: Silence as Resistant *Punctum* in Abbas Kiarostami's *The Chorus* (1982), *Homework* (1989) and *Close-Up* (1990)

In the mid-to-late 1990s, Abbas Kiarostami (1940–2016) was easily the most high-profile director of what was known at that time as the 'New Iranian Cinema', culminating in his being awarded the Palme d'Or at Cannes in 1997 for *Taste of Cherry* (1997), a provocative film about a man who drives around in his truck in search of someone who will take on the macabre job of burying him under a cherry tree after he commits suicide. Kiarostami had already gained a strong international reputation since the first European screening of his work in Locarno in 1989 and is perhaps best known critically for his so-called 'Koker Trilogy' – *Where Is the Friend's House?* (1987); *Life, and Nothing More . . .* (1992, aka *And Life Goes On*) and *Through the Olive Trees* (1994) – which are all set in the same northern Iranian village. This success has led to a certain schizophrenic split in his reputation. On the one hand we have the western film festival circuit, where Kiarostami is often seen as the Iranian equivalent of Antonioni or Godard – indeed Godard is once reported to have said at Cannes that 'Cinema starts with D. W. Griffith and ends with Kiarostami' (cited in Mulvey 1998: 24), presumably referring to conventional *narrative* cinema (conveniently ignoring the 'cinema of attractions' and its avant-garde appropriation). This is often manifested in Kiarostami's French New Wave predilection for black and white screens, sound drop-outs and Brechtian distanciation devices such as revealing his film crew on the set or making personal appearances by interviewing his own actors.

On the other hand we have Iran itself – a self-confessed cinephile nation – where he not only draws on the specific pre- and post-Revolutionary political and cultural context (the Shah was overthrown on 11 February 1979) but was heavily involved in making children's education films for Kānun (aka Kānoon) at the beginning of his career. Agnès Devictor explains the context:

> One pre-Revolution public production company continued to work after the Revolution: the famous Center for the Intellectual Development of Children and

> Young Adults (*Kānun-e parvareš-e fekri-e kudakān va nowjavānān*). The center, created by the Shahbanu [Farah Pahlavi], and its Department of Cinema opened in 1969 [other sources say 1965] and was overseen during its first several years by Ebrahim Foruzesh and Abbas Kiarostami. It was an active producer of children films and at the same time of auteur films. Many of the most famous Iranian directors worked with the Center at some point between 1970 and the late 1990s. Among them were Bahram Beyza'i, Daryush Mehrju'i, and Amir Naderi. It did not close during the Revolution. But during the late 1990s, its production declined. (2015: 16)

Equally important is the influence of modern Iranian poetry, especially the works of Sohrab Sepehri and Forugh Farrokhzad, whose respective poems, 'Where Is the Friend's House?' and 'The Wind Will Carry Us' also happen to be the titles of two of Kiarostami's most popular films. Farrokhzad, who sadly died in 1967 at the young age of thirty-two, was not only a famous author but also made one film, *The House Is Black* (1963), a twenty-minute short that many critics argue was hugely influential on an entire generation of Iranian film-makers, including Kiarostami. 'Indeed,' as the exceptional Kiarostami scholar Godfrey Cheshire notes,

> *The House Is Black*, with its sonorous, quasiliturgical narration over images of a leper colony, formulates and advances a very specific idea of *poetic cinema*, one that incorporates both actual verbal poetry and an approach to cinematic construction based on the example of poetry. (2000: 8)

Cheshire goes on to argue that this influence consists of a double register, a combination of classical Persian and Arabic poetry along with Modernist forms derived from French and English precursors, particularly the works of William Carlos Williams, Marianne Moore, Ezra Pound and Wallace Stevens. Cheshire hits the nail on the head when he states that,

> If you wanted to reduce Kiarostami to a single idea, you would not be far wrong in saying that he has spent his career developing a cinematic equivalent of Iranian modernist poetry. To suggest why, it's first necessary to note that poetry pervades the educations and consciousnesses of Iranians, from virtually all social strata, to a far greater extent than in the West. (2000: 8)

Indeed, the impact of Iranian Modernist poetry hit the iconoclastic tendencies of the nation's youth at exactly the same time that the New Wave and the Beat Generation impacted the West. Cheshire argues that,

> For a young Iranian in the Sixties, entering the cinema inspired by and infused with the creative spirit of poets like Forugh Farrokhzad was hardly an anomaly; it was an

eminently sensible way of approaching an imported medium through the precepts of one's own culture. (2000: 8)

Kiarostami himself acknowledges this influence, arguing that, unlike the novel, the poem is inherently incomplete and non-linear, riddled with gaps and fissures that can defy convenient interpretation, not unlike Deleuze's 'irrational cuts' as temporal interstices in the time-image. To be more specific, we could also argue that Kiarostami sees this poetic image as a variation on Deleuze's 'noosign', 'an image which goes beyond itself towards something which can only be thought' (Deleuze 1989: 335). As Kiarostami states,

> What happens between the lines of a poem occurs in only one place: inside our heads. Why can't cinema be the same? If a level of incomprehension is inherent in poetry, why can't it be so with cinema? Why can't a film be experienced like a poem, an abstract painting, or a piece of music? Cinema will never be considered a major art form unless the possibility of incomprehension is accepted as a positive attribute. (Cited in Cronin 2015: 20)

In short, Kiarostami is very much against spoon-fed cinema: he likes his films to be half-finished, vague, ambiguous, calling on the audience to work hard to overcome their temporary confusion, even to the point of falling asleep if necessary. In short Kiarostami likes to 'show by not showing' so that he can tap into the inner reaches of the spectator's mind (a latent or virtual chaoid that even the viewer didn't know was there). This explains his predilection for open endings, for as he argues, 'What film starts at the beginning of a character's life and ends with the end of that life? Everyone has a past and future we never see' (Cronin 2015: 19). To put it another way, watching a film isn't like doing a crossword puzzle, where even the most cryptic of clues leads to a definitive answer. Instead,

> The identity of a film is established by whoever is watching it, which means there are as many meanings as there are members of the audience. A film shouldn't have a solid structure or a clear-cut conclusion. There should be holes and fissures into which the audience can climb. It's a never-ending game. I encourage you to leave things unsaid as much as possible. (Cronin 2015: 24)

It's also worth noting that even Kiarostami's Brechtian tendencies towards *V-Effekt* and self-reflexivity have an Iranian source in the form of Taazieh (*taziyeh*), the traditional folk theatre that depicts the Shi'ite account of the murder of Imam Hossein, the son of Muhammad, by the tyrant Yazid. This is performed annually on the anniversary of the event and is notorious for 'baring the device' on a number of occasions. As Kiarostami describes a performance that he himself witnessed,

> In the scene of Yazid's and Imam Hossein's battle, Imam Hossein's sword suddenly became bent because it was made of very cheap, soft metal. Yazid went to him and took his sword and put it on a big stone and straightened it with another stone and gave it back to him and then they continued fighting. And at the moment Yazid is supposed to chop off Imam Hossein's head, they were served tea, and Yazid signalled with a nod for his to be placed next to him as he continued with the decapitation. These things really helped me. I saw how nothing could affect this scene. (Hamid 1997: 24)

The French philosopher, Jean-Luc Nancy, one of the most insightful commentators on Kiarostami's work, frames this poetic and theatrical structure in terms of the insistence of cinema which partakes of its specific 'evidence', whereby

> Cinema (and with it television, video, and photography: in Kiarostami's films they play a part that is not accidental) makes evident a conspicuous form of the world, a form or a sense. Evidence always comprises a blind spot within its very obviousness: in this way it leans on the eye. The 'blind spot' does not deprive the eye of its sight: on the contrary, it makes an opening for a gaze and it *presses* upon it to look. (Nancy 2001: 12)

The whole objective of Kiarostami's films is to exert this pressure – whether through sound/silence or image/black screen – whereby overt 'lies' and misdirection can reveal an even deeper truth. Indeed, Kiarostami himself once admitted that 'We can never get close to the truth except by lying' (cited in Cheshire 1996: 42). This is not unlike the analogy of the hermit's cave in Nietzsche's *Beyond Good and Evil*:

> The hermit does not believe that any philosopher – assuming that every philosopher was first of all a hermit – ever expressed his real and ultimate opinions in books: does one not write books precisely to conceal what one harbors? Indeed, he will doubt whether a philosopher could possibly have 'ultimate and real' opinions, whether behind every one of his caves there is not, must not be, another deeper cave – a more comprehensive, stranger, richer world beyond the surface, an abysmally deep ground behind every ground, under every attempt to furnish 'grounds'. Every philosophy is a foreground philosophy – that is a hermit's judgment . . . ([1886] 1966, section 289: 229)

In Kiarostami's cinema, it is the audience's role to be an active 'spelunker', to break through the wall of Plato's cave of illusions to discover a non-representational, non-illusionary world in an extra-formal sense where we can discover art and reality's innermost depths. As Nancy argues,

> That is why the recurring attempt to compare cinema with Plato's cave is inaccurate: precisely, the depths of the cave attest to an outside of the world, but as a negative, and this sets up the discrediting of images, as we know, or it demands a consideration for images that are loftier and purer, named 'ideas'. Film works the opposite way: it does not reflect an outside, it opens an inside onto itself. The image on the screen is itself the idea. (2001: 46)

A useful method for applying this Nietzschean 'gay science' (the allusion to Godard's *Le Gai Savoir* is deliberate) is through Roland Barthes's distinction between the *studium* and the *punctum* in his 1980 book, *Camera Lucida*, published in France two months prior to his death. Although Barthes was writing specifically about still photography, his insights are equally applicable to cinema, particularly as Kiarostami's often radical construction of probing blind spots in conventional narrative were designed to simultaneously challenge and surrender to the political and cultural status quo (and its corresponding censorship) in post-Revolutionary Iran. Stated simply, the *studium* is the cultural, political and linguistic interpretation of a photograph, the elements of its contact that make it immediately recognisable and 'readable', the way, say, a photograph or filmic establishing shot of the Eiffel Tower immediately signifies Paris and a certain lifestyle. As Barthes puts it, it's a kind of 'average' affect that we derive from a certain cultural training. Although deriving from the Latin word *studium*, it

> doesn't mean, at least not immediately, 'study', but application to a thing, taste for someone, a kind of general, enthusiastic commitment, of course, but without special acuity. It is by *studium* that I am interested in so many photographs, whether I receive them as political testimony or enjoy them as good historical scenes: for it is culturally (this connotation is present in *studium*) that I participate in the figures, the faces, the gestures, the settings, the actions. (Barthes [1980] 1981: 26)

According to Barthes, the *studium* is

> of the order of *liking*, not of *loving*; it mobilizes a half desire, a demi-volition; it is the same sort of vague, slippery, irresponsible interest one takes in the people, the entertainments, the books, the clothes one finds 'all right'. ([1980] 1981: 27)

In short, the *studium* is a kind of aesthetic contract between the image-maker and the spectator, a shared civility and understanding that, in Kiarostami's case, would placate the censors and a hyper-critical public, but also give him the opportunity to challenge it from within.

The latter is the role of the *punctum*, whose job is to break or punctuate the *studium*. However, the *punctum* is outside the control of both auteur and audience (just as Kiarostami likes it), for as Barthes argues,

> This time it is not I who seek it out (as I invest the field of the *studium* with my sovereign consciousness), it is this element which rises from the scene, shoots out of it like an arrow, and pierces me. A Latin word exists to designate this wound, this prick, this mark made by a pointed instrument: the word suits me all the better in that it also refers to the notion of punctuation, and because the photographs I am speaking of are in effect punctuated, sometimes even speckled with these sensitive points; precisely, these marks, these wounds are so many *points*. This second element which will disturb the *studium* I shall therefore call *punctum*; for *punctum* is also: sting, speck, cut, little hole – and also a cast of the dice. A photograph's *punctum* is that accident which pricks me (but also bruises me, is poignant to me). ([1980] 1981: 26–7)

The *punctum* can often take the form of a minor detail that both attracts and annoyingly sidelines the audience (the inexplicable focus on an aerosol can, which, as we shall see in *Close-Up*, prevents us from seeing a key narrative event in the film), but also an extra-formal chasm/chaoid that instead of sucking us into an internal abyss in the sound-image relationship, actually springs out and pricks us like a projectile, wounding us intellectually so that we are forced into a completely new and different temporality. As Barthes puts it, 'I now know that there exists another *punctum* another "stigmatum" than the "detail". This new *punctum*, which is no longer of form but of intensity, is Time, the lacerating emphasis of the *noeme* ("*that-has-been*"), its pure representation' ([1980] 1981: 96). It is the latter that underpins Kiarostami's use of silence – in different ways for different purposes – in the three films that we will discuss in this chapter: *The Chorus* (1982), *Homework* (1989) and *Close-Up* (1990).

The Chorus (*Hamsarayan*), based on an idea by M. J. Kahnamui, was Kiarostami's last short film for Kānun and was set in Rasht, the capital of Gilan province which borders the Caspian Sea to the north. The film's opening credits are seen over an image of blank staff paper/sheet music (as if waiting for a yet-to-be-written score) accompanied by a complete sound drop-out. Thus Kiarostami establishes silence both visually and literally as a kind of phenomenological ground zero right from the start, as if what follows will consist of various contrasts of sound in different degrees of counterpoint. We then cut to a static shot down a narrow alleyway, paint peeling off crumbling walls covered in graffiti, clearly indicating an impoverished working-class neighbourhood. We then hear the sound of an approaching horse and cart which gets louder as it reaches the camera before swerving off to the left. After following its progress through various back alleys for almost two minutes, we cut to an angle behind the driver's head as the horse and cart stalls behind an elderly man walking leisurely in front of them, blocking the way. The driver suddenly starts to shout: 'Get out of the way, old man [. . .] Get out of the way.' We cut to a side view as the man spins round just as the horse and cart pass him from right to left. At the same time the sound drops out as the film takes on his subjective sonic point of view, for we now see that his hearing aid is dangling loose from his ear socket. Indeed, he is so hearing-impaired that it is obvious that he hasn't heard a thing. He adjusts the aid and his subjective sense of sound returns so that he and the audience hear the loud rumbling of the cart's wheels and the horse's hooves. He sits on a step, takes off his left shoe, shakes it, puts it back on, stands, ties his lace and exits the frame to the left.

This opening scene has an obvious ambivalence: on one hand the old man clearly has an aversion to the sounds of the city, otherwise why would he walk along a narrow alley without his hearing aid? On the other hand it shows that he is also at risk – he needs the aid in order to avoid being hit by local horse-drawn traffic. We then see him walk through an open-air bazaar, highlighted by the shouts and cries of the local vendors as he buys a broom and some radishes from the bustling stalls, making little or no eye contact with the vendors or the customers. This man is clearly isolated from the world, with or without his hearing aid. He then stops to wake up a napping shoemaker, sitting next to his last in a doorway. It's amazing that the latter can even relax let alone sleep given the racket made by his neighbouring coppersmiths as they hammer hardware into shape under ethereal yellow lights in their workshop. The old man gives the shoemaker his shoe for a quick repair and the two try to make polite conversation as the ambient sound rises to a crescendo. Suddenly, it all seems too much for the old man and once again he removes his hearing aid, causing a brief sound drop-out before he replaces it and the cacophony is restored. Kiarostami then retains the sound of the man's sonic subjectivity as he makes his way home: he stops to routinely feed some pigeons in the town square, then stops in front of a shop window filled with ornate mirrors and bright yellow lights that give an uncanny religious aura to the image. As we see his face reflected in a mirror to the left and the back of his head in the foreground to the right, the shot eerily conjures up the similar shot of Peter Lorre's Beckert in *M* as he sees a potential child victim reflected in the mirror. However, seducing little girls is far from the old man's mind as he adjusts his glasses and moves to the other side of the street to check out another market stall specialising in lamps. Unfortunately they are too expensive: 1,400 tomans!

He eventually reaches his house and after greeting an acquaintance pushing a cart of fresh vegetables he makes his way into the inner courtyard. Kiarostami is careful to accentuate the sound of his footsteps as well the street noise in the background, as if to stress his heightened audio acuity due to the sensitive mediation of the hearing aid. In other words, it's possible that he is hyper-sensitive to sound and it may be affecting his cognitive abilities as well as his ability to cushion the intrusive sounds of the modern world. This is borne out after he enters his living room and is immediately greeted by the loud sound of a jackhammer outside on the street. He places his brush and radishes on the window ledge to the left, looks out onto the street and immediately removes his hearing aid. Unlike in *Homework* and *Close-Up*, this isn't expressed by a complete sound dropout but rather an extremely reduced and muffled ambience, for we can still hear the very faint sound of the jackhammer, which continues throughout the interior scenes that follow. After hanging up his hat and coat, he boils a pot of water for his tea, sits on the bed and starts to nibble on the radish leaves. The overall effect is that of a hermetically sealed life that is artificially sealed off from the modern world (especially the sounds of urban redevelopment) that perhaps reflects the alienation of an older generation seeking shelter from a world of clamour and disjuncture. Babak Tabarraee, for example, sees definite political connotations in this 'noise'-silence dialectic, for *The Chorus* was made during what he calls Kiarostami's 'political period' (1979–84),

> which is three years after the Revolution and its bloody aftermath of executions and terrors and retaliations, shortly after the American hostage crisis, and during the third year of the horrible Iran–Iraq war (1980–1988). Considering all these, it is meaningful to see how Kiarostami manipulates his audience: By contrasting all those annoying and horrible noises of outside to a comfortable silence, and then making us listen from the old man's point of audition and therefore aligning us with him, Kiarostami leads the audience to a level of identification, empathy or sympathy, with the old man. So, at the very least, his motivation for 'choosing silence' is justified. (Tabarraee 2013: 76)

Unfortunately, the old man has forgotten that his two grandchildren are coming home from school and will be coming round to visit. As a precursor to the authoritative regimentation of education highlighted in *Homework*, Kiarostami contrasts the annoying noise of the jackhammer with the children – all wearing hijab head scarves – exiting the school onto the street as they are closely monitored by a supervisor/teacher standing in the doorway, presumably making sure that they 'behave themselves' even when they're outside the institution's purview. Eventually the two granddaughters reach the old man's front door as other pedestrians enter the shot from both directions. Suddenly, we cut to a close-up as one of the girls reaches up to ring the doorbell with a long flat stick. However, instead of hearing the bell ring, we cut back to the grandfather's living room and his hearing-impaired subjectivity – what Gérard Genette would call his inner focalisation – as he continues to eat his radishes accompanied by the faint sound of the jackhammer off-screen. In other words, he hasn't heard the doorbell and neither have we, the audience.

The last seven minutes of the film cut back and forth between the comparative silence of the grandfather eating, smoking, pouring his tea, checking his pocket watch – 'Where are those girls!!' – and the grandchildren shouting 'Grandpa, come and open the door' as they throw stones up at his window in order to grab his attention as the sound of the jackhammer persists throughout. However, with each cut back to the street, the number of children increases as the grandkids' schoolmates join them in solidarity until at the very end there is a full chorus of chants loud enough to penetrate even the old man's sonic inhibitions. Thus he vaguely hears their pleadings and puts his hearing aid back into his ear to confirm his suspicions. After a brief flutter we hear the full sound of the chant, he stubs out his cigarette and goes to the window. He looks down and Kiarostami cuts to a point-of-view shot through the glass: the gathered throng of the children's chorus completely fills the frame as they continue their chant in the street below. We then cut to a reverse angle through the glass on the grandfather, smiling. Fade to black.

Again, Tabarraee sees a political connotation in the film's ending, accentuating the generation gap between the solitary 'deafness' of the older political generation and the collective solidarity of the young – the Iran-to-come. In his opinion the film seems to be saying that:

> *to conquer an old man's deafness, what we need is a chorus of young people.* I do not mean to reduce the film to a propaganda tool, but then again, considering the populist slogans of the time, and the frequent repetition of terms such as 'alliance', 'unity', and 'solidarity' both among the officials and the masses of a war-struck country, this simple message can bring out two different political readings: one that sees it as an enforcement of life and hope despite the hardship (also a major theme in the last two films of the Koker trilogy), and one that sees it as an act of opposition and protest to the deafness and silence of the official 'powers' in that critical period, which is something that again we can see seven years later, in his first rendition of the 'false documentary' period, *Homework* (1989). (2013: 76)

This is obviously a very valid argument – you can't shut your ears to political and economic realities no matter how unpleasant and uncomfortable they are. However, by ending with what amounts to a shot-reverse shot between the grandfather acknowledging the outdoor chorus and the exterior suturing him into its own world through the recognition of his integrated place in the larger *mise-en-scène*, Kiarostami gives the suggestion of two subjectivities in conversation, much like the over-the-shoulder reverse angle of conventional editing. It's a known fact that Kiarostami almost never uses this form of montage, preferring to put himself in the place of the one asking the questions, not another diegetic character.

This argument is also reinforced by the fact that the film's silences are not absolute but relative: the chorus and the jackhammer are not eliminated by the grandfather's subjectivity but rather muffled and mollified, made temporarily bearable until the old man can be reintegrated into both his immediate family and the wider social community. In a Barthesian sense, Kiarostami isn't using the silence as a *punctum* – a prick or wound that forces us to think outside the narrative through a poetically inspired space or fissure – but rather as a *studium*, a softening, enveloping space where everything is integrated into a 'likeable' and docile whole. While on one level we may criticise *The Chorus*'s ending as being overtly sentimental, a more accurate Barthesian reading might call it a *unary* image:

> The Photograph is unary when it emphatically transforms 'reality' without doubling it, without making it vacillate (emphasis is a power of cohesion): no duality, no indirection, no disturbance. The unary Photograph has every reason to be banal, 'unity' of composition being the first rule of vulgar (and notably, of academic) rhetoric: 'The subject,' says one handbook for amateur photographers, 'must be simple, free of useless accessories; this is called the Search for Unity.' ([1980] 1981: 41)

What could be more conciliatory than a deaf grandfather who is brought out of seclusion by the love of his grandchildren and the collective participation of their loyal schoolmates?

As Kiarostami himself put it,

> For a short you need only one idea. My film *The Chorus* is seven(teen) minutes long and based on the simple concept that a man can't hear what is going on unless he is wearing a hearing aid. Don't complicate things. Don't waste a second. Cut to the chase. (Cited in Cronin 2015: 47)

No kidding!

To appreciate how much *The Chorus* is a film grounded in the *studium* rather than the *punctum* it may be worth making a quick comparison with an episode of the popular TV show, *The Magicians* (2015–20) which also features a hearing-impaired character.

Based on the novels by Lev Grossman and co-written by David Reed and series co-creator Sera Gamble, 'Six Short Stories About Magic' (Series 3, Episode 8) consists of half a dozen 'vignettes' that focus on six different characters as they plan to retrieve a special key from the underworld 'Neitherlands Library'. Unlike Akira Kurosawa's *Rashomon* (1950), where the rape of a bride and the murder of her samurai husband are recalled, in turn, by four different contradictory perspectives, in this case the contrasting subjectivities dovetail with each other in order to clarify the narrative rather than obscure it. The key protagonist for our purposes is Harriet, played by the hearing-impaired actress Marlee Matlin, who was awarded the Best Actress Oscar for her stellar performance with William Hurt in Randa Haines's *Children of a Lesser God* (1986). Harriet's story is particularly important because we discover that the chief librarian is actually her mother, played by Mageina Tovah, with whom she has a fundamental disagreement: while Harriet wants the library to be opened up as part of a free flow of information, her mother feels that it would be disastrous if the books fell into the wrong hands so she has effectively shut it down. To temporally reinforce the rift, mother and daughter exist in different time frames: the stubborn, conservative mother never ages, while we see Harriet confront her in 1952 as a young girl (played by Winter Sluyter-Obidos), in 1965 as a teenager (Stephanie Nogueras) and finally in 2007 and 2018 as Marlee Matlin.

According to David Reed, the latter's hearing impairment – she is completely deaf in her right ear, 80% in her left ear – was seen as a great character resource so they decided to write a segment exclusively from her point of view.[1] Because *The Magicians* is rooted in horror and thus exploits the subjective register, especially in regard to the supernatural, it seems logical that the audience is only truly scared when we're locked inside someone's focalised view of the world, which in Harriet's case would be exacerbated by the sequence's relative silence. Because Harriet isn't completely deaf it was decided to replicate what she can hear by recording the sound normally and then re-recording it 'mutely' by covering the microphone with bubble wrap and duct tape. As a result, throughout the nine-minute segment most of our sense of sensation is through vibration rather than actual audio as we rely exclusively on subtitles and sign language to follow the narrative. Significantly, the episode reverses the dialectic between isolation and public communication explored by Kiarostami in *The Chorus* by making the protective, closed-off librarian mother, wracked with fear,

---

[1] Phone interview with the author, 8/9/2019.

have 'normal' hearing while the impaired Harriet, embracing chance and change, is open to anything.

The most interesting part of the episode – presented last in the sequence of six – is that Harriet's story, told in muffled silence, actually repeats segments of the previous characters' stories so that we have already witnessed certain scenes sonically when we subsequently hear them in silence, urging us to identify more closely with the 'cushioned' comfort zone created by Harriet's focalisation on one level but also making us aware that there is another mode of subjectivity that might put her in danger. This is borne out in a key scene featuring a Bridge to the Mirror World, built by Harriet's cohort, Victoria (Hannah Levien) which consists of a 'floor' of lights anchored by an entrance/exit made of a mirror that melts into liquid when a character passes through it, much like the 'dissolving' mirrors that act as gateways to the underworld in Jean Cocteau's *Orphée* (1950). As Harriet and Victoria make their escape after their confrontation with the mother, they pass through the mirror onto the bridge but another Neitherlands librarian and 'traveller' between worlds, Gavin (Daniel Nemes) is in hot pursuit and throws a large trash can through the mirror glass to destroy the bridge. It's at this exact moment that the sound returns, shocking the audience with the vibration and ear-splitting noise of shattered glass as the fragments float in slow motion over Harriet and Victoria, stranded in limbo on the bridge. This is the segment's *punctum*, piercing the silence audibly but also taking the appropriate visual form of a projectile, as if we and the characters were being pricked out of our safety zone and forced to encounter another, more dangerous plane of immanence: death. This is exactly what *The Chorus*'s ending avoids, for it is loyal to the benign *studium* that integrates the silences with the life-affirming collective whole. Which isn't to say that Kiarostami doesn't pursue this issue further, because both *Homework* (*Mashgh-e Shab*) and *Close-Up* (*Nema-ye Nazdik*) not only use silence as a *punctum* but the latter also adopts *The Magicians*' use of multiple focalisations to tell its story from different perspectives and subjectivities to the point where truth and lie are deliberately muddied so that an even higher truth may emerge from the deliberate confusion wrought by poetic art.

The latter position is clearly stated by Kiarostami in a 1994 *BOMB* Magazine interview with Akram Zaatari in which he admits that

> Our work starts with a lie on a daily routine basis. When you make a film you bring elements from other places, other environments, and you gather them together in a unity that really doesn't exist. You're faking that unity. (1994–5: 13)

Discussing *And Life Goes On* and *Through the Olive Trees*, he indicates how he constantly changed the motivation of the romantic couple in the film's main relationship, to the point that his own son complained that he kept lying to his audience. However, Kiarostami sees this as a constructive discussion:

> My son concluded that perhaps if we analyze different aspects of the lie, then we can arrive at the truth. In cinema anything that can happen would be true. It doesn't have to correspond to a reality, it doesn't have to 'really' be happening. In cinema, by fabricating lies we may never reach the fundamental truth, but we will always be on our way to it. We can never get close to the truth except through lying. (1994–5: 13)

This suggests that there is a strong Nietzschean undercurrent to Kiarostami's commitment to an ambiguous poetic incommensurability where, as we have seen, the possibility of incomprehension is accepted as a positive attribute. Nietzsche himself outlines this position clearly in his early 1873 essay, 'On Truth and Lying in an Extra-Moral Sense', where in an oft-cited statement he raises the key question:

> What is truth? A mobile army of metaphors, metonyms, anthropomorphisms, in short, a sum of human relations which were poetically and rhetorically heightened, transferred, and adorned, and after long use seem solid, canonical, and binding to a nation. Truths are illusions about which it has been forgotten that they *are* illusions, worn-out metaphors without sensory impact, coins which have lost their image and now can be used only as metal, and no longer as coins. ([1873] 1989: 250)

Kiarostami applies this bifurcation between truth and lie not only to the principal subjects of both *Homework* and *Close-Up* but also his own cinematic practice.

In the case of *Homework*, this also applies to the principles of documentary film-making as a whole. Although the film takes on certain trappings of direct cinema and *cinéma vérité* it should more accurately be described as a pseudo- or meta-documentary that constantly questions the truth value of its own assumptions, largely because the film is not only about the oppressive and authoritarian nature of the Iranian education system in the immediate aftermath of the Iran–Iraq War, but is also influenced by the personal difficulties with homework assignments of Kiarostami's own son, Bahman. The latter actually attended the Shahid Massoumi School in Tehran where the film is shot and he makes a brief appearance in its opening sequence, although he declined to appear in the series of interviews that followed. According to Godfrey Cheshire, Kiarostami's two children,

Bahman and his older brother Ahmad, were the main reason he remained in Iran at the time of the Revolution:

> he told me in a 1994 interview, 'because an internal revolution was taking place in my household: I was getting separated from my wife and was going to take care of my two sons, so it was impossible for me to think of leaving the country'. (1996: 41)

This degree of parental duty heavily influenced Kiarostami's overall approach to the film, for as he admitted to Phillip Lopate,

> Let me start by saying that this was the most difficult film I ever had to make. My son was having this problem doing his homework, and that's why I decided to go to his school and see about a solution. But while doing that, I ran into so many other kids having similar problems, it was so alarming to just sit there and hear their problems. (Lopate 1998: 353–4)

Kiarostami wasn't even thinking about cinema at that point, simply shooting a film to help understand a problem: 'To call this movie a "research" – this is not the way you do research, it's not the right methodology. But if you were to call it "film", then it's not really film, it's more like "research" (*laughs*)' (Lopate 1998: 353).

Kiarostami metacommunicates these contradictions in the opening sequence of the film as he films a group of first and second graders on their way to school. At one point a group of boys approach the camera and ask him, 'Excuse me sir, what film is this?' Kiarostami's voice-over responds: 'It's a film about homework [. . .] homework assignment. What school do you go to?' After the boys respond, 'Shahid Massoumi', Kiarostami asks them the key question that is repeated in interviews throughout the film: 'Have you done your homework?' They all say they have but Kiarostami wants confirmation (as if he already assumes that they're lying). They assure him they're telling the truth and Kiarostami lets them go: 'Go to school now, we're coming too.'

However, before Kiarostami and his crew can move on, a man's voice-over asks him whether he is shooting a children's movie and whether it's a feature film. As Kiarostami stated in his interview with Lopate, he's not sure whether it's a documentary or fiction: 'You can't tell until the film's made.' It turns out that the man (who Alberto Elena argues is actually the school's headmaster: [2002] 2005: 62) is already familiar with Kiarostami's work, having seen his *The First Graders* (*Avaliha*, 1984) – which featured a relatively sympathetic treatment of the school administration so it's likely that the headmaster gave *Homework* his blessing as a result. Kiarostami explains that the film doesn't have a theme at this point:

> I don't work from a script. It's based on impressions [. . .] I've only started today. To tell you the truth, I came across a problem when I was helping my own child with his homework. Homework's supposed to be for kids but adults are even more involved. So I thought I'd bring a camera over and see what's happening here. See if it's only my child's problem, my own problem [. . .] or the educational system's.

In short, 'It's a research project. You could say it's a visual study of pupils' homework assignments.'

The formal structure of this research takes the basic cinematic form of parallel editing, cross-cutting occasional inserts of the boys gathered in the playground like troops on parade as they mindlessly recite Islamic chants while performing calisthenics, with twenty-eight interviews of first and second graders along with two of their parents. Thus in the first pre-interview scene they shout 'Islam is victorious!'; 'Down with the East and the West'; and after a command to say their prayers, chant in unison: 'O Allah! Bless Mohammed and his household . . . In the name of God the Merciful, the Compassionate . . . Save those who believe and do good works . . . And exhort one another to truth . . .' This combination of religious fervour and military discipline is a clear reflection of how the school organises its lessons – in other words, lots of dictation and rote learning with very little creative thinking and improvisation. This is more than expressed by the children in their interviews as they answer Kiarostami's set question: 'Why don't you do your homework on time?' The recurring litany is that they are assigned far too much homework, and their fathers, many of whom are illiterate because it is a working-class neighbourhood, lack the basic knowledge and skill-set to help them. In addition, their mothers are busy cooking while their siblings are either absorbed in their own work or are unwilling to help. Plus there's a savage trickle-down effect whereby the overworked parents take out their frustrations on their kids. Failure to do homework or obtain the highest passing grade – a 20 – is invariably punished by beatings, usually a whipping with the father's belt. Thus every kid knows what 'punishment' is – we often see it in the form of cuts and bruises on their faces – but no one can define 'reward' or 'encouragement' (except one boy who knows all too well – 'Cookies. Two cookies!').

The key problem is that the children are too leery (or, as we shall see, petrified) to voice their real opinions of the situation. They put up with their parents' abuse in the same way that they accept their teachers' institutionalised cruelty, leading them to blatantly lie when asked a simple question like: 'Which do you like best, cartoons or homework?' Every child says they prefer 'homework' to watching cartoons on TV. Clearly there's a double register here, for Kiarostami's 'documentary' camera is recording a lie but expressing a truth insofar as the children are in a very real double bind. As Peter Matthews points out,

> So it appears that a good part of the tuition consists in learning to stifle their natural instincts and master the meek deportment officially demanded of them. These children don't lack all individuality; it only seems so. For a primary socialisation has already taught them that survival depends on gauging the distance between private desire and acceptable public face. (2002: 32)

Again, Nietzsche explains the motivation of this tendency in 'On Truth and Lying in an Extra-Moral Sense' when he states:

> We still do not know where the desire for truth originates; for until now we have heard only of the obligation which society, in order to exist, imposes: to be truthful, i.e., to use the customary metaphors, or in moral terms, the obligation to lie according to an established convention, to lie collectively in a style that is mandatory for everyone. Now, of course, man forgets that this is his situation; so he lies in the designated manner unconsciously and according to centuries-old habits – and precisely by this unconsciousness, by this forgetting, he arrives at his sense of truth. ([1873] 1989: 250)

In this sense Kiarostami has extracted the lies that reveal the truth, calling out the education system that purports to *teach* its students but instead *terrorises* them. It's the institution that is the lie, with the children acting as its mere mouthpieces.

This is also true when the children appear to offer up 'truthful' and honest responses to Kiarostami's questions, such as 'What do you want to be after you leave school?' One boy answers: 'A pilot.' When Kiarostami asks why, he replies: 'To kill Saddam. Saddam is cruel, because he destroys houses [. . .] He ruins them.' Sensing that the boy is clearly expressing militaristic indoctrination, not his own true ambitions, Kiarostami adds: 'And if Saddam is dead by then, what will you be?' After the boy has difficulty finding the right word, Kiarostami says it for him: 'So you want to be a physician.' 'Yes. A pilot and a physician, both.' Kiarostami then slam cuts to the children lined up in the schoolyard, shouting in unison: 'Islam is victorious! Down with the East and the West!' Even more sinister, another boy proclaims that he wants to be a *komiteh* agent – a member of one of the terrifying local groups who patrolled neighbourhoods, streets and factories during the Revolution as a means of arresting and jailing drug addicts and other criminals. In the school context, when asked who should be punished, the future *komiteh* agent says 'bad boys: if they don't listen to their mum and dad . . . or if they don't listen to what the teacher says . . . or if they don't listen to what the headmaster says. Then . . . they must be punished.'

Kiarostami also shows how this attitude is inexorably handed down from one generation to another. He asks one boy if, when he grows up, he would punish his own child with a belt if he didn't do his homework. He replies that because his dad doesn't beat him, he wouldn't harm his own son. 'What if your dad had beaten you?' asks Kiarostami, hypothetically. 'I'd beat him too,' says the boy. Kiarostami is alarmed: 'You'd beat your son? It's not his fault . . . your dad shouldn't have beaten you up.' 'Well, I would beat him up.' It turns out that the boy in question is the class monitor and he believes strongly in punishment – as opposed to conciliation or collective cooperation – as a means of keeping discipline. Kiarostami's fellow film director Mehrnaz Saeed-Vafa makes a key point in this respect by arguing that all these attitudes are related to the war context:

> Another monumental addition to the film is the question of war, including religious martyrdom and the preparation of the young generation for the enemy. One can conclude that both the beatings of the children and their training to become warriors are their real homework and the goal of their education. (2003: 73)

One immediately thinks of Ernst Jünger's utopian 'second consciousness' that we discussed in Chapter 1, whereby, in this case, it is the nation's youth – through education – who are integrated into the machinic assemblage through 'total mobilisation', in this case both religious and military.

In addition to creating a hardened generation of future combatants, there is also the question of survival, channelling real fear into a diversionary tactic where outward conformity to the system's rules – both in school and in the brutal context of familial abuse – acts as a delaying tactic to buy time in order to fight another day. This is, of course, a classic Brechtian manoeuvre based on the survivalist strategies outlined in Jaroslav Hašek's *The Good Soldier Švejk* (1921), the inspiration for one of Brecht's own plays but also one of his Mr Keuner short stories, 'Measures Against Power'. Keuner was in an auditorium speaking out against Power before an invited audience when people started to leave – it turns out that Power was standing directly behind Keuner on stage. '"What were you saying?" Power asked him, somewhat threateningly. "I was speaking out in favor of Power," replied Mr Keuner' ([1965] 2001: 3). After leaving the hall, Keuner's students righteously questioned his lack of backbone and, as if speaking for the first graders in Kiarostami's film, he replied, 'I don't have a backbone to be broken. I'm the one who has to live longer than Power' ([1965] 2001: 3). To illustrate his point, he then tells an oft-quoted story of a certain Mr Eggers whose apartment was forcefully appropriated during a time of unrest by an agent acting on behalf of the city authorities. Ordering Eggers to serve him, feed him and bathe him, the agent throws down the gauntlet: 'Will you be my servant?' Then, as Keuner relates the outcome:

> Mr. Eggers covered the agent with a blanket, drove away the flies, watched over his sleep, and, as he had done on this day, obeyed him for seven years. But whatever he did for him, one thing Mr. Eggers was very careful not to do: that was, to say a single word. Now, when the seven years had passed and the agent had grown fat from all the eating, sleeping, and giving orders, he died. Then Mr. Eggers wrapped him in the ruined blanket, dragged him out of the house, washed the bed, whitewashed the walls, drew a deep breath and replied: 'No.' ([1965] 2001: 4)

This of course resonates heavily with the dilemma of Kiarostami's schoolkids, who are in a similar no-win situation. All they can do is hold out until they leave school and the confines of the family home, for only then can they safely say: 'Cartoons!'

It's significant that the teachers and parents are not the only 'bad guys' in this scenario, for Kiarostami also includes himself and his crew in an interesting self-indictment, where the cinematic apparatus is also presented as an authority figure by showcasing the interviews themselves as something of an intimidating inquisition. As Matthews rightly argues,

> The question-and-answer format is Kiarostami's sly parody of an educational system that force-feeds knowledge and rules out imaginative participation. The homework comprises masses of dictation – which, the film implies, is likewise dictation to the masses. It's plausible too that this self-reflexive text is entering a caveat against documentary, whenever it suppresses art, creativity, for a bureaucratic administering of the facts. (2002: 32)

Fortunately, Kiarostami at least foregrounds his own negative role as an authority figure by making his pseudo 'documentary' both self-reflexive and self-critical.

Firstly, he regularly intercuts shots of the camera and his cinematographer, Iraj Safavi in order to suture the children into the mechanism of the filmed interview. One is reminded of the similar frontal shots of Dziga Vertov's brother, Mikhail Kaufman in *Man with a Movie Camera* (1929) as well as Vertov's own recipe for the kino-eye itself: 'I have placed you, whom I've created today, in an extraordinary room which did not exist until just now when I also created it' (Vertov 1984: 17), thereby underlining the artificiality of the entire interview experience. There are also several shots of

Kiarostami himself, trying to encourage the children to tell the truth, and although he may have hoped to help them relax in front of the camera, according to Elena, 'he was later accused of terrifying the children with his abrupt manner and his dark glasses, as though he were a common gangster or a police inspector' ([2002] 2005: 63). The shots of Safavi and Kiarostami also evoke Godard's 'Camera Eye' sequence in *Loin du Vietnam* (*Far from Vietnam*, 1967) where he points his Mitchell camera directly at the audience and speaks of the impossibility of capturing or understanding the Vietnam War from the safe confines of a film-making intellectual in Paris. As he puts it: 'it seemed difficult to address certain topics, to speak of bombs when they don't fall on your head and you speak in the abstract'.

If we enfold this back into Kiarostami's own position vis-à-vis the children, he may be foregrounding his own inability to relate to their dilemma as a film director (as opposed to a sympathetic father, for he is fully aware of his son's own difficulties with his homework) and this Brechtian distancing is his one concession to expressing this *aporia* between cine-realism and real life. It also raises the question of why we never see the second cinematographer – presumably either Ali Asghar Mirzaie or Farhad Saba – who is shooting the inserts, in the specific context of the interviews themselves. Elena notes:

> In fact, as he later confessed to Stéphane Goudet, this device was only thought of after the event, when at the editing stage the director decided to incorporate some form of 'punctuation marks' between the interviews, and proceeded to film the (fictitious) reverse-angle shots in his own home. ([2002] 2005: 62)[2]

There's also another obvious manipulation: it's evident that we are not seeing the interviews in their original order because there is a noticeable degeneration in the children's psychological demeanour as the film progresses, marking a transition from the confident, playful and smiling interviewees in the first half to the nervous, fidgety and outright distressed subjects in part two. This is clearly the result of editing the raw footage, suggesting that Kiarostami was trying to build up a negative momentum, all the better to rescue it at the last minute – which is where his silent *punctum* plays a key role. Another possible contrivance is the interview with the first father, a man in his fifties, who tells us that

> My child doesn't go to this school but I live around here. I've come to discuss transferring him to this school. I heard you're making a film about homework and I thought I'd come and discuss some problems with you.

---

[2] Stéphane Goudet (1997: 98).

Those of us who know Kiarostami's films are immediately thinking: 'How convenient! He just happened to be passing . . .!' Whether the man is a real parent or an actor reading a prepared script is really beside the point because he is clearly standing in for Kiarostami's own position, for when we cut to reverse shots of the director he is invariably nodding in agreement.

The father says he has lived for many years in foreign countries and has observed their educational systems with great interest. They either have no homework at all, as in the US and Canada, or in countries like England they eschew rote learning and use homework assignments to encourage the children's creativity in handicrafts, geography and composition. In contrast, Iranian children (as we have seen in the interviews) are under great pressure and although teachers may know how to tackle the problem the parents have no idea what to do. As he puts it,

> What we actually do is dump our own frustrations on the children and we end up with an indignant, surly and defensive generation susceptible to every possible mental problem. With such pressure and unhappiness imposed on our kids we'll end up with a generation lacking in any creativity. capable only of copying.

Instead teachers and children alike must use their imagination, parents must leave their kids to do their own homework in their own time, as well as take the time to be instructed in new methods:

> The point is: if I'm supposed to be qualified to teach my children at home then what's the teacher training college for? If that's not the case they should send me on a training course so I know what to do.

He also correctly notes that the twenty-first century will see radical change, especially given the influence of computers and new technologies. He concludes,

> What I'm getting at refers to the proverb of the Indian telling the British not to give him the fish out of the river but rather teach him how to catch it. We shouldn't give our children the fish. We should teach them how to catch it. We must teach them how to think. But with our system of education the children might learn everything, though I doubt it, but they certainly won't learn how to think.

The common sense of these arguments is obvious and Kiarostami clearly sets them up in counterpoint to what we have learned from the children's personal experience, both at home and at school. As if to underline the contrast, one of the last boys to be interviewed – Madjid (one of the few identified with a first name) – is also the most distressed. According to his best friend, Molaie, his female teacher has been punishing those who have been misbehaving and failing in their studies – including Madjid – by beating them with a ruler. When the ruler broke she threatened to use a cane from now on and Madjid is understandably frightened. Added to that, he is also intimidated by Kiarostami and his camera and refuses to be interviewed unless Molaie is present. He starts to cry so Kiarostami lets him go – for now. Molaie subsequently explains that Madjid is always frightened – obviously when the kids are called out for punishment, but also when the bell rings and during break. Kiarostami says they have no rulers so why is he scared of his crew? Molaie: 'He thought you have a ruler hidden here somewhere and you'd bring him in and beat him up after you closed the door.' Molaie himself doesn't believe it and is not scared himself so Kiarostami lets him go.

This is clearly edited out of order as a lead-in to the key scene that follows: another playground religious assembly where the boys are lined up in formation to celebrate Hazrat Fatemieh, the wife of Hazrat Ali, the first Imam of the Shi'a Muslims. The supervising teacher and lead singer tells them he is about to sing 'In the rose-garden of the Martyrs'. We pan left across the children as they join in but instead of the respectful dignity for the occasion expected by the school authorities we immediately notice that it's pure chaos: the boys wave their arms and beat their chests, turn sideways, wander about and tease each other mercilessly. Suddenly Kiarostami's voice-over cuts in as he makes both an apology and an attempted redress:

> In spite of the great care taken by the authorities to assure the proper run of the ceremony, due to the children's mischievous manner and lack of comprehension, it was performed inappropriately. Out of respect for the ritual, we opted to delete the sound from this section of the film.

We then get one minute fifteen seconds of dead air as the camera focuses exclusively on the children, their fears and apprehensions cast to the winds as they turn a solemn rite into pure carnival. They still slap their chests as the ritual requires but increasingly out of sync with each other, they laugh at jokes, pick at each other's hair and generally use the whole performance as a collective catharsis. The sequence ends with a gradual fade-in of the teacher singing before we cut to an interview with Madjid's father.

The silent sequence works on two contradictory levels. Firstly, as a mechanism to placate the censors and show Kiarostami's sympathy for the school authorities, the image acts as a *studium*, an attempt to show the film-makers' respect for the ritual and reintegrate it back into the 'everydayness' of school life. This reinforces the need for strict discipline while at the same time understanding that 'boys will be boys' and will tend to misbehave. In short, no real harm done. On the other hand, and this is clearly Kiarostami's intent, the sequence acts as a jarring *punctum*, drawing the audience into complete solidarity with the children and forcing us to focus on the sheer affective joy in their body language and their faces. This is a prime example of Kiarostami as a cinema poet, for it is in the gap opened up by the *punctum* that we gain a jarring insight into untrammelled thought, beyond the truth and falsehood framed by (in this case, religious) symbols and metaphors. In other words, the scene breaks through institutional barriers like the fist smashing through the Union Jack at the end of Godard's *British Sounds*. One is also reminded of Deleuze's pronouncement on the body as a catalyst for thought in *Cinema 2* when he states:

> Give me a body, then: this is the formula of philosophical reversal. The body is no longer the obstacle that separates thought from itself, that which it has to overcome to reach thinking. It is on the contrary that which it plunges into or must plunge into, in order to reach the unthought, that is life. Not that the body thinks, but, obstinate and stubborn, it forces us to think, and forces us to think what is concealed from thought, life. Life will no longer be made to appear before the categories of thought; thought will be thrown into the categories of life. (1989: 189)

The silence as *punctum* thus makes a complete mockery of Kiarostami's statement of 'respect for the ritual' and shows it, as Cheshire admits, for what it really is: 'a wily end run round the censors. But as soon as you sense who this passage is not aimed at, you have to wonder who its intended audience is. Non-fundamentalist Iranians? Other filmmakers? Cinephiles in the West? Future generations?' (Cheshire 1996: 32).

Cheshire makes a good point and once again raises the dialectic that we discussed at the beginning of this chapter between Kiarostami's reputation on the Western film festival circuit and his position as a revered post-Revolutionary director in Iran. One could argue that both sides of the equation saw the silent sequence as a *punctum* but only the Iranian authorities saw it as completely subversive. Far from buying in to Kiarostami's attempts to placate the censors by foregrounding the silence as a benign, almost humorous *studium*, they cut the scene from all copies to be screened in Iran itself and then banned the whole film for three years before agreeing to authorising it for adult viewing only (Elena [2002] 2005: 66). However, it's important not to overplay the importance of the censored scene because it too acts as a lead-in to the film's coda and its focus on the distressed Madjid. Firstly we see an interview with his father, who again reiterates that the parents are too unfamiliar with new teaching methods and in their confusion transfer extra stress onto their children. This led to

Madjid withdrawing and losing interest in studying. His anxiety increased and he probably came to see his father as an aggressor rather than an asset. As the father explains,

> Since I didn't want our arguments to affect the other children I would take him into another room and perhaps close the door. That, obviously, made him even more anxious. Of course I did nothing to hurt him in that room except to help him with his lessons or to repeat the sentences to him loudly. Yet the child's mind was elsewhere. He kept expecting the door to open and for someone to come in and rescue him, free him from captivity.

This helps to explain why Madjid is petrified of being alone with Kiarostami and his crew, once again with the door closed, and why he needs Molaie at his side. Kiarostami relents and lets Molaie join him but Madjid is still tense because their religion class is about to start and neither he nor Molaie have done their homework. Madjid is anxious to leave at once but Kiarostami asks him to repeat one of his lessons for the camera. He says he can recite 'O Lord', a life-affirming prayer in radical contrast to the warlike chants that we heard during the playground sequences:

> Oh, Lord of the beautiful stars,
> Oh, Lord of the many-coloured universe,
> Thou, who hast created Venus,
> Thou, who hast created the Sun and the Moon,
> the mountains and the oceans,
> the lovely colours of the trees,
> the tiny wings of butterflies,
> and the nests of birds,
> eyes for us to see them,
> rain and snow,
> heat and cold,
> Thou, who hast made all these things,
> Thou, who hast granted all my wishes,
> Fill our hearts with joy and happiness. (Elena [2002] 2005: 66–7)

Madjid has clearly absorbed the words and for the first time appears calm and at one with the world. Kiarostami appropriates the poem for his own ends by freeze-framing on the two school friends as a post-synched chorus continues the hymn over the closing credits, creating a new immanent whole out of a series of disconcerting chaotic fragments that folds the collective camaraderie of the boys from the earlier silent sequence into an affective embrace of the once-marginalised Madjid, who is now accepted (at least by the film) as 'one of the lads'.

Kiarostami explores this rehabilitation of the marginalised – in this case through the transformative power of an art that lies beyond truth and lie – even further in *Close-Up*, which is widely recognised by most critics as his cinematic masterpiece. Based on an actual incident from 1989, the film is a literal recreation of the story of Hossein Sabzian, an impoverished and unemployed Turkish print shop worker who is separated from his wife and lives with his son at his mother's house. Like most Iranians at that time, Sabzian is an ardent cinephile with a particular admiration for the popular Iranian director Mohsen Makhmalbaf, specifically his compelling 1989 film, *The Cyclist*, which focuses on Nasim (Moharram Zaynalzadeh), an equally poor Afghan refugee who rides his bicycle non-stop – to the point of exhaustion – for an entire week to raise money for his dying wife's life-saving surgery. As if guided by the hands of fate, Sabzian happens to be riding a bus with a copy of the published screenplay of Makhmalbaf's film when a Mrs Ahankhah (also Turkish) sits next to him and reveals that she too is familiar with the film. Sabzian – without so much as a pause for reflection – tells her that he himself is Makhmalbaf and, after signing the book with Makhmalbaf's name, gives her his copy of the script. During their conversation he learns that her sons – Mehrdad and Monoochehr – are also film lovers and they were all extremely impressed by *The Cyclist*. As their conversation progresses we also discover a strong class angle: although the Ahankhahs are clearly bourgeois and live in a comfortable town home in northern Tehran, the elder son – Monoochehr – is a mechanical engineer who is unable to find work in his field and is currently working in a bakery in Mazandaran. The younger brother – Mehrdad – is a civil engineer who has just graduated but he hasn't found a related job either. Instead he helps out at a computing firm. The daughter is a student who has just taken her university entrance exams. It's clear that the shrewd Sabzian has gleaned a certain 'precariat' commonality that he shares with the children which might be exploited for his own artistic (as opposed to financial) gain.

Sure enough, once again posing as Makhmalbaf, he visits the Ahankhah family home and exploits their common interest in film by saying that he wants to use their house as a major location in his next film – *The House of the Spider* (*Khane-ye ankabut*)[3] and to use the two brothers as actors. Extremely flattered, the family agrees and rehearsals begin. However, there are early signs that Sabzian is not who he claims to be: he borrows 1,900 tomans from Mehrdad to pay for a cab fare and never pays

---

[3] Sabzian later told the magazine *Sorush* that the film's proposed title was *Misfortune* (*Ghessavat*) (Elena [2002] 2005: 231 n. 8).

it back. The father, Abolfazl Ahankhah starts to suspect that Sabzian's professed 'location scouting' in the family home is in fact a front for 'casing the joint' with a view to robbing them. He shares his suspicions with a family friend, Ahmad Mohseni, who also has doubts. The evidence mounts when the family comes across a magazine photograph showing a younger Makhmalbaf with darker hair. Sabzian admits that he dyes it, but has no explanation for not knowing that *The Cyclist* had just won an award at the Rimini Film Festival. As the father explains to Mohseni: 'He stood there dazed, unable to respond. He got out of it in his own cunning fashion, saying the award wasn't for the film but for the musical score.'

Meanwhile, Mr Ahankhah has invited a *Sorush* magazine journalist, Hossain Farazmand, to look into the case and he confirms that Sabzian is indeed an impostor. As the police come to arrest Sabzian, Farazmand takes several pictures for his upcoming article titled 'Bogus Makhmalbaf Arrested'. This is the written source for *Close-Up*, although there is some doubt as to the film's actual provenance. Writing in 1999, nine years after the film's release, Godfrey Cheshire states that,

> Although it goes against the film's aura of good will to point this out, Kiarostami and Makhmalbaf actively detest each other, and have through much of the last two decades. *Close-Up* marks a brief and curious respite in their mutual loathing. The hostility evidently began with Makhmalbaf, who spent part of the '80s vituperatively denouncing pre-revolutionary directors, including Kiarostami, as decadent, bourgeois remnants of the old regime. ([1999] 2010: unpaginated)

Apart from their age and class difference – the middle-class Kiarostami was forty-nine when *Close-Up* was in production, the lower class Makhmalbaf was thirty-two – there was also a political and religious divide. Makhmalbaf had been a rabid opponent of the Shah and after participating in a terrorist action was imprisoned and tortured for several years. Freed by the Revolution, he became a radical Islamist and vented his ire against pre-Revolutionary directors like Kiarostami before becoming more interested in humanist class issues such as impoverishment and self-sacrifice, the very elements that made him a hero for Sabzian. The rift with Kiarostami was gradually patched up over the years and when Cheshire interviewed the two directors in the summer of 1997 they gave very different accounts of their introduction to Farazmand's published account of Sabzian's fraudulent ruse: 'Where they diverge is over the issue of who had the crucial copy of *Sorush* magazine, and who first thought of making a movie about the strange case of the Makhmalbaf impersonator' (Cheshire [1999] 2010: unpaginated).

On one hand, Makhmalbaf claimed that he had an advance copy of the magazine and was already planning to make the movie adaptation. Kiarostami agreed that it was an amazing story but argued that Makhmalbaf couldn't be the director as he was an intrinsic part of the narrative. Kiarostami's version is that *Sorush* had already hit the newsstands and he knew all about the incident. He persuaded Makhmalbaf to borrow a car and join him in some preliminary research: a visit to the police station where Sabzian was being held, pending trial, and then to the Ahankhahs' house to interview them. As Cheshire tells the story:

> Kiarostami goes to the door and announces himself. The daughter of the family asks skeptically for some ID. They have just gotten rid of a fake Makhmalbaf, she says, they certainly don't need a fake Kiarostami. Kiarostami doesn't have an ID, but he says he has something just as good: Makhmalbaf, who is sitting in the car. He produces Makhmalbaf and the family – one can imagine their initial befuddlement – admits the two filmmakers. Tea is served and the conversation runs late into the night. By the end of the evening, as Makhmalbaf tells it, Kiarostami has very adroitly bamboozled everyone concerned, including him, into playing roles in the film. ([1999] 2010: unpaginated)

Bamboozling or not, Kiarostami's plan to have everyone play themselves in his film recreation – which would necessarily be a documentary/fiction hybrid – would necessitate the full cooperation of all parties. Thus he visits Sabzian in prison and gets his endorsement to tell the story and also play himself playing Makhmalbaf. Kiarostami also receives permission from the judge, Haj Ali Reza Ahmadi, to record the trial, where Sabzian will be tried for fraud and attempted fraud (but not robbery). Jonathan Rosenbaum rightly sees a huge class-based irony in this arrangement (which Kiarostami was undoubtedly aware of), for

> Film, as we see it here, enables people to cross class barriers, in their imaginations when they watch films and, in this case, in life when a poor man impersonates a famous film director. It becomes an instrument of empowerment as well as a double-edged sword: Sabzian goes to jail for impersonating someone else, but Kiarostami gets prizes and recognition for persuading Sabzian, the Ahankhahs, the reporter, the judge, and others to impersonate themselves. (2003: 17)

As we shall see in more detail, Sabzian reveals his motivations for his imitation as a sincere love for Makhmalbaf's film, *The Cyclist*, and cinema/art as a whole. As a witness for the plaintiffs, Mehrdad recounts Sabzian's visits to the house to direct rehearsals for his film and his father's gradual suspicions of his true identity, leading eventually to his arrest. The turbaned judge is extremely kind and sympathetic, taking into account

Sabzian's circumstances as a young unemployed father with no prior record and his obviously sincere remorse. He asks the family if they would be willing to pardon Sabzian.

They (reluctantly) agree provided he becomes a productive member of society, although, as Cheshire argues, 'Kiarostami himself orchestrated what happened in the courtroom, including the family's forgiveness (they actually wanted Sabzian to be locked up)' ([1999] 2010: unpaginated). If Cheshire is right, then the film's coda is a complete fabrication on all levels. After the trial, Kiarostami stage-manages a meeting between the real Makhmalbaf and his *doppelgänger* outside the jail house. As the stirring theme music of Kiarostami's *The Traveler* (1974) fades in on the soundtrack – a particular favourite of Sabzian's – Makhmalbaf gives him a ride back to the Ahankhahs' house on his motorbike. After stopping to buy some flowers (as with Mehrdad and the taxi fare, Sabzian has to borrow the money) they are greeted at the front gate by Mr Ahankhah who, ever the cinephile, embraces the real Makhmalbaf as Sabzian asks for forgiveness. After Makhmalbaf says, 'This isn't the old Mr Sabzian. I hope you'll see him in a new light', the father generously replies: 'I hope he'll be good now and make us proud of him.'

The story – although undoubtedly bizarre – sounds relatively straightforward when outlined in a linear fashion, but Kiarostami complicates matters by not only editing the footage out of chronological order but also muddying the difference between diegetic re-enactment and a direct cinema documentary approach, especially in the trial scenes.

Again, according to Cheshire, the current theatrical version of *Close-Up* (as well as the Criterion DVD) is very different from its first New York screenings at the Human Rights Watch Film Festival in 1991 and the Walter Reade Theater in 1992. As Cheshire explains:

> The earlier version was more chronological, beginning with the incident of Sabzian meeting the woman on the bus. Kiarostami changed the movie, he told me, after seeing it projected at a festival in Munich where the projectionist accidentally mixed up the reels. Rather than being offended, he decided he liked the scrambled chronology better and reedited the film accordingly. When I expressed surprise at this, he replied matter-of-factly that a movie is good or a movie is bad, and neither fact is affected by the order the reels are shown in. (Godard is one of the few filmmakers who would surely agree). ([1999] 2010: unpaginated).

As a result, the bus encounter between Sabzian and Mrs Ahankhah is moved to the middle of the film as a flashback during the trial and the film opens, *in medias res*, with the journalist, Farazmand, riding in a taxi with the two arresting police officers as they make their way to the Ahankhah household to take Sabzian into custody.

The sequence is bizarre on a narrative level but brilliantly constructed on an aesthetic plane, raising a number of performative and phenomenological questions without providing easy answers. The first obvious uncertainty that arises is: why are the police officers riding in a taxi with a reporter instead of in an official police car? Don't the police have their own vehicles? Apparently they do but that doesn't answer the question. Secondly, Farazmand, a would-be Oriana Fallaci (an Italian journalist famous for her impassioned coverage of war and revolution) seems to be running the show and provides us with all the exposition on the case. Given *Close-Up*'s central theme of impersonation and the credibility of the creative lie, we immediately wonder whether Farazmand – the source of the film's narrative – is an objective resource or simply a journalistic hack in search of a self-aggrandising scoop. Thirdly, the taxi driver, a retired fighter pilot, quips that 'I'm part of the ground forces now.' Farazmand – always on the ball – thinks that would make a good story too: 'air forces on the ground, ground forces in the air'. Fourthly, the driver doesn't seem to know the route to the Ahankhahs' house and, as in almost every Kiarostami film it seems, they have to stop to ask directions three times before they find the right location. Finally, when they arrive at the house, Farazmand enters without the two policemen so that he can obtain a copy of the official complaint and ID papers from Mr Ahankhah.

In a Hollywood film we would then cut to the interior in order to witness the arrest but instead Kiarostami gives us two and a half minutes of small talk between the taxi driver (Hooshang Shamaei) and the policemen while we wait for the reporter to return. When he emerges with Mr Ahankhah and the complaint, the policemen join them as they re-enter the grounds. Finally: we're going to see some action and also catch our first glimpse of Sabzian himself! Unfortunately, no such luck. Instead, the camera stays on the taxi driver as he does a U-turn in front of the main gate, stops and gets out of the cab. He looks around and then gazes skyward to take in a jet's vapour trail as it cuts vertically across the screen (as a former flyer, is he nostalgically yearning for his younger self?) before walking over to a large pile of leaves and garden mulch. He picks out a couple of red flowers but in doing so dislodges an aerosol can onto the street and it rolls off to the right. He kicks it like a football and Kiarostami holds on the can for forty seconds as it rolls down the gradient of the street, away from the camera, before it comes to a stop by the kerb.

On one level, Kiarostami is equalising elements that make up a phenomenology of the world, paying more attention to the aerosol can – focusing on the 'object's view of things' à la Francis Ponge – than to the fate of the film's main *human* character. Moreover, he is as much interested in the sound generated by the rolling can as he is in capturing its visual trajectory. As David Johnson notes,

> here, in a scene emptied of narrative drive, we are asked merely to perceive; we are asked to listen to this sound and consider it in its own right. What does an aerosol can really sound like? Like this, the scene seems to say, much like an old children's toy ('A cow says "*Moo*").' (2008: 296)

Kiarostami's own explanation is much simpler, entailing a deliberate shift in focus from the activity going on inside the house to the relative inactivity on the street:

> The scene in all my films that provokes the most queries is the shot near the start of *Close-Up* of a can rolling down a street. The number of theories I have heard about that single moment! People don't believe me when I explain where this image came from. They expect something terribly profound, but the truth is there was a slope in front of the house where we were filming. The important events of the story were taking place inside and I wanted to represent the inactivity of the man standing outside. I created a scene where he would cause an empty spray can to roll gently down the hill. I just liked the image and figured I wouldn't have many other opportunities to capture a shot like that, one I knew would somehow get audiences involved. We also had time to kill and a few feet of film in the camera. A deadly combination. (Cited in Cronin 2015: 93)

The scene also fits Kiarostami's predilection for using black leader to stand in for scenes that have nothing to do with the film's ostensible plot. As he told Phillip Lopate, 'Some places in a movie there should be nothing happening, like in *Closeup*, where somebody kicks a can. But I needed that. I needed that "nothing" there' (1998: 356). As a poetic device, the aerosol can also acts as an interstice, opening up a gap for multiple interpretations: everyone is free to think what they want. As he explained to Miriam Rosen, 'The danger comes when someone wants to say, "No, my interpretation is the only right one"' (1992: 39).

However, Kiarostami doesn't stop there because after Farazmand and the two policemen escort Sabzian to the taxi after his arrest, the reporter suddenly realises that he has forgotten his tape recorder. Thus instead of accompanying Sabzian to the police station and catching our first glimpse of the would-be Makhmalbaf, we instead spend three and a half minutes watching Farazmand's unsuccessful attempts to borrow a recorder from one of the Ahankhahs' neighbours. Eventually he succeeds and in his delight he playfully kicks the same aerosol can. Rolling much faster than before, we follow its course for a few moments before cutting to a close-up of a printing press, presumably churning out Farazmand's story and thereby kick-starting the film we are watching. Gilberto Perez rightly argues that this is not a cause and effect connection between the aerosol can and the press but a metaphor:

> ... the unremarkable detail of everyday life given the kick, the spin of publication. Or the resonance of art: in Kiarostami's hands that aerosol can becomes remarkably expressive. It becomes expressive not so much within the story as in what it tells about the telling of the story, as a representation of the means of representation: expressive in the characteristic manner of modernism. The detail of naturalism is treated with the self consciousness of modernism and turned into a metaphor for the means of art. (1998: 264–5)

It's the spray can's connection to poetry (via Ponge) and to art (via its metacommunicative double register) that makes it a *punctum* rather than a *studium*, a pin prick that generates a spatio-temporal vector linking multiple facets of both the diegesis and the film's production as a whole that expresses our running theme of the truth value of the creative lie.

During his trial, Sabzian admits to the court that on the day of his arrest,

> In my notebook, on the last day, the day I was arrested, under Mr Ahankhah's address, I wrote 'the tragic finale', that this was the end of a tragedy. That's what I sensed and wrote. I'm sure they read it at the police station. I was certain I'd be arrested that day because of the money I'd received and the fact I'd spent the night there. But I couldn't stop myself from going there.

Kiarostami re-enacts the arrest sequence as a trial flashback, thus giving the film audience the scene that they were denied during the film's opening focus on the taxi driver and the aerosol can. However, the power of the *punctum* carries over into this scene as we are forced to share Sabzian's nervousness and trepidation. In many ways this is an acting *tour de force* on Sabzian's part. On one level he is the post-trial 'real' Sabzian acting a pre-trial 'Sabzian' impersonating Makhmalbaf for the benefit of the Ahankhah family. He is also acting – putting on a front – by pretending to be calm and relaxed when he knows full well that he is about to be arrested. Ivone Margulies makes a very interesting point when she argues that:

> Because this scene shows us the drama that was unfolding inside the house as we waited with the cab driver in the street at the beginning of the film, it retroactively feeds dramatic momentum into a rather banal, gratuitous moment – the kicking of the can by the cab driver. By showing this scene from two different perspectives – one in which we know nothing, another in which we know too much – Kiarostami turns witnessing into a clear, costly embarrassment: faced with the scene's elaborate deceit and stark pathos, we almost wish for the earlier, blocked, more innocent view. (2003: 237)

In this way, the power of the aerosol can as a poetic *punctum* is reinforced as a metaphor for Sabzian's ill-fated venture, linking inside (the arrest) and outside (the waiting), subject and object in a pure poetics of both time-image (simultaneity) and movement-image (contrasting actions). David Johnson also sees this combination of unfolding and enfolding in terms of a clear contrast in sound: from the loud rattle of the can on the street to the barely perceptible dialogue in the house as the family await the arrival of the police we become increasingly aware of the materiality of speech as a form of testimony, a testimony that is denied during the arrest sequence but highlighted and celebrated, as we shall see, during the trial.

There is a third and extremely important level of *punctum* that reinforces the link between the can and the arrest and that is the performative register in-itself. Kiarostami admitted to Lopate that recreating the arrest scene in the family's house *after* the trial was extremely difficult. An uncomfortable Sabzian waited silently outside the door prior to the shoot,

> ... because he felt that the kind of authority that had helped him get into the house the first time wasn't there anymore. So I went up to him and said, 'Hey, don't be embarrassed. You didn't even lie to these people. Didn't you tell them you're going to bring your film crew to film them? That's what you did!' (*laughter*) So that took care of *his* problem. He felt better and he went in. Then I had difficulty just thinking about what I had done, what I had told him. I was about to cry. And I paced around the place where they kicked the can before I could go in. (Cited in Lopate 1998: 360)

This is a telling statement on several levels. Firstly, Kiarostami seems to endorse the creative lie by arguing that Sabzian delivered on his promise to the Ahankhah family, even if he did it in a roundabout way that added to their understandable embarrassment at being duped. Kiarostami also seems to be aware that he too is an exploiter, forcing Sabzian to re-enact an episode that must have been a crushing disappointment, shattering all his dreams of being a great director. Significantly, in order to feel some sense of remorse, Kiarostami returns to the scene of the can-kicking episode (which is diegetically simultaneous in time to the scene he is about to shoot) so that its initial Ponge-like role as an objective *punctum* is supplemented by yet another level of poetic resonance – the responsibility of the artist (in this case Kiarostami *and* Sabzian) as a creative *affective* force. In this respect the whole film constructs a plane of consistency where everyone concerned is a conceptual persona – i.e. everyone acts out their real-life role in scare quotes – for the furtherance of a Spinozist ethics of interrelated affects that, in Nietzsche's words, are 'beyond good and evil'. In short, in *Close-Up*, the chaoid is made up of multiple doublings that potentially reverberate all the way to infinity.

This basic philosophy is the central focus of the trial sequence which, like the rest of the film, deliberately muddies the difference between 'authentic' direct cinema and artificial contrivance. As Kiarostami explains:

> For the trial scene, I planned on having three cameras inside the courtroom. One was for a close-up of the defendant Hossein Sabzian, the second for a wider shot of the courtroom, the third to emphasize the relationship between Sabzian and the judge. Almost immediately, one of the cameras broke and another was so noisy I had to turn it off. We ended up having to move our single workable camera from one spot to the next, which meant missing a continuous shot of Sabzian. This is why, when the trial ended after only one hour and the judge left because he was so busy, we filmed with Sabzian, behind closed doors, for another nine hours. I talked with him and suggested what he might say on camera. We ended up recreating most of the trial in the judge's absence. The occasional shots of him that I inserted into *Close-Up*, to make it seem as if he had been present the whole time, constitute one of the biggest lies in any of my films. (Cited in Cronin 2015: 8)

Although this explanation contradicts most commentators' view that Kiarostami used two cameras, one to capture the courtroom as a whole in long shot, the other to focus on Sabzian in close-up (thus the inspiration for the film's title), it doesn't undermine the basic formal dialectic between the letter of the law and sincere personal belief based on Kiarostami and Sabzian's complicit cinephilia, whereby the idea of who is the original and 'authentic' Makhmalbaf becomes irrelevant. The close-up camera is thus designed to allow Sabzian – fed by direct questions from an acousmatic Kiarostami – to inform the trial and filmic audience of 'facts' and feelings that may be legally dubious but are nonetheless aesthetically 'true'. As Margulies rightly argues: 'Kiarostami's intervention transforms the trial from an accusation of fraud into an exploration into the nature of belief' (2003: 239).

Perhaps Sabzian's key line of defence in the trial is that 'When spite comes along, art dons a veil', suggesting that the veil is his persona as Makhmalbaf but is doubled and tripled when he plays Sabzian playing Makhmalbaf playing a scared Sabzian in Kiarostami's film. The spite is the law, the family he cheated, the film's audience and the plight of the underclass in contemporary Iran. Stating his feelings directly to the close-up camera, he admits that,

> Every time I feel sad in prison I think of the Koran verse that says, 'Speak Allah's name, and your heart will be consoled', but I feel no consolation. Whenever I feel depressed or overwhelmed, I feel the urge to shout to the world the anguish of my soul, the torments I've experienced, all my sorrows – but no one wants to hear about them. Then a good man comes along who portrays all my suffering in his films, and I can go see them over and over again. They show the evil faces of those who play

with the lives of others, the rich who pay no attention to the simple material needs of the poor. That's why I felt compelled to take solace in that screenplay. I read it, and it brings calm to my heart. It says the things I wish I could express.

Although on one level Sabzian aspires to be the Makhmalbaf who directed *The Cyclist*, he seems to take even greater solace in portraying the role as an actor rather than as a director: 'I think I could express all the bad experiences I've had, all the deprivation I've felt with every fibre of my being. I think I could get these feelings across through my acting.' When an off-screen Kiarostami suggests that he's acting (for the courtroom) as he says those very words, Sabzian draws a clear distinction between representation as performance and true affect:

I'm speaking of my suffering. I'm not acting. I'm speaking from the heart. This isn't acting. For me, art is the experience of what you've felt inside. If one could cultivate that experience, it's like when Tolstoy says that art is the inner experience cultivated by the artist and conveyed to his audience. Given the positive feelings I've experienced, as well as the deprivation and suffering, and my interest in acting, I think I could be an effective actor and convey that inner reality.

The incommensurable nature of this inner reality is expressed in the film's finale – the touching meeting of Sabzian and his hero – where the reverberating *punctum* of the aerosol can/arrest scene is unfolded further to include Makhmalbaf himself, who is affectively linked with Sabzian through the film's idiosyncratic silences. The meeting is shot using a 'hidden' camera in a pseudo-*cinéma vérité* style through the windshield of a van as Kiarostami and his crew observe Makhmalbaf pulling up on his motorcycle and overshooting his designated parking spot. A voice says: 'I can't see him. Stop rolling?'

Then a voice that we assume to be Kiarostami says, 'We can't redo this shot. Now I see him – behind the taxi.' Then just as Makhmalbaf appears into the frame the sound engineer says that they have just lost sound: 'It's either the jack or Mr Makhmalbaf's lapel mike. It's old equipment. It has a loose wire.' Kiarostami admits that it's fifteen years old (suggesting that they're not a well-financed film crew) but fortunately the sound returns (at least for the crew) as we cut to Makhmalbaf and Sabzian embracing. Their emotional meeting – Sabzian is in tears – is then interrupted, as in the case of *Homework*, by multiple technical drop-outs and we only catch fragments of their conversation as Makhmalbaf leads him to his motorcycle so that they can make their trip together to visit the Ahankhahs. However, we do hear one telling line as Makhmalbaf asks Sabzian: 'Do you prefer being Makhmalbaf or Sabzian? Even I'm tired of being Makh . . .', suggesting that the distinction between the 'legitimate' artist and his simulacrum double isn't so clear-cut after all. The drop-outs continue as we follow their journey from the perspective of the van – either through the windscreen or reflected in the right-side wing mirror. At one point Makhmalbaf piques our interest by asking Sabzian: 'When you met that woman on the bus . . .' but the sound drops out before we can hear his reply. The silence continues as they arrive at the flower market and there is only intermittent sound as Sabzian buys the bouquet to present as his *mea culpa* gift to the Ahankhahs. As if to prove that he is a more discerning director (and art director) than his double, Makhmalbaf tells Sabzian to substitute red flowers for his original choice of yellow blooms, even though the latter knows the family far better than his idol. Interestingly, the van and Kiarostami's camera seem to have arrived at the market long before our protagonists. Was this a deliberate attempt to bare the cinematic device, or because they wanted extra time to set up a deliberately framed long shot? If so, why does it look like contrived surveillance camera footage?

There's clearly something not quite right about the authenticity of this sequence – as an audience we're denied the satisfaction of truly enjoying this long-delayed meeting between the two 'directors' and it smacks of a deliberate recycling of the *punctum* effect of the equally frustrating aerosol can sequence. And so it proves to be true, for the faulty sound microphone is a deception – a deliberate fake – set up because of the original sound recording's discrepant focus on Makhmalbaf, thereby turning a conversation into a monologue. As Kiarostami explains:

> I was following in a car, listening to them talking, and quickly realised that nothing they were saying would fit in the film. The problem was that Makhmalbaf knew he was being recorded but Sabzian didn't. It was just two opposing monologues rather than a dialogue I could use. The fake director was too real and the real director was too fake. Beyond that, we were wrapping up production, and leaving in unedited dialogue between the two of them would have shifted the film in a new direction. The narrative had to be progressively directed towards a climax, not opened up. The dialogue as spoken would also have made Makhmalbaf the hero, but I wanted Sabzian to be at the story's centre from start to finish. (Cited in Cronin 2015: 27)

Apparently, the editor refused to go along with Kiarostami's decision to slice up the recording so he did it himself. He argues,

> Today I consider it one of the most important moments in any of my films, especially whenever anyone complains because they want to know what Makhmalbaf and Sabzian are saying to each other. The audience has been primed, pushed to think about things beyond the frame of the film. They want to know what lies off-screen, which means they have to fill in the gaps themselves. (Cited in Cronin 2015: 28)

There is, however, another gap that neither the film nor Kiarostami fills in. Drawing upon a 1996 *Positif* interview with Makhmalbaf by Stéphane Goudet, Alberto Elena gives us a completely different perspective. According to Makhmalbaf,

> This was the second sequence that was filmed, right after the trial. In fact, while we were on the motorbike, Sabzian was telling me the whole time that he didn't want to take part in the film, and I was trying to convince him that it would be worthwhile. (Goudet 1996: 22; Elena [2002] 2005: 233)

This view is more than borne out by Sabzian's embittered retrospective opinion of Kiarostami in Mamhoud Chokrollahi and Moslem Mansouri's 1996 documentary, *Close-Up Long Shot*, where he states that:

> The only thing the movies did for me was to portray me as a con artist. If that's the case, everyone's a con artist. That family wanted to use Mohsen Makhmalbaf to gain prestige. That's a kind of con. Maybe I toyed with their feelings but their actions speak for themselves. Or that reporter who wanted to break the story so he could become another Oriana Fallaci, using me as his bridge, his stepladder to success – that's another kind of con. Even Kiarostami himself, who heard of my case through that reporter [. . .] found an interesting subject, and won international acclaim for it. When you think of it, he conned me. He's a con artist too.[4] (Chokrollahi and Mansouri 1996)

Hamid Naficy makes a key point when he argues that the film is acting less on an aesthetic level than a mystical one, for by deliberate dropping out the sound and encouraging the audience to fill in the gaps,

> Kiarostami has acted like Sabzian: by engaging in a game of pretense. Unlike Sabzian, however, he does not confess on film to his fraud. Perhaps with this ruse he is telling us that the content of their conversation is not important; what is important is that the lover and the beloved, the fan and the star, the disciple and the master are united – a classic trope in Persian mystic poetry and philosophy. (2005: 803)

It is through this creation of a mystical 'whole' that the film enfolds its resistant *puncta* back into an enveloping *studium*, an aesthetic that combines elements of naturalism and Modernism, transcendence and immanence, realism and self-reflexivity, in short, a chaoid cinema that lies beyond truth and lie in an extra-formal sense.

---

[4] Sadly, Sabzian suffered respiratory failure on the Tehran metro in August 2006 and slipped into a coma before passing away on 29 September. It seems oddly ironic that his impersonation of Makhmalbaf began on a bus and his life ended on the metro, as if public transport became a moving frame for his lifelong dream to be a director. (Ferguson 2006).

CONCLUSION

'The Abyss Also Looks into You': From Syncinema to 'Sin' Cinema in Mike Figgis's *Leaving Las Vegas* (1995) and Harmony Korine's *Trash Humpers* (2009)

It's traditional for conclusions to make some attempt to tie up loose ends and summarise the key themes of the book while avoiding a sense of stifling 'closure'. After all, it's important to raise new questions and encourage further debate and research beyond the confines of the study. However, in this case, where loose ends play an invaluable role in the work's deterritorialising strategies – a case of pursuing vectors and singularities to the point of creating an endless number of ever-mutating assemblages – it makes far more sense (or non-sense) to replace a conventional conclusion in favour of revisiting a couple of the book's themes and putting a new spin on them, a case of re-unfolding an already enfolded entity like a supple, transmutable topology. It's with this goal in mind that we will re-explore Syncinema ('*séance de cinéma*') and 'sin' cinema in new contexts: commercial and legal, through the work of Mike Figgis and Harmony Korine.

As we saw in Chapter 3 with the deliberately provocative films of Maurice Lemaître and Guy Debord, Syncinema focuses less on the diegetic filmic event as a seductive photographic reproduction and more on the cinema screen as a defamiliarising performative and exhibitionary frame, much like Filippo Tommaso Marinetti's Futurist Theatre. However, Syncinema in its early days took place within the relatively 'safe' confines of the ciné-club circuit where audiences were already primed for excessive avant-garde experimentation, even to the point of being soaked with ice water as they lined up outside the theatre. That's all well and good, but what about commercial cinema, particularly Hollywood film and its corporate control, both on the level of studio production and cinema-chain exhibition? As one might expect, the basic tenets of Syncinema and Hollywood film are completely incompatible – at least in principle.

We have first-hand knowledge of this from a 2017 entry by Zack Sharf in the online magazine *IndieWire* entitled '"The Last Jedi" Has Such An Unconventional "Star Wars" Moment That AMC Theaters Are Warning Fans, No, the sound in your theater isn't cutting out by accident during

"The Last Jedi"'. Sharf is, of course, referencing Rian Johnson's Walt Disney production of *Star Wars: Episode VIII – The Last Jedi* (2017), which had opened on 17 December. Audiences had been extremely confused by the soundtrack dropping out for ten seconds at the exact moment when Laura Dern's Vice Admiral Holdo sacrifices her life to save the Resistance by flying her spaceship at light-speed directly into the First Order's Mega Destroyer, thereby allowing the Resistance's space pods to escape to safety. The combination of the sonic vacuum effect and the sight of the shattered debris of the Destroyer is particularly powerful, punctuated by another explosion as the sound returns. In a series dominated by John Williams's insistent (albeit catchy) scoring, this moment is a welcome anomaly. The film's VFX supervisor, Ben Morris, admitted at the time,

> That's never really happened in 'Star Wars' before. We had always hoped that would resonate, both as a story beat and as a striking visual, and when I heard all of the cries and gasps in the silence, it was just fantastic. We realized that it worked. (Cited in Sharf 2017: unpaginated)

However, according to Sharf there was also a major backlash:

> apparently some fans have been complaining and blaming the theater for a sound issue. Complaints were apparently so consistent that an AMC Theater decided to print out and post signs warning fans in advance about the moment, saying the silence is very much an intentional creative decision made by director Rian Johnson. (2017: unpaginated)

Three days later, Jenna Marotta followed up the story with a new *IndieWire* piece describing the latest developments: 'AMC Removes "Spoiler" Signage, Warning "The Last Jedi" Audiences of Key Climactic Moment'. Thanks to the reproduction of an online post by Kevin Church, we also got to see a photo of the 'spoiler' sign itself:

> PLEASE NOTE: THE LAST JEDI contains a sequence at approximately 1 hour and 52 minutes into the movie in which ALL sound stops for about 10 full seconds. While the images continue to play on the screen you will hear nothing. This is intentionally done by the director for a creative effect. (Marotta 2017: unpaginated)

Church slyly added his own opinion with his post: 'AMC, you need to stop allowing cretins into your theaters' (Marotta 2017: unpaginated). According to Marotta, the sign was posted at two of AMC's 660 locations and was removed before social media coverage could spread the 'spoiler' like wild fire. Finally, in an interesting addendum, she notes that, 'According to *Variety*, police officers were called one week ago to calm patrons at a Burbank, California screening of the film after the audio dropped out for 10 minutes, and the theater declined to restart the feature' (2017: unpaginated).

It's clear from this example that contemporary audiences – understandably suspicious of spoilers that ruin the suspense of many films and TV programmes – are also ill-equipped to deal with anything that seems to disrupt their absorption in the cinematic spectacle.

So how does an innovative and experimental 'sound-conscious' (but also mainstream) director like Mike Figgis tackle these limitations? This is all the more pertinent because Figgis is an extremely accomplished musician and composer (he is close friends with his regular collaborator, Sting) who started out playing keyboards in Brian Ferry's first band (i.e. pre-Roxy Music) before getting into experimental theatre with *The People Show* (Deutsch et al. 2008: 163). Indeed, as Figgis explained in a 2008 interview with *The Soundtrack* journal:

> The thing that attracted me to film in the first place was sound; by the time I actually got to make films and got to the sharp end of it, which was post-production, I was determined not to relinquish any element of *that*. There were things I knew about, I knew how to do, and the idea of handing that over to a stranger who was sort of an employee, to say this is sad, this is tense, this is like poster-colour as opposed to watercolour. It was something that I hadn't been aware of until I was within the system. (Deutsch et al. 2008: 164)

Figgis became quickly aware that the soundtrack – particularly the film's score – was always considered by the studios to be out of the hands of the director. The score is what he calls 'the cheap psychology of the film or, at its best, the very subtle underscoring of the existing psychology of the film' (Deutsch et al. 2008: 164). We've just noted how important John Williams's scores are to the *Star Wars* franchise (to the point of being shockingly missed when the sound drops out during a dramatic moment), but Figgis sees him as the studios'

> Norwich Union insurance policy because they know if the film is flagging, that Williams is such a consummate technician, and brilliant at his job, that he can fill the room with a certain kind of a manufactured, ersatz-type tension that will fix the problems that they perceive to be existing in the film. (Deutsch et al. 2008: 164)

Figgis's understandably guarded position vis-à-vis the soundtrack is due to his original background in sound design. He is consequently very mindful of how the Hollywood system stifles creativity and innovation, and he therefore tries to avoid all attempts to use scoring and sound effects as a form of 'Mickey Mousing', an overt rhythmic reinforcement of the movement-image through over-synchronisation that dates back to 1930s animation. It should come as no surprise to learn that one of Figgis's life-long ambitions was to achieve a legitimate sound drop-out in a commercial film that would defy these conventions, in short, to have *nothing* on the soundtrack. In a 16 April 1998 lecture at the Institute Français in London, Figgis explained the problem in detail:

> There's one specific thing that was a big moment for me in terms of film-making and, in particular, in terms of sound. It was something I'd wanted to do my entire film career, which is basically have *nothing* on the soundtrack. Every time I've tried to do that in the past, a sound person has said, 'No, you can't have *nothing* on a soundtrack. If you want silence, you have to approximate silence with what's called "room tone". It's like quiet white noise. But you can't have zero.' There are two things you can't do in film: one – never ever look into the lens directly; it's almost like a biblical statement. Never have your actor look into the lens, it's too frightening for the audience, always have them look slightly to the left or slightly to the right. And the other thing you can never do is have silence. (Figgis 2003: 1)

Needless to say the sound technicians stubbornly refused to budge from what they considered to be a technical truism, for as Figgis argues,

> Well, why not? Why not look in the lens and why not have silence? And you ask people and they say, 'Well, because, you know, the way equipment is, you've got to have something on the soundtrack that tells you it's silence, but it's got to be a noise', which seemed pretty silly to me. (2003: 1)

Figgis finally achieved his goal with *Leaving Las Vegas* (1995), an MGM/United Artists release based on the autobiographical novel by John O'Brien. A key reason why Figgis could manipulate the film sonically was because it was filmed in super 16mm instead of 35mm, a low-budget medium that tied it more to an art-house production context. As he explained in the same Institut Français lecture:

> In the low-budget *Leaving Las Vegas* the sound was done in a tiny space in the middle of Soho – no big post-production. They made sure the mix sounded good in a big space and it was gorgeous. And so I thought, 'My time has come. I'm going to have real silence.' That means, take the faders on the mixer to zero and have nothing going through any of the pots. (2003: 2)

Significantly, Figgis only used complete silence in one scene but, as we shall see, it was an early moment that resonated throughout the film, not only because of Figgis's brilliant sound and image design but also as a result of stellar performances by Nicolas Cage (who won the Best Actor Academy Award for his role) and Elisabeth Shue (nominated for Best Actress).

Cage plays Ben Sanderson, an alcoholic who works behind the scenes in the Hollywood film industry. He is clearly on a downward spiral to oblivion: he has broken up with his wife and family, lost his job and alienated most of his friends. He decides to drink himself to death but with no fixed time limit decides to enjoy the few weeks or months that he has left by moving to Las Vegas, where the bars stay open 24/7. Living on his sizeable severance check, he checks into a motel called 'The Whole Year Inn' (although from Ben's perspective it reads, 'The Hole You're In'). Shortly after his arrival on the Vegas Strip, Ben (habitually drunk) almost runs down an attractive woman named Sera (Shue) on a crosswalk. They exchange words and she walks angrily away, giving him the finger as she makes her way to the other side of the street. It turns out that she is a prostitute working for a brutal Latvian pimp named Yuri Butsov (Julian Sands), who beats her up and, as we see in flashback, savagely cut her buttocks with a knife. However, it turns out that a group of Polish mobsters, who Ben had seen briefly at a petrol station in the desert, are after Yuri (probably a turf war or a question of unpaid debts) so he mercifully ends his personal and business relationship with Sera for fear that the Poles may hurt her. Cut scenes from the original script tell us that the Poles end up murdering Yuri, although we never see it depicted on-screen. As Figgis explains:

> I had to avoid creating a scenario where the audience expects Yuri to jump out and be a threat to Ben's and Sera's love affair. This was not the nature of the story. On the other hand, he has to be strong enough to be believable as her pimp. I didn't want to show him being killed and I dropped the sequence where we see the gangsters' car driving into the desert with the body [scene 82 in original]. By bringing in Sting's version of 'My One and Only Love' as Yuri looks up at the gangsters at the door, we have already crossed over into the love story and never given him a second thought. The other thing I loved about Yuri's tale was that it reminded me of Hemingway's *The Killers*, which is one of my favourite American stories. I made him more philosophical than John O'Brien had and suggested to Julian that he accept his fate. (Figgis 2002: 308–9)

Indeed, after Yuri is killed, Ben and Sera are free to develop their relationship without compromise. It begins as a client–hooker liaison – he offers her $500 to come to his room for an hour and although Sera agrees, it turns out that Ben does not want sex. Instead, he seems to be more interested in a loving friendship: as they talk they develop a strong connection and Sera eventually invites him to move into her apartment. However, there are strict conditions on both sides: he tells her that she must never ask him to stop drinking; she asks Ben never to question or criticise her occupation as a prostitute. Right from the start, their fates are therefore fixed and unchanging: this is not a film about character development so much as a narrative about accepting the trajectory of your lot in life, even if that means staring into the abyss at all times. Needless to say, Sera's innate compassion forces her to beg Ben to seek medical help and he spitefully responds by picking up another prostitute at a casino, as if to test her seemingly feigned disinterest as a sexual being. From his point of view she fails the test: after catching them in her bed she kicks Ben out and as if in revenge she agrees to sleep with three college students at the Excalibur Hotel. Unfortunately she has no inkling of their savage perversity: they want her to 'service' all three of them at once while they film her on video. She only agrees to 'one at a time' but acquiesces when they up the price. Unfortunately they want to practise anal sex on her. She refuses but they brutally gang-rape her, filming the whole proceedings.

Things go from bad to worse when the following morning, a bruised and battered Sera is evicted by her landlady and after receiving a desperate phone call from Ben she arrives at his motel room to witness his last hours on his deathbed. After they make love for the first and only time, he dies, leaving Sera to reveal her true feelings to her therapist as the camera holds on her distraught face:

> I think the thing is, we both realised that we didn't have that much time and I accepted him for who he was. And I didn't expect him to change. And I think he felt that for me too. I liked his drama and he needed me. And I loved him. [Jazz piano up.] I really loved him.

The film ends with Sting once again singing 'My One and Only Love' as we see a slow-motion close-up of a smiling Ben at night against the twinkling Las Vegas lights which freeze-frames just prior to the closing credits: 'Every kiss you give / Sets my soul on fire / I give myself in sweet surrender / My one and only love.'

The key scene featuring Figgis's long-desired sound drop-out occurs in Los Angeles, just prior to Ben's leaving for Las Vegas. He is sitting next to an older man at the bar in a strip joint as jazz plays on the soundtrack. Figgis cuts back and forth between the stripper and Ben drinking (as if the alcohol is turning him on far more than the woman's body). Suddenly, an already intoxicated Ben downs an entire bottle of scotch and Figgis resorts to ten seconds of silence which creates such a sonic vacuum that we affectively share Ben's shock as he gasps for air, teetering on the bar stool as if he were suffering a heart attack. Our fears are (partially) eased as the music fades back up and we cut to Ben driving, his mouth still open as he sucks in air. He stops to chat with another prostitute but he is barely audible as he slurs his words. The jazz reaches a crescendo as we cut to him crossing the street: at least he's not driving!

This raises a couple of key questions: how did this scene play with the actual pre-release audience? Did it have the desired Syncinema effect of pushing the audience out of both their diegetic and exegetic comfort zones? According to Figgis:

> What I discovered when I started to tour with *Leaving Las Vegas* in America was that this moment in the film – in a crowded cinema, with a good sound system – was extremely uncomfortable when he's so distressed. And suddenly, it's so quiet in the cinema that you can literally hear everything, and you don't have the protection of this sound blanket of mush, or just ambient noise, or whatever, which we come to expect of a soundtrack. And I loved it. I thought that was exactly what I wanted, but it was even much more powerful than I thought it would be in my imagination. I know the film really well; I get really tense in my stomach when that scene comes on, because there's nowhere to go. It's like that moment when suddenly you're talking animatedly and then everybody stops talking and you realize your voice is a bit too loud. So, one of the most important things about *Leaving Las Vegas*, for me, was that I got to have real silence in a film. (Figgis 2003: 2)

A major contributor to this effect was the technological influence of Dolby sound systems, for as Michel Chion explains,

> Dolby cinema [. . .] introduces a new expressive element: the silence of the loudspeakers, accompanied by its reflection, the attentive silence of the audience. Any silence makes us feel exposed, as if we were laying bare our own listening, but also as if we were in the presence of a giant ear, tuned to our slightest noises. We are no longer merely listening to the film, we are as it were being listened to by it as well. (Chion 2003: 151)

In other words, this heightened level of what Paul Théberge calls 'attentive silence' (2008: 55) creates both audience discomfort and a higher affective intensity, leading to greater identification with the characters while they, in turn, pay closer attention to us.

There is also a distinct Nietzschean element present in this *aporia*, for as the philosopher famously states in *Beyond Good and Evil*, 'Whoever fights monsters should see to it that in the process he does not become a monster. And when you look long into an abyss, the abyss also looks into you' ([1886] 1966: 89). Ben's alcoholism – a form of self-inflicted abuse – and Sera's inability to escape the class and economic entrapment of prostitution – external abuse (often physical as well as mental) – are in their different ways an encounter and negotiation with the abyss. However, rather than dive nihilistically into chaos, the couple create a chaoid of love and friendship – not unlike the Greeks' definition of philosophy as the pleasure of forming associations (plus a concomitant pleasure in breaking them up through fissures such as rivalry, or even hatred). As Deleuze and Guattari argue in a key passage in *What is Philosophy?*,

> The three disciplines advance by crises or shocks in different ways, and in each case it is their succession that makes it possible to speak of 'progress'. It is as if the *struggle against chaos* does not take place without an affinity with the enemy, because another struggle develops and takes on more importance – the struggle *against opinion*, which claims to protect us from chaos itself. (1994: 203)

Figgis's affirmative view of silence is critical here, for it has long been seen as cinema's equivalent of the rent or fissure until the commentator (as narrative) enters the scene to patch it back up again by returning it to opinion/doxa. *Leaving Las Vegas* eschews this solution by having Ben follow his 'destructive' course to the bitter end and, more importantly, have Sera affirm their love and friendship to her therapist. Moreover, instead of ending with a Freudian judgement (Oedipal or otherwise), the unseen therapist is also reduced to silence and the so-called 'talking cure' is instead presented as an uninterrupted monologue: a pure expression of becoming-as-desire.[1]

While Figgis began his career in music and sound design, Harmony Korine got his start in writing, most notably the screenplay for Larry Clark's *Kids* (1995), a film about Manhattan youth culture and the AIDS crisis. In 1997 he wrote and directed *Gummo* before having underground success with the Dogme 95-inspired *Julien Donkey-Boy* (1999), followed by the far more commercial *Mister Lonely* (2007). Recorded over already-used VHS tape, edited in the VCR and presented as a 'found footage' home movie artefact, *Trash Humpers* has all the visual and sonic glitches associated with decaying video: faded and blurred colour, bar rolls, drop-outs, skewed tracking and inserted PLAY and REW commands that suggest that we are watching a compilation tape composed of seven separate home

---

[1] What we actually see is Elisabeth Shue in different costumes doing a camera test shot the week before filming started. She improvised answers to questions posed to her by Figgis who stood in for the absent therapist. This allowed her to get into character and for hidden emotions that were crucial to her character to come out of the sessions. 'None of these therapy scenes appeared in the first cut of the film,' admits Figgis. 'This was deliberate. I wanted to be absolutely sure that they were needed. Afterwards we quickly made a second pass and added everything. [. . .] I'm beginning to realize the power of the word in film. Someone talking about sex is stronger than seeing sex. The same is true about death' (Figgis 2002: 301).

movies. Korine explained the origin of *Trash Humpers* to Bilge Ebiri in a 2009 interview for *New York* Magazine:

> I would walk my dog at night back behind the alleyways in the neighborhood where I live in Nashville. And sometimes I would see these trash bins propped up against garages or lying on the ground. These overhead lights would be shining on them, giving them a real dramatic effect. The trash bins began to resemble human forms to me — almost like a war zone where the trash bins had been molested and beaten up and stuff. Sometimes, the way they were propped, they looked very humpable. Then I remembered that in my neighborhood growing up, there were these elderly peeping toms who would stare into my neighbor's window. They lived in an old person's home down the road, and they would come out at night. And I just put these ideas together. (Ebiri 2009: unpaginated)

As we shall see, the fact that these images are grounded in childhood memories gives Korine free play to mix fantasy with horror, retrogressive infantile sexuality (controlled by adults) with adult perversions (inspired by juvenile misbehaviour).

There are four main characters: a woman, Momma (Rachel Korine), and three men, Travis (Travis Nicholson), Buddy (Brian Kotzur) and Hervé (Korine himself). All are relatively young, so in order for them to appear as elderly 'white trash' (what Floridians call 'crackers'), they each wear a latex mask and a wig that makes them look old and decrepit (despite their often agile body movements). As Korine explains the origin of 'the look':

> I made these really crude masks that resemble burn victims – faces that were sort of melting – and my friends and I would go out wearing them late at night in the back alleyways near my house. We'd fool around and I'd take pictures using bad disposable cameras. I didn't really know what I was doing; I was just trying something out. But when I looked at the images all together there was something interesting there. It felt like found footage, a found object – the sort of thing you'd find buried in the dirt in a zip-lock bag, or shoved up the guts of a horse. (Cited in Sciortino 2010: unpaginated)

Although the film's ostensible plot is somewhat scattershot, there are recurring themes and vignettes that provide a loose narrative continuity. Firstly, there is of course the humping, and it's not only trash cans. In fact, the group will hump pretty much anything that's vertical: trees, lamp posts, telegraph poles, mail boxes, fences and walls. A key influence here is the performance artist Paul McCarthy, whom, as Nikolaj Lübecker (2015: 149) points out, Korine met in Los Angeles and later collaborated with in James Franco's *Rebel* (2012), a multimedia homage to James Dean which included works by Douglas Gordon, Terry Richardson, Aaron Young and Ed Ruscha. The key McCarthy museum project in this case is *The Garden*

(1991–92), a room-sized thicket of trees, rocks and grass that is actually an appropriated stage set from the TV western *Bonanza*. As in *Trash Humpers*, a robotic man vertically fornicates a tree while a younger man (perhaps his son) horizontally humps a hole in the ground as if they were involved in some ecosophical forest ritual. As Cary Levine describes the scene,

> While the father figure monotonously humps his stump, the motor that thrusts his pelvis in and out is visible, and its drone permeates the room. Similarly, the figures themselves are at once realistic and conspicuously artificial. Their movements are spasmodic, their flesh sickly – detailed, but waxy and buckling at the joints – somewhere between department store mannequin and Madame Tussaud statue. (2013: 139–40)

Levine then makes the key argument that the father–son relationship is yoked to rites of passage handed down from one generation to another, but that McCarthy lampoons them by making them seem like crimes against nature. Korine playfully adapts this scenario by making his own zombie-like humpers commit urban 'crimes' in the trashy back alleys of Nashville, as if sexuality – in both cases – were enacted for our own perverse voyeurship.

While the humping continues throughout the film, there are other motifs that paint a much darker side. Firstly, the film opens with Momma and one of the men defecating in a driveway. We also see them ritualistically smashing TV sets and boom boxes, setting off fireworks, indulging in 'spanking' sessions with overweight prostitutes, enjoying extremely racist and homophobic jokes with a comedian friend, all of which lack a punch line. They also force two performers who impersonate the original Siamese twins, Chang and Eng, with sock puppets to eat a stack of pancakes covered in dish soap instead of syrup, while another performer explains to us the advantages of living life without a head ('people would weigh eight-to-eleven pounds less; and best of all, no one would get dizzy again'). While all of this evokes the camp elements of John Waters's *Pink Flamingos* (1972) and the graphic sexual imagery of Jack Smith's *Flaming Creatures* (1963), Korine told Eric Kohn in a *New York Press* interview that,

> The only movie that I was actually thinking about as a reference was the William Eggleston movie *Stranded in Canton*. It has this liquid home movie photography and an accidental narrative. He just walked around filming his friends in black and white video. It's very fluid. (Kohn [2009] 2015: 185)

The Memphis-born Eggleston is most well known for his expressive colour photography and for taking the cover photo of Big Star's *Radio City* album (indeed band member Alex Chilton appears in the original uncut version of the film). Korine was clearly attracted not only to the free-form nature of Eggleston's film and its interviews with musicians like the Delta bluesman Furry Lewis, but also the white trash 'geek show' episode when a seemingly deranged man bites the head off a live chicken (thus the term 'geek', which can apply to a computer expert or a carnival show performer in equal measure: something Korine doubtless appreciated).

However, *Trash Humpers*'s main undercurrent is murder and child abuse, which takes it far beyond the limits of a mere 'freak show'. Firstly, Korine's hand-held camera discovers a naked corpse in the woods and simply leaves it there with no attempt to call the police. Secondly, one of the group's male performers who, dressed in a woman's skirt, improvises a Ginsberg-like Beat poem on the joys of trash humping, winds up lying in a pool of blood in their kitchen, his head smashed in. Finally, there is a constant use of baby dolls as props for acts of violence. Thus a young boy smashes a doll's head with a hammer or suffocates it in cling wrap, while Momma, either solo or with her friends, ties the dolls to BMX bikes and drags them over gravel and grass or through puddles as they cycle around in circles. These actions are often accompanied by diametrically opposed refrains which Momma sings and hums in her broken Southern accent. The first is 'Three Little Devils' which, like the song accompanying the children's elimination game during the opening sequence of Fritz Lang's *M*, takes the form of a macabre lullaby:

> three little devils jumped over the wall
> la la la di da da
> three little devils jumped over the wall
> knocked off your head and killed you all
> and laugh if I doodle da day
> oh Mr Devil you surely love me
> la la la di da da
> oh Mr Devil you surely love me
> strangled your child right under the tree
> and laugh if I doodle da day

This is, of course, the perfect accompaniment to the doll abuse but it also acts as a cushioning effect, sublimating psychopathic behaviour – the film's ostensible abyss – to a form of enacted theatre that distances the diegetic participants and the viewer from their own libidinal pathologies.

The second lullaby – 'Sleep my Darlin'' – seems to be in counterpoint to the first, for its lyrics are traditional parental reassurances that there's nothing to fear and that the child will be safe throughout the night before waking to greet the dawn:

> Sleep my darlin', and it's going to be fine.
> you will see, that you'll be mine.
> Sleep my baby, the whole night through,
> and don't let the bedbugs bite you.
> Sleep my darlin', and don't wake,
>   until the morn' comes, and the day breaks.
> Sleep my baby, the whole night through.
> And know that I love you.

However, this turns out to be a completely misguided reading, because at the end of *Trash Humpers* Momma is seen stalking the back alleys at night before breaking into a suburban house and stealing a baby. She sings the loving lullaby as she walks the child in its pram before stopping under a streetlight and the film ends with a freeze frame as we catch a glimpse of the innocent baby's face. Lübecker offers an interesting positive reading of this scene:

> Could it be that the baby should be seen as the possibility for a new beginning – not least for the trash humpers? With her gentle singing Momma calms the crying baby. At the end, she does become a 'momma'; there is an element of fulfillment. The camera moves gently around her, the scene is intimate, almost everything but the child and Momma is in the dark. Furthermore, it is tempting to speculate and suggest that this scene is transcended by extra-diegetic circumstances: it is shot by Korine himself, his wife Rachel plays Momma, and at the time of shooting they had just had their first daughter (it is possible that she is the baby in the film). (2015: 159)

We no longer think of Korine's laughably grotesque characters but instead embrace a tender, self-reflexive family scene designed to divert our previously held prejudices against 'white trash'. On the other hand, it's more likely that we are thinking of the horror and devastating dismay felt by the parents of the (diegetic) baby as well as the latter's fate, for having witnessed what the humpers have already done to the doll substitutes, 'We may now fear that the kidnapped baby will get a similar treatment' (Lübecker 2015: 159).

In an excellent article on the film's 'subversive vocality', Shaun Inouye argues that Korine exacerbates this ambivalently displaced violence towards children through the film's discrepant soundtrack, by

> intentionally decoupling the voice from the body and divesting it of its linguistic capabilities, *Trash Humpers* presents a version of vocality regressed to a pre-lingual state, before its ideological subjugation to the body through language. This, in turn,

informs the childlike rendering of the trash humpers, who seem to revel in libidinal fixations of the past. By utilizing the voice as a non-verbal, autonomous entity, *Trash Humpers* demonstrates the voice's capacity to incite meaning outside the image, and furthers Korine's stature as a boundary pushing film-maker. (2012: 37–8)

Thus Korine often refuses to show who is actually speaking at any given time – especially in group shots or when he is speaking off-screen as the cameraman – so that the film's voices are examples of what Michel Chion calls the *acousmêtre*:

> The *acousmêtre* is this acousmatic character whose relationship to the screen involves a specific kind of ambiguity and oscillation [. . .] We may define it as neither inside nor outside the image. It is not inside, because the image of the voice's source – the body, the mouth – is not included. Nor is it outside, since it is not clearly positioned offscreen in an imaginary 'wing', like a master of ceremonies or a witness, and it is implicated in the action, constantly about to be part of it. This is why voices of clearly detached narrators are not *acousmêtres*. (1994: 129)

In other words, language is largely disembodied throughout *Trash Humpers* so its specific ties to the elderly – whether psychologically or affectively – is displaced both diegetically and conceptually. In addition, the characters are not linguistically articulate: they exclaim expressively through song and dance, wild yelps (epitomised by Korine's own ear-splitting Banshee laugh), repetitive mantras like 'Make it! Make it! Don't take it!'[2] and atavistic cries. As Inouye explains,

> for the trash humpers, laughter (or the vocal signatures of laughter) is not an involuntary reaction but an exercised affront, utilized precisely because of its regressive qualities, in that it is distinctly human yet exemplary in its remoteness from human language (2012: 46–7)

The crux of Inouye's argument is that this disembodied characteristic of speech-as-pure sound takes the humpers back to their pre-linguistic childhood, a remnant of the past that still haunts their present-day 'adulthood'. Once again it evokes a Paul McCarthy performance-video, this time co-starring Mike Kelley, titled *Family Tyranny* (1987), which was performed live at Rosamund Felsen Gallery in Los Angeles. The work's main theme

---

[2] As Korine explained: 'I knew this guy who was in a cast for six months, but he kept lifting weights with his left arm. When he got his cast off, his right arm was like a twig, but his left arm was insanely muscular. I could never get that out of my mind. He would sit there coaching basketball and go, "Make it! Make it! Don't take it!" But sometimes he would do it with his strong arm, and sometimes with his twig arm. I never forgot that' (cited in Kohn [2009] 2015: 186).

is the subjugation of childhood instincts as a form of perversity and whose only cure is systematic and obligatory indoctrination. Heavily influenced by R. D. Laing's explorations into social conditioning as both tyrannical and depraved, as Levine rightly argues:

> *Family Tyranny* dramatizes this socializing enterprise, transforming a cliché of father–son bonding into a traumatic lesson in ritualized abuse. In the opening scene, a shirtless father (played by McCarthy) punishes his son – actually a Styrofoam head on a stick – for being a 'very bad boy'. 'My daddy did this to me, you can do this to your son', he repeatedly chants while driving a funnel into the boy's mouth and forcing a lumpy mayonnaise-based concoction down his throat. As in many of his works dating back to the mid-1970s, force-feeding is a metaphor for acculturation. (2013: 165)

Later, Kelley appears on stage to play the son and unfortunately fails to escape this abject paternalism. McCarthy then symbolically abuses a plastic doll – 'daddy's little boy' – (very reminiscent of those in *Trash Humpers*) and quietly intones 'I'm sooorry, I'm sooo sorry'. In effect, *Trash Humpers* reverses this tyranny: not by having children abuse the 'parents' but by having the adults *haunted* by their own childhood and re-enacting the abuse as hybrid adults/children (which in a way makes them even scarier).

This is why the film's climax – the kidnapping – is so affecting, for the baby doll has now been replaced by a real infant. As Inouye argues,

> Taken from the idyllic place of the home and brought into the dystopic world of the trash humpers, the baby becomes a literal manifestation of a past brought violently into the present – a past made abhorrent in the act of remembrance. (2012: 48)

However, while it would be easy to read Momma's appropriation of the child as a physical reinforcement of the difference between babies and adults (thus returning to a psychological, Freudian norm), the soundtrack continues to muddy the difference, for after Momma finishes singing her loving lullaby, 'the baby begins making inchoate vocal noises. Yet we do not hear a baby's voice: indistinguishable from the vocality that Korine has agonizingly attuned us to, what we hear are, rather, the trash humpers' (2012: 48).

If sound is used to fuse childhood with adulthood in similar pre-lingual expressions of atavism, silence is used to draw attention both to the apparatus and the humpers' role as criminals. The judicious use of sound dropout at the exact point where the VCR starts to play a new video, indicated by a grey screen bearing the word 'PLAY' or a blue screen with 'REW' for rewind, sets up a new context for the role of the video beyond what is actually shown on-screen (or monitor). The videos – either separately or dubbed onto a single tape – are now crucial evidence of two murders and a kidnapping, involving not only the characters in the narrative but the conspiratorial role of the diegetic trash-humper cameraman (Korine himself) and actual director (also Korine), who bear witness to the crimes but have so far (we assume) neglected to report them. As Korine admitted to Ebiri, he thought of *Trash Humpers* as a 'found object' (perhaps discovered on a garbage heap like Godard's *Weekend*, or, as he argued, in a ditch), and like all found objects it doesn't come with a legal copyright or court warning. When Ebiri playfully suggests that he should 'pretend like the print of your film got lost and that you were going to project this random old tape you found instead', Korine replies:

> I thought of doing that, actually. Then the few people I showed it to told me that there's no way anyone would believe I didn't make it. We thought of not putting titles or anything at all on the film. There was even a conversation at one point about just making a bunch of copies and leaving them on the sidewalk somewhere, and seeing what would happen. Leave it in front of some restaurant or an old person's retirement home or a police station or something. But I just didn't have the patience or the trust for something like that. (Cited in Ebiri 2009: unpaginated)

It's interesting that Korine thought about anonymously dropping off the tape with the police (as part of the project's humorous self-reflexivity), but of course he didn't do it.

As Korine told the audience during a Q&A session at the Film Society of Lincoln Center in New York in 2009, 'It's a movie that I probably will throw away someday' (cited in Lim 2015: 189). Maybe, but if we follow the logical topological vector indicated by the film's silences, the ultimate destination of *Trash Humpers* is not a film or video archive, a collector's shelf or Korine's trash can, but a brown envelope filed away in a District Attorney's office, ready to be used in a murder and kidnapping trial. We have thus moved, if you'll pardon the pun, from Figgis's variation on Syncinema to 'sin' cinema, from the movie theatre or art gallery to the court of law, not unlike *M*'s Beckert, with his endless psychological screening of a snuff film and eventual trials (kangaroo and legitimate).

Filmic silence thus moves to another point in the multiplicity in the form of what Americans call Miranda Rights or their British version – the right to remain silent (imagine Helen Mirren in voice-over from *Prime Suspect*): 'You do not have to say anything, but it may harm your defence if you do not mention when questioned something which you later rely on in court. Anything you do say may be given in evidence.' Silence is now a matter of legal survival, a defence tactic not to be messed with. The abyss – now shifted from the characters' eccentric negotiation with their pre-linguistic childhood to the prospect of a lengthy jail sentence – suddenly stares starkly back at us, no longer as 'time past' but 'doing time'. Of course, as John Cage constantly reminds us, there's no such thing as silence, for even after we ponder this new appalling reality – are we complicit in the crime simply by enjoying the absurdity of Korine's characters and dismissing their actions as freakishly regressive? – we make a sound simply by hearing our hearts race and blood pulsate, and ultimately by closing this book. Then we open up another vector, to another text (filmic or written), that awaits our attention. So: see you in court (hopefully not Judge Himmler's as he bangs his gavel and cries out: 'Silence!!!').

Bibliography

Abidor, Mitchell (2018), 'What the Non-Revolution of May '68 Taught Us', *New York Times*, 5 May, <https://www.nytimes.com/2018/05/05/opinion/sunday/may-1968-france.html> (last accessed 24 August 2020).
Alpers, Svetlana (1983), *The Art of Describing: Dutch Art in the Seventeenth Century*, Chicago: University of Chicago Press.
Althusser, Louis [1969] (1971a), 'Ideology and Ideological State Apparatuses (Notes towards an Investigation', in Ben Brewster (trans.), *Lenin and Philosophy and other Essays*, London: New Left Books and New York: Monthly Review Press, pp. 127–86.
Althusser, Louis [1966] (1971b), 'A Letter on Art in Reply to André Daspre', in Ben Brewster (trans.), *Lenin and Philosophy and Other Essays*, London: New Left Books and New York: Monthly Review Press, pp. 221–7.
Althusser, Louis (1976), *Essays in Self-Criticism*, trans. Grahame Lock, London: New Left Books.
Althusser, Louis [1965] (1990), *For Marx*, trans. Ben Brewster, London and New York: Verso.
Aron, Raymond (1964), *La lutte de classes: Nouvelles leçons sur les sociétés industrielles*, Paris: Gallimard.
Artaud, Antonin (1972), 'Distinction between Fundamental and Formal Avant-Garde', in Alastair Hamilton (trans.), *Collected Works*, Vol. 3, London: Calder and Boyars.
Artaud, Antonin (1976), 'To Have Done with the Judgment of God, a radio play (1947)', in Susan Sontag (ed.), *Antonin Artaud: Selected Writings*, Berkeley and Los Angeles: University of California Press, pp. 555–74.
Atack, Margaret (1999), *May '68 in French Fiction and Film: Rethinking Society, Rethinking Representation*, Oxford: Oxford University Press.
Avellar, José Carlos (2005), 'Vento, barravento [Glauber and Godard at the gates of the Lumière factory]', in Jane de Almeida (ed.), *Grupo Dziga Vertov*, São Paulo: witz edições, pp. 78–86.
Barthes, Roland [1953] (1984), *Writing Degree Zero*, in Annette Lavers and Colin Smith (trans.), *Writing Degree Zero & Elements of Semiology*, London: Jonathan Cape, pp. 1–73.

Barthes, Roland [1957] (1972), *Mythologies*, trans. Annette Lavers, New York: Hill and Wang.
Barthes, Roland (1977), *Image, Music, Text*, trans. Stephen Heath, New York: Hill and Wang.
Barthes, Roland [1975] (1980), 'Upon Leaving the Movie Theater', in Theresa Hak Kyung Cha (ed.), Bertrand Augst and Susan White (trans.), *Apparatus*, New York: Tanam Press.
Barthes, Roland [1980] (1981), *Camera Lucida*, trans. Richard Howard, New York: The Noonday Press.
Bateson, Gregory (2000), 'Toward a Theory of Schizophrenia', *Steps to an Ecology of Mind*, Chicago and London: University of Chicago Press, pp. 201–27.
Bazin, André (1967a), 'Painting and Cinema', in Hugh Gray (trans.), *What Is Cinema?* Vol. 1, Berkeley and Los Angeles: University of California Press, pp. 164–9.
Bazin, André (1967b), 'Theater and Cinema: Part Two', in Hugh Gray (trans.), *What Is Cinema?* Vol. 1, Berkeley and Los Angeles: University of California Press, pp. 95–124.
Benjamin, Walter [1936] (1969) 'The Work of Art in the Age of Mechanical Reproduction', in Hannah Arendt (ed.), *Illuminations: Essays and Reflections*, New York: Schocken Books, pp. 217–42.
Benjamin, Walter (1998), *Understanding Brecht*, trans. Anna Bostock, London and New York: Verso.
Berardi, Franco 'Bifo' (2012), *The Uprising: On Poetry and Finance*, South Pasadena: Semiotext(e).
Berg, Gretchen [1965] (2003), 'The Viennese Night: A Fritz Lang Confession, Parts One and Two', in Barry Keith Grant (ed.), Glenwood Irons (trans.), *Fritz Lang Interviews*, Jackson: University Press of Mississippi, pp. 50–76. Originally in *Cahiers du Cinéma* 169 (August 1965): 42–61 (Part One); and 179 (June 1966): 50–63 (Part Two).
Bergson, Henri [1907] (1983), *Creative Evolution*, trans. Arthur Mitchell, Lanham, MD: University Press of America.
Bergson, Henri [1896] (1991), *Matter and Memory*, trans. Nancy Margaret Paul and W. Scott Palmer, New York: Zone Books.
Berréby, Gérard (ed.) (1985), *Documents Relatifs à la Fondation de L'Internationale Situationniste*, Paris: Éditions Allia, pp. 111–23 (for Debord's 'Hurlements en faveur de Sade', originally published in *Ion*, No. 1 (April 1952): 219–30), and p. 109 (for Debord's 'Prolégomènes à tout cinéma futur', originally published in *Ion*, No. 1 (April 1952): 219).
Betz, Mark (2009), *Beyond the Subtitle: Remapping European Art Cinema*, Minneapolis: University of Minnesota Press.
Bonitzer, Pascal [1978] (2000), 'Deframings', trans. Chris Darke, in David Wilson (ed.), *Cahiers du Cinéma*, Vol. 4 1973–1978: *History, Ideology, Cultural Struggle* (An anthology from *Cahiers du Cinéma* nos 248–92, September 1973–September 1978), London and New York: Routledge, pp. 197–203.

Borges, Jorge Luis (1970), 'Pierre Menard, Author of the *Quixote*', trans. James E. Irby, in Donald A. Yates and James E. Irby (eds), *Labyrinths*, Harmondsworth: Penguin Books, pp. 62–71.
Brecht, Bertolt (1964), 'The Modern Theatre is the Epic Theatre (Notes to the Opera *Aufstieg und Fall der Stadt Mahagonny*)', in John Willett (trans. and ed.), *Brecht on Theatre*, London: Methuen, pp. 33–42.
Brecht, Bertolt (1978), 'Short Description of a New Technique of Acting Which Produces an Alienation Effect', in John Willett (trans. and ed.), *Brecht on Theatre*, London: Methuen, pp. 136–47.
Brecht, Bertolt (1987), *Poems 1913–1956*, eds John Willett, Ralph Manheim and Erich Fried, New York: Routledge.
Brecht, Bertolt [1965] (2001), *Stories of Mr. Keuner*, trans. Martin Chalmers, San Francisco: City Lights Books.
Brecht, Bertolt (2016), *Bertolt Brecht's Me-ti: Book of Interventions in the Flow of Things*, ed. and trans. Antony Tatlow, London: Bloomsbury Methuen Drama.
Brown, Royal S. (1972), 'Introduction: One Plus One Equals', in Royal S. Brown (ed.), *Focus on Godard*, Englewood Cliffs: Prentice-Hall, pp. 5–19.
Burch, Noël (1991), 'Fritz Lang: German Period', trans. Tom Milne, in *In and Out of Synch: The awakening of a cine-dreamer*, Aldershot: Scolar Press, pp. 3–31.
Cabañas, Kaira M. (2014), *Off-Screen Cinema: Isidore Isou and the Lettrist Avant-Garde*, Chicago and London: University of Chicago Press.
Cage, John [1961] (1973), *Silence: Lectures and Writings by John Cage*, Hanover, NH: Wesleyan University Press.
Carroll, Kent E. (1972), 'Film and Revolution: Interview with the Dziga-Vertov Group', in Royal S. Brown (ed.), *Focus on Godard*, Englewood Cliffs: Prentice-Hall, pp. 50–64.
Carroll, Noël (1978), 'Lang, Pabst, and Sound', in *Ciné-Tracts: A Journal of Film and Cultural Studies* (Montreal), Vol. 2, No. 1 (Fall): 15–23.
Cawkwell, Tim (2016), 'Little Dog for Roger by Malcolm', on website *Tim Cawkwell's Cinema*, <https://www.timcawkwell.co.uk/little-dog-for-roger> (last accessed 26 July 2018).
Cheshire, Godfrey (1996), 'Abbas Kiarostami: A cinema of questions', *Film Comment*, Vol. 32, No. 4, July/August: 32–43.
Cheshire, Godfrey [1999] (2010), 'Godfrey Cheshire on *Close-up*', 29 March 2010. Reprinted from 29 December 1999 issue of *New York Press*, <https://www.slantmagazine.com/film/godfrey-cheshire-on-close-up-abbas-kiarostami-1990/> (last accessed 24 December 2018).
Cheshire, Godfrey (2000), 'How to Read Kiarostami', *Cinéaste*, Vol. 25, No. 4: 8–15.
Chion, Michel [1990] (1994), *Audio-Vision: Sound on Screen*, ed. and trans. Claudia Gorbman, New York: Columbia University Press.
Chion, Michel (2003), 'The Silence of the Loudspeakers', in *Soundscape: The School of Sound Lectures, 1998–2001*, London and New York: Wallflower Press, pp. 150–4.

Chion, Michel (2009), *Film, A Sound Art*, trans. Claudia Gorbman, New York: Columbia University Press.

Chokrollahi, Mamhoud and Moslem Mansouri (1996), *Close-Up Long Shot*, documentary film includes interview with Hossein Sabzian.

Collet, Jean [1964] (1972), 'No Questions Asked: Conversation with Jean-Luc Godard on *Bande à part*', in Royal S. Brown (ed. and trans.), *Focus on Godard*, Englewood Cliffs: Prentice-Hall, pp. 40–5. From *Télérama*, No. 761 (16 August 1964): 49–50.

Conley, Tom (2000), 'The Film Event: From Interval to Interstice', in Gregory Flaxman (ed.), *The Brain is the Screen: Deleuze and the Philosophy of Cinema*, Minneapolis: University of Minnesota Press, pp. 303–25.

Cournot, Michel (1972), 'A Leap into Emptiness: Interview with Suzanne Schiffmann, Continuity Girl for *Alphaville*', in Royal S. Brown (ed.), *Focus on Godard*, Englewood Cliffs: Prentice-Hall, pp. 46–9.

Cronin, Paul (ed.) (2015), *Lessons with Kiarostami*, New York: Sticking Place Books.

Daney, Serge [1976] (2000), '"Theorize/Terrorize" (Godardian Pedagogy)', trans. Annwyl Williams, in David Wilson (ed.), *Cahiers du Cinema, Vol. 4 (1973–8): History, Ideology, Cultural Struggle*, New York and London: Routledge/British Film Institute, pp. 116–23. (Originally appeared as 'Le thérrorisé: pédagogie godardienne', *Cahiers du Cinéma*, January 1976: 262–3).

de Almeida, Jane (2005), 'A Friend of Glauber [and Godard]: special article for the newspaper Folha de São Paulo', in Jane de Almeida (ed.), *Grupo Dziga Vertov*, São Paulo: witz edições, pp. 48–54.

de Baecque, Antoine (2010), *Godard: biographie*, Paris: Grasset & Fasquelle.

Debord, Guy [1967] (1983), *Society of the Spectacle*, trans. Fredy Perlman and Jon Supak, Detroit: Black and Red.

Debord, Guy (2002), 'One More Try If You Want to Be Situationists (The SI *in* and *against* Decomposition)', trans. John Shepley, in Tom McDonough (ed.), *Guy Debord and the Situationist International: Texts and Documents*, Cambridge, MA: MIT Press, pp. 51–9.

Debord, Guy (2003), *Guy Debord: Complete Cinematic Works*, trans. Ken Knabb, Oakland: AK Press.

De Landa, Manuel (1991), *War in the Age of Intelligent Machines*, New York: Zone Books.

DeLanda, Manuel (2002), *Intensive Science and Virtual Philosophy*, London and New York: Continuum.

Deleuze, Gilles [1976] (1995) 'Three Questions on Six Times Two', in Martin Joughin (trans.), *Negotiations, 1972–1999*, New York: Columbia University Press, pp. 37–45. Originally published as 'Trois questions sur *Six fois deux*', in *Cahiers du Cinéma*, No. 271, November 1976.

Deleuze, Gilles (1983), *Nietzsche and Philosophy*, trans. Hugh Tomlinson, New York: Columbia University Press.

Deleuze, Gilles (1986), *Cinema 1: The Movement-Image*, trans. Hugh Tomlinson and Roberta Galeta, Minneapolis: University of Minnesota Press.

Deleuze, Gilles (1988a), *Bergsonism*, trans. Hugh Tomlinson and Barbara Habberjam, New York: Zone Books.
Deleuze, Gilles (1988b), *Spinoza: Practical Philosophy*, trans. Robert Hurley, San Francisco: City Lights Books.
Deleuze, Gilles (1989), *Cinema 2: The Time-Image*, trans. Hugh Tomlinson and Roberta Galeta, Minneapolis: University of Minnesota Press.
Deleuze, Gilles (1991a), 'Coldness and Cruelty', in *Masochism*, New York: Zone Books, pp. 7–138.
Deleuze, Gilles (1991b), *Bergsonism*, trans. Hugh Tomlinson and Barbara Habberjam, New York: Zone Books.
Deleuze, Gilles (1992), 'Ethology: Spinoza and Us', in Jonathan Crary and Sanford Kwinter (eds), *Zone 6: Incorporations*, New York: Zone Books.
Deleuze, Gilles (1997), 'The Exhausted', in Daniel W. Smith and Michael A. Greco (trans.), *Essays Critical and Clinical*, Minneapolis: University of Minnesota Press.
Deleuze, Gilles (2000), *Proust and Signs*, trans. Richard Howard, Minneapolis: University of Minnesota Press.
Deleuze, Gilles (2001), 'Immanence: A Life', in Anne Boyman (trans.), *Pure Immanence*, New York: Zone Books.
Deleuze, Gilles (2006a), 'The Rich Jew', in Ames Hodges and Mike Taormina (trans.), David Lapoujade (ed.), *Two Regimes of Madness*, New York: Semiotext(e), pp. 135–8.
Deleuze, Gilles (2006b), 'What is a Dispositif?', in Ames Hodges and Mike Taormina (trans.), David Lapoujade (ed.), *Two Regimes of Madness*, New York: Semiotext(e), pp. 338–48.
Deleuze, Gilles and Claire Parnet (1987), *Dialogues*, trans. Hugh Tomlinson and Barbara Habberjam, New York: Columbia University Press.
Deleuze, Gilles and Félix Guattari (1983), *Anti-Oedipus: Capitalism and Schizophrenia*, trans. Robert Hurley, Mark Seem and Helen R. Lane, Minneapolis: University of Minnesota Press.
Deleuze, Gilles and Félix Guattari (1987), *A Thousand Plateaus: Capitalism and Schizophrenia*, trans. Brian Massumi, Minneapolis: University of Minnesota Press.
Deleuze, Gilles and Félix Guattari (1994), *What is Philosophy?*, trans. Hugh Tomlinson and Graham Burchell, New York: Columbia University Press.
Deutsch, Stephen, Larry Sider and Dominic Power (2008), 'The thing that attracted me to film in the first place was sound: An Interview with Mike Figgis', *The Soundtrack*, Vol. 1, No. 3: 163–74.
Devictor, Agnès (2015), 'Iranian Film Policy in a Global Context', in Peter Decherney and Blake Atwood (eds), *Iranian Cinema in a Global Context: Policy, Politics, and Form*, New York and London: Routledge, pp. 13–32.
Dixon, Wheeler Winston (1997), *The Films of Jean-Luc Godard*, New York: State University of New York Press.

Drabinski, John (2008), 'Separation, Difference, and Time in Godard's *Ici et ailleurs*', *SubStance*, Vol. 37, No. 11: 148–58.
Ebiri, Bilge (2009), 'Harmony Korine on How Fatherhood Influenced His New Movie About Having Sex With Garbage Cans', *New York Magazine*, 9 October, <https://www.vulture.com/2009/10/harmony_korine_on.html> (last accessed 31 October 2018).
Eisenstein, Sergei, Vsevolod Pudovkin and Grigori Alexandrov (1957), 'Appendix A: A Statement', in Sergei Eisenstein, Jay Leyda (trans. and ed.), *Film Form: Essays in Film Theory*, New York: Meridian Books, pp. 257–9.
Elcott, Noam M. (2008), 'Darkened Rooms: A Genealogy of Avant-Garde Filmstrips from Man Ray to the London Film-Makers' Co-Op and Back Again', *Grey Room*, No. 30 (Winter): 6–37.
Elena, Alberto [2002] (2005), *The Cinema of Abbas Kiarostami*, trans. Belinda Coombes, London: SAQI and the Iran Heritage Foundation (originally Madrid: Ediciones Cátedra).
Elshaw, Gary (2000), 'The Depiction of Late 1960s Counter Culture in the 1968 Films of Jean-Luc Godard', MA thesis, Film. Faculty of Humanities and Social Sciences, Victoria, NZ: University of Wellington.
Emmelhainz, Irmgard (2009), 'From Third Worldism to Empire: Jean-Luc Godard and the Palestine Question', *Third Text*, Vol. 23, No. 5, September: 649–56.
Fanon, Frantz (1966), *The Wretched of the Earth*, trans. Constance Farrington, New York: Grove Press.
Fargier, Jean-Paul and Bernard Sizaire (1969), 'Deux Heures avec Jean-Luc Godard', *Tribune Socialiste* 396, 23 January: 18. Reprinted in Godard (1985).
Fehsenfeld, Martha and Lois More Overbeck (eds) (2009), *The Letters of Samuel Beckett, Volume 1: 1929–1940*, Cambridge: Cambridge University Press.
Ferguson, Coco (2006), 'The Most Fatal Attraction: Kiarostami's *Close-Up* revisited', *Envy*, Issue 6, <https://new.bidoun,org/issues/6-envy> (last accessed 20 September 2020).
Field, Allison (1999), '*Hurlements en faveur de Sade*: The Negation and Surpassing of "Discrepant Cinema"', *SubStance*, No. 90: 55–70.
Figgis, Mike (2002), '*Leaving Las Vegas*', in *Collected Screenplays 1*, London: Faber and Faber, pp. 195–293.
Figgis, Mike (2003), 'Silence: The Absence of Sound (Thursday 16 April, 1998, Institut Français, London)', in Larry Sider, Diane Freeman and Jerry Sider (eds), *Soundscape: The School of Sound Lectures, 1998–2001*, London and New York: Wallflower Press, pp. 1–14.
Fink, Daniel (1971), 'Vermeer's Use of the Camera Obscura – A Comparative Study', *The Art Bulletin*, Vol. 53: 493–505.
Foucault, Michel (1972), *The Archaeology of Knowledge & The Discourse on Language*, trans. A. M. Sheridan-Smith, New York: Pantheon Books.

Foucault, Michel (1977), 'The Confession of the Flesh', in Colin Gordon (ed.), *Power/Knowledge: Selected Interviews & Other Writings, 1972–1977*, New York: Pantheon Books, pp. 194–228.

Foucault, Michel (1984), 'Nietzsche, Genealogy, History', in Paul Rabinow (ed.), Donald F. Bouchard and Sherry Simon (trans.), *The Foucault Reader*, New York: Pantheon Books, pp. 76–100.

Foucault, Michel (1989), *The Order of Things*, London and New York: Routledge.

Foucault, Michel (2007), *Security, Territory & Population: Lectures at the College de France 1977–1978*, ed. Michel Senellart, trans. Graham Burchill, New York and Basingstoke: Palgrave Macmillan.

Frampton, Hollis (1976), 'Notes on Composing in Film', *October*, 1 (Spring): 104–10.

Frampton, Hollis (2009a), 'Impromptus on Edward Weston: Everything in its Place', in Bruce Jenkins (ed.), *On the Camera Arts and Consecutive Matters: The Writings of Hollis Frampton*, Cambridge, MA: MIT Press, pp. 67–87.

Frampton, Hollis (2009b), 'For a Metahistory of Film: Commonplace Notes and Hypotheses', in Bruce Jenkins (ed.), *On the Camera Arts and Consecutive Matters: The Writings of Hollis Frampton*, Cambridge, MA: MIT Press, pp. 131–9.

Frampton, Hollis (2009c), '*Zorns Lemma*: Script and Notations', in Bruce Jenkins (ed.), *On the Camera Arts and Consecutive Matters: The Writings of Hollis Frampton*, Cambridge, MA: MIT Press, pp. 192–202.

Frampton, Hollis (2009d), 'Talking about *Magellan*: An Interview', in Bruce Jenkins (ed.), *On the Camera Arts and Consecutive Matters: The Writing of Hollis Frampton*, Cambridge, MA: MIT Press, pp. 232–52.

Frampton, Hollis (2009e), 'Text of Intertitles for *Gloria!*', in Bruce Jenkins (ed.), *On the Camera Arts and Consecutive Matters: The Writing of Hollis Frampton*, Cambridge, MA: MIT Press, pp. 253–4.

Freud, Sigmund (1921), 'Introduction', in Sándor Ferenczi, Karl Abraham, Ernst Simmel and Ernest Jones (eds), *Psycho-Analysis and the War Neuroses*, London, Vienna and New York: International Psycho-Analytic Press.

Fry, Nicholas and Jean-Luc Godard (1972), 'Wind from the East', in Marianne Sinclair and Danielle Adkinson (trans.), *Weekend/Wind From the East: Two Films by Jean-Luc Godard*, New York: Simon and Schuster, pp. 120–88.

Gardner, Colin (2013), 'Constructing a Cinema of Minorities: "Staying Put", *Memories of Underdevelopment* and the Invention of a People Yet to Come', in Giorgio Hadi Curti, Stuart Aitken and Jim Craine (eds), *The Fight to Stay Put: Social Lessons Through Media Imaginings of Urban Transformation and Change*, Media Geography at Mainz, Vol. 3, Stuttgart: Franz Steiner Verlag, pp. 75–90.

Gardner, Colin (2017), 'From Weimar to Los Angeles: Cold War Hysteria and the Politics of Paranoia in Joseph Losey's *M* (1951)', in Kimberly Drake (ed.), *Critical Insights: Paranoia, Fear and Alienation*, Ipswich, MA: Salem Press/Grey House Publishing, pp. 137–53.

Gellen, Kata (2015), 'Indexing Identity: Fritz Lang's M', *Modernism/modernity*, Vol. 22, No. 3, September: 425–48.
Gidal, Peter (1985), 'Interview with Hollis Frampton', *October* 32 (Spring): 93–117.
Godard, Jean-Luc (1964), 'The Characters According to Godard'. Excerpts from Godard's character descriptions from the original pressbook printed by Unifrance/Gaumont for the theatrical release of *Bande à part*, 1964. Criterion DVD booklet, pp. 4–5.
Godard, Jean-Luc (1967), 'Lutter sur deux fronts', conversation with Jean-Luc Godard by J. Bontemps, Jean-Louis Comolli, Michel Delahay and Jean Narboni, *Cahiers du Cinéma*, No. 194, *Octobe*: 12–27 and 66–70.
Godard, Jean-Luc (1968), 'Three Thousand Hours of Cinema', in Toby Mussman (ed.), Jane Pease (trans.), *Jean- Luc Godard: A Critical Anthology*, New York: E. P. Dutton & Co., Inc., pp. 293–9. Beginning excerpt from Godard's journal, originally published in *Cahiers du Cinéma*, November 1966.
Godard, Jean-Luc (1971). 'Dans la société moderne, la prostitution est l'état normal' ('In Modern Society, Prostitution is the Normal State'), in *2 ou 3 choses que je sais d'elle*, Paris: Points Seuil/Avant-Scène, p. 120.
Godard, Jean-Luc (1972a), '*Works of Calder* and *L'Histoire d'Agnès*', in Jean Narboni and Tom Milne (eds), *Godard on Godard*, New York: Viking Press, pp. 19–20. Originally published in *Gazette du Cinéma* 4, October 1950.
Godard, Jean-Luc (1972b), 'My Approach in Four Movements', in Jean Narboni and Tom Milne (eds), *Godard on Godard*, New York: Viking Press, pp. 239–42. Originally published in *L'Avant-Scène du Cinéma* 70, May 1967.
Godard, Jean-Luc [1956] (1972c), 'Montage my Fine Care', *Cahiers du Cinéma* 65, December 1956, in Jean Narboni and Tom Milne (eds), *Godard on Godard*, New York: Viking Press, pp. 39–41.
Godard, Jean-Luc [1965] (1972d), 'Let's Talk About Pierrot', *Cahiers du Cinéma* 171, October: 18–35, in Jean Narboni and Tom Milne (eds), *Godard on Godard*, New York: Viking Press, pp. 215–34.
Godard, Jean-Luc (1984a), 'A Woman is a Woman', in Jan Dawson (trans.), *Three Films*, London: Lorrimer Publishing, pp. 17–55.
Godard, Jean-Luc (1984b), 'Two or Three Things That I Know About Her', in Marianne Alexandre (trans.), *Three Films*, London: Lorrimer Publishing, pp. 122–78.
Godard, Jean-Luc (1985), *Jean-Luc Godard par Jean-Luc Godard*, ed. Alain Bergala, Paris: Éditions de l'Étoile.
Goldmann, Lucien [1964] (1975), *Towards a Sociology of the Novel*, trans. Alan Sheridan, New York: Tavistock Publications.
Goodwin, Michael, Tom Luddy and Naomi Wise (1970), 'The Dziga Vertov film group in America', in *Take One. The Film Magazine*, Vol. 2, No. 10, March/April: 8–27. The extended draft version of the same interview – 'The Dziga Vertov Film Group in America: an Interview with Jean-Luc Godard and Jean-Pierre Gorin', in *Cinefiles* <https://webapps.cspace.berkeley.edu/cinefiles/

imageserver/blobs/d9557f1a-7fba-426d-b95b/content/linked_pdf>, (last accessed 11 March 2018).
Goudet, Stéphane (1996), 'Entretien avec Mohsen Makhmalbaf: Prises de position et prises de pouvoir', *Positif*, No. 422, April: 21–2.
Goudet, Stéphane (1997), 'Entretien avec Abbas Kiarostami: Manipulations', *Positif*, No. 442, December: 79–104.
Graham, Peter (1968), *The New Wave*, London: Martin Secker and Warburg; New York: Doubleday & Co.
Guattari, Félix [1992] (1995), *Chaosmosis: An Ethico-Aesthetic Paradigm*, trans. Paul Bains and Julian Pefanis, Bloomington and Indianapolis: Indiana University Press.
Guattari, Félix (2008), *The Three Ecologies*, trans. Ian Pindar and Paul Sutton, London: Continuum.
Guattari, Félix (2013), *Schizoanalytic Cartographies*, trans. Andrew Goffey, London: Bloomsbury.
Guevara, Che (2003), 'Create Two, Three, Many Vietnams' (message to the Tricontinental Conference, April 1967), in David Deutschmann (ed.), *Che Guevara Reader: Writing on Politics and Revolution*, North Melbourne, Australia: Ocean Press, pp. 350–62.
Guimarães, António Sérgio Alfredo (2009), 'Frantz Fanon's Reception in Brazil', *Lusotopie*, Vol. 16, No. 2: 157–72.
Gunning, Tom (2000), *The Films of Fritz Lang: Allegories of Vision and Modernity*, London: British Film Institute Publishing.
Gunning, Tom (2006), 'The Cinema of Attraction(s): Early Film, Its Spectator and the Avant-Garde', in Wanda Strauven (ed.), *The Cinema of Attractions Reloaded*, Amsterdam: Amsterdam University Press, pp. 381–8.
Gunning, Tom (2015), 'Applying Color: Creating Fantasy of Cinema', in Tom Gunning, Joshua Yumibe, Giovanna Fossati and Jonathon Rosen (eds), *Fantasia of Color in Early Cinema*, Amsterdam: Eye Filmmuseum, Amsterdam University Press.
Guzzetti, Alfred (1981), *Two or Three Things I Know About Her: Analysis of a Film by Godard*, Cambridge, MA and London: Harvard University Press.
Hamid, Nassia (1997), 'Near and Far', *Sight and Sound*, Vol. 7, No. 2, February: 22–4.
Hayes, Kevin J. (2000), '*Une femme est une femme*: A Modern Woman's Bookshelf', *Film Criticism*, Vol. 25, No. 1 (Fall): 65–82.
Heidegger, Martin (1977), 'The Letter on Humanism', in David Farrell Krell (ed.), Frank A. Capuzzi, J. Glenn Gray, and David Krell (trans.), *Martin Heidegger: Basic Writings*, New York: Harper and Row, pp. 193–242.
Heidegger, Martin (1993), 'The Question Concerning Technology', in David Farrell Krell (ed.), William Lovitt and David Krell (trans.), *Martin Heidegger: Basic Writings*, San Francisco: Harper San Francisco, pp. 311–41.
Heymann, Werner Richard (1931), 'Sound Film Music as a New Musical Form', trans. Alan Lareau, in *Film und Ton* (weekly insert in *Licht-Bildbuehne*),

No. 31, 1 August 1931, <https://www.heymann-musik.de/_Etexte.htm> (last accessed 7 September 2020).

Hoberman, J. [1998] (2004), 'A Woman Is a Woman', Criterion DVD booklet, pp. 5–7.

Inouye, Shaun (2012), 'Debasing the voice: Subversive vocality in Harmony Korine's *Trash Humpers*', *The Soundtrack*, Vol. 5, No. 1: 37–49.

Isou, Jean Isidore (1952), 'Esthétique du Cinéma', *Ion* No. 1, April: *Centre de Création: Numéro Spécial sur le Cinéma*: 7–154.

Isou, Isidore (1964), 'Traité de bave et d'éternité', in *Oeuvres de spectacle*, Paris: Gallimard, pp. 7–88.

Isou, Isidore (2019), 'Treatise on Venom and Eternity', in Julian Kabza (ed.), Ian Thompson, Anna O'Meara, Nadege LeJeune, Catherine Goldstein and Julian Kabza (trans.), *Treatise on Venom & Eternity*, Ann Arbor: Annex Press, unpaginated throughout.

Jacob, Gilles (1972), 'Atonal Cinema for Zombies', in Royal S. Brown (ed.), *Focus on Godard*, Englewood Cliffs: Prentice-Hall, 147–58.

Johnson, David T. (2008), 'Critical Hearing and the Lessons of Abbas Kiarostami's *Close-Up*', in Jay Beck and Tony Grajeda (eds), *Lowering the Boom: Critical Studies in Film Sound*, Urbana and Chicago: University of Illinois Press, pp. 289–98.

Johnson, Randal (1984), *Cinema Novo x 5: Masters of Contemporary Brazilian Film*, Austin: University of Texas Press.

Jorn, Asger (ed.) (1964), *Contre le Cinéma*, Aarhus: Institut Scandinave de vandalisme comparé.

Joyce, James (1961), *Ulysses*, New York: Random House.

Jünger, Ernst (1926), 'Grolkstadt und Land', *Deutsches Volkstum* 8: 577–81; in Werneburg (1992), pp. 42–64.

Jünger, Ernst (1930), 'Krieg und Lichtbild' ('War and Photography') in *Das Antlitz des Weltkrieges*, Berlin: Neufeld & Henius, chapter 2.

Kaes, Anton (1993), 'The Cold Gaze: Notes on Mobilization and Modernity', in *New German Critique*, Special Issue on Ernst Jünger, No. 59 (Spring/Summer): 105–17.

Kaes, Anton (2001), *M* (revised edition), London: BFI/Palgrave.

Kleist, Heinrich von (2004), 'The Puppet Theatre', in David Constantine (trans.), *Selected Writings*, Indianapolis: Hackett Publishing, pp. 411–16.

Knabb, Ken (ed. and trans.) (1989), *Situationist International Anthology*, Berkeley: Bureau of Public Secrets.

Köhler, Wolfgang (1964), *Psychologie de la forme: Introduction à de nouveau concepts en psychologie*, Paris: Gallimard.

Kohn, Eric [2009] (2015), 'His Humps', in Eric Kohn (ed.), *Harmony Korine: Interviews*, Jackson: University Press of Mississippi, pp. 184–6. (From *New York Press*, 30 September 2009.)

Kovács, András Bálint (2007), *Screening Modernism: European Art Cinema 1950–1980*, Chicago: University of Chicago Press.

Kuntzel, Thierry (1978), 'The Film-Work', trans. Lawrence Crawford, Kimball Lockhart and Claudia Tysdal, *Enclitic*, Vol. 2, No. 1 (Spring): 39–62.
Kustow, Michael (1968), 'Without and Within: Thoughts on Politics, Society, and the Self in Some Recent Films', in Toby Mussman (ed.), *Jean-Luc Godard: A Critical Anthology*, New York: E. P. Dutton & Co., Inc., pp. 284–92. (Excerpts from an article originally in *Sight and Sound*, Summer 1967.)
Landy, Marcia (2001), 'Just an image: Godard, cinema and philosophy', *Critical Quarterly*, Vol. 43, No. 3: 9–31.
Lang, Fritz [1931] (2001), 'My Film *M*: A Factual Report', in Rolf Aurich, Wolfgang Jacobsen and Cornelius Schanuber (eds), Robin Benson, Nicole Gentz, Catherine Kerkhoff-Saxon, Jane Paulick and Steve Smith (trans.), *Fritz Lang: His Life and Work. Photographs and Documents*, Berlin: Jovis Verlag, pp. 138–40. Originally published in the German newspaper *Die Filmwoche*, No. 21, 20 May 1931. Also in the Criterion DVD booklet, pp. 8–11.
Lefebvre, Henri (1991), *The Production of Space*, trans. Donald Nicholson-Smith, Cambridge, MA and Oxford: Blackwell.
Le Grice, Malcolm (1972), 'Real Time/Space', *Art and Artists Magazine*, December: 39–43.
Le Grice, Malcolm (1977), *Abstract film and beyond*, Cambridge, MA: MIT Press.
Le Grice, Malcolm (2001), *Experimental Cinema in the Digital Age*, London: BFI Publishing.
Le Grice, Malcolm (2014), Malcolm Le Grice's Official Website <https://www.malcolmlegrice.com/1960s>; <https://www.malcolmlegrice.com/1970s> (last accessed 26 July 2018).
Lemaître, Maurice [1952] (1999), 'Le film est déjà commencé?: Organisation d'une Séance de cinéma', in *Le film est déjà commencé: Séance de Cinéma*, preface by Isidore Isou, Paris: Cahiers de L'Externité, pp. 95–183.
Lesage, Julia (1974), 'Godard-Gorin's *Wind from the East*: Looking at a film politically', *Jump Cut*, No. 4: 18–23, <http://www.ejumpcut.org/archive/onlinessays/JC04folder/WindfromEast.html> (last accessed 4 March 2021).
Lesage, Julia (1979), *Jean-Luc Godard: A Guide to References and Resources*, Boston: G. K. Hall.
Levin, Thomas Y. (2002), 'Dismantling the Spectacle: The Cinema of Guy Debord', in Tom McDonough (ed.), *Guy Debord and the Situationist International: Texts and Documents*, Cambridge, MA: MIT Press, pp. 321–453.
Levine, Cary (2013), *Pay For Your Pleasures*, Chicago and London: University of Chicago Press.
Levitin, Jacqueline (2014), 'One or Two Points About *Two or Three Things I Know About Her*', in Tom Conley and T. Jefferson Kline (eds), *A Companion to Jean-Luc Godard*, Chichester: Wiley Blackwell, pp. 243–62.
Lim, Dennis (2015), 'Q&A at New York Film Festival for Trash Humpers', in Eric Kohn (ed.), *Harmony Korine: Interviews*, Jackson: University Press of Mississippi, pp. 187–92. (Recorded at the Film Society of Lincoln Center, October 2, 2009.)

Lopate, Phillip (1998), 'Interview with Abbas Kiarostami', in *Totally, Tenderly, Tragically: Essays and Criticism from a Lifelong Love Affair with the Movies*, New York and London: Anchor Books/Doubleday, pp. 352–67.
Lübecker, Nikolaj (2015), *The Feel-Bad Film*, Edinburgh: Edinburgh University Press.
Lundy, Craig (2012), *History and Becoming: Deleuze's Philosophy of Creativity*, Edinburgh: Edinburgh University Press.
Lyons, Alice (2016), 'A Keyboard Mind: Hollis Frampton's *Gloria!* as Lyric Poem', originally published, 11 March, 2016, The Poetry Foundation/*Poetry* Magazine, <https://www.poetryfoundation.org/harriet/2016/03/a--keyboard-mind-hollis-framptons-gloria-as-lyric-poem> (last accessed 7 March 2018).
MacBean, James Roy (1975), *Film and Revolution*, Bloomington and London: Indiana University Press.
MacCabe, Colin with Mick Eaton and Laura Mulvey (1980), *Godard: Images, Sounds, Politics*, Bloomington: Indiana University Press.
MacCabe, Colin (2004), *Godard: A Portrait of the Artist at Seventy*, New York: Farrar, Straus and Giroux.
Macciocchi, Maria Antonietta (1973), *Letters from Inside the Italian Communist Party to Louis Althusser*, trans. Stephen M. Hellman, London: New Left Books.
MacDonald, Scott (1995), *Screen Writings: Scripts and Texts by Independent Filmmakers*, Berkeley and Los Angeles: University of California Press.
MacDonald, Scott (n.d.), 'Zorns Lemma', <http://hollisframpton.org.uk/zlessay.htm> (last accessed 7 September 2018).
Macherey, Pierre (1978), *A Theory of Literary Production*, trans. Geoffrey Wall, London: Routledge and Kegan Paul.
MacKenzie, Scott (2014), *Film Manifestos and Global Cinema Cultures: A Critical Anthology*, Berkeley and Los Angeles: University of California Press.
Manceaux, Michèle (1972), 'A Movie is a Movie: Interview with Jean-Luc Godard on *Une Femme est une femme*', in Royal S. Brown (ed. and trans.), *Focus on Godard*, Englewood Cliffs: Prentice-Hall, pp. 28–36. Combination of two interviews with Godard from *L'Express*, 12 January 1961: 36–8; and 27 July 1961: 32–4.
Mao Tse-tung (1941), 'Reform Our Study', in *Selected Works,* Vol. III, *China,* Peking: Foreign Languages Press, pp. 22–3.
Mao Tse-tung (1957), 'On the Correct Handling of Contradictions Among the People' (27 February), <https://www.marxists.org/reference/archive/mao/selected-works/volume-5/mswv5_58.htm> (last accessed 2 March 2018).
Margulies, Ivone (2003), 'Exemplary Bodies: Reenactment in *Love in the City, Sons,* and *Close-Up*', in Ivone Margulies (ed.), *Rites of Realism: Essays on Corporeal Cinema*, Durham, NC: Duke University Press, pp. 217–44.
Marinetti, Filippo Tommaso (1914), 'Futurism and the Theatre: A Futurist Manifesto', trans. D. Nevile Lees, *The Mask: A Quarterly Journal of the Art of the Theatre*, Vol. 6, No. 3, January 1914: 188–93.

Marks, Laura U. (2009), 'Information, secrets, and enigmas: an enfolding-unfolding aesthetics for cinema', *Screen*, Vol. 50, No. 1 (Spring): 86–98.
Marks, Laura U. (2010), 'Experience—Information—Image: A Historiography of Unfolding in Arab Cinema', in Dina Iordanova, David Martin-Jones and Belén Vidal (eds), *Cinema at the Periphery*, Detroit: Wayne State University Press, pp. 232–53.
Marotta, Jenna (2017), 'AMC Removes "Spoiler" Signage Warning "The Last Jedi" Audiences of Key Climactic Moment', *IndieWire*, 28 December, <https://www.indiewire.com/2017/12/star-wars-the-last-jedi-amc-signs-spoiler-1201911549/> (last accessed 12 March 2021).
Marshall, Phoebe (2015), *The Cinétracts: Cinema's Radical Return to Zero*. MA thesis, Program in the Humanities, University of Chicago.
Martin, Adrian (2012), 'Hanging Here and Groping There: On Raúl Ruiz's "The Six Functions of the Shot,"', in *Screening the Past*, Issue 35, La Trobe University, <http://www.screeningthepast.com/2012/12/hanging-here-and-groping-there-on-raul-ruiz%E2%80%99s-%E2%80%9Cthe-six-functions-of-the-shot%E2%80%9D/> (last accessed 14 June 2020).
Martin-Jones, David (2011), *Deleuze and World Cinemas*, London and New York: Continuum.
Martin-Jones, David (2019), *Cinema Against Doublethink: Ethical Encounters with the Lost Pasts of World History*, London and New York: Routledge.
Massumi, Brian (2002), *Parables for the Virtual: Movement, Affect, Sensation*, Durham, NC and London: Duke University Press.
Matthews, Peter (2002), 'A Little Learning', *Sight and Sound*, Vol. 12, No. 6, June: 30–2.
Merleau-Ponty, Maurice (1964), *Sense and Non-Sense*, trans. Hubert L. and Patricia Allen Dreyfus, Evanston: Northwestern University Press.
Mulvey, Laura (1998), 'Kiarostami's uncertainty principle', *Sight and Sound*, Vol. 8, No. 6, June: 24–7.
Nancy, Jean-Luc (2001), 'The Evidence of Film: Abbas Kiarostami', in trans. Verena Andermatt Conley, *The Evidence of Film: Abbas Kiarostami*, Brussels: Yves Gevaert Publisher, pp. 8–79.
Naficy, Hamid (2005), '*Close-Up* (1989): Questioning Reality, Realism, and Neorealism', in Jeffrey Geiger and R. L. Rutsky (eds), *Film Analysis: A Norton Reader*, New York and London: W. W. Norton & Company, pp. 794–812.
Narboni, Jean and Tom Milne (eds) (1972), 'Interview with Jean-Luc Godard' (*Cahiers du Cinéma* 138, December 1962: 20–39), in *Godard on Godard*, New York: The Viking Press, pp. 171–96.
Nietzsche, Friedrich [1901] (1935), *La Volonté de Puissance*, trans. Geneviève Bianquis, Friedrich Würzbach edition, Paris: Gallimard.
Nietzsche, Friedrich [1886] (1966), *Beyond Good and Evil*, trans. Walter Kaufmann, New York: Vintage Books.
Nietzsche, Friedrich [1883] (1976), 'Thus Spoke Zarathustra', in Walter Kaufmann (trans.), *The Portable Nietzsche*, New York: Viking Penguin, pp. 103–439.

Nietzsche, Friedrich (1983), 'On the Uses and Disadvantages of History for Life', in R. J. Hollingdale (trans.), *Untimely Meditations*, Cambridge: Cambridge University Press.

Nietzsche, Friedrich [1873] (1989), 'On Truth and Lying in an Extra-Moral Sense', in Sander L. Gilman, Carole Blair and David J. Parent (trans. and ed.), *Friedrich Nietzsche on Rhetoric and Language*, New York and Oxford: Oxford University Press.

O'Rawe, Des (2006) 'The Great Secret: Silence, Cinema, Modernism', *Screen*, 47.4 (Winter): 395–405.

Paillet, Marc (1964) *Gauche: année zero*, Paris: Gallimard.

Penley, Constance (1977), 'The Avant-Garde and Its Imaginary', *Camera Obscura*, Vol. 1 No. 2: 2–33.

Perez, Gilberto (1998), *The Material Ghost: Films and Their Medium*, Baltimore: Johns Hopkins University Press.

Pipolo, Tony (1988), 'The Spectre of JOAN OF ARC: Textual Variations in the Key Prints of Carl Dreyer's Film', *Film History*, Vol. 2, No. 4, November–December: 301–24.

Pisters, Patricia (2012), *The Neuro-Image: A Deleuzian Film-Philosophy of Digital Screen Culture*', Stanford: Stanford University Press.

Ragona, Melissa (2004), 'Hidden Noise: Strategies of Sound Montage in the Films of Hollis Frampton', *October*, Vol. 109 (Summer): 96–118.

Reader, Keith (2007), 'Godard and Asynchrony', in Michael Temple, James S. Williams and Michael Witt (eds), *For Ever Godard*, London: Black Dog Publishing, pp. 72–93.

Remes, Justin (2015), *Motion(less) Pictures: The Cinema of Stasis*, New York: Columbia University Press.

Remes, Justin (2016) 'The Sleeping Spectator: Nonhuman Aesthetics in Abbas Kiarostami's *Five: Dedicated to Ozu*', in Tiago de Luca and Nuno Barradas Jorge (eds), *Slow Cinema*, Edinburgh: Edinburgh University Press, pp. 231–42.

Remes, Justin (2020), *Absence in Cinema: The Art of Showing Nothing*, New York: Columbia University Press.

Rocha, Glauber (1970a), 'Beginning at Zero: Notes on Cinema and Society', trans. Joanne Pottlitzer, *The Drama Review: TDR*, Vol. 14, No. 2: Latin American Theatre (Winter): 144–9.

Rocha, Glauber (1970b), 'O último escândalo de Godard' ('Godard's Latest Scandal'), *Manchete*, No. 928, 31 January: 52–3. Translated by Stoffel Debuysere with help from Mari Shields, in the context of the research project 'Figures of Dissent' at KASK School of Arts, Ghent, <https://www.sabzian.be/article/godard%E2%80%99s-latest-scandal> (last accessed 15 September 2019).

Rocha, Glauber [1965] (2019a), 'An Aesthetics of Hunger', in Ismail Xavier (ed.), Stephanie Dennison and Charlotte Smith (trans.), *On Cinema*, London and New York: I. B. Tauris, pp. 41–6.

Rocha, Glauber [1969] (2019b), 'Tropicalism, Anthropology, Myth, Ideography', in Ismail Xavier (ed.), Stephanie Dennison and Charlotte Smith (trans.), *On Cinema*, London and New York: I. B. Tauris, pp. 100–4.

Rocha, Glauber (2019c), 'Positif' (1967 interview with Glauber Rocha by Michel Ciment), in Ismail Xavier (ed.), Stephanie Dennison and Charlotte Smith (trans.), *On Cinema*, London and New York: I. B. Tauris, pp. 58–75.

Rocha, Glauber (2019d), 'Tricontinental (1967)', in Ismail Xavier (ed.), Stephanie Dennison and Charlotte Smith (trans.), *On Cinema*, London and New York: I. B. Tauris, pp. 51–8.

Rocha, Glauber (2019e), 'Discussion of the Concept of Aesthetics and its Political Function', in Ismail Xavier (ed.), Stephanie Dennison and Charlotte Smith (trans.), *On Cinema*, London and New York: I. B. Tauris, pp. 106–13.

Rocha, Glauber, Gary Crowdus, Wm Starr, Ruth McCormick and Susan Hertelendy (1970), 'Cinema Novo Vs. Cultural Colonialism: An Interview with Glauber Rocha', *Cinéaste*, Vol. 4, No. 1 (Summer): 2–9, 35.

Rosen, Miriam (1992), 'The Camera of Art: An Interview with Abbas Kiarostami', *Cinéaste*, Vol. 19, Nos. 2–3: 38–40.

Rosenbaum, Jonathan (2003), 'Abbas Kiarastami', in Mehrnaz Saeed-Vafa and Jonathan Rosenbaum (eds), *Abbas Kiarostami*, Urbana and Chicago: University of Illinois Press, pp. 1–44.

Roud, Richard (1967), *Godard*, Bloomington and London: Indiana University Press.

Rowbotham, Sheila (2000), *Promise of a Dream: Remembering the Sixties*, London: Penguin.

Ruiz, Raúl (2004), 'The Six Functions of the Shot', trans. Carlos Morreo, in Helen Bandis, Adrian Martin and Grant McDonald (eds), *Raúl Ruiz: Images of Passage*, Melbourne: Rouge Press/International Film Festival of Rotterdam, pp. 57–68.

Ryan, Michael P. (2013), 'Fritz Lang's Radio Aesthetic: *M. Eine Stadt sucht einen Mörder*', *German Studies Review*, Baltimore Vol. 36, No. 2, May: 259–79, 495.

Saeed-Vafa, Mehrnaz (2003), 'Abbas Kiarostami', in Mehrnaz Saeed-Vafa and Jonathan Rosenbaum (eds), *Abbas Kiarostami*, Urbana and Chicago: University of Illinois Press, pp. 45–78.

Sanbar, Elias (1991), 'Vingt et un ans après' ('21 Years After'), *Trafic*, No. 1 (Winter): 109–19.

Sciortino, Karley (2010), 'Harmony Korine and Rita Ackermann', *AnOther*, 3 December, <https://www.anothermag.com/art-photography/654/harmony-korine-and-rita-ackermann> (last accessed 24 March 2021).

Serisuelo, Marc (2014), 'Jean-Luc, Community and Communication', trans. T. Jefferson Kline, in Tom Conley and T. Jefferson Kline (eds), *A Companion to Jean-Luc Godard*, Chichester: Wiley Blackwell, pp. 296–317.

Sharf, Zack (2017), '"The Last Jedi" Has Such An Unconventional "Star Wars" Moment That AMC Theaters Are Warning Fans, No, the sound in your theater isn't cutting out by accident during "The Last Jedi"', *IndieWire*, 25 December,

<https://www.indiewire.com/2017/12/star-wars-last-jedi-sound-holdo-sacrifice-amc-theaters-1201910923/#!> (last accessed 22 September 2020).
Shilina-Conte, Tanya (2015), 'Black Screen, White Page: Ontology and Genealogy of Blank Space', Special Issue on 'Writing in Film', *Word & Image: A Journal of Verbal/Visual Enquiry* 31, No. 4, October–December: 501–14.
Shilina-Conte, Tanya (2016), 'How It Feels: Black Screen as Negative Event in Early Cinema and 9/11 Films', Special Issue on 'Film and Phenomenology', *Studia Phaenomenologica* 16: 409–38.
Shilina-Conte, Tanya (2022), *Black Screens, White Frames: The Interstices of Cinema*, Oxford: Oxford University Press.
Shohat, Ella and Robert Stam (1994), *Unthinking Eurocentrism: Multiculturalism and the Media*, London and New York: Routledge.
Sobchack, Vivian (1992), *The Address of the Eye: A Phenomenology of Film Experience*, Princeton: Princeton University Press.
Sparavigna, Amelia Carolina (2014), 'Robert Grosseteste's Thought on Light and Form of the World', *International Journal of Sciences*, Vol. 3, No. 4, April: 54–62.
Spinoza, Benedict de (1994), *A Spinoza Reader: The* Ethics *and Other Works*, ed. and trans. Edwin Curley, Princeton: Princeton University Press.
Spiteri, Raymond (2003), 'Surrealism and the Political Physiognomy of the Marvellous', in Raymond Spiteri and Donald LaCoss (eds), *Surrealism, Politics and Culture*, Aldershot: Ashgate.
Stam, Robert (1976), '*Land in Anguish*: Revolutionary Lessons', *Jump Cut, A Review of Contemporary Media*, Nos 10–11, June: 49–51.
Stam, Robert (1997a), 'Racial Representation in Brazilian Cinema and Culture: A Cross-Cultural Approach', in Michael T. Martin (ed.), *New Latin American Cinema, Volume Two: Studies of National Cinemas*, Detroit: Wayne State University Press, pp. 335–64.
Stam, Robert (1997b), *Tropical Multiculturalism: A Comparative History of Race in Brazilian Cinema and Culture*, Durham, NC and London: Duke University Press.
Stam, Robert and Ismail Xavier (1990), 'Transformation of National Allegory: Brazilian Cinema from Dictatorship to Redemocratization', in Robert Sklar and Charles Mussers (eds), *Resisting Images: Essays on Cinema and History*, Philadelphia: Temple University Press, pp. 279–307.
Stamelman, Richard (1974), 'From Muteness to Speech: The Drama of Expression in Francis Ponge's Poetry', in *Books Abroad*, Vol. 48, No. 4 (Autumn): 688–94.
'Stella' [1966] (2009), 'A Working Woman', trans. Nicholas Elliott, in the Criterion DVD booklet 2009, pp. 10–13. Originally published in *Le Nouvel Observateur*, 4 May 1966: 16. A letter in response to Catherine Vimenet's articles of 23 and 29 March that year.
Sterritt, David (ed.) (1998), *Jean-Luc Godard: Interviews*, Jackson: University Press of Mississippi, pp. 69–84.

Sterritt, David (2018), 'Godard, Gorin, and Company', in *Quarterly Review of Film and Video*, Vol. 35, No. 4: 418–21.
Tabarraee, Babak (2013), *Silence Studies in the Cinema and the Case of Abbas Kiarostami*, MA Thesis in Film Studies, Vancouver: The University of British Columbia.
Théberge, Paul (2008), 'Almost Silent: The Interplay of Sound and Silence in Contemporary Cinema and Television', in Jay Beck and Tony Grajeda (eds), *Lowering the Boom: Critical Studies in Film Sound*, Urbana and Chicago: University of Illinois Press, pp. 51–67.
Thomsen, Christian Braad (1974), 'Jean-Pierre Gorin interviewed: Filmmaking and history', *Jump Cut*, No. 3: 17–19.
Ulman, Erik (2005), 'Jean-Pierre Gorin', in Jane de Almeida (ed.), *Grupo Dziga Vertov*, São Paulo: witz edições, pp. 34–46.
Uroskie, Andrew V. (2011), 'Beyond the Black Box: The Lettrist Cinema of Disjunction', *October* 135 (Winter): 21–48.
Vaneigem, Raoul (1983), *The Revolution of Everyday Life*, Donald Nicholson-Smith (trans.), London: Left Bank Books and Rebel Press.
Vertov, Dziga (1984), *Kino-Eye: The Writings of Dziga Vertov*, ed. Annette Michelson, trans. Kevin O'Brien, Berkeley and Los Angeles: University of California Press.
Viany, Alex (1970), 'The Old and the New in Brazilian Cinema', *The Drama Review: TDR*, Vol. 14, No. 2 (Winter): Latin American Theatre: 141–4.
Viegas, Susana (2016), 'Gilles Deleuze and early cinema: The modernity of the emancipated time', *Early Popular Visual Culture*, Vol. 14, No. 3: 234–50.
Viénet, René (1967), 'Les situationnistes et les nouvelles formes d'action contre la politique et l'art' ('The Situationists and the New Forms of Action against Politics and Art'), *Situationist International (internationale situationniste)* [SI Journal], No. 11, October 1967: 32–6, cited in Knabb (1989), pp. 213–16.
Vimenet, Catherine (1966), 'Les Étoiles filantes' ('Shooting Stars'), 23 March, and 'Prostitution dans les grands ensembles?' ('Prostitution in the "Grands Ensembles"?'), 29 March and 10 May in *Le Nouvel Observateur*.
Virilio, Paul (2002), 'The Overexposed City', in Gary Bridge and Sophie Watson (eds), *The Blackwell City Reader*, Oxford: Blackwell Publishing, pp. 440–8.
von Harbou, Thea (1968), *M, a Film by Fritz Lang*, trans. Nicholas Garnham, New York: Simon and Schuster.
von Harbou, Thea (1973), '*M*', in *Masterworks of the German Cinema*, introduction by Roger Manvell, New York: Harper & Row.
Weiss, Allen S. (1985), 'Frampton's Lemma, Zorn's Dilemma', *October* 32 (Spring): 119–28.
Werneburg, Brigitte (1992), 'Ernst Jünger and the Transformed World', trans. Christopher Phillips, *October* 62 (Autumn): 42–64.
White, Jerry (2013), *Two Bicycles: The Work of Jean-Luc Godard and Anne-Marie Miéville*, Waterloo, ON: Wilfred Laurier University Press.

Witt, Michael (2014), 'On and Under Communication', in Tom Conley and T. Jefferson Kline (eds), *A Companion to Jean-Luc Godard*, Chichester: Wiley Blackwell, pp. 318–50.
Wollen, Peter (1982), 'The Two Avant-Gardes', in *Readings and Writings: Semiotic Counter-Strategies*, London: Verso, pp. 92–104.
Xavier, Ismail (1997), *Allegories of Underdevelopment: Aesthetics and Politics in Modern Brazilian Cinema*, Minneapolis: University of Minnesota Press.
Xavier, Ismail (2004), 'Prefácio', in G. Rocha, *Revolução do Cinema Novo*, São Paulo: Cosac Naify.
Zaatari, Akram and Abbas Kiarostami (1994–5), 'Interview with Abbas Kiarostami', *BOMB*, No. 50 (Winter): 12–14.

Index

Abidor, Mitchell, 204
action committees 196–7, 209; *see also* May '68
aesthetics of hunger, 149, 166, 169, 188, 248, 250; *see also* Rocha
affects, 7, 9–10, 11–12, 47, 53, 180, 214, 313; *see also* Spinoza
Ahankhah, Abolfazi, 307, 309, 310, 312
Ahankhah, Mahrokh, 306, 309
Ahankhah, Mehrdad, 306, 308, 309
Ahankhah, Monoochehr, 306
Ahmadi, Haj Ali Reza, 308
Alea, Tomás Gutiérrez, 155, 157
   Memories of Underdevelopment (1968), 155, 157
Alexandrov, Grigori, 22
Alfonso, Yves, 257
Algiers/Algerian War, 126, 128, 152, 220
Alighieri, Dante, 61, 70, 94
   Divine Comedy, 61, 70
Alleg, Henri, 136
   La Question, 136
Alpers, Svetlana, 193
Althusser, Louis, 18, 192, 227–31, 234, 240, 241, 247–8, 250, 251, 255
   apparatus, 228
   ideology, 228, 251
   'Ideology and Ideological State Apparatuses (Notes towards an investigation', 250
   Ideological State Apparatus (ISA), 174, 228–9, 231, 234, 247, 254, 256, 259, 261
   interpellation, 192, 212, 228–9, 231, 234, 238, 239, 242, 246–7, 251, 259
   Pour Marx, 228
   Reading Capital, 247–8
   Repressive State Apparatus (RSA), 229, 259
   see also Balibar
Alves, Castro, 161
   The People in Power, 161

Anger, Kenneth, 97
Antonioni, Michelangelo, 277, 283
Apollinaire, Guillaume, 95
Aristotle, 49, 59
   hylomorphic model, 49, 59
Aron, Raymond, 134, 137, 139
   On Classes: Further Lessons on Industrial Societies, 134, 137
Arraes, Miguel, 158
Artaud, Antonin, 99, 104, 125, 256
   To have done with the judgment of God (1947), 99
Atack, Margaret, 131
Atelier de recherché cinématographique (ARC), 196
attraction-image, 267–8; *see also* Gunning: 'cinema of attractions'
Attree, Michael, 268
Auschwitz, 127, 147, 226
Autant-Lara, Claude (et al)
   L'Amour à travers les ages (1967), 107
   see also Godard: *Anticipation*
Autonomia Movement, 255
Autran, Paolo, 155, 165
Aznavour, Charles, 110, 115, 116

Bach, Johann Sebastian, 124
Baiack (actor), 172
Bakhtin, Mikhail, 181
Balhaus, Carl, 29
Balibar, Étienne, 247, 248n
   Reading Capital, 247–8
   see also Althusser
Ball, John, 208
Barcelloni, Gianni, 240
Bardot, Brigitte, 107
Barrault, Jean-Louis, 81
Barthes, Roland, 104, 110, 116, 129, 130, 137, 147–8, 189, 229, 278, 287–8, 292
   Camera Lucida, 287
   empire of signs, 105
   'The Fashion System', 129

Image, Music, Text, 104
lexia, 104
Mythologies, 104
punctum, 287–8, 292, 294, 301, 304, 312–13, 315–16, 317
rhetoric of the image, 104–5, 116, 130
semiology, 104
studium, 287–8, 292, 294, 303–4, 312, 317
'Upon Leaving the Movie Theatre' (1975), 278
Writing Degree Zero, 147
Bateson, Gregory, 37, 179
 double bind, 37
 the three ecologies, 179
Bauhaus, 271
Bay State Primer, 55, 59, 65
Bazin, André, 16–17, 190, 232, 269
Bazzini, Sergio, 240
Beat Generation, 284, 328; *see also* Ginsberg
The Beatles, 216
Beckett, Samuel, 13, 54, 55, 66
Beethoven Ludwig van, 54, 134, 135, 140, 145, 147
 String Quartet No. 12 in E Flat Major, Op. 127, 147
 String Quartet No. 16 in F Major, Op. 135, 134, 140, 145
 Symphony No. 7 in A Major, Op. 92, 54
Belmondo, Jean-Paul, 109, 114–15, 121
Bengell, Norma, 178
Benjamin, Walter, 34, 113
 'The Work of Art in the Age of Mechanical Reproduction', 34
Berardi, Franco 'Bifo', 153, 180, 255
 Radio Alice, 255
 semiotic insolvency, 153
Berg, Gretchen, 25
Bergman, Ingmar, 26, 149
Bergson, Henri, 10–12, 14, 19, 119, 264–6, 268, 281
 Creative Evolution, 264–5
 Matter and Memory, 10, 265–6, 281
 qualitative multiplicity, 119, 264–5
 quantitative multiplicity, 119, 264
Berna, Serge, 74, 78
Bernstein, Eduard, 233
Bernstein, Michèle, 100–1
Berto, Juliet, 136–7, 141, 190, 199, 256, 260–2
Bertolucci, Bernardo, 199
Betz, Mark, 126

Beylot, Pierre, 204–5, 206
Beyza'i, Bahram, 284
Bhabha, Homi, 171
 'mimic man', 171
Big Star, 327; *see also* Chilton, Eggleston
Billy the Kid (William H. Bonney), 117
biogram, 14–15, 68, 85, 89, 94, 146, 226, 249, 276; *see also* topology
Black Lives Matter, 260, 262; *see also* Floyd, Taylor
Black Panthers, 188, 256, 261
Black September Massacre, 188, 218, 224
Blasing, Mutlu Konuk, 71
Blin, Bernard, 81
Blümner, Rudolf, 30
Bologna Uprisings, 1977, 255
Bolsonaro, Jair, 149, 155, 158
Bonitzer, Pascal, 15–16
 deframing, 15–16
Borderie, Bernard, 116, 235
 Angélique (1964), 235
 Poison Ivy (1953), 116
Borges, Jorge-Luis, 14, 55, 72–3
 'The Garden of Forking Paths', 14
 'Pierre Menard, Author of the *Quixote*', 73
Bornay, Clovis, 165
Boucicault, Dion, 67
Boulez, Pierre, 5
Bourseiller, Christophe, 128
Bourseiller, Marie, 128
Bradbury, Ray, 139
 A Medicine for Melancholy, 139
Brakhage, Stan, 276
 Mothlight (1963), 276
Brasseur, Claude, 117
Brecht, Bertolt, 18, 20, 92, 97, 103, 107, 110, 113, 116, 119, 122, 131–2, 150, 154, 160, 164, 166, 169, 170, 174, 182, 192, 206, 210, 230, 232, 237, 238, 241, 244, 248, 283, 285, 299, 301
 Epic Theatre, 18, 113, 119, 166
 gest, 113
 'Hollywood', 107
 Lehrstücke (Teaching plays), 113
 A Man's a Man (1926), 113
 'Measures Against Power', 299–300
 Me-ti: Book of Interventions in the Flow of Things, 237
 Mother Courage and Her Children (1939), 113, 116
 Verfremdungseffekt, 18, 103, 122, 174, 206, 285

Bresson, Robert, 16
Breton, André, 76, 127
   Lost Steps, 76
   Nadja, 127
Brezhnev, Leonid, 222, 233
Brialy, Jean-Claude, 109
Brizola, Leonel, 158
Brogli, Giulio, 172
Brook, Peter, 217
   Marat/Sade (1967), 217
   see also Peter Weiss
Brunoy, Blanchette, 81
Buñuel, Luis, 22, 79
   L'Âge d'Or (1930)
Burch, Noël, 16, 38, 106
   The Large Form, 106
Burron, Paul, 188, 231, 236, 238–9; see also Dziga Vertov Group
Butler, David
   Sunny Side Up (1929), 274

Cabañas, Kaira M., 75, 81, 84–5, 91, 99, 102
Cabral, Pedro, 164–5
Cage, John, 3–5, 75, 274–5, 332
   4' 33" (1952), 3, 275
   Silence, 3
Cage, Nicolas, 321–2
Calder, Alexander, 142
Candomblé, 154
cannibalism (anthropophagy), 21, 81, 154, 177, 178–9
Capa, Robert, 156
carnivalesque, 148, 154, 157, 163, 181, 184, 186, 303; see also syncretism, trance
Carroll, Noël, 22
Carvana, Hugo, 156, 171
Castellari, Enzo G., 268
   Keoma (1976), 268
Castello Branco, Carlos, 182, 183
Castoro, Rosemarie, 60
Castro, Fidel, 195
Cavalcanti, Emanuel, 161
Cawkwell, Tim, 272–3
Cendrars, Blaise, 81
Cervantes, Miguel de, 73
   Don Quixote, 73
Cézanne, Paul, 141
Chabrol, Claude, 201
Chahine, Youssef, 159
chaoids, 6, 9, 19, 44, 47, 58, 64–5, 74, 77, 122, 125, 128, 230, 275, 285, 288, 313, 317, 324
   and cycle, 65
   plane of composition, 6, 9–10, 37, 41, 43, 55, 61, 72, 80, 83, 100, 101, 109, 125, 128, 133, 160, 230, 234
   plane of immanence/consistency, 6, 7–8, 9–13, 19–21, 37, 43, 51, 61, 72, 73, 80, 100, 101, 103, 109, 119, 125, 128, 133, 144, 146, 160, 179–80, 186–7, 213, 230, 234, 250, 259, 263, 294, 313
   plane of organisation, 6
chaos, 6, 9–12, 44, 47, 58–60, 64–5, 83–4, 160, 162, 180, 186, 305, 324–5
Chaplin, Charlie, 79
Charisse, Cyd, 117
Charonne Métro massacre, 220
Chateaubriand, Assis, 156
Chernyshevsky, Nikolái, 200
Cheshire, Godfrey, 284, 295, 304, 307, 308, 309
Cheyney, Peter, 116
Chicago Eight Conspiracy Trial, 256–7
Chilton, Alex, 328
Chion, Michel, 2–3, 39–40, 118, 324, 330
   acousmêtre, 330
   Audio-Vision: Sound on Screen, 2
Chokrollahi, Mamhoud, 317
   Close Up Long Shot (1996), 317
   see also Mansouri
Church, Kevin, 319
Chytilova, Vera, 235
Ciment, Michel, 166
Cinema Nôvo, 149–52, 185, 250
cinéma vérité, 15, 295, 315
Clair, René, 22, 79, 89
   À Nous la Liberté (1931), 22
   Entr'Acte (1924), 89
Clark, Larry, 325
   Kids (1995), 325
   see also Korine
Clerc, François, 278
Cocteau, Jean, 81, 294
   Orphée (1950), 294
Cohn-Bendit, Daniel, 195, 240, 241, 247
Cold War, 153, 155, 157, 249, 250, 263
Collin, Marc, 120
Collins, Alf, 67
   Murphy's Wake (1903), 67
Colpeyn, Louisa, 117
Coltrane, John, 275
Columbus, Christopher, 164
Confédération Générale du Travail (CGT), 197, 200, 204, 206, 231, 236

Constantine, Eddie, 116
Conte, Richard, 1
Cook, Peter, 120n
Corbucci, Sergio, 268
   Django (1966), 268
Corneille, Pierre, 171
Corrieri, Sergio, 157
Costa-Gavras, 245
   Z (1969), 245
Covid-19 pandemic, 149
Crook, Mackenzie, 264n
   Detectorists (2014–17), 264n
Cross, Fanny Elizabeth Catlett, 68, 70
Cuban Missile Crisis, 155, 157
Cummins, Peggy, 78

Dada, 79, 93
Dalí, Salvador, 79
Dall, John, 78
Daney, Serge, 221
Darget, Chantal, 117
Dars, Jean-François, 197
Darwish, Mahmoud, 223
Dassin, Jules, 3
   Rififi (1955), 3
David, Jacques-Louis, 113, 120
   Madame Recamier (1800), 113
   Oath of the Horatii (1784), 120
Davis, Miles, 275
Davis, Rennie, 256
Day, Sir Robin, 211
   Panorama, 211
Dayan, Moshe, 222
Dead Territory, 4
Dean, James, 326
de Andrade, Joaquim Pedro, 177
   Macunaíma (1969), 177
de Andrade, Oswald, 81, 177, 186
   'Cannibalist Manifesto', 81, 177, 178
de Baecque, Antoine, 218
Debord, Guy, 2, 5, 64n. 74–81, 84, 89, 92, 95–8, 100–1, 102, 103, 106, 109, 111, 122, 173, 199, 206, 270, 318
   Contre le Cinéma, 74
   Howlings for Sade (*Hurlements en faveur de Sade*, 1952), 2, 64n, 74–81, 84, 89, 92, 95–8, 100–1
   'Prolégomènes a tout cinéma futur', 76, 79
   Society of the Spectacle, 74, 81, 206
   see also Lettrist International, Situationist International, spectacle
decolonisation, 150, 152–3

de Diesbach, Sébastien (S. Chatel), 102
de Gaulle, Charles, 128, 129, 199, 205
Delacroix, Eugène, 234
DeLanda, Manuel, 8n, 47
Deleuze, Gilles, 4, 6, 7, 10, 13, 14–16, 18–20, 34–5, 41, 56, 58, 61, 64–5, 84, 101, 106, 108–9, 124, 126, 127, 128, 153, 154, 157, 158, 159, 166, 175, 179–80, 186, 189, 213, 217, 225, 234, 238, 246, 255, 263–7, 271, 276, 277, 281, 285, 304
   action-image, 20, 263, 268, 276
   affection-image, 124, 125
   apparatus, 35
   Bergsonism, 126, 264
   category, 238–9
   chronosign, 18–19, 263
   Cinema 1: The Movement-Image, 20, 58, 263, 266–7
   Cinema 2: The Time-Image, 4, 14, 18, 41, 108, 153, 225, 263, 277, 304
   'cinema of the speech act', 166
   event, 84
   hyalosign, 4
   irrational cuts/interstices, 19–20, 23, 55, 77, 108–9, 110, 125, 128, 188, 189, 217, 220, 222, 225–6, 230, 247, 263, 277, 285, 311
   micro-fascism, 34
   mnemosign, 90
   movement-image, 19, 20, 58, 61, 106, 127, 226, 263–8, 313, 320
   noosign, 18, 285
   onirosign (deam image), 226
   'people to come', 153–5, 157–9, 161, 164, 167, 186, 239
   perception-image, 265, 276
   Proust and Signs, 56
   recollection-image, 281
   Spinoza: Practical Philosophy, 179
   stammering/stutter, 62, 213–14, 217, 226, 228, 255
   time-image, 4, 18, 41, 70, 90, 126, 226, 263–5, 267–8, 277, 285, 313
   transcendental empiricism, 126
   transcendental field, 186–7
   Two Regimes of Madness, 34
   see also Guattari
Deleuze, Gilles & Félix Guattari, 4–5, 6, 7–13, 16, 18, 20, 21, 25, 37, 46–7, 49, 53, 55, 61, 62, 77, 99, 103, 186, 247, 325
   aesthetic figures, 10

Deleuze & Guattari (*cont.*)
  aggregates 46, 48, 53, 189
  Anti-Oedipus, 8–9, 99, 247
  assemblage, 7, 8n, 25, 28, 33, 46, 47–8, 146, 263, 271, 318
  Body without Organs (BwO), 7–8, 37, 48, 49, 53, 99, 160
  celibate machine, 8
  conceptual personae, 9, 12, 73, 147, 186, 313
  desiring-machines, 46, 49, 51, 247
  deterritorialisation, 13, 20, 35, 43, 51, 55, 58, 100, 131, 144, 154, 199, 228, 247, 252, 276, 278, 318
  disjunctive synthesis, 37
  immanence, 6, 7, 8, 10, 11, 21, 45, 46, 49, 51, 58, 62, 126, 127, 133, 158, 180, 185–7, 199, 219
  longitudes and latitudes, 7
  machinic phylum, 25, 35–7, 46–9, 51, 53, 109, 135, 146, 155, 173, 175, 255, 270
  minor literature, 153
  miraculating machine, 8
  multiplicity, 18, 35, 62, 64, 119, 180, 189, 214, 217, 219, 225, 238, 263, 332
  paranoiac machine, 8
  plateau, 230
  reterritorialisation, 43
  singularities, 25, 36, 46–8, 49, 53, 135, 142, 146, 154, 158, 166, 189, 224, 225, 271, 318
  smooth and striated space, 64
  stratigraphic, 10, 12–13, 77, 199
  A Thousand Plateaus (*Mille Plateaux*), 4, 7, 46
  transversality, 12–13, 46
  war machine, 7
  What is Philosophy?, 6, 8, 9, 11, 12, 77, 103, 325
  see also chaoids
de l'Isle-Adam, Auguste Villiers, 78
Dellinger, David, 256
Delouvrier, Paul, 128–30
Del Rey, Geraldo, 181
del Sol, Luis, 114
Demongeot, Catherine, 111, 112
Demoule, Michel, 201
Demy, Jacques, 100
  The Umbrellas of Cherbourg (1964), 110
Denke, Karl, 25
Dern, Laura, 319
Derocles, Thierry, 201
Derrida, Jacques, 106
de Sade, Marquis, 75, 78, 95, 100, 101, 102, 180
de Saussure, Ferdinand, 62, 134, 191
Descartes, René, 9, 134, 141
de Souza, Modesto, 163
Devictor, Agnès, 283
Díaz, Porfirio, 155
Diên Biên Phu, 82, 121
Dietrich, Marlene, 170
discrepant cinema/montage; *see also* Isou
dispositif; *see also* Foucault
Di Stéfano, Alfredo, 114
Dixon, Wheeler Winston, 232, 240
Donlevy, Brian, 1
dos Palmares, Zumbi, 172
dos Santos, Nelson Pereira, 150, 177
  How Tasty Was My Little Frenchman (1971), 177
Doublier, Francis, 278
  Arroseur et arrosé (1895), 278
  see also Louis Lumière
do Valle, Mauricio, 181
doxa, 6, 9, 20, 92, 141, 189, 194, 229, 325; see also Barthes
Drabinski, John, 217, 221
Dreke, Victor, 169
Dreyer, Carl Theodor, 22, 124
  The Passion of Joan of Arc (1928), 124
  Vampyr (1932), 22
Dreyfus, Alfred, 256
Dubček, Alexander, 231, 235, 242
  'Prague Spring', 231, 242
Dubois, Marie, 116
Duchamp, Marcel, 50
Dufrêne, François, 83, 95, 97
Duperey, Anny, 139
Duras, Marguerite, 102
Dussel, Enrique, 168, 183
Duval, Benoît, 278
Dziga Vertov Group, 18, 104, 132, 148, 188, 190, 196, 203, 207, 218, 222, 225, 227, 229, 232
  British Sounds (*See You at Mao*, 1970), 143, 207–17, 221, 226, 227, 239, 241, 304
  Here and Elsewhere (*Ici et Ailleurs*, 1976), 121, 188, 217, 219–26
  Jusqu'à la victoire (1970), 188, 218, 256
  Pravda (1970), 227, 228, 231–40, 241, 257
  Struggle in Italy (*Lotte in Italia*, 1971), 192, 228, 242, 250–6
  Tout va bien (1972), 203, 227, 232

Vladimir and Rosa (1971), 136, 192, 228, 256–62
Wind from the East (*Le vent d'est*, 1970), 122, 228, 231, 232, 240–50
see also Burron, Godard, Gorin, Miéville, Roger, Wiazemsky

Eastwood, Clint, 240
Eaton, Mick, 232
Ebiri, Bilge, 326, 332
Eggleston, William, 327
   Stranded in Canton (2005), 327
Eisenstein, Sergei, 17–18, 22, 79, 149, 164, 169, 230, 232, 244
   The General Line (1929), 244
   montage of attractions, 17, 230, 244
   Potemkin (1925), 17, 164, 244
Elcott, Noam, 273, 275
Elena, Alberto, 296, 301, 317
Elshaw, Gary, 202
Emmelhainz, Irmgard, 220
Engels, Friedrich, 238
Establet, Roger, 248n
États Généraux du Cinéma, 201
ethology, 7, 101; see also Uexküll
Extinction Rebellion, 262

Falconetti, Maria, 124–5
Falkenberg, Paul, 23
Fallaci, Oriana, 310, 317
Fanon, Frantz, 151–2, 155, 159, 161, 167, 176
   Wretched of the Earth, 151–2
   see also violence as catharsis
Farazmand, Hossain, 307, 309–12
Farrell, Charles, 274
Farrokhzad, Forugh, 284
   The House Is Black (1963), 284
   'The Wind Will Carry Us', 284
Faustino, Mário, 159
Feiffer, Jules, 137–8
Fellini, Federico, 149
Fernandel (Fernand Joseph, Désiré Contandin), 102
Ferry, Brian, 320
Field, Allison, 77, 96, 97
Figgis, Mike, 6, 44n, 318, 320–5, 332
   Leaving Las Vegas (1995), 44n, 318, 321–5
Filho, Jardel, 155, 165
Fink, Daniel, 193n
Fischinger, Oskar, 276
   An Optical Poem (1938), 276

Flaherty, Robert, 132
flâneurie, 126–7
Flaubert, Gustave, 135
   Bouvard et Pécuchet, 135
Fleming, Victor
   Gone with the Wind (1939), 216, 241, 244
Flötner, Peter, 51
   Menschenalphabet (1534), 51
Floyd, George, 260
the fold (enfolding and unfolding); see also Leibniz
Fonda, Jane, 232
Ford, John, 76, 149, 240
   Fort Apache (1948), 240
   My Darling Clementine (1946), 240
   Rio Grande (1950), 76
   She Wore a Yellow Ribbon (1949), 240
Forman, Milos, 235
   Taking Off (1971), 235
Foruzesh, Ebrahim, 284
Foucault, Michel, 21, 32, 34–5, 141, 201, 208, 228
   archive, 208
   dispositif, 34–5, 37, 40, 42, 45–6, 48, 51, 52, 107, 108, 135, 155, 202, 220, 228, 247
   episteme, 201
   genealogy, 21
Frampton, Hollis, 5, 23, 53–73, 74, 94, 101, 150, 267
   axiomatic structures, 56–9, 62
   'For a Metahistory of Film: Commonplace Notes and Hypotheses', 63, 72
   Gloria! (1979), 24, 54, 60, 65–73, 74, 94, 267
   'Impromptus on Edward Weston: Everything in its Place', 54–5
   infinite cinema, 55, 58, 60, 63, 64, 68
   Magellan Cycle (1974–84), 65–6
   'Notes on Composing in Film', 56
   set theory, 55, 57, 64, 65, 66
   universal film archive, 60, 66, 68, 70, 72, 150
   Zorns Lemma (1970), 54–65, 74, 101
Franco, James, 326
   Rebel (2012), 326
Freisler, Roland, 257
French New Wave Cinema, 102, 108, 120, 149, 250, 283, 284
French Revolution, 223
Freud, Sigmund, 9, 36–7, 45, 199, 210, 211, 228, 325, 331

Freud (*cont.*)
   death drive (Thanatos), 37, 78
   dementia praecox, 9
   Eros, 78
   Oedipus Complex, 45–6
   Psycho-Analysis and the War Neuroses, 36–7
Frey, Sami, 117
Froines, John, 256
Furey, Finbar, 66, 69

Galbraith, John Kenneth, 235
Gallimard 'Idées' book series, 134, 144, 147, 148
Galton, Francis, 42
Gamble, Sera, 293
Garnett, Tony, 207
Garrincha, 181
Gaynor, Janet, 274
Gellen, Kata, 42–3
Genette, Gérard, 291
   focalisation, 291, 293
Gennat, Ernst, 28
Gérson, 181
A Gesture Fight in Hester Street (1900), 66
Getino, Octavio, 240
   Hour of the Furnaces (1968), 240
   see also Solanas
Gidal, Peter, 263, 268
Gilliatt, Penelope, 209
Ginsberg, Allen, 328
Girard, Danièle, 119
Gnaß, Friedrich, 29
Godard, Jean-Luc, 3–4, 6, 15, 18, 20, 52n, 64n, 89, 102–48, 149, 150, 151, 171, 181, 182, 188–226, 227, 230, 231–2, 234, 238–41, 244–6, 250, 251, 254–61, 271, 277, 283, 287, 301, 304, 309, 332
   Alphaville (1965), 107, 116, 135
   Anticipation, ou l'Amour en l'an 2,000 (1967), 107
   Band of Outsiders, (*Bande à part* 1964), 3, 107–8, 116–22, 123, 127, 188, 257
   Breathless (*À bout de souffle*, 1960), 102, 115, 121, 203
   'Camera Eye' in *Loin du Vietnam* (1967), 139, 301
   Ciné-Tract #23 (1968), 196–9
   Les Carabiniers (1963), 90, 121, 150
   La Chinoise (1967), 121, 136, 137, 188, 199, 245
   Contempt (*Le Mépris*, 1964), 107, 119
   Un Film comme les autres (*A Film Like Any Other*, 1968), 190, 200–7, 227
   Le Gai Savoir (1969), 103, 136, 140, 148, 151, 171, 188, 190–200, 201, 203, 207, 259, 287
   Made in U.S.A. (1966), 103, 148, 149, 245
   A Married Woman (*Une femme mariée*, 1964), 106, 107
   Masculin Féminin (1966), 245
   My Life to Live (*Vivre sa vie*, 1962), 107–8, 110, 122–8
   One Plus One (*Sympathy for the Devil*, 1968), 207
   Pierrot le Fou (1965), 103, 121, 122, 238
   Six fois deux / Sur et sous la communication (1976), 213
   2 or 3 Things I Know About Her (*Deux ou trois choses que je sais d'elle*, 1967), 107–8, 122, 128–47, 188, 191, 192, 194, 195, 233, 245
   Weekend (1967), 137, 148, 203, 209, 238, 245, 257, 332
   A Woman is a Woman (*Une femme est une femme*, 1961), 107–8, 109–16, 119, 120, 121, 134, 181
   see also Dziga Vertov Group, Gorin, Miéville
Goebbels, Joseph, 244
Goldmann, Lucien, 134–5
   Sociology of the novel, 134
Gomes, Carlos, 166
Goodis, David, 116
   Shoot the Piano Player, 116
Goodwin, Michael, 200
Gordon, Douglas, 326
Gorin, Jean-Pierre, 6, 18, 105, 121, 132, 188, 192, 203, 215–16, 217–18, 223, 227, 230, 232, 238, 241, 245, 250–2, 254–7, 259–61, 271
   'A French Movie', 227
   see also Dziga Vertov Group, Godard
Goudet, Stéphane, 301, 317
Goulart, João, 122, 149, 156, 158
Gracindo, Paulo, 156
Gramsci, Antonio, 174, 228, 229
   hegemony, 174, 228, 229
grands ensembles, 129, 131, 132, 133, 135, 146; see also Habitation à Loyer Modéré (HLM)
Grandstand (TV programme), 71
Grieg, Edvard, 25
   Peer Gynt Suite No. 1, Op. 46, 25, 27–8, 30, 37, 43, 49, 51

Griffith, D. W., 87–8, 244, 266, 267, 283
  Intolerance (1916), 87–8, 244
Grosseteste, Robert, 55, 59–60, 65
  On Light, or the Ingression of Forms (1225), 55, 59, 65
Grossman, Lev, 293
Grossmann, Carl, 25–6, 41
Gründgens, Gustav, 29
Guattari, Félix, 4–5, 6, 45, 56, 58, 153, 178, 179, 180, 182, 224, 255
  assemblages of enunciation, 46
  chaosmosis, 46
  ecosophy, 45, 56, 58, 60, 65, 101, 155, 177, 178, 179–81, 182, 224, 327
  heterogenesis, 46
  points of singularity, 46
  post-media poetics, 159, 178
  Radio Tomato, 255
  Schizoanalytic Cartographies, 178
  semiotic fluxes, 46
  The Three Ecologies, 56, 224
  see also Deleuze
Gudgin, Tim, 71
Guevara, Che, 167–8, 169, 170, 171, 173, 176, 177, 181, 194, 197–8, 199
  'Le Socialisme et l'Homme à Cuba', 197
  Tricontinental Manifesto, 167–8, 173
Guimarães, António Sérgio Alfredo, 152
Gunning, Tom, 38, 44, 267, 280
  cinema of attractions, 263, 267, 276, 277–9, 283
Guy, Alice, 278
  Arroseur et arrosé (1895), 278
  see also Louis Lumière
Guzzetti, Alfred, 132, 134, 135, 137, 146, 147

Haarmann, Fritz ('The Ogre of Hanover'), 25, 41
Habitation à Loyer Modéré (HLM – Housing at Moderate Rent), 128–9, 139, 194, 200, 233; *see also* grands ensembles
Haines, Randa, 293
  Children of a Lesser God (1986), 293
Halford, Marilyn, 279
Hammond, Roger, 268
hapticity, 42–3
Harbou, Thea von, 25, 28
Hašek, Jaroslav, 299
  The Good Soldier Švejk, 299
Hayden Tom, 256, 257
Hayes, Kevin J., 112, 116

Heath, Edward, 212
Hegel, Georg Wilhelm Friedrich, 236
Heidegger, Martin, 133, 137, 141, 281–2
  'The Letter on Humanism', 133
Hein, Birgin and Wilhelm, 271
  Rohfilm (*Raw Film*, 1968), 271–2
Hemingway, Ernest, 322
  The Killers, 322
Henderson, Ray, 274
Henry, Buck, 235
Heraclitus, 65
Heymann, Werner Richard, 24
Hippler, Fritz, 53
  The Eternal Jew (*Der ewige Jude*, 1940), 53
Hiroshima, 127, 147
Hitchcock, Alfred, 109
Hitchens, Dolores, 117
  Fools' Gold, 117
Hitler, Adolf, 170–1, 215, 222, 225, 226
Hoberman, Jay, 116
Hoffman, Abbie, 256
Hoffman, Julius, 256, 257
Holliman, Earl, 1
Homer, 199
Hurt, William, 293
Husák, Gustáv, 231
Hussein, King of Jordan, 218
Hussein, Saddam, 298
Husserl, Edmund, 141

indexicality, 42–3
Inouye, Shaun, 329, 330, 331
Iran–Iraq War, 290
Iser, Wolfgang, 111; *see also* Reception Theory
Isou, Jean Isidore, 2, 57, 74, 77, 79–84, 85–6, 88, 94, 95, 97, 98, 100, 101, 102, 193
  amplic phase of cinema, 79, 80, 91, 95, 97, 102, 103
  chiselling phase/editing of cinema, 57, 80–1, 85–6, 90, 92, 98, 102
  discrepant cinema/montage, 2, 5–6, 79–83, 85, 90, 92, 95, 98, 100, 163, 244
  Esthétique du Cinéma, 80, 100
  On venom and eternity (*Traité de bave et d'éternité*, 1951), 2, 74, 79, 80–4, 85–6, 88, 94, 95, 98, 100, 102, 193
  pellicules brossées (chiselled or painted filmstrips), 81–3, 85, 94, 241
Italian Neorealism, 263
Itzenberger, Markus, 4

Jacob, Gilles, 148
Jakobson, Roman, 189
Jameson, Fredric, 134
    'Prison House of Language', 134, 229
Jauss, Hans Robert, 111; *see also* Reception Theory
Jawhariyya, Hany, 218
Jeanson, Blandine, 137
John, Georg, 27
Johnson, Boris, 181
Johnson, David, 311, 313
Johnson, Jimmy, 120
Johnson, Lyndon Baines, 128, 137
Johnson, Randal, 156, 171, 182, 185, 186
Johnson, Rian, 319
    Star Wars: Episode VIII – The Last Jedi (2017), 319
Joyce, James, 6, 66, 68, 72–3, 76, 90, 94, 95
    Finnegans Wake, 66, 68, 72, 94
    Ulysses, 66, 76, 95
Jünger, Ernst, 32–5, 40, 52, 299
    'Big City and the Countryside', 32
    second consciousness, 33, 42, 135, 299
    total mobilisation, 33–4, 40, 52, 299
    Typus, 33–4, 36, 37, 42, 47
    'War and Photography', 32
    'The Worker,' (*Der Arbeiter*), 33–4

Kaes, Anton, 23, 28n, 31, 32–4, 36, 38, 50
Kahnamui, M. J., 288
Kant, Immanuel, 264
Kānun (Centre for the Intellectual Development of Children and Young Adults), 283–4, 288
Karina, Anna, 107, 109, 116, 117, 121, 122
Karmitz, Marin, 201
Kasavubu, Joseph, 169
Kaufman, Mikhail, 230
Kaun, Axel, 54
Kautsky, Karl, 233
Kelley, Mike, 330–1
    Family Tyranny (1987), 330–1
Kemp, Paul, 29
Khrushchev, Nikita, 136
Kiarostami, Abbas, 5, 6, 15, 20, 283–92, 293, 294, 295–317
    The Chorus (*Hamsarayan*, 1982), 288–92, 293, 294
    Close-Up (*Nema-ye Nazdik*, 1990), 15, 288, 290, 294, 295, 305–17
    The First Graders (*Avaliha*, 1984), 296
    Five: Dedicated to Ozu (2003), 5, 16

Homework (*Mashgh-e Shab*, 1989), 288, 290, 291, 294, 295–305, 315
'Koker Trilogy', 282, 291
Life and Nothing More . . . (*Zendegi va digar hich*, aka *And Life Goes On*, 1992), 283, 295
Taste of Cherry (*Ta'm e guilass*, 1997), 283
Through the Olive Trees (*Zire darakhatan zeyton*, 1994), 283, 295
The Traveler (*Mossafer*, 1974), 309
Where Is the Friend's House (*Khane-ye doust kodjast?*, 1987), 283
Kiarostami, Ahmad, 296
Kiarostami, Bahman, 295–6
Klein, Mélanie, 199; *see also* Rivière
    L'amour et la haine, 199
Kleist, Heinrich von, 51, 53
    Penthesilea, 53
    'The Puppet Theatre', 51
Köhler, Wolfgang, 134
    Psychologie de la forme, 134
Kohn, Eric, 327
Kolldehoff, Reinhard, 170
Korda, Alexander, 1926
    A Modern Du Barry (1926), 24
Korine, Harmony, 6, 44n, 318, 325–33
    Gummo (1997), 325
    Julien Donkey-Boy (1999), 325
    Mister Lonely (2007), 325
    Trash Humpers (2009), 44n, 318, 325–33
Korine, Rachel, 326, 329
Kosygin, Alexei, 233
Kotzur, Brian, 326
Kunstler, William, 257
Kuntzel, Thierry, 26
Kurosawa, Akira, 293
    Rashomon (1950), 293
Kürten, Peter ('The Vampire of Düsseldorf'), 25, 28n, 31
Kustow, Michael, 131

Labarthe, André S., 123
Lacan, Jacques, 14, 228
Lacerda, Carlos, 149
Laing, R. D., 331
Landgut, Inge, 27
Landow, George, 271–2
    Film in which there appear Sprocket Holes, Edge Lettering, Dirt Particles, etc. (1966), 271
Landy, Marcia, 190, 246

Lang, Fritz, 5, 22–53, 68, 82, 107, 108, 114, 155, 184, 202, 328
   M (1931), 22–53, 68, 82, 108, 114, 155, 202, 289, 328, 332
   Metropolis (1927), 34, 184
   Spies (*Spione*, 1928), 24
   The Testament of Dr. Mabuse (1933), 22
Laverne, Jean-Pierre, 137
Leão, Danuza, 156, 178
Léaud, Jean-Pierre, 171–2, 189, 190, 199, 200
Lebel, Jean-Patrick, 136
Lefebvre, Henri, 35–6
   abstract space, 35–6
Legrand, Michel, 110, 123
Le Grice, Judith, 279
Le Grice, Malcolm, 6, 263, 265, 267, 268–82
   Abstract Film and Beyond, 272
   After Lumière – L'Arroseur Arrosé (1974), 268, 270, 278–82
   Little Dog for Roger (1967), 268, 270, 271–6, 277
   'Real Time/Space', 269
   Threshold (1972), 270, 276–8
LeGros, Albert J., 81
Leibniz, Gottfried Wilhelm, 14, 19, 21
   the fold (enfolding and unfolding), 19–21, 43, 58, 60, 68, 74, 105, 115, 128, 146, 301, 313, 315, 317, 318
Lemaître, Maurice, 5, 74, 79–80, 82–95, 98, 100, 102, 111, 241, 244, 270, 318
   Has the Film Started Yet? (*Le film est déjà commence?*, 1951), 74, 85–95, 98, 100, 244
   syncinema (*séance de cinéma*), 5, 44, 74, 84–6, 88, 89, 91, 94, 98, 102, 111, 119, 270, 275, 318, 324, 332
Lenin, Vladimir, 171, 200, 211, 222, 226, 232–3, 237–8, 243, 258
Leone, Sergio, 170, 240
   A Fistful of Dollars (1964), 240
   For a Few Dollars More (1965), 240
   The Good, the Bad and the Ugly (1966), 170
Lesage, Julia, 117, 197, 248
Lettrism, 2, 5, 21, 64n, 74–7, 79–80, 82–4, 86, 93, 94, 95, 98, 100, 101, 102
   Ion Journal, 76, 79–80, 97, 270
   mégapneumie, 98, 100
   Potlatch, 97
Lettrist International, 100; *see also* Debord

Levellers, 208–9
Levien, Hannah, 294
Levin, Thomas Y., 79–80, 95
Levine, Cary, 327, 331
Levitin, Jacqueline, 128n
Lévy, Raoul, 139
Lewgoy, José, 155
Lewis, Furry, 328
Lewis, Joseph H., 1, 76
   The Big Combo (1955) 1–2, 9, 61, 76
   Gun Crazy (1950), 76, 78
Libaux, Oliver, 120
Lincoln, Abraham, 171
Lingen, Theo, 29
Loach, Ken, 207
Lo Duca, Joseph-Marie, 124–5
Loos, Theodor, 42
Lopate, Phillip, 296, 311, 313
Lords of the New Church, 120
Lorre, Peter, 27, 53, 289
Losey, Joseph, 33n
   M (1951), 33n
Louys, Pierre, 136
   Aphrodite, 136
Lübecker, Nikolaj, 326, 329
Lubitsch, Ernst, 109
   Heaven Can Wait (1943), 109
   Ninotchka (1939), 109
   To Be or Not To Be (1942), 109
Luddy, Tom, 200
Lumière, Auguste and Louis, 69, 150, 263, 267, 278–9
   Arroseur et arrosé (1895), 278
   see also Alice Guy
Lumumba, Patrice, 169, 173, 190
Lundy, Craig, 9–12
Luxemburg, Rosa, 233, 237
Lyons, Alice, 70–2

MacBean, James Roy, 209, 210, 212, 239, 251, 256
MacCabe, Colin, 105, 106, 197, 210, 231, 232, 240, 241, 246, 257
McCarthy, Joseph, 33n
McCarthy, Paul, 326–7, 330–1
   Family Tyranny (1987), 330–1
   The Garden (1991–2), 326–7
Macciocchi, Maria Antonietta, 231
MacDonald, Ramsay, 215
MacDonald, Scott, 60, 66
Macherey, Pierre, 230, 248n
Magalhães, Ana Maria, 178
Magellan, Ferdinand, 65

The Magicians TV series (2015–20), 292–4
  'Six Short Stories About Magic' (Series 3, Episode 8), 293–4
Makhmalbaf, Mohsen, 306, 307–9, 312, 314–17
  The Cyclist (*Bicycleran*, 1989), 306, 307, 308, 315
Mallarmé, Stéphane, 148
Malle, Louis, 111
  Zazie dans le Métro (1960), 111
Malraux, André, 15
Manne, Shelly, 1
Man Ray, 271
  Retour à la raison (1923), 271
Mansouri, Moslem, 317
  Close Up Long Shot (1996), 317
  see also Chokrollahi
Mao Tse-tung, 21, 103, 172, 193, 194–5, 196, 201, 215, 232, 236, 239, 246–7, 253
  'On the Correct Handling of Contradictions Among the People', 196
  'Reform Our Study', 194
Marcellin, Raymond, 258
Marco, Armand, 188, 217; see also Dziga Vertov Group
Marc'O (Marc-Gilbert Guillaumin), 79, 83, 86, 95–6
Marcuse, Herbert, 191
  One Dimensional Man, 191
Margulies, Ivone, 312, 314
Marinetti, Filippo Tommaso, 88–9, 318
  'Futurism and the Theatre: A Futurist Manifesto', 88
Marinho, José, 162
Marker, Chris, 102, 196–7, 204, 234, 239
  Ciné-Tract #3 (1968), 204
  Ciné-Tracts (1968), 196–7, 200
  Société pour le Lancement des Oeuvres Nouvelles (SLON), 196
  Sunday in Peking (1956), 239
Marks, Laura U., 19–21, 74, 250
Maron, Hanna, 26
Marotta, Jenna, 319
Marshall, Phoebe, 197
Martin, Adrian, 19
Martin, Arthur W., 66
  A Wake in 'Hell's Kitchen' (1900), 66, 69
Martin, Gérard, 188, 240; see also Dziga Vertov Group
Martin-Jones, David, 168, 266–8

Marx, Karl, 103, 106, 209, 211, 215, 228
  Base/Superstructure, 228
  The Communist Manifesto, 208
  Ideology as false consciousness, 228
  Das Kapital, 248
Marx Brothers, 256
  Animal Crackers (1930), 256
  Monkey Business (1931), 256
Marxism, 79, 107, 113, 141, 149, 152, 154, 155, 163, 178, 180, 196, 199, 206, 210, 211, 215, 217, 228, 231, 234, 240, 243–4, 250, 251, 252–3, 262
Marxism-Leninism (Maoism), 169, 172, 188, 195, 203, 216, 219, 227, 231, 232, 236–7, 238, 239–41, 247, 248, 256
Massumi, Brian, 13–14, 146, 226
Matlin, Marlee, 293
Matter, Herbert, 142
  Works of Calder (1950), 142
Matthews, Peter, 298, 300
Maurois, André, 81
May '68, 103, 131, 188, 190, 197, 199, 200, 202–3, 205, 222, 231, 240, 242, 255
Mehrju'i, Daryush, 284
Meir, Golda, 222, 225, 226
Meira, Tarcisio, 181
Méliès, Georges, 79, 256, 263, 267
  L'Affaire Dreyfus (1899), 256
Menzer, Ernest, 117, 257
Meredith, Burgess, 142
  Works of Calder (1950), 142
Méril, Macha, 106
Merleau-Ponty, Maurice, 140, 141, 143
  La Phénoménologie de la perception, 141
  Sens et nonsense, 141
  see also phenomenology
Mesquita, Júlio, 156
Michelmore, Cliff, 211
  Tonight, 211
Midgette, Allen, 242, 243, 245, 248
Miéville, Anne-Marie, 121, 188, 213, 217, 218, 220–6;
  Six fois deux/Sur et sous la communication (1976), 213
  see also Dziga Vertov Group
Milani, Francisco, 162
Miller, Claude, 136
Mirren, Helen, 332
  Prime Suspect TV series (1991–2006), 332
Mirzaie, Ali Asghar, 301
Mitterand, François, 189
Moholy-Nagy, Laszlo, 271

Mohseni, Ahmad, 307
Monet, Claude, 242
Montaigne, Michel de, 123, 124, 177
  'Des Cannibales', 177
Montand, Yves, 203, 232
Montsoret, Robert, 128
Monty Python, 120
Moore, Marianne, 284
Moreau, Jeanne, 116
Moro, Aldo, 255
Morris, Ben, 319
Motörhead, 275
Mozart, Wolfgang Amadeus, 193
  Piano Sonata No. 8 in A Minor, K. 310, 193
Mulvey, Laura, 232
Murnau, F. W., 24
  Faust (1926), 24

Naderi, Amir, 284
Naficy, Hamid, 317
Nancy, Jean-Luc, 286–7
Narboni, Jean, 137
Nazi Germany, 33, 52, 153, 235
Nebenzal, Seymour, 25
Nedjar, Claude, 257
Nemes, Daniel, 294
New Iranian Cinema, 283
Newman, Barnett, 145
Nicholson, Travis, 326
Niemeyer, Oscar, 179, 181
Niépce, Nicéphore, 192–3
  View from his Window at Le Gras, 192
Nietzsche, Friedrich, 9–10, 21, 64–5, 83, 103, 189, 190, 196, 286–7, 295, 298, 313, 324
  amor fati, 64
  Beyond Good and Evil, 286, 324
  dice throw, 64–5
  Eternal Return, 21, 64–5, 67, 74, 89, 190, 282
  The Gay Science (*Die Fröhliche Wissenschaft*), 190, 287
  'On Truth and Lying in an Extra-Moral Sense', 295, 298
  powers of the false (creative lie), 189, 196, 310, 312–13, 317
  ressentiment, 10
  untimely, 103
  La Volonté de Puissance (*Will to Power*), 65
Nixon, Richard, 212, 222
Nogueras, Stephanie, 293

Nouvelle Vague (band), 120
Novotný, Antonín, 235

O'Brien, John, 321, 322
  Leaving Las Vegas, 321
  see also Figgis
Odemar, Fritz, 29
O'Rawe, Des, 75
Organisation Armée Secrète (OAS), 126
Orientalism, 249
Ozu, Yasujiro, 16
  'pillow shots', 16

Pabst, G. W., 31
  Westfront 1918 (1930), 31
Pahlavi, Farah, 284
Pahlavi, Mohammad Reza (Shah of Iran), 283
Paillet, Marc, 148
  Gauche: année zero (*The Lowest Point of the Left*), 148
Pain, Mélanie, 120
Palance, Jack, 107
Palestine Liberation Organisation, 217
  Fatah, 217–18, 219, 223
  fedayeen, 218, 219, 223–5
panoptic surveillance, 31–3
Papon, Maurice, 220
Parain, Brice, 123
Paris-Match, 104–5, 116, 140
Pasolini, Pier Paolo, 178, 180, 183, 184
  Gospel According to St. Matthew (1964), 178
Pedro, Antônio, 152
Peirce, Charles Sanders, 20, 43, 58, 192
  firstness, secondness and thirdness, 20, 58
  iconic signs, 192–3
  indexical signs, 43, 192–3
  symbolic signs, 193
Pelé, 181
Penley, Constance, 271
Perez, Gilberto, 312
Pernoud, Laurence, 112
  J'Attends un Enfant, 112
Petrovicho, Carlos, 185
phenomenology, 140–2, 144, 195, 281–2, 288, 310
  epoché, 141
  see also Husserl, Merleau-Ponty, Ponge
Picasso, Pablo, 81
pieds-noirs, 129, 135
Pipolo, Tony, 124

Pisters, Patricia, 277
  neuro-image, 277
Pitanga, Antonio, 181, 182
Platan, Karl, 30
Plato, 9, 59, 65, 128, 141, 286–7
Pompidou, Georges, 212
Ponge, Francis, 140, 141–3, 144–6, 147–8, 195, 310, 312, 313
  Le Parti Pris des Choses, 141
  see also Godard, phenomenology
Pons, Isabelle, 188, 249; see also Dziga Vertov Group
Pontecorvo, Gillo, 245
Pope John XXIII, 180
Popular Front (France), 222
Porter, Edwin S., 267
  The Great Train Robbery (1903), 267
Portinari, Beatrice, 70
Potter, Dennis, 207
Potter, Sally, 268
Pound, Ezra, 70, 73, 284
Powell, Enoch, 212, 215
Pozzesi, Paolo, 242
prostitution, 52, 105, 106–7, 108, 109–10, 119, 123–4, 127, 128–31, 135, 139, 143, 147, 233, 322–4, 327
Proust, Marcel, 94, 120, 259
Pudovkin, Vsevolod, 22
  The Deserter (1933), 22
Puskás, Ferenc, 114

Quadros, Janio, 158
Quant, Mary, 145
Queneau, Raymond, 112, 127
  Odile, 127
  Zazie dans le Métro (1960), 112, 127
Quijano, Carlos, 198

Raban, William, 268, 278
radio sound techniques, 23, 26, 38, 82–3, 202
Ragona, Melissa, 55
Rancière, Jacques, 231, 248n
Rassimov, Rada, 170
Ray, Nicholas
  Rebel Without a Cause (1955), 119
Reader, Keith, 121
Rebot, Saddy, 123
Récamier, Juliette, 113
Reception Theory, 111; see also Iser, Jauss
Red Brigades, 255
Reed, David, 293
Reineri, Madeleine, 77–8, 96

Remarque, Erich Maria, 31
  All Quiet on the Western Front, 31
Remes, Justin, 5
Resnais, Alain, 102, 127, 196, 277
  Muriel (1963), 128
Reston, Telma, 161
return to zero, 128, 137, 147–9, 150, 155, 188, 191, 200, 207, 217, 226, 250, 288;
  see also Barthes, Godard, Kiarostami, Paillet, Rocha
Ribeiro, João Ubaldo, 182
Richardson, Terry, 326
Rivette, Jacques, 256
  Duelle (1976), 256
  Noroît (1976), 256
Rivière, Joan, 199
  L'amour et la haine, 199
  see also Klein
Robbe-Grillet, Alain, 55
Robison, Arthur, 24
  The Last Waltz (*Der letzte Walzer*, 1927), 24
Rocha, Glauber, 6, 21, 114, 122, 148, 149–87, 188, 199, 215, 248, 249–50
  'An Aesthetic of Hunger', 151, 152, 159
  Age of the Earth (*A Idada da Terra*, 1980), 114, 150, 160, 165, 171, 177–87
  Antonio das Mortes (1969), 154, 249
  'Beginning at Zero: Notes on Cinema and Society', 149–50
  Black God, White Devil (1964), 154, 166, 167
  Earth Entranced (*Terra em Transe*, 1967), 150, 154, 155–67, 170, 178, 179
  The Lion Has Seven Heads (*Der Leone Have Sept Cabeças*, 1970), 154, 167, 169, 170–7
  'Tricontinental', 169
Rocha, Glauce, 155
Rochet, Waldeck, 242, 244, 247
Roger, Jean–Henri, 188, 207, 231–2; see also Dziga Vertov Group
Rogers, Shorty, 1
room tone, 3, 22, 321
Rosen, Miriam, 311
Rosenbaum, 308
Rosenthal, Barbara, 74–6, 78, 95
Rossellini, Roberto, 149
Rouch, Jean, 109, 132
Roud, Richard, 106
Rousseau, Jean-Jacques, 119, 190
  Émile, 190
  The Social Contract, 190

Rowbotham, Sheila, 210
   'Women: the struggle for freedom', 210
Roxy Music, 320
Rubin, Jerry, 256
Ruiz, Raúl, 17–19, 86
   'Six Functions of the Shot', 17–18
Ruscha, Ed, 326
Ruttman, Walther, 23n, 50
   Berlin, Symphony of a Big City (*Berlin Die Sinfonie der Großstadts*, 1927), 50
   Weekend (1930), 23n
Ryan, Michael P., 23, 38

Saba, Farhad, 301
Sabzian, Hossein, 306–17
Sacher-Masoch, Leopold von, 180
Saeed-Vafa, Mehrnaz, 299
Safavi, Iraj, 300–1
Saint-Just, Louis-Antoine de, 76
   'Laws of Ventôse', 76
Samba, Miguel, 172
Sanbar, Elias, 225
Sanborn, Keith, 75
Sands, Julian, 322
Sarraute, Nathalie, 4
Sartre, Jean-Paul, 76, 140, 152, 153, 195
   Roads to Freedom trilogy, 76
Satie, Erik, 279–80
   Gnossienne #1, 279–80
Schiffman, Suzanne, 135
Schlegel, Friedrich, 56–7, 128
Schreber, Daniel, Paul, 9
Schultze, Johann Heinrich, 193
Scott-Heron, Gil, 216
Seale, Bobby, 256
Segolo, Andre, 171
Seko, Mobutu Sese, 169
Sembene, Ousmane, 20, 23
   Borom Sarret (1963), 23
   Xala (1975), 20, 171
Sepehri, Sohrab, 284
   'Where Is the Friend's House?', 284
Série Noire, 116, 117, 122
Serisuelo, Marc, 258
Servan-Schreiber, Jean-Jacques, 235
Shakespeare, William, 69, 121, 157, 205–6
   The Tempest, 69
Shamaei, Hooshang, 310
Sharf, Zack, 318–19
Shilina-Conte, Tanya, 5
   This Video Does Not Exist, 5
Shohat, Ella, 156, 179
Shue, Elisabeth, 321–2, 325n

Šik, Ota, 235
Simenon, Georges, 133
   Banana Tourists, 133
'sin' cinema, 44, 107, 318, 332
Situationist International, 74, 77, 81, 96, 101, 102, 103, 109, 206, 216, 270
   dérive, 78
   détournement, 76–7, 81, 92, 95, 100, 101, 103, 109, 120, 216
   situations, 75–6, 78–9, 99
   spectacle, 104, 106, 109, 122, 199, 202, 205, 206, 223, 267–8
   see also Debord
Sluyter–Obidos, Winter, 293
Smith, Jack, 327
   Flaming Creatures (1963), 327
Smith, O. C., 233
Soares, Joffre, 154
Sobchack, Vivian, 282
Socrates, 9–10, 94
Solanas, Fernando, E., 240
   Hour of the Furnaces (1968), 240
   see also Getino
Sorin, Raphaël, 188; *see also* Dziga Vertov Group
Sosin, Daniel, 24
Sparavigna, Amelia, 59
Spinoza, Baruch, 7–8, 126, 143, 153, 179–80, 186, 187, 230, 313
   Ethics, 8
   potentia, 7
   substance, 8
Spiteri, Raymond, 127
Spivak, Gayatri Chakravorty, 208
   subaltern, 207–8, 209
Stahl-Nachbaur, Ernst, 28
Stakhanov, Aleksey, 235
Stalin, Joseph, 153, 194, 195, 203, 245, 246–7
Stam, Robert, 151, 156, 158, 164, 165, 166, 170, 177, 178, 179
Stamelman, Richard, 141
Staquet, Georges, 117
Stein, Franz, 28
'Stella', 129; *see also* Godard
Sterritt, David, 203
Stevens, Wallace, 284
Stewart, Garrett, 71
Sting (Gordon Sumner), 320, 322, 323
Straub, Jean-Marie, 199
subjectivity, 7, 45, 126
Surrealism, 79, 93, 271
synaesthesia, 14

syncinema (*séance de cinéma*); *see also* Lemaître

syncretism, 148, 152, 154, 156, 165, 169, 178, 181, 182, 185, 195; *see also* carnivalesque

Taazieh (*taziyeh*) folk theatre, 285–6
Tabarraee, Babak, 290, 291
Tarr, Béla, 19, 269
  'endurance-image', 269
Tautin, Gilles, 203–5, 206
Taylor, Breonna, 260
Taylorism (after Frederick W. Taylor), 36, 52, 143, 175, 235
Teitelbaum, Irving, 207
Teitelbaum, Mo, 207, 210
Tharp, Twyla, 60
Théberge, Paul, 324
Thomsen, Christian Braad, 218, 227
time of Aion, 6, 11, 84
time of Chronos, 6, 11, 84
Tinti, Gabriele, 171
Tiradentes, 181
Tolstoy, Leo, 315
topology, 13–14, 16, 18, 19, 92, 100, 109, 131, 133, 146, 226, 318, 332; *see also* biogram
Tostão, 181
Tovah, Mageina, 293
trance, 150, 151, 153, 157–8, 164–6, 180, 187; *see also* carnivalesque, syncretism
tricontinental revolution, 167–70, 172, 173, 176–8, 195, 199; *see also* Che Guevara, Rocha
Trodd, Kenith, 207
tropicalism, 151, 177–80, 250
Truffaut, François, 111, 116, 119
  Jules et Jim (1962), 116
  Shoot the Piano Player (1960), 116
Trump, Donald, 181, 262
Tudor, David, 3
Tullio-Altan, Cristiana, 242–5, 251, 254, 256
Twiggy (Lesley Hornby), 145
Tyler, Wat, 208

Uexküll, Jacob von, 7, 101; *see also* ethology
Uroskie, Andrew V., 84, 86, 92

Valadão, Jece, 181
Van Cleef, Lee, 1
Vaneigem, Raoul, 206, 207

Vargas, Getulio, 158
Vauselle, Bernard, 204
vector space/time, 13–16, 18, 19, 35, 43, 46, 60, 68, 86, 89, 92, 94, 104, 109, 113, 115, 119, 121, 131, 133, 135, 144, 146, 154, 155, 160–1, 164, 165, 173, 183, 192, 196, 199, 213, 217, 226, 228, 236, 238, 249, 252, 255, 263, 279, 312, 318, 332
  centrifugal, 15–18, 21, 22, 57, 89, 252, 253, 259, 260
  centripetal, 15–18, 21, 22, 57, 88–9, 252
  vectors of subjectification, 182, 224
  see also topology
Verdi, Giuseppe, 166
  Otello, 166
Vermeer, Johannes, 193, 194
  Girl With the Pearl Earring, 194
  The Lace-maker, 193
  The View of Delft, 193
Vertov, Dziga, 22, 232, 243, 245, 270, 300
  The Eleventh Year (1927), 245
  Enthusiasm (1930), 22
  Kino-Eye, 271, 300
  Man with a Movie Camera (1929), 271, 300
  Three Songs of Lenin (1934), 22
Viegas, Susana, 266
Viénet, René, 103
Vietnam War, 121, 128, 130, 131, 133, 137, 139–40, 147, 167–8, 188, 195, 199, 201, 215, 222, 301
Villa-Lobos, Heitor, 156, 159, 167, 182
  Bacchianas, 155
Vimenet, Catherine, 129
violence as cathartic decolonising catalyst, 151–3, 155, 158, 159, 161–2, 164–5, 167, 173–4, 176–7; *see also* Che Guevara, Deleuze, Fanon, Rocha
Virilio, Paul, 32
  'The Overexposed City', 32
  War and Cinema, 32
Vivaldi, Antonio, 95, 124
Vlady, Marina, 128, 130, 132
Volonté, Gian Maria, 240, 241
Vulpiani, Mario, 240

Wallerstein, Immanuel, 168
Warhol, Andy, 242, 275
  Chelsea Girls (1966), 275
Waters, John, 327
  Pink Flamingos (1972), 327
Weather Underground, 256

Weiner, Lee, 256
Weiss, Allen, 58, 59
Weiss, Peter, 217
  Marat/Sade (1963), 217
Wernicke, Otto, 28
Wiazemsky, Anne, 188, 231, 241–3, 247, 248, 251, 252, 256; *see also* Dziga Vertov Group
Widmann, Ellen, 26
Wieland, Joyce
Wiene, Robert, 79
Wilde, Cornel, 1
Williams, John, 319, 320
Williams, William Carlos, 284
Wilson, Harold, 212
Wise, Naomi, 200
Witt, Michael, 225
Wollen, Peter, 189

Wolman, Gil J., 74–9, 95, 98–9, 100
  anticoncept, 99
  L'Anticoncept (1952), 74, 79, 98–9, 100
  'Physical Phase' of cinema, 98
Woolf, Virginia, 13
world systems analysis, 168–9, 183; *see also* Dussel, Wallerstein

Xavier, Ismail, 152, 157, 160, 178

Young, Aaron, 326

Zaatari, Akram, 294
Zaynalzadeh, Moharram, 306
Zeno, 264
Zola, Émile, 122
Zorn, Max, 57
  lemma, 57